LAW, STATE AND RELIGION IN THE NEW EUROPE: DEBATES AND DILEMMAS

Edited by

LORENZO ZUCCA

and

CAMIL UNGUREANU

CAMBRIDGE
UNIVERSITY PRESS

CAMBRIDGE UNIVERSITY PRESS
Cambridge, New York, Melbourne, Madrid, Cape Town,
Singapore, São Paulo, Delhi, Tokyo, Mexico City

Cambridge University Press
The Edinburgh Building, Cambridge CB2 8RU, UK

Published in the United States of America by Cambridge University Press, New York

www.cambridge.org
Information on this title: www.cambridge.org/9780521198103

© Cambridge University Press 2012

This publication is in copyright. Subject to statutory exception
and to the provisions of relevant collective licensing agreements,
no reproduction of any part may take place without the written
permission of Cambridge University Press.

First published 2012

Printed in the United Kingdom at the University Press, Cambridge

A catalogue record for this publication is available from the British Library

Library of Congress Cataloguing in Publication data
Law, state and religion in the new Europe : debates and dilemmas /
[edited by] Lorenzo Zucca, Camil Ungureanu.
p.   cm.
Includes bibliographical references and index.
ISBN 978-0-521-19810-3 (hardback)
1. Freedom of religion–Europe.   2. Religion and law–Europe.
3. Church and state–Europe.   I. Zucca, Lorenzo.   II. Ungureanu, Camil.
KJC5156.L39 2012
342.408′53–dc23
2011042608

ISBN 978-0-521-19810-3 Hardback

Cambridge University Press has no responsibility for the persistence or
accuracy of URLs for external or third-party internet websites referred to in
this publication, and does not guarantee that any content on such websites is,
or will remain, accurate or appropriate.

BLACKBURN COLLEGE
LIBRARY
BB50417
Acc. No
Class No. U.C.L 342.408 SZUC
Date 22.3.12

a Francesca (L. Z.)
To my mother (C. U.)

CONTENTS

Introduction   1
CAMIL UNGUREANU

PART I   19

1   Religion and political liberty in Italian republics
    (in the thirteenth to the fifteenth centuries)   21
    MAURIZIO VIROLI

2   Two stories about toleration   49
    RAINER FORST

3   Natural reason, religious conviction, and the justification
    of coercion in democratic societies   65
    ROBERT AUDI

4   The 'other' citizens: religion in a multicultural Europe   93
    MALEIHA MALIK

5   Islam and the public sphere: public reason or public
    imagination?   115
    CHIARA BOTTICI AND BENOIT CHALLAND

PART II   135

6   Law v. religion   137
    LORENZO ZUCCA

7   Unveiling the limits of tolerance: comparing the
    treatment of majority and minority religious symbols
    in the public sphere   160
    SUSANNA MANCINI AND MICHEL ROSENFELD

8   Objective, critical and pluralistic? Religious education and
    human rights in the European public sphere   192
    IAN LEIGH

9   Religion and (in)equality in the European framework   215
    AILEEN MCCOLGAN

10 Is there a right not to be offended in one's religious
    beliefs?   239
    GEORGE LETSAS

11 Religious pluralism and national constitutional traditions
    in Europe   261
    DANIEL AUGENSTEIN

    PART III   281

12 Rights, religion and the public sphere: the European Court
    of Human Rights in search of a theory?   283
    JULIE RINGELHEIM

13 Europe and religion: an ambivalent nexus   307
    CAMIL UNGUREANU

    Index   334

~

Introduction

CAMIL UNGUREANU

The present book is based on a workshop that brought together legal and political theorists to discuss tensions and dilemmas raised by religion with respect to secular law and political authority. The interdisciplinary workshop was organized in Florence, at the European University Institute in 2008. Florence is an ideal *locus symbolicus* for such an intellectual enterprise. At the height of its cultural and political power, Florence was torn by the political–religious conflict between the Guelfs and the Ghibellines, a conflict whose early stages were immortalized by Dante's *Divine Comedy*. The Ghibellines strongly believed that the Emperor should represent the ultimate political authority, while the Guelfs wanted a central political role for the Catholic Church, and viewed the Pope as having both spiritual and temporal authority. This political–theological conflict, which forced Dante into exile away from his beloved Florence, was acrimonious and violent. Nonetheless, the conflict also nourished a range of novel political ideas concerning the relation between state and church. Machiavelli, together with other outstanding fellow Florentines, stands for one beginning of modernity and modern political thought in Europe. He proposed novel views on the nature of authority before Europe's wars of religion and the influential work of Hobbes, Locke (see Chapter 1) and Bayle (see Chapter 2).[1]

The relation between religion and secular state as a central question for modernity has, however, been at points obscured and masked by other problems. During the Cold War, the question was, by and large, eclipsed by the gigantomachia between capitalism and communism, and its perception was shaped by the conviction that modernization would cause the ineluctable decline of religion.[2] This teleological image of modernization

---

[1] M. Viroli, *Machiavelli's God* (Princeton University Press, 2010).

[2] For a *locus classicus* of this belief in contemporary sociology, see P. L. Berger, *The Sacred Canopy: Elements of a Sociological Theory of Religion* (Garden City, NY: Doubleday, 1967).

as secularization has recently been discarded by influential sociologists. Scholars such as P. Berger or J. Casanova have replaced the theory of secularization with that of desecularization or deprivatization of religion.[3] From this perspective, the fact that religion has returned to the public sphere brings into question the notion of the incompatibility between modernity and religion, and leads to the image of "multiple modernities."[4] Nonetheless, the now-popular idea of the "return of religion" is in part an academic myth. Religion is not like a volcano that, dormant for some time, is erupting over again. During the Cold War, religiosity did not shrink in a decisive way. Moreover, its hostility to religion notwithstanding, communism represented, with its myths, rituals and messianic "structure," a continuation of religious experience, and a substitute for and a distortion of it. It is not surprising that the communist experience was analyzed, by J. Benda and E. Voegelin to M. Eliade and R. Aron, as a "secular religion."

In the vacuum left by the collapse of communism in 1989, the issue of religion in the public sphere has reassumed a central place in current debates, and compelled scholars into rethinking their empirical and theoretical tools. As Pippa Norris and Ronald Ingelhart argue, religiosity is globally on the rise.[5] There appears to be, however, a notable exception: the European continent. In Europe, churchgoing has been in decline and the number of non-believers or those who are indifferent is on the rise.[6] The empirical hypothesis of secularization remains open, yet not even the recent history of Europe has, in fact, confirmed the teleological saga of the linear decline of religion. Europe has become increasingly secularized, in the sense that "society has gradually emancipated itself from religion without necessarily denying it."[7] In many European countries the power of institutional religion has declined, while the interest in individualized

---

[3] Berger has turned upside down his earlier theory of secularization in Berger (ed.), *The Desecularization of the World* (Washington, DC: Ethics and Public Policy Center, 1999). See also P. Berger, G. Davie and E. Fokas, *Religious America, Secular Europe?: A Theme and Variations* (Aldershot: Ashgate, 2008) and J. Casanova, *Public Religions in the Modern World* (University of Chicago Press, 1994).

[4] See P. J. Katzenstein, "Multiple Modernities as limits to secular Europeanization?" in P. J. Katzenstein and T. A. Byrnes (eds.), *Religion in an Expanding Europe* (Cambridge University Press, 2006), pp. 1–42.

[5] P. Norris and R. Ingelhart, *Sacred and Secular: Religion and Politics Worldwide* (Cambridge University Press, 2004).

[6] G. Davie, *Europe: The Exceptional Case. Parameters of Faith in the Modern World* (London: Darton, Longman and Todd Ltd, 2002).

[7] O. Roy, *Secularism Confronts Islam* (New York: Columbia University Press, 2007), p. 15.

religious and spiritual searches has increased. Immigration and globalization have also contributed to the growth of a more diverse religious environment. For example, Islamic and Pentecostal beliefs have become more commonplace in several nations. As Charles Taylor points out, the secularization of Europe is accompanied "by a new placement of the sacred or spiritual in relation to individual and social life. This new placement is now the occasion for re-compositions of spiritual life in new forms, and for new ways of existing both in and out of relation to God."[8]

At the political–legal level, religious claims have become ever more visible in the public sphere. Initially private and social matters have been gradually turned into European contentious issues benefiting from the generous coverage of the mass media. This is not only because religious organizations and movements have found new "windows of opportunity" of lobbying for their interests and values in Brussels or Strasbourg. In effect, a variety of sub-state, state, international and supranational actors have, in spite of their often divergent interests, contributed to defining religious issues in terms of political and legal rights. The resulting process of politicization and juridification of religion has generated an ambivalent "culture of litigation." This "culture" can undermine the art of political compromise and reasonable legal accommodation of pluralism. Consider how the veil, initially a non-issue in the primary school Châtelaine in the canton of Geneva (Switzerland), was turned into a hard-fought political problem in the Swiss public space, and what's more, into the first "veil case" at the European Court of Human Rights (ECtHR).[9] After her conversion to Islam, a Swiss citizen and teacher (Ms. Dahlab) started to wear the veil at the end of the scholastic year 1990–91. It was understood that Dahlab was fulfilling her professional responsibilities without ever attempting to persuade her students towards her religious convictions. Nor did her wearing of the veil provoke complaints from colleagues or parents. However, in 1995, the local teaching inspector brought the fact that Ms. Dahlab was wearing the veil to the attention of the General Department of the Primary School Teaching of the canton of Geneva. This apparently insignificant event snowballed into a bitter public debate and a legal case that culminated in the case being brought to the ECtHR. In the end, the decision of the Court in the case *Dahlab* v. *Switzerland* (2001) supported the stance of the Swiss authorities: in line with the State Council of Geneva, the ECtHR argued, inter alia, that Mrs. Dahlab's

---

[8] C. Taylor, *A Secular Age* (Cambridge, MA: Harvard University Press, 2007), p. 437.
[9] Eur. Ct. H. R., *Dahlab* v. *Switzerland*, 15 February 2001.

wearing of the veil amounted to nothing less than a threat to "public order and public safety."[10]

In the Dahlab affair, the "security state" and its imagination created the conflict and prescribed a disciplinary antidote for it. Nonetheless, this is not to suggest that conflicts involving religion are merely fabricated by imagination. The fact remains that the inherited compromises and agreements about the place of religion in the secular state have been challenged in virtually all corners of the European continent. In particular, Europe is being confronted with the crisis of its two opposite models of integration: assimilationist (France, Turkey) and multicultural (UK, Holland).[11] On the one hand, France's laic model aims at creating a single overarching community where everyone assimilates into the republican and national values. The state plays a central role in creating the public sphere as a *locus* of militancy for public virtues and republican values. The state, public sphere and citizenship are largely "co-substantial": the public sphere is not primarily an independent and external check on a state contemplated with the distrustful eyes of the liberal citizen. To the contrary, the public sphere is part of the statehood, that is, it constitutes a space where the state and its republican citizens pursue their "mission" of safeguarding the public virtues and goods. The laic state does not grant recognition to ethnic and cultural–religious minorities: in order to become a *citoyen*, individuals are required to strip themselves of their attachments to any ethnic or cultural–religious group. By keeping their cultural–religious differences in the private sphere, individuals are regarded as being able to reach reconciliation in virtue of the consensus over the republican values. However, the French republican model attempts to define away conflicts by imposing a non-negotiable primacy of republican–national values over any other values. Therefore, it is a paternalistic model in so far as it imposes top-down solutions without room for genuine dissent and reasonable exceptions. Furthermore, the laic model works, in practice, more like a partial disestablishment regime in which the Catholic Church has been privileged by the state.[12]

---

[10] *Ibid.*

[11] C. Joppke, "The retreat of multiculturalism in the liberal state: theory and policy," *British Journal of Sociology* 55(2) (2004), 237–57.

[12] See C. Laborde, "Virginity and Burqa: Unreasonable Accommodations? Considerations on the Stasi and Bouchard-Taylor Reports" (2008), available at www.laviedesidees.fr/ Virginity-and-Burqa-Unreasonable.html?lang=fr (last accessed September 5, 2011) and C. Laborde, *Français, encore un effort pour être républicains!* (Paris: Seuil, 2010); J. Baubérot, *Laïcité 1905–2005: entre passion et raison* (Paris: Seuil, 2004).

The multicultural model attempts to keep conflicts at bay and bring about reconciliation by supporting the development of "public spaces" of cultural–religious difference within which everyone can practice her own values. This model has the merit of emphasizing the salience of the recognition of the plurality of communities in the age of "galloping pluralism" (Charles Taylor).[13] But this model has, especially in its radical version, turned out to be over-optimistic as to the possibility of avoiding segregation, integrating the newcomers with their differences, and reconciliation.

The current conflicts have shaken the trust in the immediate feasibility of solutions based on reconciliation through multicultural recognition and assimilation in the public sphere.[14] Following D. Grimm, the conflicts involving religion can be broadly divided into freedom-centered and equality-centered: a believer or a religious group may claim a liberty that is not granted by the general laws, or they may claim equality rights that are not prescribed by the general laws. In the first case, the demand is either to extend or to restrict the generally guaranteed freedom in accordance with a religious commandment, duty or tradition. Think of conflicts over the ritual killing of animals, polygamy, consumption of drugs in a ritual, interruption of work for purposes of prayer, wearing a turban while driving, blood transfusions, and so on.[15] In the second case, the issue is either the equal treatment of various religious groups or the application of the equality principle within a religious group. Consider the debates and conflicts over whether all religious communities enjoy the same rights or whether indigenous religious beliefs may be privileged, namely the construction of mosques in non-Islamic countries, the call of the muezzin (just as the Christian churches ring their bells), public display of religious symbols, state subsidies for religious activities, the recognition of the religious holidays of the newcomers, and the equal treatment of various religious heritages in education.[16]

There are no transparent solutions at hand for solving such conflicts, which are often marked by dilemmatic situations, that is different if not

[13] Taylor, *A Secular* Age, p. 401. See also B. Parekh, *Rethinking Multiculturalism: Cultural Diversity and Political Theory* (Basingstoke: Macmillan, 2000).
[14] See also M. Rosenfeld, "Equality and the Dialectic between Identity and Difference," in O. A. Payrow Shabani (ed.), *Multiculturalism and Law – A Critical Debate* (Cardiff: University of Wales Press, 2007), pp. 157–81.
[15] For more details, see Dieter Grimm's categorization of conflicts involving religion and law, in Grimm, "Conflicts between general laws and religious norms," *Cardozo Law Review* 30 (2008–2009), 2369–82.
[16] *Ibid.*

divergent imperatives. Such dilemmatic situations question and undercut the goodwill confidence in the mainstream philosophies of reconciliation through public reason (Habermas' dialogical postsecularism; Rawls' political liberalism) – philosophies that regard aporias as a marginal exception and dissensus as subordinate to disagreement.[17] Rights and values, pluralism and identity, justice and efficacy, autonomy and tradition, integration and toleration cannot always be balanced without the loss and sacrifice of something valuable. Consider again the headscarf. When the headscarf is converted into a contentious legal issue, a court needs to balance between gender equality and freedom of religion, non-domination and pluralism. Nonetheless, the headscarf has a plural meaning: it can signify subordination, but it can also be a means of expressing one's freedom of religion.[18] This entails that legal decisions which often follow an either/or logic cannot be taken without risk, sacrifice and loss, as they can either leave certain women unprotected or, to the contrary, curtail the free exercise of religion on the part of autonomous women.

The lack of consensus over such conflicts raises a vital concern: how it is possible to design anew stable and fairer agreements within the space of a *complex center* wherein there is no "single ideal solution" (Habermas) between the extremes of assimilationism and radical multiculturalism? In contrast to the public reason approaches (Habermas, Rawls), this concern involves a rethinking of the heritage of the Enlightenment in a more pluralistic and situational way (see Chapter 7) and taking history more seriously (see Chapter 1 and Chapter 4). It also gives a central salience to persistent disagreements (see Chapter 3) and also takes into account the importance of emotions and imagination (see Chapter 1 and Chapter 5).

This search for a theoretical renewal encounters specific layer difficulties when we move beyond the nation state and focus on the European institutions. Europe is marked by the debate and confrontation between different models of democracy, law and religion – from the model of a Christian Europe (Weiler)[19] to that of a postsecular (Habermas)[20] or laic one (see Chapter 13). This is unsurprising given the practical and

---

[17] J. Rawls, *Political Liberalism* (New York: Columbia University Press, 1993); J. Habermas, "Reconciliation through the public use of reason: remarks on John Rawls' Political Liberalism," *Journal of Philosophy* 92 (1995), 109–31.

[18] See, for instance, G. Jonker and V. Amiraux (eds.), *Politics of Visibility: Young Muslims in European Public Spaces*, (London: Transaction Publishers, 2006).

[19] See J. Weiler, *Un'Europa Cristiana. Un saggio esplorativo* (Milan: Rizzoli, 2003); Weiler, "State and Nation; Church, Mosque and Synagogue—the trailer," *I-CON* 8 (2010), 157–66.

[20] J. Habermas, *Between Naturalism and Religion* (Cambridge: Polity, 2008).

normative questions and dilemmas that mark the current European predicament: how to square the development of a consistent European approach to religion beyond the nation state, with the recognition of the often conflictive diversity of the continent's models? Where is the appropriate border between judicial interventionism and judicial restraint, excessive interference and moderation, the *esprit géometrique* and the *esprit de finesse*?

The present book brings together contributions that deal with this cluster of questions and dilemmas in three parts. Part I includes political–theoretical reflections which stand for different schools of thought, i.e. republicanism (see Chapter 1), liberalism (see Chapter 3), Critical Theory (see Chapter 2 and Chapter 5), post-colonial thought and multiculturalism (see Chapter 4). Part II analyzes concrete legal conflicts from different theoretical perspectives. It starts from a typology of conflicts (see Chapter 6), and centers on representative issues such as religious symbols (see Chapter 7), free speech and religious offense (see Chapter 10), education (see Chapter 8), equality and discrimination (see Chapter 9) or social cohesion (see Chapter 11). Part III focuses on the merits and ambivalences of the emergent European legal and political discourses on religion (see Chapter 12 and Chapter 13).

The present book adopts a pluralistic and interdisciplinary perspective, including contributions from different schools of thought (e.g. analytical, historical) and fields of research (e.g. political theory, legal analysis). In *Political Liberalism* (1993), Rawls points out that, when consensus is fractured and conflict emerges, we need to climb up the ladder of abstraction so as to gain more clarity in the principles that orientate us in grappling with concrete dilemmas. Rawls writes: "(i)n political philosophy the work of abstraction is set in motion by deep political conflicts ... We turn to political philosophy when our shared political understandings, as Walzer might say, break down, and equally when we are torn within ourselves."[21] In Rawls' post-Hegelian understanding, philosophizing is meant to reinstate the consensus by a process of reconciliation with the "reason" embedded in our political tradition.[22] However, going up the ladder of

---

[21] Rawls, *Political Liberalism*, p. 49.

[22] Rawls draws on M. Hardimon's interpretation of Hegel's view as a philosophy of reconciliation. See esp. Rawls' *Lectures on the History of Political Philosophy*, ed. S. Freeman (Cambridge, MA: Harvard University Press, 2002). For a critique of the reduction of Hegel's view as a "philosophy of reconciliation," see Ch. Menke, *Tragödie im Sittlichen: Gerechtigkeit und Freiheit nach Hegel* (Frankfurt am Main: Suhrkamp), 1996.

abstraction in search of reconciliation is *one* limited way of conceiving legal–political theorizing. Probing afresh into the history of our current predicament and revitalizing "lost" traditions, bringing to light persistent dilemmas hidden behind the smokescreen of a reconciling reason, imagining innovative legal–political arrangements, deepening a sense of protest against some of well-entrenched traditions of our situation, correspond to alternative styles of reflection pursued in this book. Even if the representatives of these styles and their followers have often treated each other in a dismissive way, to conceive the relation between their approaches as one of incommunicability or mutual exclusion is artificial. Consider the seemingly opposed approaches of J. Rawls and Q. Skinner. In *Political Liberalism*, Rawls pursues his analytical approach under the form of "political constructivism." Political constructivism neither is able nor does it wish to bracket the question of history, as it is aimed to make explicit and to systematize what is implicit and unsystematic in a historical tradition. It is significant that Rawls opposes his "political constructivism" as based on a specific historical tradition, to Kant's ahistorical "moral constructivism." In turn, Skinner's historicist approach cannot avoid making general theoretical assumptions. In fact, Skinner's "revolution" in studying political ideas as "performances" in specific historical contexts was inspired by philosophers such as Wittgenstein, Austin or Davidson.[23] What's more, as Skinner makes the case that the concept of freedom initially formed in the context of the Roman republican period answers better the contemporary predicament than the liberal or socialist ones, he cannot avoid a degree of trans-contextual generalization and theoretical constructivism. The point is not that there is or should be a harmony between these different approaches. To the contrary, it is most likely that a relation of tension will remain between them, and so it should be. However, my suggestion is that these authors emphasize one of the different dimensions – history or structure, context or theoretical generalization and construction, factual research or imagination and so on – that constitute the *inner* and *open dialectic* of any legal–political and historical research. It is therefore more useful to see these methods and styles of investigation from a pluralist perspective, namely in a relation of mutual check and learning, rather than in one of incommunicability and reciprocal exclusion.

The pluralist perspective that informs the present enterprise is all the more salient given the need for more interaction and collaborative

---

[23] See especially the essays in Q. Skinner's *Visions of Politics: Regarding Method*, vol. I. (Cambridge University Press, 2002).

projects between legal and political theorists working on religion – above all in Europe. The relative absence of such enterprises is due, in general, to the protocols of overspecialization, homologation and promotion in the current university system.[24] The relative lack of interdisciplinary projects applies much more to Europe's academic space than to the American one, as the European "cultural wars" and the resulting jurisprudential religion are more recent phenomena.[25] At the same time, in Europe an asymmetry between legal and political theorists is notable: there are probably more legal theorists who are well versed in the normative issues of political justice than there are political theorists who are experts in legal issues. Somehow understandably, there are not so many political theorists who choose to acquaint themselves with the intricate technicalities and meanders of the jurisprudential traditions.

In a letter written in 1929, the US Supreme Court Justice Oliver Wendell Holmes famously states: "I have said to my brethren many times that I hate justice, which means that I know if a man begins to talk about that, for one reason or another he is shirking thinking in legal terms."[26] Nonetheless, while justice and law, political and legal theory are relatively autonomous, building a "wall of separation" between them is unsustainable, not least because the border between law and politics has become ever more complex. In Europe particularly, there are at least two interrelated reasons for this complexity. The first is the European passage from government to multi-layered governance. Religious organizations and movements have been contributing to this shift by "going" European, and thus by rendering more complicated the traditionally binary relation between state and church. Likewise, various European institutions (the European Parliament, the European Commission, the Council of Europe, etc.), have become increasingly involved with religion. This trend, which includes the recent institutionalizing of the dialogue with religious organizations by the Lisbon Treaty (article 17-C), will probably gain more importance in the future. Second, in the past decades there has been a global trend of judicialization of politics at

---

[24] See T. D. Campbell, "Legal studies" in R. Goodin and P. Pettit (eds.), *A Companion to Contemporary Political Philosophy* (Basic Blackwell, 1995), pp. 183–211; K. E. Whittington, R. D. Kelemen and G. A. Cadeira (eds.), *The Oxford Handbook of Law and Politics* (Oxford University Press, 2008).

[25] The first case decided under Article 9, European Convention on Human Rights (ECHR) – which protects freedom of religion – was *Kokkinakis* v. *Greece*, in 1993 (Eur. Ct. H. R., *Kokkinakis* v. *Greece*, 25 May 1993).

[26] Letter to John C. H. Wu, 1 July 1929, in *Justice Holmes to Dr. Wu: An Intimate Correspondence 1921–32* (New York: Central Books, 1947).

the international and supranational level that has affected Europe as well. "Judicialization" is a particular dimension of the broader process of juridification: it refers to the increasing reliance on courts and judicial means for addressing public policy questions and political controversies.[27] This raises the normative question of democratic legitimation, given the transfer of power from representative institutions to courts and judiciaries whose members are not always elected in transparent ways. With respect to religion, the process of judicialization enforces, especially after 9/11, the political or "militant dimension" of the Convention system.[28] This can be seen from the ECtHR's concern with fundamentalist and other "threats" to public order posed by certain religious symbols, forms of speech or behaviour. Naturally, grasping such questions regarding the dynamic interaction and unstable borderline between politics and law requires the collaborative effort between political and legal theory and case study.

Part I, dedicated mostly to contributions focused on political ideas, begins with Maurizio Viroli's reflections on the history of the idea of a republican or civil religion. Viroli's contribution is part of his broader agenda of unearthing forgotten treasures of European thought, his most recent interest being in placing the notion of republican religion at the heart of a republican revival. Methodologically, Viroli develops the historical and linguistic turn of the Cambridge School, and examines political ideas not only on the basis of major political texts but also of cultural artefacts such as Ambrogio Lorenzetti's representative painting in the Sala dei Nove of Siena's Palazzo Pubblico. In recent years Viroli has interpreted Machiavelli as a key figure for the Western history of the relationship between politics and religion, an aspect that has escaped the recent historiography on republicanism. In contrast to Q. Skinner and J. G. A. Pocock, Viroli develops S. Wolin's observation that American Christianity can be considered "a Machiavellian civil religion."[29] For Viroli, the Founding Fathers and

---

[27] Tom Ginsburg, "The Global Spread of Constitutional Review" in K. E. Whittington, R. D. Kelemen and G. A. Cadeira (eds.), *The Oxford Handbook of Law and Politics* (Oxford University Press, 2008), pp. 81–99. See also B. Iancu (ed.), *The Law/Politics Distinction in Contemporary Public Law Adjudication* (Utrecht: Eleven International Publishing, 2009).

[28] For the idea of militant democracy and ECtHR's approach to religion, see P. Macklem, "Guarding the Perimeter: Militant Democracy and Religious Freedom in Europe," Working Paper Series, University of Toronto, 2010.

[29] Viroli, *Machiavelli's God*, p. 25. S. Wolin, *Tocqueville between Two Worlds: The Making of a Political and Theoretical Life* (Princeton University Press, 2001), pp. 297–8.

Tocqueville unwittingly pursued an idea of a "religion of liberty" theorized in depth by Machiavelli. However, by pleading for a republican religion, Machiavelli was not originating a new theory but he was in fact keeping alive and reinforcing a well-established language of republican religion, which Viroli masterfully reconstructs in his contribution. Finally, Viroli deplores the fact that, starting from the sixteenth century, the religion of the Counter-Reformation destroyed the idea of republican religion, and held Italy in a state of slavery for centuries.

In the interdisciplinary tradition of the Critical Theory, Rainer Forst combines historical and philosophical analysis in order to pursue his long-term reflection on toleration.[30] Forst proposes a fresh reading of Bayle as the first to have developed a universalist theory of tolerance. The strength of Bayle's theory lies in the combination of epistemological and moral arguments to find a "universal, neutral ground for tolerance" independent of what Rawls would call comprehensive doctrines, religious or not. For Bayle, practical reason is a "natural light" able to reveal certain moral truths to every sincere person, regardless of his or her faith, even including atheists. The resulting principles of moral respect and of reciprocity cannot be trumped by religious truths, given that reasonable religious faith is aware that ultimately it is based on personal faith and trust. Bayle, in Forst's view, did not advance a skeptical argument; rather his claim was that the truths of religion were of a different epistemological character than truths arrived at by the use of reason alone. On this basis, Forst argues for a conception of toleration as respect, which moves away from the paternalistic components of a liberalism based on the concept of autonomy. However, tolerance as respect is permanently put at risk by subtle forms of paternalist toleration. This entails, in Forst's view, that toleration should be considered a "dialectical concept."

Robert Audi's contribution brings together moral, legal and political theorizing in order to carry on his influential endeavour of advancing a liberal understanding of the relationship between the secular state and religion. Audi refines his arguments as developed in his long-term dialogue with liberals such as Rawls, on the one hand, and "revisionist"

---

[30] See, R. Forst, *Toleranz im Konflikt: Geschichte, Gehalt und Gegenwart eines umstrittenen Begriffs* (Frankfurt/Main: Suhrkamp, 2003) (Engl. transl. forthcoming with Cambridge University Press). See also R. Forst, "Toleration, Justice and Reason" in C. McKinnon and D. Castiglione (eds.), *The Culture of Toleration in Diverse Societies* (Manchester University Press, 2003), pp. 71–85; Forst, "The Limits of Toleration," *Constellations* 11(3) (2004), 312–25.

critics such as P. Weithman or N. Wolterstorff, on the other.[31] At the state
level, Audi proposes three guiding principles, namely governmental protection of religious liberty, government's equal treatment of different religions and state neutrality. At the non-state level, Audi develops an ethics
of citizenship that takes seriously the contributions of the religious people
in the public sphere as well as the rational disagreement (as distinguished
from actual disagreement). This ethics is based on four principles. The
first is Audi's famous principle of secular rationale, which he defends
from criticism and qualifies. Audi argues inter alia for the non-exclusive
character of the principles, since it "does not even rule out having *only*
religious reasons for lifting oppression or expanding liberty" (Chapter 3).
In fact, Audi adds a "counterpart" to the principle of secular rationale,
namely the principle of the religious rationale, which calls on religious
citizens to find "adequate religious reasons" before supporting coercive
laws or public policies. These two principles should be complemented,
in Audi's view, by the principles of rational disagreement and toleration.
Both these principles require that citizens abstain from coercion "where
apparent epistemic peers argue for liberty" (Chapter 3). As a result, Audi's
revisited version of liberalism is not restrictive with respect to religion
and religious reasons, as it gives them an important place at the various
levels of the public sphere.

But do such analytical clarifications of liberalism hide a bias to be
unearthed by the examination of the historical context? By pointing out
the importance of the colonial legacy, and by drawing on multiculturalism
and post-colonial literature, Maleiha Malik examines the "blind spots"
of liberalism in Europe. Malik points out that the increasing importance of religion in the European public sphere is fundamentally linked to
the migration of former "colonial subjects" after the Second World War.
From Malik's perspective, the scholastic distinctions between religious
and secular reason may not be able to give a full account of the political
realities of a post-colonial state.[32] It is only by analyzing the post-colonial

---

[31] From Audi's prolific work, see *Religious Commitment and Secular Reason* (Cambridge
University Press, 2000); R. Audi and N. Wolterstorff, *Religion in the Public Square*
(Lanham, MD: Rowman and Littlefield, 1997).

[32] See also other instructive contributions by M. Malik, e.g. Malik, "'The Branch on
Which We Sit': Multiculturalism, Minority Women and Family Law" in A. Diduck and
K. O'Donovan (eds.), *Feminist Perspectives on Family Law* (Abingdon: Routledge, 2006),
pp. 221–3; "Feminism and its 'Other': Female Autonomy in an Age of 'Difference,'"
Cardozo Law Review 30 (6) (2009), 2613–28.

that we can have a proper grasp on controversial issues such as the Islamic headscarf and sharia.

In their contribution, Chiara Bottici (a philosopher) and Benoit Challand (a sociologist and expert in Islam) opt for a contextual approach to the current predicament of Islam in Europe. On the theoretical side, the chapter is the development in a new field of Bottici's *A Philosophy of Political Myth*.[33] For Bottici and Challand, the public reason approach is unsatisfactory in empirical and normative terms. Bottici and Challand suggest that imagination should help to recover the hidden meaning behind religious *topoi*. Imagination does not impose asymmetrical burdens; both religious and non-religious people have to step outside of their boundaries and attempt to interpret each other message in a more empathic way. On account of this notion of imagination, Bottici and Challand look into resources inside the Islamic traditions that may nourish such processes and ultimately prove beneficial for building and expanding democratic practices.

Part II of the book deals with the link between theory and case-analysis, focusing on different legal trends in Europe, both at the state level and beyond the state. Susanna Mancini and Michel Rosenfeld's reflection on the transformation of Enlightenment and religious symbols is an authentic tour de force that combines philosophical issues, counterfactual reasoning and legal case-analysis. For Mancini and Rosenfeld, the revival of religion and postmodern thought are real challenges for an Enlightenment tradition based on a clear-cut distinction between reason and faith in addition to a secularism that is inhospitable to religiosity. In line with philosophers such as J. Derrida, J. Habermas or C. Taylor, Mancini and Rosenfeld aim to provide a more open and pluralistic understanding of the heritage of the Enlightenment so as to avoid the extremes of religious fundamentalism and antireligious secularism.[34] For them, the distinction between reason and faith remains relevant, but "it must be conceived as much more fluid and uncertain" (Chapter 7). It is also necessary to revisit secularism given the "futility of pursuing a

---

[33] C. Bottici, *A Philosophy of Political Myth* (Cambridge University Press, 2007).

[34] See as well M. Rosenfeld, "A Pluralist Critique of the Constitutional Treatment of Religion" in András Sajó and Sholomo Avineri (eds.), *The Law of Religious Identity: Models for Post-Communism* (The Hague: Kluwer Law International, 1999), pp. 39–40; M. Rosenfeld, "Derrida's Ethical Turn and America: Looking Back from the Crossroads of Global Terrorism and the Enlightenment," *Cardozo Law Review* 27 (2005), 815–45; S. Mancini, "The Power of Symbols and Symbols as Power: Secularism and Religion as Guarantors of Cultural Convergence," 30 (6) *Cardozo Law Review* (2009), 2629–68.

neutral areligious ideal" (Chapter 7). Secularism remains a fundamental principle of our constitutional democracies, but it needs to be perceived from a "situational and relational" perspective. This revisited secularism "is above all pluralist." From this standpoint, Mancini and Rosenfeld are critical of the jurisprudence concerning religious symbols, given that it "reveals a tendency to counter or minimize pluralism" instead of seeking "reasonable accommodation" of the different religious communities existent in a polity. The authors make, in this context, the distinction between the symbols of the majority (crucifix) and of the minority (e.g. the Islamic headscarf), noting that, as a general tendency, the courts have developed argumentative strategies so as to favor the majorities over the minorities.

By pointing out that, in the existing literature, "conflict" has become a catch-all term, Lorenzo Zucca embarks on proposing a typology of conflicts between law and religion, in addition to clarifying strategies for dealing with them. Zucca is concerned with practical conflicts. Zucca builds his typology of practical conflicts on the basis of two criteria. On the one hand, there are norms that belong to the same system of rules, and norms that belong to different systems of rules (such as a domestic and a foreign law system). This entails a first category of conflicts, "from within" and "from without." On the other hand, Zucca distinguishes between duty-imposing and power-conferring norms, such as the right to be protected against racial or religious hatred, and the right to freedom of speech. Zucca rejects aggressive secularism, and opts for a "robust secularism" as a central pillar polity free of (islamo)-phobias.

In his contribution, Ian Leigh deals with one of the most controversial issues concerning religion, namely its place in the educational process. In states with an established church, what is a fair balance between the recognition of the importance of the majority religion and that of minority religions in the educational process? When should non-believers and atheists be granted exemptions? Leigh examines these thorny questions by comparing documents such as the Organization for Security and Co-operation in Europe's (OSCE) "Toledo Guiding Principles on Teaching about Religion and Beliefs in Public Schools" with the jurisprudence of the ECtHR, more specifically its decisions *Folgerø and others* v. *Norway* (2007)[35] and *Zengin* v. *Turkey* (2007)[36] concerning religious education

---

[35] Eur. Ct. H. R. (Grand Chamber), *Folgerø and others* v. *Norway*, 29 June 2007.
[36] Eur. Ct. H. R. (Former 2nd section), *Hasan and Eylem Zengin* v. *Turkey*, 9 October 2007.

and the right to exemption. Leigh criticizes the recent assertiveness of the ECtHR as undermining the pluralism of existing traditions and systems of education.[37] The Court's detailed scrutiny of curricula is questionable not only because it fails to provide clear principles of examination but also because it can generate a pernicious culture of litigiousness. Therefore, for Leigh, "more modest and less interventionist approach from Strasbourg" (Chapter 8) would be more adequate. In fact, such a minimal approach respectful of pluralism is advanced by the OSCE.

George Letsas is critical of the ECtHR on the matter of free speech and its limits (art. 10 of the European Convention). Starting with *Otto-Preminger-Institute* v. *Austria* (1994)[38], the ECtHR has taken religious offense or offense against religious feelings as a ground for restricting freedom of speech. Is there anything special about religion, so that religious feelings are granted particular protection? From a liberal standpoint, Letsas argues that there is no legal right not to be offended in one's religious beliefs. For Letsas, there is no special characteristic about religion that would make religious people and communities liable for specific protection.

Aileen McColgan deals with the expansion of the EU and domestic anti-discrimination legislation beyond the sphere of employment so as to cover new territory such as religion. Should the courts and the judiciaries grant protections against discrimination to religious organisations? Should freedom of religion trump equality claims? In tackling these questions, McColgan does not limit her analysis to examining different legal trends in Europe, but she also engages with the communitarian and multiculturalist arguments in favor of granting a special status to religious organizations. While McColgan acknowledges the importance of culture and the legitimacy of granting limited exemptions, she argues that allowing religious exemptions to prohibitions on discrimination may serve to undermine those prohibitions. McColgan is in favor of the ECtHR's approach whereby the accommodation of individual or collective religious practice is a "qualified right at best" (Chapter 9). Granting statutory exemptions undermines not only equality but also multiculturalism, since it can lead to a situation in which individuals inside those groups protected by exemptions are, by virtue of the exemptions themselves, discriminated against.

---

[37] For Leigh's broader view on law and religion, see the masterful R. Ahdar and I. Leigh, *Religious Freedom in the Liberal State* (Oxford University Press, 2005).

[38] Eur. Ct. H. R., *Otto-Preminger-Institut* v. *Austria*, 20 September 1994, *Serie* A, 295.

Daniel Augenstein focuses on the tension between religious pluralism and social cohesion in European human rights jurisprudence.
Comparing the German, French and British interpretation of the "social
cohesion limitation" of freedom of religion, Augenstein argues that, at the
national level, concerns for social cohesion stem from negative and defensive societal attitudes towards religious diversity that are difficult to reconcile with the normative premises of religious pluralism in a democratic
society. In addition, Augenstein examines this tension by looking into the
jurisprudence of the ECtHR and the European Court of Justice (ECJ). For
Augenstein, the ECJ, as part of the EU, is a better site for making religious
pluralism possible within a wider project of political integration.

In Part III, Julie Ringelheim reflects on the main legal normative principles of the ECtHR. Does the ECtHR have a guiding theory? This is a
question that cannot be answered in a straightforward way. Ringelheim
identifies state neutrality, autonomy of religious communities vis-à-vis the
state, secularity of the foundations of the law, secularism and pluralism as
guiding principles of the ECtHR.[39] However, in building a model between
religion and the secular state, the ECtHR faces at least two difficulties.
First, its role is subsidiary with respect to the national authorities. Second,
according to the working method of the judges, their understanding of
religious freedom can only be developed on a casuistic basis. This is a
problem since it implies that the variety of factual circumstances charac-
terizing each case is a constant challenge to the edification of a consistent
framework of adjudication. Despite its ambiguities, overall the jurisprudential activity of the Court "contributes to the building of a European
public sphere" (Chapter 12).

Camil Ungureanu broadens the discussion by dealing with four
approaches that aim at providing orientation to the European institutions faced with renewed claims of religion: a Christian Europe, laïcité,
liberal constitutionalism and dialogical postsecularism. In so doing,
Ungureanu combines political–philosophical analysis with the investigation into aspects of European discourses on religion by focusing
mainly on the European Court of Human Rights and the Council of
Europe. At the European level important steps have been taken in developing an "approach" based on the minimal principles of freedom, of
religion and state neutrality, in addition to those of pluralism and dialogue. Nonetheless, institutions such as the ECtHR have, at key moments,

---

[39] See also J. Ringelheim, *Diversité culturelle et droits de l'homme. La protection des minorités par la Convention européenne des droits de l'homme* (Brussels: Bruylant, 2006).

undermined the principles of minimal liberal constitutionalism, pluralism and dialogue. In particular, Ungureanu underlines that, with some exceptions, the ECtHR has generally taken a black-and-white approach to Islam and, in turn, it has been over-protective with respect to Christian majorities.

Acknowledgments

The 2008 workshop "Religion in the Public Sphere" (Florence) was sponsored by the European University Institute (EUI). Special thanks are due to Yves Mény, the ex-president of the EUI. The Centre of European Law at King's College and Professor Martin van Gelderen from the European University Institute also contributed to the organization of the workshop. Camil Ungureanu also wishes to acknowledge the support of the Spanish Ministry of Education, Project CSO2009-13143, "Religious pluralism and political decentralization in Europe: towards a post-secular model?" (Director: Ferran Requejo).

PART I

1

Religion and political liberty in Italian republics (in the thirteenth to the fifteenth centuries)

MAURIZIO VIROLI

Between the thirteenth and the fifteenth centuries a particular kind of civil Christianity flourished in Italian city republics. It was a religiosity that cultivated charity, and the principle that only a good citizen, who loves and serves the common good, can be a good Christian. That kind of civil Christianity also preached that Christian virtue is strength: not the strength to endure oppression and resign oneself to corruption, but the strength to resist those men who want to impose their dominion, and to fight against the bad custom of placing particular and personal interests above the public good. It also affirmed that of all the forms of government the republican one is the most grateful to God, for God created us in His own image, and hence wants that we live free. It exhorted us to a sacred respect of the laws and taught us that the citizen who governs well and serves the common good with all his strength renders himself similar to God and deserves perennial glory. Indeed, the conflicts that opposed the Italian republics and the Church of Rome were not only political conflicts, but also conflicts between two interpretations of Christianity. When the Florentine magistrates of the fourteenth century challenged the papal interdict by saying that they loved their fatherland more than their souls, they were not, nor did they feel they were, pagan or atheist, but rather true Christians fighting against the corrupt Christianity of the papacy. At the root of the first experiment in political and civil liberty of Italy's history, there lay a civic interpretation of Christianity.

And yet, notwithstanding the intensity and spread of such a civic understanding of Christianity, even the best scholars of republicanism have not seen it, or have seen but a few aspects of it. The great works on Italian republicanism – one could say with a little daring – report the situation that Tocqueville observed, regarding Europe as a whole at the beginning of the nineteenth century: those who are interested in republicanism are not interested in religion, and those who are interested in religion are not interested in republicanism. The religious dimension of Italian republicanism is therefore almost completely absent from the comprehensive narrations of Italian political thought. This chapter intends to offer a contribution to the history of the birth, development and decline of the first form of the religion of liberty in the post-classic world.

1   Under God

The first assemblies of citizens that, in the eleventh and twelfth centuries, gave birth to the communes in northern and central Italy gathered in churches. Even when public authorities built their own palaces, public council meetings were always preceded by religious ritual. Furthermore, the commune contributed to the consecration of the city through paintings and sculptures of the saints, especially those patron saints who had defended the community from external or internal enemies, and who hence had an explicitly civic meaning. The cities were religious, and so were the communes.

The religious dimension of the Italian commune was further reinforced with the shift from a government of consuls and Podestà – the supreme magistrate who represented the commune and carried out important administrative and judicial tasks – to the experiment of real popular governments, that is to say governments by the people's councils. Whereas the first communal statutes, until the beginning of the twelfth century, contained very few references to God, Christ and the saints, these are plentiful in later statutes. In Vicenza, to cite but one example, the statutes of 1264 open with an oath that invokes God, celebrates the divine creation that gave birth to mankind and celebrates the commune as the arrival point of God's project in the world. The commune comprised people with religious, military and professional associations. They scrupulously kept and promoted a religious and civic dimension, held their meetings in churches, after mass, and diligently attended to the worship of the patron saints. The commune's religious identity and republicanism went hand in hand: both gave birth to a republican religion.[1]

One can find evidence of this already in the treaties that explained the functions and duties of the Podestà. These texts insist upon the virtues

---

[1] A. Thompson, O.P., *Cities of God. The Religion of the Italian Communes 1125–1325* (University Park, PA: The Pennsylvania State University Press, 2005) Chapter 3, "The Holy City," pp. 103–40.

that the Podestà and the other communal magistrates have to possess so
that the city can live in peace and flourish in liberty. Although the texts
often have the character of practical handbooks that teach the Podestà
how to speak on various occasions and how to behave at home and in public, their authors also emphasize the religious significance of the supreme
magistrate's office and of the communal government. The most ancient of
the handbooks for the Podestà, the anonymous *Oculus pastoralis*, written
around 1220, places emphasis on the sacred dimension of the republican
regime and of the authority that administers justice. After quoting the
canonical "there is no authority except from God" (Rm 13:1), the author
adds that such a principle holds also for the city's rector; he then adapts
to the republican Podestà the verse of Proverbs 20:8 ("A king enthroned
on the judgment seat / with one look scatters all that is evil") and finally
paraphrases the letter of Paul to the Romans, to argue that the subjects
must revere with sincere faith those rectors who have been elected to
govern.[2] In his first speech, the Podestà must invoke God's grace to perform the task that the citizens have entrusted to him, and which he gladly
accepted. The handbook also recommends that, at the end of the speech,
the Podestà utters words of praise and reverence to "our Lord Jesus Christ,
true son of God, and to his holy mother, madonna Saint Mary," as well to
revered saints of the city.[3] The republican government comes from God,
and to God, to his glory and praise, it must be first directed.[4] If the city
that the Podestà prepares to rule is lacerated by civil strife, as was common in thirteenth-century Italy, he must appeal to the Gospel in order to
exhort us to peace and concord, and cite Luke's famous passage: "Glory to
God in the highest heaven, / and on earth peace for those he favors" (Lk
2:14).

The republic needs God's help. Hoping to obtain it, the ruler must have
a sincere fear of God, and must observe the Catholic faith, remembering
the Scripture: "But Yahweh's face is set against those who do evil, / to cut
off the memory of them from the earth" (Ps 34:16).[5] The author of the
Oculus pastoralis also draws the warning from the Bible that the weighti-
est decisions must be deliberated by the council and, once the decision has
been taken, one must execute them firmly, despite the people's uproar.[6]
Within the council, the one who rules must take advantage, above all, of

---

[2] (*Oculus pastoralis*, vol. I, 1–11); quoting from *Oculus Pastoralis*, in D. Franceschi (ed.),
Memorie dell'Accademia delle Scienze di Torino (Turin: Accademia delle scienze, 1966),
XI, pp. 1–75.

[3] *Ibid.*, vol. III, pp. 58–61.   [4] *Ibid.*, vol. IV, pp. 81–9.

[5] *Ibid.*, vol. II, pp. 1–15.   [6] *Ibid.*, vol. III, pp. 59–68.

the wise and elderly, as again the Bible teaches us: "Do not dismiss what the old people have to say, / for they too were taught by their parents; / from them you will learn how to think" (Si 8:9). He must also always remember that wisdom keeps cities free. This principle of fundamental import for the republican government also comes from the Bible: "There was once a small town, with only a few inhabitants; a mighty king made war on it, laying siege to it and building great siege-works round it. But there was in that town a poverty-stricken sage who by his wisdom saved the town" (Qo 9:14–15). If instead the ruler makes the mistake of trusting foolish councilors, he will bitterly regret it, for "Sand and salt and a lump of iron / are a lighter burden than a dolt" (Si 22:15).[7] Lastly, the ruler must always remind the magistrates appointed to the civil tribunals of the words of the Book of Wisdom: "Love uprightness you who are rulers on earth" (Ws 1:1).[8]

One of the ruler's most important duties is to be able to talk to the people when soldiers die. On these sad occasions the Podestà must remind the citizens that man's life on earth is just conscript service (Jb 7:1) and that man's duty is to fight against pride, vainglory, avarice and envy. The Podestà must then explain that the soldier who falls for his country emigrates from earth to God ("ad Deum"). In order to assuage the suffering, he must quote the Bible, where it admonishes that "Everything goes to the same place, / everything comes from the dust, / everything returns to the dust" (Qo 3:20), and that man is "fleeting as a shadow, transient" (Jb 14:2).[9] Weeping is human, and Jesus himself wept before the suffering of Mary, Lazarus' sister (Jb 11:33–35). But the ruler of a city must teach with humane words that persisting in weeping will not make the beloved one come to life again. It would be wiser to once more consider the Old Testament's words: "Yahweh gave, Yahweh has taken back. Blessed be the name of Yahweh!" (Jb 1:21).[10] In the practice of the public rite, an essential moment of the republican religion, it is therefore the Bible that teaches the fittest words to instill into the citizens the courage and wisdom that is indispensable to a free life.

The work closes with an invective of Justice against bad rulers, who, longing for vainglory, break human and divine laws, unmindful of the sacred principle of loving justice. Their bad conduct offends not only men but also God: it violates the principles of human justice and provides the

---

[7] *Ibid.*, vol. II, pp. 45–56.   [8]*Ibid.*, vol. II, pp. 125–30.
[9] *Ibid.*, vol. IV, pp. 43–5 and pp. 80–96.
[10] *Ibid.*, vol. V, pp. 205–10.

example of a way of life that is antithetical to Christian principles. Christ had admonished that "You are light for the world. A city built on a hill-top cannot be hidden. No one lights a lamp to put it under a tub; they put it on the lamp-stand where it shines for everyone in the house. In the same way your light must shine in people's sight, so that, seeing your good works, they may give praise to your Father in heaven" (Mt 5:14–16). The ruler who oppresses his subjects through an excessive desire for power spreads darkness on earth, and extinguishes in their hearts the love for God, which is the highest and most sacred good. The principle of justice must be sacred in the republican government too.[11] Even in the most pragmatic of the handbooks on the Podestà, *De regimine et sapientia potestatis*, written in verses by justice Orfino da Lodi (*c*.1195–1251), one finds precise religious warnings, first of all that God and Christ teach chiefs and kings to "institute the laws," and that not only Wisdom and Philosophy but also Theology regulate the creation of civil laws, which "uprightly orders every single precept." The first precept of the art of governing is that the Podestà "fears God and observes the commandments of the law."[12] When the Podestà sits as a judge in civil and penal proceedings, he must be a "sharp interpreter of the laws, following Heaven's precepts."[13]

Much more ambitious and refined, the *Liber de regimine civitatum*,[14] written by Giovanni da Viterbo probably in 1240, is even richer in considerations about the republican religion. The author begins his treaty with an invocation to God and adds that he intends to treat, with the help of divine grace, the topic of the republican cities' government and magistrates, with a special focus on their customs. When he explains what he means by "government," he quotes, after Horace, the Psalms (Ps 124:1), to emphasize that only God guards the cities. To clarify what he means by "Podestà," he mentions, after Cicero's *De Officiis*,[15] the Gospel of John (19:11) – "You would have no power over me at all if it had not been given you from above" – as well as other sources of the Old Testament that attest the divine foundation of sovereign power. Aware of the sacred character of his office, the Podestà must solemnly swear on the Gospels and invoke

[11] *Ibid.*, vol. VI, pp. 265–75.

[12] O. da Lodi, *De regimine et sapientia potestatis*, ed. S. Pozzi, (Lodi: Archivio Storico Lodigiano, 1998), pp. 310–15, 410–15 and 465.

[13] *Ibid.*, pp. 822–3.

[14] Giovanni da Viterbo, *Liber de regimine civitatum*, ed. Gaetano Salvemini, in *Bibliotheca iuridica medii aevi*, 3 vols., ed. Augusto Guadenzi (Bologna, 1901), vol. III, pp. 215–80.

[15] Cicero, *De Officiis*, ed. and trans. Walter Miller (London, 1913).

God's help in order to be able to perform honorably the difficult task that he has agreed to carry on his shoulders.

Giovanni da Viterbo assures that the Podestà can count on God's help only if he sincerely fears Him. The Wisdom Books affirm that "By me monarchs rule and princes decree what is right" (Pr 8:15). All men's efforts would be vain without God's help. This concept, of the utmost significance for the republican ideology of the thirteenth and following centuries, is drawn from the Bible: "If Yahweh does not guard a city / in vain does its guard keep watch" (Ps 127:1). This implies that the Podestà must have a sincere Catholic faith, be religious and never forget that "Like flowing water is a king's heart in Yahweh's hand" (Pr 21:1). If the Podestà is instead disloyal to God, he will lose upright reason and be abandoned to degrading passions (Rm 1:26). Corrupt rulers, blinded by pride, seek glory, but do not realize that all they obtain is mere vainglory, as it does not come from God.

After a lengthy treatment of the virtues of the Podestà, Giovanni da Viterbo makes clear that the sovereign's power, similar to the priest's power, is a gift of God, which greatly elevates the condition of the one who receives it. He then explains that Christian, pagan and Hebrew authors all agree that sovereign power is good inasmuch as it comes from God, who is perfect goodness. The exercise of sovereign power, however, can be bad: "They have set up kings, / but without my consent, / and appointed princes, / but without my knowledge. / With their silver and gold, / they have made themselves idols, / but only to be destroyed" (Hos 8:4). Without engaging the tricky question of the obligation to obey corrupt sovereigns, Giovanni da Viterbo strongly reaffirms that the Podestà must always have God and justice before his eyes.

An encyclopedia in wide circulation in the Middle Ages, the *Livres dou Tresor*, (c.1260) written by the magistrate and master of rhetoric Brunetto Latini (c.1220 to c.1294–95), contains what is perhaps the most influential treatment of the republican religion. In the third book, Latini begins first by mentioning the Aristotelian idea that the government of the city "is the noblest and highest science, and the noblest occupation on earth," and then Cicero's definition that "the city is an association of men who live in the same place and in accordance to a single law."[16] As he goes on to explain what are the pillars of a ruler, he relies on biblical sources to emphasize that "all dominions and dignities are conferred upon us by our

---

[16] B. Latini, *Tresor*, ed. P. G. Beltrami, P. Squillaccioti, P. Torri and S. Vatteroni (Turin: Einaudi, 2007), vol. III, 73, p. 791.

sovereign Father, who, in the sacred order of earthly things, wanted that the cities' government be founded on three pillars, that is justice, reverence, and love." Justice, in particular, must be fixed in the ruler's heart so firmly that he shall guarantee everyone's right, and shall "turn neither to right nor to left" (Pr 4:27). He finally quotes the Apostle to admonish us that our Lord be loved, as reverence is "the only thing in the world which augments the faiths' merits and overcomes every sacrifice."[17]

Among the ruler's virtues, besides the political virtues of justice, fortitude, prudence and temperance, Latini also indicates the theological virtues of faith, hope and charity. About faith, he observes that "God is well praised and glorified when he is believed in accordance with truth and that only at that point can God be rightly entreated and prayed [to]." Without faith, he adds, no one can please God. Faith must be translated into deeds, but many Christians, Latini laments, greatly depart from Christian truth in their lives.[18] Man must trust that God will pardon him, but "must take great care not to persist in sin."[19] About charity, Latini writes that she is "lady and queen of all virtues and represents the bond of perfection, for it binds together the other virtues." As the Apostle Paul teaches us when he affirms that, were he to give away his own body to be burned, it would be of no use without charity: man has no virtues at all "if he lacks charity and love for men." Charity means loving God and one's neighbor. Jesus Christ, Latini emphasizes, is God and man, and hence whoever hates man does not truly love Jesus Christ."[20]

When Latini expounds which are the qualities that the ruler must possess, he makes sure to include in his long list that the ruler "shall have pure faith in God and in men, for without faith and loyalty justice cannot be preserved."[21] Governing well is a task that gives great honors, but is also very demanding: "Only Jesus Christ's nobleness makes man worthy of such offices." Whoever accepts to govern in full liberty and awareness, must confide in Christ and the sovereign Father, be religious with respect to God and the Holy Church, and remember that in the law the judge is said to be consecrated. The *Digest* states that "one properly calls you priests." Elsewhere, the law says that the judge is consecrated in God's presence, and that he is on earth "like a God."[22]

As soon as he arrives in the city, the ruler must talk to the magistrates and to the citizens, and in his speech he cannot forget – Latini urges – to

---

[17] *Ibid.*, vol. III, 74, p. 793.   [18] *Ibid.*, vol. II, 126, p. 625.
[19] *Ibid.*, vol. II, 128, p. 627.   [20] *Ibid.*, vol. II, 127, p. 625.
[21] *Ibid.*, vol. III, 75, p.797.   [22] *Ibid.*, vol. III, 79, pp. 808–9.

invoke Jesus Christ, the glorious Virgin Mary and Saint John, the city's patron and guide. After having sworn, he must go to church, hear Mass and pray to God and the saints.[23] There is nothing better for a prince of the earth "than following the right faith and true doctrine." The ruler of the republic must therefore have a pure soul and intention, and must always keep his hands "clean before God."[24]

What emerges from the first writings of the thirteenth century on government is a republican religion founded on the principle that the commune is under the protection of God, Christ and the patron saints. Divine help is the true bulwark against sedition, discord, tyranny and war – the mortal enemies of republican liberty. The man who undertakes the task of governing acquires a dignity that renders him similar to God, and that imposes on him to always follow the virtues, both political and theological. Prominent among these is charity for God and men. Beyond charity, the ruler must respect justice, which is meant as God's command. The principles of republican government, therefore, are not only moral and political maxims dictated by reason and prudence, but real religious principles.

2   Images of the civil religion

Through the treaties on government, the concept of civil religion spread within republican cities' culture and custom. But even more effective were the images that expressed those concepts. Whereas the concepts expounded in the treaties talked first and foremost to reason, paintings struck the eyes, and from the eyes touched the passions. Rulers of republics were aware of the strength of the image, especially when accompanied by clear words, written in big and visible characters, preferably in vulgar Italian. For this reason, rulers ordered from valid artists a great number of works that explained to the magistrates and citizens who went to public palaces what were the principles of republican good government. The message that came from the walls of the city government's most important halls was both political and religious at the same time. These works exhorted the people to love and respect justice, follow civil virtues, serve the common good, avoid discord and hate tyranny. That is to say, they taught the people to consider civic duties as real religious duties: as God's and Christ's commandments, not just the advice of human wisdom.

---

[23] *Ibid.*, vol. III, 84, p. 823.   [24] *Ibid.*, vol. III, 97, pp. 844–5.

In Simone Martini's wonderful *Maestà*, in Siena's Palazzo Pubblico (1315), Christ holds the scroll with the Book of Wisdom's words: "Diligite iustitiam qui iudicatis terram." The Madonna, too, talks with severe language to the magistrates who pass by her to reach the Sala dei Nove. The Virgin says that she loves good advice more than flowers, and that she suffers because men too often prefer their own advantage to the common good: "The angelic little flowers, roses and lilies, / with which the celestial meadow is adorned, / delight me no more than the good advice. / However, sometimes I see the one who, for his own advantage, / disregards me and deceives my land, / and the worse he speaks the more he is praised. Beware, anyone who condemns this" ["Li angelichi fiorecti, rose e gigli, / onde s'adorna lo celeste prato, / non mi dilettan più che i buon' consigli. / Ma talor veggio chi per proprio stato / disprezza me e la mia ter[r]a inganna, / e quando parla peggio è più lodato. / Guardi ciascun cui questo dir conda[n]na"]. Siena is the Virgin's land, and whoever offends or deceives the republic offends the Virgin, and behaves as a bad Christian.

The Virgin herself commands us not to follow the men who speak against the common good. The fresco's political and religious teaching is rendered even clearer by its inscription, "Responsio Virginis ad dicta santorum," which is the reply from the Virgin to the pleas that, on their knees, the four saints (Ansano, Savino, Crescenzio and Vittore) address to her on the city's behalf. The four saints' words are lost, but the Virgin's words are still readable within the frame's lower border: "My beloved, bear in mind / that as you wish I will meet / your pious honest prayers. / However, if the powerful will vexate the weak, / by burdening them with disgrace or harm, / do not pray for them / or whoever else deceives my land" ["Diletti miei, ponete nelle menti / che li devoti vostri preghi onesti / come vorrete voi farò contenti. / Ma se i potenti a' debil' fien molesti, / gravando loro con vergogne o danni, / le vostre orazion non son per questi / né per chiunque la mia terra inganni"]. Christ's Mother is saying to Siena's magistrates and citizens that she sides with the weak people offended, molested and oppressed by the powerful, and that she is not willing to listen to prayers for those powerful people who deceive her and her land. If they want to be heard, even the saints, like the other citizens, must take justice's side. A perfect civic warning, but also a religious warning, both because the Virgin is speaking, and because her words pose a specific condition in order to receive divine help: "you can count on my protection and my benevolence if and only if you will behave like good citizens."

The principles of republican religion emerge also from Ambrogio Lorenzetti's (1258–1348) great painting in the Palazzo Pubblico's Sala dei Nove, where the city's supreme magistracy met. In this work, finished between 1337 and 1340, the artist draws both from the Greek and Roman tradition, and from biblical sources. We can see this in the image of Justice, which is the foundation of the common good and of good government. She draws inspiration from divine Wisdom, which is in heaven, at the same height as the theological virtues – faith, hope and charity. Between Wisdom and Justice, as an ideal link between the two, lie the Book of Wisdom's words, as in Simone Martini's '*Maestà*': "Diligite iustitiam qui iudicatis terram." For her link with divine wisdom, justice itself has a quasi-divine status. Lorenzetti defines her "holy virtue." It is from her that republican government takes a distinct religious dimension.

The republican religion emerges also from the majestic figure that dominates the central part of the painting. It represents Siena's commune: its dress has the city's colors; at its feet one sees the twins suckling the she-wolf – a clear example of Siena's boasted Roman origin. The figure is an old man, that is, a *sena* person; the letters CSCV (*Commune Senarum Civitas Virginis*) encircle his head; on the shield one sees the image of the Virgin with the baby Jesus. The old man's head is as high as the theological virtues and the celestial figures. Lorenzetti wants to impart the teaching that a well-governed commune is under the Virgin's protection and respects the principles of justice. Besides being the representation of the Commune of Siena, the majestic figure is also a judge, and as such acquires a further religious significance. As we have already seen, the treaties on civil government maintain that the judge is "like a God on earth," for, by judging in conformity with justice, the judge brings divine wisdom into the city. He certainly is the supreme judge, but he is also bound by the laws and statutes that, with solemn oath, he has declared to respect and apply. From this point of view, the sovereign and free commune is the opposite of tyranny, which is not subjected to any statues and laws and, on the contrary, crushes justice under its heel. For this quasi-divine character, the commune and its representatives must be looked at with a devotion similar to that which one owes God, just as in the fresco the citizens who go in procession towards the ruler do (especially those who are closer to him).

Another concept of the republican religion concerns the principle of the common good. In this respect a quarrel has been going on about the meaning of the majestic figure. In 1958 Nicolai Rubinstein argued that the image is the pictorial translation of the Aristotelian concept of common good, as the basis and criterion of good government "in its Thomistic-Aristotelian meaning." Lorenzetti wanted Siena's governors and citizens to always have before their eyes the warning that the common good must always prevail, if one wishes the city to enjoy the benefits of good government.[25] Against this interpretation, Quentin Skinner has argued, in various studies published between 1987 and 1999, that the proper intellectual context by which one can understand the meaning of Lorenzetti's painting is not Thomistic–Aristotelian, but rather the pre-humanistic treaties on city government of the thirteenth century. According to Skinner, the majestic figure is not the representation of the common good, but the symbolic representation of the kind of ruler that the city needs in order to live in justice and enjoy the common good.

Consequently, Rubinstein and Skinner also interpret in a different way the fundamental inscription that Lorenzetti placed at the basis of the fresco's central section, and which reads: "Wherever it rules, this holy virtue [justice] induces to unity the many souls. And these, gathered for this reason, make a common good for their lord" ["Questa santa virtu [la giustizia] laddove regge induce adunita lianimi molti. Equesti accio riccolti un ben comun perlor sigror sifanno"]. According to Rubinstein, this sentence affirms that, wherever the holy virtue of justice rules, it induces many souls to unity, and that these people, gathered thus, give themselves the common good as their lord. According to Skinner, however, the sentence affirms that wherever the holy virtue of justice rules, it induces many souls to unity, and these people, gathered thus, create through their lord a common good.[26] In my own judgement, the majestic central figure represents the common good, besides being the representation of the sovereign commune and of the judge. The most important proof of this is the inscription that Lorenzetti placed at the base of the painting of tyranny. It describes what happens when justice is crushed and tied up, and when the citizens pursue their private advantage instead of aiming at the common good: "Wherever justice is tied up. No one ever with the common good / is in keeping. Nor does he follow a straight way. But tyranny imposes itself"

---

[25] N. Rubinstein, "Political Ideas in Sienese Art: The Frescoes by Ambrogio Lorenzetti and Taddeo di Bartolo in the Palazzo Pubblico," *Journal of the Warburg and Courtauld Institutes* 21 (1958), 179–207; on this theme, see M. M. Donato's excellent study, "Ancora sulle 'fonti' nel Buon Governo di Ambrogio Lorenzetti: dubbi, precisazioni, anticipazioni," in S. A. Braccesi and M. Ascheri (eds.), *Politica e cultura nelle repubbliche italiane dal medioevo all'età moderna*, ed. by S. A. Braccesi e M. Ascheri (Romea: Istituto Storico Italiano per l'Età Moderna e Contemporanea, 2001), pp. 43–79.

[26] Q. Skinner, *Visions of Politics*, vol. II, *Renaissance Virtues* (Cambridge University Press, 2002), p. 99.

["Ladoue sta legata la iutitia. Nesun albe(n) comune giamay / sacorda. Ne tira adritta corda. P(er)o convie(n) che tirannia / sormonti"].

Where justice is sovereign, the citizens agree on the common good and enjoy good government; where justice is oppressed, the citizens are not in keeping with the common good and tyranny emerges, with its dreadful string of vices. The message could not be clearer, and in order to keep it thus, we must interpret the majestic figure as the representation of the common good, and read it as the pictorial transcription of a political principle that derives from the Aristotelian tradition. This interpretation allows us to grasp a further meaning of the majestic figure that has a great relevance for the republican religion's birth.

Once more, the Aristotelian context is a precious guide. In the first pages of the *Nicomachean Ethics* (1094 1–10),[27] Aristotle writes in fact that the common good is not only better, but also more divine than the individual good: "melius vero ac divinius," as we can read in William of Moerbeke's Latin translation, which circulated at Lorenzetti's times. In his comment, Thomas Aquinas explained that Aristotle meant that the city's common good is more divine than the individual good because it is similar to God in its being the universal cause of all goods.[28] The idea that the common good is divine became almost a common place of fourteenth-century republican political thought. From this idea derived the conviction that the magistrates who serve the common good make themselves similar to God.

Lorenzetti renders these concepts figuratively, by elevating the central figure to the height of the theological virtues, and by putting on its head, as a guide and inspiration, *caritas*. In the Aristotelian tradition, *caritas* is the passion that encourages us to put the common good above the individual one. Remigio de' Girolami (1235–1319), who was Thomas's disciple and Santa Maria Novella's prior, writes in *De bono pacis* that charity does not seek one's own good, but places the common good before one's own good.[29] In *De bono communi*, he points at

---

[27] Aristotle, *Nicomachean Ethics*, trans. Roger Crisp (Cambridge University Press, 2000).

[28] See also T. Aquinas, *Summa Theologiae*, Pars Prima Secundae, Questio 97, art. 4 (CreateSpace, 2009).

[29] "Caritas non quaerit quae sua sunt," quod hoc sit est intelligendum, quia caritas communia propriis anteponit"; R. de' Girolami, 'De bono pacis,' in M. C. De Matteis, *La "teologia politica comunale" di Remigio de' Girolami* (Bologna: Pàtron Editore, 1977), pp. 56–7. See also C. T. Davis, "An Early Florentine Political Theorist: fra Remigio de' Girolami," in *Proceedings of the American Philosophical Society*, LIV (Philadelphia: 1960), pp. 662–76. On the relationship between civic conscience and charity of country, see A. Bosisio, "Milano e la sua coscienza cittadina nel Duecento" in *"Atti dei Convegni del Centro Studi sulla Spiritualità medievale,"* XI, (Todi: Università degli Studi di Perugia, 1972), pp. 47–93.

charity as civil life's foundation, and emphasizes that love of country is a Christian duty founded upon man's natural inclination, and upon God's love.[30] Inasmuch as the common good, as Aristotle teaches us in the *Nicomachean Ethics*, is the best and most divine good, those who love the common good get closer to God. Another disciple of Thomas, Tolomeo da Lucca, affirms in the *De regimine principum* that the love of country is charitable love of the common good, which renders one's soul strong, and is perfectly coherent with God's love; in fact, it is its necessary consequence.[31] Unlike Augustine, Tolomeo does not acknowledge any difference between the pagans' and the Christians' *caritas patriae*. He places charity at the highest rank in the hierarchy of virtues, and assigns to love of country the same rank. In the most influential texts of medieval political thought, love of country assumes, therefore, the meaning of charitable love of the common good, which makes man closer to God.

After having explained the nature of charity, Tolomeo expounds its political and moral effects. Charity for the fatherland inspired the Romans to govern well ("ad bene regendum"), and for this reason they deserved to become the masters of the world. He also adds the noteworthy specification that love of country shares to some degree in the divine nature ("partecipabant quandam naturam divinam"). As God is the universal cause of all things, love of country is directed towards the community and the people's good. In support of his thesis, Tolomeo quotes the classic episodes of Marcus Curtius, who hurled himself into the abyss; Attilius Regulus, who preferred to save his country rather than his life; and Fabricius, who was not corrupted by gold. The person who really loves his country and diligently looks after the common good, becomes God's deputy and shares in divine nature, thereby fulfilling God's commandment to love God and one's neighbor with all one's heart, soul and strength.

---

[30] R. de' Girolami, "*De bono communi*," in M. C. De Matteis, *La "teologia politica comunale" di Remigio de' Girolami* (Bologna: Patron Editore, 1977), p. 43. See also C. T. Davis, "Remigio de' Girolami and Dante: a Comparison of their Conceptions of Peace" in *Studi Danteschi*, 36, ed. Michele Barbi (Florence: G C. Sansoni, 1959), 105–36, and Davis, *An Early Florentine Political Theorist: Fra Remigio de' Girolami*.

[31] "Amor patriae in radice charitatis fundatur, quae communia propriis, non propria communibus anteponit"; T. da Lucca, "*De regimine principum*," in R. Spiazzi (ed.), *Divi Thomae Aquinatis Opuscula Philosophice* (Turin: Marietti, 1954), p. 299. Augustine disapproves of the ancients' love of country in *De civitate Dei*, V, 12; see also C. T. Davis, "Ptolemy of Lucca, and the Roman Republic," *Proceedings of the American Philosophical Society*, 118 (Philadelphia: 1974), 30–50.

The concept of love of country as a love that renders man similar to God resurfaces in Dante's *Convivio* (IV, V, 13–14). For Dante, love of country is a love that God instills in some men and that renders them divine:

> If we consider, then, [Rome] in its adolescence, after its royal tutelage was emancipated, since Brutus first consul until Caesar first supreme prince, we find her exalted through citizens not human, but divine, in whom a love not human, but divine, was inspired in loving [her]. And this could not be but for a special end, intended by God in such a celestial infusion. Who can affirm that it was without divine inspiration that Fabricius could reject an almost infinite quantity of gold because he did not want to abandon his country? And Curius, tempted by the Samnites' corruption, who for charity of country rejected a great quantity of gold, stating that Roman citizens wanted to possess not gold, but the possessors of gold? And Mucius, who set fire to his own hand, as he had missed his attempt to free Rome? Who will say of Torquatus, who condemned to death his own son for love of the common good, that he could endure this sufferance without God's help?[32]

Back to Lorenzetti's painting, we notice that *caritas* is the highest of all virtues, and, although it is a theological virtue, it has a worldly content, as well as a strong erotic meaning. Lorenzetti paints it red, love's color, perhaps after Dante's inspiration: "tanto rossa / Ch'a pena fora dentro al fuoco nota" (*Divina Commedia: Purgatorio*, XXIX, 121). Charity is veiled, to be more seductive. In her right hand she holds an arrow pointed downwards, one of the most typical symbols of love piercing someone's heart. In her left hand, she carries a burning heart, to point to charity as *amor concupiscentiae*, a real erotic passion.[33] Lorenzetti admonishes that, in order to make the common good triumph and to save the city from the horrors of tyranny, it is necessary that the ruler is guided by political virtues, but, above all, by a charity that makes him love the common good with intense passion.

---

[32] D. Alighieri, *Opere minori*, Tomo I. Part II, ed. C. Vasoli and D. De Robertis (Milan-Naples: Riccardo Ricciardi Editore, 1988), pp. 571–3. Petrarca considers instead the ancients' love (charity) of country as an imperfect love, and does not accept the idea of a specifically Christian patriotism. See C. Trinkaus, *In Our Image and Likeness. Humanity and Divinity in Italian Humanist Thought* (London: Constable, 1970), vol. I, p. 37–8. In *De vita solitaria*, however, he maintains that nothing is more suitable for man, and nothing renders him more similar to God, than operating for the common good: "'quid aut homine dignius aut similius Deo est, quam servare et adiuvare quam plurimos?'"; Petrarca, "De vita solitaria" in *Prose*, ed. G. Martellotti (Milan and Naples, 1955), pp. 322 and 328.

[33] R. Freyan, "The evolution of the Caritas figures in the thirteenth and fourteenth centuries," *Journal of the Warburg and Courtauld Institutes* XI (1948), 68–82.

The same principles of republican religion emerge from the "Cycle of Famous Men," which Taddeo di Bartolo (1362–1422) painted between 1413 and 1414 in the Anticapella placed between the Hall of the Nine and the Council Hall. Like Lorenzetti's "Buongoverno," the cycle lies at the centre of Siena's institutional space. Guide to the entire cycle is Aristotle. Taddeo di Bartolo means to say that we have to turn to the Greek master if we want to understand the principles of good government, and learn the lessons of the great men and the virtues in the Anticapella. One reads in the inscription that introduces the painting: "Magnus Aristotles ego sum, qui carmine seno, / Est etenim numerus perfectus, duxit ad actum / Quos virtus tipi signo viros, quibus atque superne / Res crevit Romana potens, celosque subivit."[34] Aristotle teaches the way to preserve liberty and to reach to the sky, following the sacred traces of the great men. Taddeo di Bartolo teaches that the men who pursue virtues and defend liberty acquire a quasi-divine splendor.

Great Roman figures reinforce Aristotle's words. First among them is Cicero;[35] next to him is Cato, who asserts the principle that liberty requires devotion, even at the cost of one life.[36] The sacred republican principle of serving one's country and the common liberty meets a spectacular divine confirmation by the representation of "Religion," placed on top of the arch that leads to the chapel. Underneath it lies the map of Rome, to signify the link with the civil ethos that the pagan religion could instill in the hearts of the Romans. However, its message is unmistakably Christian: "Omne quodcumque facitis in verbo aut in opera / In nomine domini Iesu Christi facite." If they will follow the example of Roman and biblical heroes, and if they will always act as good Christians, the republic's magistrates will be able to serve the common good, defend liberty, and rise to the sky in glory.[37] This is the lesson of Aristotle and the Romans, but above all the

---

[34] *Un ciclo di tradizione repubblicana nel Palazzo Pubblico di Siena. Le iscrizioni degli affreschi di Taddeo di Bartolo (1413–1414)*, ed. R. Funari (Siena: Accademia Senese degli Intronati, 2002), p. 5.

[35] *Ibid.*, p. 25.   [36] *Ibid.*, p. 31.

[37] To be sure that this political and religious lesson would be really clear, Taddeo places a long inscription, in vernacular, on the main wall: "You who rule, mirror yourselves in these men / If you want to rule for thousands of years, / Pursue the common good and do not be led astray ... The more you will remain united the more you will be powerful / And will rise to the sky full of glory / As the great people of Mars did, / a people which had won the whole world, / but then, as they had factions / Lost liberty everywhere [Specchiatevi in costoro voi che reggete / Se volete regnare mille et mille anni, / Seguite il benune et non v'inganni ... Sempre magiori sarete insieme uniti / Et saglirete al cielo pieno d'ogni gloria / Si come fecie il gran popolo di marte, / El quale avendo del mondo victoria, / Perché infra loro si furo dentro partiti / Perdé la libertade in ogni parte]."

lesson of the Christian religion. Serving the common good is the true way to be Christians.

If we move from Siena to Florence, the artistic representations that were meant to give a religious significance to republican liberty are equally splendid and meaningful. One of the most important examples, because of its artistic value and the eloquence of its political message, is the statue of David, which Donatello began to sculpt in 1409, and which was transferred to Palazzo Vecchio's Sala dei Gigli in 1416. David is the biblical hero who decides to confront alone, armed only with a sling, the gigantic Goliath, and who overcomes him. The religious character of the statue's message emerges not only from the choice of a biblical hero, but also from the explicit reference to God's help for those who fight for liberty, as one can grasp from the inscription placed at the base of the statue: "Pro patria fortiter dimicantibus etiam adversus terribilissimos hostes deus prestat auxilium."[38]

Equally strong is the pedagogical message contained in the statue of Judith and Holofernes, completed by Donatello in 1464, the year of the death of Cosimo il Vecchio, the founder of the Medicean regime. The Florentines who, in 1494, inspired by Savonarola's preaching, had established a republican government, grasped a strong civic message in the statue, and decided to transfer it to a podium in the Palazzo Vecchio, where everybody could admire it. The Florentines knew well the biblical story of Judith, Manasseh's wonderful wife, who, after having been left a widow, wore a sackcloth next to the skin, "without anyone finding a word against her, so devoutly did she fear God" (Jdt 8:8). Judith invoked the "God of the humble, / the help of the oppressed, the support of the weak, / the refuge of the forsaken, / the Saviour of the despairing" (Jdt 9:11), so that He would help her to free the people of Israel from the oppression of the Assyrians, whose chief was Holofernes. She then "removed the sackcloth she was wearing and taking off her widow's dress, she washed all over, anointed herself plentifully with perfumes, dressed her hair, wrapped a turban round it and put on the robe of joy she used to wear when her husband Manasseh was alive. She put her sandals on her feet, put on her necklaces, bracelets, rings, earrings and all her jewelry, and made herself beautiful enough to beguile the eye of any man who saw

---

[38] See H. W. Janson, *The Sculpture of Donatello* (Princeton University Press, 1963), pp. 3–7. See also N. Rubinstein, *The Palazzo Vecchio 1298–1532. Government, Architecture, and Imagery in the Civic Palace of the Florentine Republic* (Oxford: Clarendon Press, 1995), pp. 55–6.

her" (Jdt 10:3–4). Admitted into Holofernes' presence, she was invited to his table, and made him drink far more wine than he had drunk on any other day in his life. When he collapsed completely drunk on his bed, she beheaded him with his own scimitar. Judith brought the head to her fellow Israelites, who found the strength to attack the Assyrians and regain liberty. The Florentines decided to exalt Judith's deed as an example of a heroic action for the country's salvation that teaches the citizens that defending the republic against enemies and tyrants is their duty towards God.

Around the end of the fourteenth century, a "Cycle of Famous Men" was realized in the Saletta. Destroyed in 1470, it was illustrated with epigrams composed by Coluccio Salutati, the Florentine Republic's Chancellor from 1375 to 1406. The republican content of the inscriptions was very strong. Especially powerful were the references to Brutus, who, by expelling the kings, founded Roman liberty, Cicero, who died by the same sword that killed liberty altogether, and Cato, the implacable enemy of vice, who committed suicide so as not to submit himself to the tyrant.[39] The use of biblical and classical themes to exhort the people to love liberty with religious devotion is particularly evident in the paintings that Ghirlandaio made in 1482 for the Sala dei Gigli. At the centre of the painting, one finds the portrayal of St. Zanobio, flanked on the right with a lion carrying the people's banner and, on the left, with another lion carrying the banner of the city of Florence. Higher up there lie two big lunettes, with portrayals of Brutus, first consul, Mucius Scaevola, Scipio Africanus and Cicero. The inscriptions placed under these Roman heroes have a more generic republican content compared to those that Salutati had composed about a century before for a more ancient cycle. Salutati's Brutus is the founder of Roman liberty through the expulsion of the kings; Ghirlandaio's Brutus is a defender of the country. Cicero, who died together with Roman liberty, becomes Catilina's triumphant flogger.[40] The difference can be explained by the Medicean dominion of Florence. Nevertheless, the character, at once religious and republican, of the paintings' teachings is clear enough. Rather than on the inscriptions, it rests on the match of a saint, and of Christ, with the symbols of the commune of Florence and the republican heroes.

---

[39] See Rubinstein, *The Palazzo Vecchio*, pp. 52–3 and A. T. Hankey, "Salutati's Epigrams for the Palazzo Vecchio at Florence," *Journal of the Warburg and Courtauld Institutes* XXII (1959), pp. 363–5.
[40] See Rubinstein, *The Palazzo Vecchio*, p. 64.

During the 1494–1512 popular government, Florentine authorities committed themselves with renewed eagerness to decorating the Palazzo Vecchio with works of art of civic and religious inspiration. Not all of them were realized before the republic's fall in 1512, above all because of the financial straits imposed by military commitments. One of those which did not see the light was a painting of St. Ann, assigned to Fra Bartolomeo, that would have represented the saint in a very important position, for on her feast day the Florentines had rebelled against the Duke of Athens, who had become the city's tyrant. Two marble epitaphs inspired by Savonarola were put in the Consiglio Grande's hall, the kernel of the popular government. The first, in vulgar Italian, clearly referred to the expedient, used more than once in Florence's history, to call the people to the squares in order to destroy republican liberties ["chi vuol fare parlamento vuol torre al popolo e' reggimento"]. The second, in Latin, admonished that the Great Council was given by God, and anyone who tried to undo it, would come to no good.[41] The republican government's heart was thus charged by the religious dimension and it radiated from there to the whole of the republic's body.

3   Republican religion and monarchic religions

Republican religion was born and rooted in a late-medieval Europe dominated by monarchies that, from the thirteenth century, had endowed themselves with a sacred dimension similar to that of the church.[42] Jurists and political philosophers transferred to the state the concept of "corpus mysticum," which had been created to designate the church community and meant a body which cannot be seen by the eyes, but only grasped by the intellect. Applied to the state, the concept of the mystical body referred mainly, but not exclusively, to the monarchy, where the king is at the head of the mystical–political body, just like Christ, or his Vicar on earth, is at the head of the mystical body of the church. Republics too, however, are mystical bodies. The great jurist Baldus de Ubaldis (1327–1400), for instance, uses the phrase "mystical body of the people" as the equivalent of *politia*, that is political community, or any other multitude ordered by

---

[41] *Ibid.*, p. 73.

[42] The best study on monarchic sacredness is still that of the lamented C. Geertz, "Centers, Kings, and Charisma: Reflections on the Symbolics of Power" in J. Ben-David and T. N. Clark, *Culture and Its Creators. Essays in Honor of Edward Shils* (Chicago and London: University of Chicago Press, 1977), pp. 150–71.

laws and political institutions. The "breath of incense" and sacredness that invested the state when it started to be considered a mystical body also invested the republics.[43]

The spread of Aristotelianism further reinforced the state's sacred dimension. From the Aristotelian perspective, the state is a moral and political body that pursues the end of the common good, that is, as we have already seen, a divine good. Thanks to Aristotelianism, a new sacred aura thus descended upon the political community. Of course, that aura was different from the one that the church had, but it was not incompatible with it. Later on, to add to the quasi-sacred character of the political community the jurists created the metaphor of the moral and political marriage between the prince and the state: just as men are spiritually united through the mystical body whose chief is Christ, they are morally and spiritually united through the *respublica*, whose chief is the prince. Just like the prelates, at their crowning the kings received the ring, which symbolized – God witnessing – the marriage between the prince and the political community.[44]

As the centrality of the ointment testifies, the basic tenet of monarchical religion was the transformative event of God's descent to man, as opposed to the republican idea of man's elevation to God through his virtues. Echoing the ancient custom of the use of ointment for catechumens, the priests and the bishops became the essential character of the royal ointment. Through it, medieval kings became "Christs du Seigneur," defended against the devil by divine protection.[45] Kings acquired through ointment a quasi-priestly character, without ever properly becoming priests. Inasmuch as he has not received the holy orders, the king obviously cannot be a clergyman; having a wife, and a sword, prevent him from being a minor; therefore, he can be but a layman.[46] This logical argument was little appreciated by the kings, though, eager as they were to expand their power so as to undertake even priestly functions. The annointment was the quintessential royal act, to the point that not even the great feudal lords, who were constantly seeking to imitate other aspects of the kings' sacred character, ever dared embezzling such prerogative.[17]

[43] E. H. Kantorowicz, *The King's Two Bodies. A Study in Mediaeval Political Theology. With a New Preface by William Chester Jordan* (Princeton University Press, 1997), pp. 209–10.

[44] *Ibid.*, pp. 216–23

[45] M. Bloch, *Les rois thaumaturges* (Strasbourg: Librairie Istra, 1924), pp. 69–70.

[46] *Ibid.*, p. 186.   [47] *Ibid.*, p. 194.

The concept of royal religion ("religion royal") emerges with particular clarity in the *Traité du sacre*, written in 1372 by the Carmelite friar Jean Golein. Above all, the author insists upon the rite of spoliation, as a symbol of the passage from mundane condition to royal religiosity.[48] From the point of view of a more rigorous theology, like that which was established at the Council of Trent, such a doctrine seemed scandalous. How could royal annointment, since it was no sacrament, pardon a mortal sin? However, starting from the thirteenth century, one witnesses a clear effort to assimilate the condition of the temporal chief of Christianity into that of a deacon, or a sub-deacon.[49] The kings of the Middle Ages always strived to appear to their subjects as men illuminated by the glory of priesthood. As one can read in a text written in 1430, the king who has received ointment is not merely a laic person, but a mixed person.[50] Besides the oil falling from above, the spoliation and the ring, the royal religion's signs are – especially in France – the hailing of the scrofulous, Charlemagne's relics and the tradition of the Crusades. The king of France was called a holy king in a holy land, as witnessed by the royal lily, a symbol of holiness in itself, as the three petals represent faith, doctrine and military power. In the thirteenth century, when republican religion emerged in Italy, the idea of the holy king in a land devoted to the true Christian faith was generally accepted in France. "Most Christian king," "champion of faith" and "defender of the Church" became terms of common use at the beginning of the fourteenth century.[51]

We can now rather easily grasp the difference between the royal religion and the republican religion. The former celebrates an individual mystical body, that of the king; the latter celebrates a collective mystical body, that of the republic. Even in Venice, where the doge had a quasi-royal dignity, the public ceremonial aimed at celebrating the republic's excellence and the doge in that he was its representative.[52] Starting from

---

[48] "Quant le roy se despoille, c'est signifiance qu'il relenquist l'estat mondain de par devant pour prendre celui de la religion royale; et s'il le prent en tele devocion comme il doit, je tieng qu'il est telement nettoié de ses pechiez comme celui qui entre nouvellement en religion esprouvée: de quoy dit saint Bernart ou livre *de precepto et dispensacione* vers la fin: que aussi comme ou baptesme les pechiez sont pardonnez, aussi à l'entrée de la religion"; *ibid.*, p. 483.

[49] *Ibid.*, p. 201.

[50] *Ibid.*, p. 211. J. Gerson, one of the princes of Christian mysticism, utters the following words when preaching before Charles VI: "Roy tres crestien, roy par miracle consacré, roy espirituel et sacerdotal"; *ibid.* p. 213.

[51] *Ibid.*, p.10.

[52] G. Fasoli, "Liturgia e cerimoniale ducale" in A Pertusi (ed.), *Venezia e il Levante fino al secolo XV* (Florence: Leo S. Olschki, 1973), pp. 261–95.

the eleventh century (according to the sources), the new doge's investiture became – from the simple civil ceremony that it had been – also a religious one; but even then, there was no trace of divine annointment, not even when the doge's chancellery, after much indecision, adopted the formula "Dei gratia dux."[53] Some of the doge's symbols, such as the ducal horn and the pope's cap, evoked royal religiosity. Nevertheless, the Venetian doge was no sacred person and never received the ointment. In 1485 the ducal crowning was instituted by decree of Maggior Consiglio, but it was a ceremony of strictly laic character. In certain phases of Venice's history, the doges were inclined to imitate Byzantine dresses and customs, but this tendency was soon overcome and was never translated into a true sacralization.

Although the doge was no sacred person, as the Byzantine emperor or the kings of France and England were, he nevertheless had a more solemn status compared to the communes' governors, who took office right after a simple oath. His election was accompanied by propitiatory rites. In the case of Domenico Selvo's election at the end of the eleventh century, all the bishops of the region headed to the monastery of San Nicolò al Lido to pray God with litanies, masses and supplications, to give Venice's people a doge who would protect them.[54] The prayers sung for the doge summoned God's protection on him, but they did not transform him into a god in his turn. With regard to Venice, one should speak of subordination of religion to the republic, rather than of sacralization of the doge. The first Venetian humanists even subordinated all values, theological virtues included, to the republic. Giovanni Caldiera, a humanist of the fifteenth century, regarded the republic as the "living embodiment of all perfections." In his judgement, republican virtues were the same as divine virtues. God and state, patriotism and religion, harmoniously merged.[55] Once again, the state, and not the doge, undertakes a sacred value.[56]

Fundamental expressions of the republican religion were public processions. Both Florence and Venice recognized the sacredness of secular authorities, and endeavored to bestow a sacred character to their republics. The doge conferred to the Venetians a mystical and holy image that was not a relic, but a living being, elected and made sacred by the political

[53] *Ibid.*, p. 278.
[54] "ut populum Venecie regas et protegas"; *ibid.*, p. 276.
[55] E. Muir, *Il rituale civico a Venezia nel Rinascimento* (Rome: Il Veltro Editrice, 1984), pp. 218–9.
[56] M. Casini, *I gesti del principe: la festa politica a Firenze e Venezia in età rinascimentale* (Venice: Marsilio, 1996).

system.[57] The Florentines, as they were deprived of a central sacred symbol, had to look for other ones: adolescents, miraculous images, charismatic priests. The Medici were able to satisfy the Florentines' need for sacredness, but only after they had buried the republican government. The Venetians, instead, succeeded in making religion serve the republic: "accompanying temporal matters with religion has ever been our custom," Francesco Sansovino writes. Accompanying, indeed, as a servant.[58] Even in the republic that expressed the highest sacredness, no man could undertake divine status by virtue of God's grace. Rather, a citizen undertook sacred dignity insofar as he represented the republic. He retained such sacred dignity as long as he performed well his duty of serving the common good.

4   A religion that instills virtue

The most refined elaborations of republican religion are to be found in quattrocento political thought. Politicians, prophets, historians and philosophers explained that men who serve the common good render themselves similar to God. Coluccio Salutati, for instance, states several times that a good Christian has the duty to serve his fatherland with all his energies, and explains that charity of the fatherland must surpass and comprise any other affection, bond and interest.[59] *Caritas* is the foundation of patriotism and of the ideal of the Christian citizen. In his early writings, Salutati elaborates on charity without implications or religious meanings; in the years of his chancellorship, however, he clothes charity with a pronounced religious meaning. Inasmuch as all men have a natural inclination to live in society, it is against nature to cause harm to other men, or not help them. Christians have the duty to love their neighbors as themselves, and even to love their enemies – private enemies, of course, not the enemies of their country.[60] Christ, too, experienced the sentiment of love of country, and His example teaches that Christians have a stronger obligation towards the common good than other men.

For Salutati, Christians' love of country is even superior to the muchcelebrated love of country of the ancients. They did not know true charity ("vera caritas"), which originates from Christ's love and love of Christ,

[57] *Ibid.*, p. 230.   [58] *Ibid.*, pp. 234–6.

[59] *Epistolario di Coluccio Salutati*, ed. F. Novati (Rome: Istituto Storico Italiano, 1891–1911), 4 vol., I, p. 21; vol. II, p. 87; vol. III, p. 638.

[60] *Ibid.*, vol. I, pp. 253–4 and p. 318.

and commands us to love our neighbor as ourselves. A society of true friends was impossible among the ancients, and can exist only among true Christians.[61] In Salutati's view, Christian ethics was the perfection of Cicero's ideal of civil virtue. Those who live in the world and fulfill their duties towards family and fatherland are truer to the Christian spirit than the anchorites, who seek salvation in solitude.[62] A good citizen who serves his country operates similarly to divine Providence, because Providence acts for the good of the universe and desires the good of civil communities. The true Christian who serves his fatherland is thus an instrument of Providence, and thereby becomes *imago dei*: he turns from being human to being God-like.

Christian religion teaches that earthly life is a struggle, where man employs his will of good. Precisely because he was "religious, endowed with an austere and profound faith, lived with all his soul," Salutati considered his first duty as a Christian and as a citizen to always put first the struggle for liberty.[63] Salutati's was a religion in which Cicero, Seneca and the Gospel spoke the same moral language, and the ancients' moral and political wisdom acquired, in light of the Christian faith, new and more fulgent splendor.[64] When man seeks to render himself similar to his Creator, he obeys divine will; but the fatigue is his. Man's end is not to know God, but to obtain eternal beatitude by means of his good deeds on earth. The laws are a safe guide as to how to act well. They lead us to live according to virtue, show us the way to earthly happiness, and disclose the way towards eternal beatitude.[65] Through good laws, legislators make political happiness ("politica felicitas"), which evolves into eternal happiness, possible on earth.[66] Obeying the laws and serving the common good

---

[61] *Ibid.*, vol. IV, p. 20.   [62] *Ibid.*, vol. III, pp. 285–308.

[63] E. Garin, "I trattati morali di Coluccio Salutati", *"Atti e memorie dell'Accademia fiorentina di scienze morali la Colombaria,"* N.S., vol. I, 1943–1946, (Florence: Felice Le Monnier, 1947), pp. 54–88, quotation on p. 62. See also E. Garin, "I cancellieri umanisti della Repubblica Fiorentina da Coluccio Salutati a Bartolomeo Scala" in *La cultura filosofica del Rinascimento italiano* (Florence: Sansoni, 1961), p. 11.

[64] Garin *La cultura filosofica del Rinascimento italiano*, p. 128. On the evolution of Salutati's thought from Stoicism to Christianity, see R. Witt, *Hercules at the Crossroads. The Life, Works and Thought of Coluccio Salutati* (Durham, NC: Duke University Press, 1983), pp. 355–67.

[65] C. Salutati, *De nobilitate legum et medicinae*, ed. E. Garin (Florence: Vallecchi, 1947), pp. 98 and 166.

[66] To clarify this essential aspect of his Christian conception of the law and of the Christian citizen's ideal, Salutati quotes the Book of Proverbs, 29:18, "happy is he who keeps the law," and comments: "really happy when he will have lived according to the law"; Salutati, *De nobilitate legum et medicinae*, pp. 166–7.

is a duty towards God, and the right way of behaving for a man in whom God has instilled the sentiment of *caritas*.[67] This is the reason why the founder of a state and the legislator are not only loved by God, but also, through their virtue, obtain His friendship: "Is it predicated of anyone else besides legislator Moses that he talked to God face-to-face, as a man with a friend of his?"[68]

Also for Leonardo Bruni, who served as Chancellor of the Republic from 1410 to 1411, and then from 1427 to his death (1444), the good Christian ought to be a good citizen, ready to serve his fatherland, because Christ's word does not at all contrast with love of country.[69] Leon Battista Alberti, in his *Libri della famiglia*, presents care for one's country as a difficult and hard job, but one that the good citizen must accept to prevent the arrogant from dominating the republic and making all others their servants. Defending the public good, even when this requires strictness, is therefore "cosa piissima" (the most pious matter), and dear to God.[70] According to Matteo Palmieri, author of that true compendium of civic humanism that is *Vita civile*, civic duties are religious duties. The passion urging republican Rome's heroes to give their life for the liberty of all, Palmieri explains, was "pietà della patria" [piety for country], or "civile pietà" [civil piety]. "Taking care of the fatherland's well-being, preserving the city and maintaining the union and concord of the well-assembled multitudes" are the most deserving among human actions.[71] Justice, in particular, is the highest among virtues, so welcome to almighty God that throughout the Holy Scriptures "the righteous blessed and the blessed righteous are mentioned by God without differentiation."[72] Not just the Scriptures, but

---

[67] Witt, *Hercules at the Crossroads*, pp. 342–3.

[68] "loquetur ad eum Deus facie ad faciem, sicut home ad amicum suum"; Salutati, *De nobilitate legum et medicinae*, p. 55.

[69] See V. da Bisticci, *Vite di uomini illustri del secolo XV* (Florence: Rinascimento del libro, 1938), p. 456.

[70] L. B. Alberti, "*I libri della famiglia*" in *Opere volgari*, ed. C. Grayson (Bari: Laterza, 1960), pp. 182–4.

[71] "Resta dunque che in terra non si faccia niuna cosa più cara nè più accetta a Dio, che con iustizia reggere e governare le congregazioni e moltitudini d'uomini, unitamente con iustizia ragunati: per questo promette Iddio a' giusti governatori delle città, e conservatori della patria, in cielo determinato luogo, nel quale eternalmente beati vivono co' suoi santi [Nothing is therefore dearer to or more well-accepted by God than justly ruling and governing the congregations and multitudes of men who are justly assembled in unity: hence does God promise to the just governors of the cities and to the preservers of the fatherland a certain place in heaven, where they forever happy will live together with the saints]"; M. Palmieri, *Della vita civile*, ed. Felice Battaglia (Bologna: Zanichelli, 1944), p. 45.

[72] *Ibid.*, p. 168.

all divine and human laws, together with the common interest, demand that justice be honored. Those rulers of republics who honor justice perform something dearer to God than anything else.[73] This is why they shall receive eternal beatitude in heaven, as a reward for their labor.[74] Man can render himself divine and eternal through the search of perfection in all arts and deeds. Thus he realizes his true nature, lives in accordance with God's will, and obtains glory on earth.

Authentic Christianity requires that everyone fulfills his own task in life, without escaping risks and pains. Giannozzo Manetti, a man of profound faith, explains in his *Della dignità e dell'eccellenza dell'uomo* speech (1451–52) that escaping pain is not proper in the strong and magnanimous, but rather, as Aristotle says, in the weak and feeble. We cannot abandon our place in life "lest with the chief's, that is to say God's, command." Wisdom and faith command us to face with virtue the labor, struggles and pains that torment the earthly city. Manetti exalts the virtue that is translated into the strong and magnanimous operating in civil life, that virtue which one loves with the body and with the soul, and which renders the men who practice it similar to God: "Love it, observe it, I pray you, follow it, embrace it so that, by practicing it at all times you will not only be happy and blessed, but you will also become almost similar to almighty God."[75]

Lorenzo Valla (1405–57) gave solid philological grounds to the interpretation of Christianity as the religion of virtue. He starts from the assumption that Christianity's principle is charity, which he defines as love towards God and towards one's neighbor, and the master of all virtues that make men morally strong.[76] Fortitude, Valla explains, is a kind of affection that gives strength. When the Apostles received the Holy Spirit, which is charity of the Father and of the Son, they became strong so that they could spread the word of God. According to Valla, the idea of virtue, in its meaning of power and strength, is to be found in the Gospel.[77] If charity gives strength, and strength is virtue, it follows that Christianity cannot be a religion that preaches weakness and humility before the powerful of the world, but rather a religion of virtue.[78] The conviction that

---

[73] *Ibid.*   [74] *Ibid.*

[75] G. Manetti, "De dignitate et excellentia hominis" in E. Garin (ed.), *Prosatori latini del Quattrocento* (Milan-Naples: Ricciardi, 1952), pp. 459 and 485–7.

[76] L. Valla, *Scritti filosofici e religiosi*, ed. G. Radetti (Florence: Sansoni, 1953), p. 195.

[77] L. Valla, *Collatio Novi Testamenti*, ed. A. Perosa (Florence: Sansoni, 1970). The first printed edition of this work, written between 1442 and 1444, came out in Paris in 1505, thanks to an initiative of Erasmus.

[78] See Trinkaus, *In Our Image and Likeness*, I, p. 385.

true Christianity teaches virtue that will play a fundamental role in later
republican political thought is already present in one of the most authoritative voices of quattrocento humanism.

Christian religion and political virtue also went hand in hand for
Bartolomeo Sacchi, the Platina (1421–81). He was a fervent supporter of
Christian religion as the moral foundation of the republic and restated
the classical idea that virtue, the virtue of the rulers of republics in particular, makes men similar to God and opens the way to true glory. He
explains that the people love and adore like semi-gods those who excel
in virtue. The good citizen who rules a city must carry on his shoulders
a heavy burden; the reward that awaits him is the true and perfect glory
("vera ac integra Gloria") assured by God.[79]

Marsilio Ficino (1433–99) argued as well that religion preaches civil
virtues and commands love of country.[80] Civil virtue, he clarifies, consists of the following elements: prudence, which helps understand what
the country's common good is; justice, which teaches us to distribute
honors on the basis of merit; fortitude, which wins over fear; and temperance, which assists in the effort to moderate passions.[81] The Christian
religion commands us to exercise virtues ardently, not for the end of
ambition, or pleasure, or human rest: but only to fulfill God's ends and
attain salvation in the afterlife. The example of the divine idea of virtue
was Christ, who showed us what upright justice, magnanimity, temperance and meekness are.[82]

Ficino's ideal of a religion that was all resolved in *caritas* and that in the
name of *caritas* commands us to love and serve one's country, was widely
spread also in the laic confraternities of the late quattrocento. Proofs
of this are the orations by Giovanni Nesi, who served several times in
Florence's highest magistracies and was one of the most typical exponents
of a "popular" Platonism, with strong republican aspirations.[83] In the

[79] B. Sacchi (Platina), *De optimo cive*, ed. F. Battaglia (Bologna: Zanichelli, 1944), p. 206.

[80] On Marsilio Ficino's religiosity, meant as "Paul's doctrine and practice of *charitas*, i.e.
a faith in and experience of divine love, beyond any motive of separation and discord,"
see C. Vasoli, "Dalla pace religiosa alla 'prisca theologia" in *Firenze e il Concilio del 1439.
Convegno di Studi*, Florence, 29 November – 2 December 1989, ed. P. Viti, (Florence:
Leo S. Olschki, 1994), vol. I, pp. 3–25. *Libro di Marsilio Ficino Florentino Della Cristiana
Religione ad Bernardo del Nero Clarissimo Cittadino Fiorentino*, without date and place,
Proemio.

[81] *Ibid.*   [82] *Ibid.*, chapter VIII.

[83] C. Vasoli, "Giovanni Nesi tra Donato Acciaiuoli e Girolamo Savonarola. Testi editi e
inediti" in *Umanesimo e teologia*, in "Memorie Domenicane," N.S. IV (1973), pp. 103–79,
cit., p. 110.

Oratio de Caritate, delivered on February 25, 1478, Nesi emphasizes that "deus caritas est et caritas est dues," and that charity made "God descend from heaven to earth, become a man, change from immortal to mortal, and from master to slave." Likewise, charity alone "lifted man from earth to heaven, and, whereas he was mortal, bestowed eternal life upon him; and, although he was man, made him God."[84] Charity makes us "similar to our Creator," commands us to love our neighbor and makes us strong, so that we can comply with His command. Thanks to charity, cities enjoy peace and unity. It therefore deserves to be called "madre" [mother] and "forma" [form] of all virtues and, as such, be honored and pursued with all our strengths.[85]

A religion founded on charity prevents human beings from seeking salvation in contemplation and solitude, and exhorts us instead to serve the public good with wisdom and courage. For Nesi religious faith is one with the ideals of civic humanism. He affirms that Christianity – if correctly understood – requires us to serve the fatherland also in the *Oratio de humilitate*, which he delivered before the "Reverendi Padri et dilectissimi Frategli" of the Nativity confraternity on April 11, 1476. Nesi's ideas were echoed by Giovanni Pico della Mirandola in his oration *De hominis dignitate* (1486). Only to man did God concede the possibility of elevating himself to the point of imitating his Creator.[86] In these words lies the heart of the republican religion: not men rendered divine by God, but men who become divine as they serve liberty with their soul augmented and strengthened by charity.

When Niccolò Machiavelli, some thirty years later, wrote down in the *Discourses on Livy* (II. 2) his famous invocation of a Christian religion capable of instilling virtue, he was not originating a new theory but he was in fact keeping alive and reinforcing a well-established language of republican religion. His words, however, failed to help to keep alive republican religion. Starting from the sixteenth century, republican Christianity almost entirely disappeared from the culture and the customs of the Italians. Another religion, the religion of the Counter-Reformation, took its place. It was a religion that no longer taught us to love liberty and to fight with all our strength against tyranny and corruption, and to live religion as an inner faith that is translated into a concrete force operating in the world. On the contrary, it preached respect for the authority of the

---

[84] *Ibid.*, p. 150.   [85] *Ibid.*, p. 151.
[86] G. Pico della Mirandola, *De hominis dignitate*, ed. E. Garin (Florence, Vallechi, 1942), pp. 106–7.

Pope and the secular authorities, resignation to oppression and corruption, and the belief that external practices of the cult are sufficient for saving one's soul. Whereas republican Christianity was a fellow companion to liberty, the religion of the Counter-Reformation was the key ally of the powers and the powerful people that held Italy slave for centuries.

Two stories about toleration

RAINER FORST

1 An ambivalent concept

On 18 March 2011, the Grand Chamber of the European Court of
Human Rights reversed a judgment of its Chamber from 3 November
2009 in the case of *Lautsi* v. *Italy*, which had ruled that the Italian practice of displaying crucifixes in public schools violated the basic rights
to freedom of education and to freedom of thought, conscience and
religion.[1] Cases of this kind are typical in European societies[2] and they
often exhibit similar structures. Whereas one party sees the crucifix (or
cross) as a symbol of Christian faith, others reinterpret it as a symbol
of Western culture generally and of its values. The Consiglio di Stato
had accordingly held in the *Lautsi* case that the 'crucifix is capable of
expressing ... those values – tolerance, mutual respect, valorisation of
the person, affirmation of one's rights, consideration for one's freedom,
the autonomy of one's moral conscience vis-à-vis authority, human solidarity and the refusal of any form of discrimination – which characterize Italian civilisation' as well as the Italian constitution.[3] The Grand
Chamber did not quite follow that path in its judgment; rather, it argued
that the 'passive symbol' of the crucifix 'cannot be deemed to have an
influence on pupils comparable to that of didactic speech or participation in religious activities' – and that thus the issue falls within the 'margin of appreciation of the respondent State'.[4] Such cases raise a number
of important issues about the traditions of Western societies and what

---

[1] Grand Chamber of the European Court of Human Rights, Case of *Lautsi and Others* v.
Italy, 18 March 2011 (Application No. 30814/06).
[2] I discuss a similar one in the German context in 'A Tolerant Republic?' in J.-W. Müller
(ed.), *German Ideologies Since 1945. Studies in the Political Thought and Culture of the
Bonn Republic* (New York: Palgrave Macmillan, 2003), pp. 209–20.
[3] *Lautsi and Others* v. *Italy*, section 16.
[4] *Lautsi and Others* v. *Italy*, sections 72 and 70.

they mean, about religious or non-religious symbols, about state neutrality and about fairness to minorities. What is especially interesting,
however, is that both sides of the conflict claim the virtue of tolerance
for themselves: the defenders of the crucifix in the classroom see it as a
symbol of toleration and find the critique of that practice intolerant of
religion and social traditions, whereas the plaintiffs in such cases see
that symbolic practice as a sign of intolerance toward religious minorities. Obviously, then, in such conflicts toleration is an important concept, yet its application is highly contested.

But maybe it is not only its application that is disputed. For if we look at
these conflicts closely, they might also reveal an ambivalence concerning
the interpretation of what toleration essentially means. For some, it merely
implies that minorities are not forced to adopt a religion different from
their own or to revere symbols of a different faith, while for others toleration
is the virtue accompanying state neutrality. For the first party, toleration
means that the majority does have the right to determine the character of
schools, for example, as long as it leaves room for minorities to differ, while
for others that right is an unjustifiable privilege and majoritarian exercise
of domination. If that is what toleration means, they argue, Goethe was
right when he said: 'Tolerance should be a temporary attitude only: it must
lead to recognition. To tolerate means to insult.'[5] So we encounter here an
instance of a long-standing debate about toleration in our societies, a debate
that attests to the ambivalence that inheres in that concept.

To gain a deeper understanding of this ambivalence, I want to tell two
stories about toleration, a dark and pessimistic one and a bright and optimistic one, and I want to argue that from a sufficiently complex critical historical perspective, both of them are true. More than that, they are not just
historically true, they still inform the contemporary meaning and practices
of toleration. Toleration can be based on mutual respect, and it can also be
an expression of disrespect and domination. On the basis of an analysis of
this ambivalence, I will try to develop a normative justification for toleration that is based on an adequate understanding of democratic justice.

But before I start with my two stories a word about the general concept of toleration. Its core can be explained by the three components of

---

[5] 'Toleranz sollte nur eine vorübergehende Gesinnung sein: sie muss zur Anerkennung
führen. Dulden heißt beleidigen.' J. W. Goethe, 'Maximen und Reflexionen', *Werke* 6,
(Frankfurt: Insel, 1981), p. 507. I discuss the complex relation between toleration and recognition in my ' "To tolerate means to insult": Toleration, recognition, and emancipation',
in B. van den Brink and D. Owen (eds.), *Recognition and Power* (Cambridge University
Press, 2007), pp. 215–237. In the following, I rely on parts of that text.

objection, acceptance and *rejection.*[6] First, a tolerated belief or practice has to be judged as false or bad in order to be a candidate for toleration; second, apart from these reasons for objection there have to be reasons why it would still be wrong not to tolerate these false or bad beliefs or practices, that is, reasons of acceptance. Such reasons do not eliminate the reasons of objection; rather, they trump them in a given context. And third, there have to be reasons for rejection which mark the limits of toleration. These limits lie where reasons of acceptance run out, so to speak. All three of those reasons can be of one and the same kind – religious, for example – yet they can also be of different kinds (moral, religious, pragmatic, to mention a few possibilities).

Obviously, this definition is very general, and the problems begin once these components are fleshed out: What can or should be tolerated, for what reasons, and where are the limits of toleration? Toleration as such, it seems to me, is a *normatively dependent concept*, one that is in need of other, independent normative resources in order to gain a certain content and substance – and in order to be something good at all. Hence an important aspect of every story about toleration is how the three components gain substantive content.

2 The story of the permission conception of toleration

My first story about toleration starts in sixteenth-century France. In the course of the second half of that century, the party of the *politiques* gained and propagated the conviction that the principle of *une foi, une loi, un roi* could no longer be sustained, for the price to be paid for oppressing the Calvinist minority of the Huguenots was too high, economically, politically and morally. Political unity could only be saved if the aim of religious unity was to a certain extent given up; *constituenda religione* and *constituenda republica* had to be separated and the monarch had to play the role of sovereign umpire and ruler. It took, however, a long time up until 1598

---

[6] With respect to the first two components, I follow P. King, *Toleration* (New York: St. Martin's Press, 1976), Chapter 1. G. Newey, in his *Virtue, Reason and Toleration* (Edinburgh University Press, 1999), Chapter 1, also distinguishes between three kinds of reasons in his structural analysis of toleration (which, however, differs from mine in the way these reasons are interpreted). For a more extensive discussion, see my 'Toleration, Justice and Reason' in C. McKinnon and D. Castiglione (eds.), *The Culture of Toleration in Diverse Societies* (Manchester University Press, 2003), pp. 71–85, and generally my *Toleranz im Konflikt. Geschichte, Gehalt und Gegenwart eines umstrittenen Begriffs* (Frankfurt, M. Suhrkamp, 2003; transl. forthcoming with Cambridge University Press as *Toleration in Conflict*).

before Henri IV issued the famous Edict of Nantes. This Edict clearly recognized the Huguenots as French citizens, though as citizens of a second
class. They were granted the liberty to practice their religion only at specified places (not in Paris) and at certain times, and the Edict carefully
explained which public offices they could hold, where and what kinds
of schools and universities they could found and where they could build
'security zones' with armed forces. Hence the Calvinist minority became
recognized and was protected by law, but at the same time the law fixed
their position in a situation of being 'merely' tolerated, being dependent
upon the goodwill of the authority and always taking second place after
Catholics in everyday life. This kind of recognition/toleration, to be sure,
was a great advantage compared to the prior situation (and later periods
of oppression), yet it also meant a certain form of cultural and social stigmatization, political powerlessness and dependency.

This is the kind of toleration that Goethe had in mind when he spoke of
the insult of toleration, and also what Kant meant when he criticized the
'presumptuous title of tolerant' (*hochmüthig*), and what lead Mirabeau
to say that toleration is a sign of tyranny.[7] These quotations also show
that the almost 200 years between the Edict of Nantes and the French
Revolution had not altered the structure of this kind of toleration. For
example, we also find it in the Toleration Act of 1689, right after the
'Glorious Revolution', which was declared to be 'an Act for Exempting
Their Majesties Protestant Subjects, Dissenting from the Church of
England, from the Penalties of certain Laws',[8] which shows that this act
clearly defines which dissenters (Presbyterians, Independents, Baptists
and Quakers) fall under these exemptions from the – still valid – laws
of uniformity and conformity with the Church of England and which
do not (the unitarian Socinians, for example, and of course atheists).
Also, Catholics were excluded from toleration by the oath of allegiance
that subjects of the king had to take. The result is a complex picture of
inclusion and exclusion, of a majority and of various minorities, some of
which were tolerated and some of which were not. Those who were tolerated were at the same time included and excluded; they enjoyed a certain recognition and security that the others did not have, but they were

---

[7] I. Kant, 'An Answer to the Question: "What is Enlightenment?"', in I. Kant, *Political Writings*, ed. H. Reiss, tr. H. B. Nisbet (Cambridge University Press, 1991), p. 58; Comte de Mirabeau, Speech in the National Assembly on 22 August 1789, discussing the *Declaration des droits de l'homme et du citoyen*, quoted in L. Barthou, *Mirabeau* (Freeport, NY: Books for Libraries Press, 1972), pp. 195–6.

[8] See the text of the Act in O. P. Grell, J. I. Israel and N. Tyacke (eds.), *From Persecution to Toleration* (Oxford: Clarendon, 1991), pp. 411–22.

dependent upon the protection of the monarch and thus had to show extreme loyalty. A complex matrix of power had developed that worked with different forms of recognition.

The same holds true of another example, which I want to mention briefly, the so-called *Toleranzpatente* of the Habsburg Emperor Joseph II in 1781 who – in contrast to his mother Maria Theresia who wanted to enforce religious unity – understood that in a time of intense religious strife the most rational form of exercising political power was a kind of discipline and peace through granting freedom: This 'enlightened monarch' was enlightened enough to know that toleration was the more effective policy toward powerful dissenters. Thus he granted the liberty of the *Privat-Exercitium* of religious duties (not the public exercise of religion) to three minority confessions: the Lutherans, the Reformed and the Greek Orthodox. It was exactly defined what they were allowed to do. For example, their churches could have neither bells nor entrances onto the street. This form of liberty, Joseph was convinced, would produce good subjects out of religious dissenters who would automatically have become political opponents if no toleration was practised. Toleration was the price to be paid for loyalty, and on the side of the subjects, loyalty was the price to be paid for certain liberties and security. Conformity in exchange for nonconformity.

Again, what we find here is the complex mixture of freedom and domination, of inclusion and exclusion, of recognition and disrespect that characterizes this conception of toleration, which I call the *permission conception*. According to it, toleration is a relation between an authority and a dissenting, 'different' minority (or various minorities). Toleration means that the authority gives qualified permission to the members of the minority to live according to their beliefs on the condition that the minority accepts the dominant position of the authority. As long as their expression of their differences remains 'private' and within limits, and as long as these groups do not claim equal public and political status, they can be tolerated on both pragmatic and normative grounds; on pragmatic–strategic grounds because this form of toleration is regarded as the least costly of all possible alternatives and does not disturb civil peace and order as the dominant party defines it (but rather contributes to it), and on normative grounds because the authority may find it wrong (and in any case fruitless) to force people to give up their deep-seated beliefs or practices. In short, toleration means that the authority that has the power to interfere with the practices of the minority nevertheless tolerates it, while the minority accepts its dependent position. Thus, speaking in terms of the three components of toleration, all three of them are being defined by the authority alone.

As I said, it is this conception that Kant, Mirabeau and Goethe criticize; toleration appears to be a strategic or at least a hierarchical policy, and the form of recognition that is granted to minorities both gives them certain liberties *and* turns them into dependent subjects and second-class citizens. Not rights but permissions are granted, and they can always be revoked (as the Edict of Nantes was in 1685). This form of toleration had *liberating* as well as *repressive* and *disciplining* effects (the latter in Foucault's sense): liberating because it clearly was an advantage as compared to the previous oppressive policies, repressive because to be tolerated meant to accept one's weak and underprivileged position, and disciplining because those policies of toleration 'produced' stigmatized, non-normal identities that were at the same time socially included and excluded.[9] The 'toleration' of the Jews from the Middle Ages to modern times is an obvious example of such forms of excluding inclusion; toleration always had to be paid for by stigmatization and by subservience.

If we look at the present discourses and practices of toleration through the lens of what I would call a *critical theory of toleration*, based on an analysis of repressive and disciplining forms of toleration, we see that the 'dark' story is not yet over.[10] For contrary to what many believe, the end of absolutism was not the end of the permission conception; rather, it is still very active and valid in our societies, though now in a different, *democratic* form: the tolerating authority now appears as the authority of a democratic majority. Of course, the authorities I mentioned in my three examples were also backed by overwhelming religious and political majorities, but within a democratic regime things look different, for now it is part of the very self-understanding of the regime that it grants basic equal liberties to all citizens – and that the citizens recognize each other as free and equal. Yet still in many contemporary practices of toleration, the permission conception has survived. I do not want to go into the many examples one could give for that, but only mention in

---

[9] On this point, see also W. Brown, *Regulating Aversion: Tolerance in the Age of Identity Politics* (Princeton University Press, 2006).

[10] See the examples I discuss in my *Toleranz im Konflikt*, Chapter 12, and 'A Critical Theory of Multicultural Toleration' in A. S. Laden and D. Owen (eds.), *Multiculturalism and Political Theory* (Cambridge University Press, 2007), pp. 292–311. I should note here that I use the term 'repressive tolerance' in a way that differs from H. Marcuse's classic essay 'Repressive Tolerance' in R. P. Wolff, B. Moore and H. Marcuse, *A Critique of Pure Tolerance* (Boston: Beacon Press, 1965), pp. 81–118. Whereas he calls a system of toleration 'repressive' that veils unjust relations of power in an ideological way by neutralizing real opposition (in ideas and practice), I call forms of toleration 'repressive' when they help to uphold unjustifiable relations of power by forcing those who are dominated to accept their inferior position.

passing that opponents of same-sex marriage laws often speak in favour of toleration but against equal rights in such cases (compare the slogan of the Christian Democratic Union in Germany in the context of the debate about a certain form of same-sex marriage: 'Tolerance yes, marriage no!'). In the famous German (or Bavarian) crucifix case very similar to the *Lautsi* case, many citizens, politicians, courts and speakers for the churches found that to tolerate non-Christian minorities such that they are not forced to give up their beliefs is one thing, but to grant them equal public and symbolic status and remove Christian symbols from classrooms of public schools would be quite another: it would be anti-democratic, anti-religious and would jeopardize the very foundations of the Federal Republic.[11] Hence the power structure of this form of toleration is still very much at work: inclusion and exclusion, freedom and domination at the same time.

3   The story of the respect conception

But as I remarked earlier, there also is a second, more optimistic story about toleration – which begins in the Netherlands of the sixteenth century. In the course of the fights of the primarily Protestant provinces in the north against Spanish rule and the enforcement of Catholicism, we find two important developments in struggles for religious liberty, especially in the writings of the Calvinist monarchomachs such as Duplessis-Mornay. First, a natural right to religious liberty – as God-given – was proclaimed as a basic political right, and second, a king who did not respect this basic right had to be resisted, out of a sense of political *and* religious duty. Such a tyrant had broken both the *foedus* with God and the *pactum* with the people; religious liberty accordingly was not something *granted* by the rulers, it was a natural *right* given by God and thus a basic demand of political justice: there could be no legitimate state that did not grant this right. The revolutionary result of that claim was the splitting-off of the northern provinces in the 'Union of Utrecht' in 1579, leading to the new republic that would become an example of toleration in the seventeenth century.

As the story goes on, the revolutionary claim of religious and political liberty as a 'birthright' reappears in the context of the English Civil War. The opposition to the king was justified by a 'fundamental law' of justice that called for political and religious liberty; government was no longer directly instituted by God but by men in order to safeguard the natural rights given by God to men as a special kind of 'property'. In the

---

[11]   See my *Toleranz im Konflikt*, Chapter 12.

eyes of levellers like Lilburne,[12] this kind of God-given liberty meant that any exercise of power, be it religious or political, had to be justified to the people who were 'affected' (or better: 'well-affected') by the laws. The right to freedom of conscience was justified with the Protestant argument that conscience was directly bound to obey and follow God and not men: a theory of the free and at the same time unfree conscience (as the 'work of God', as Luther had said) that also figures prominently in Milton's thought and later in Locke's *Letter Concerning Toleration*. William Walwyn expressed this – in the debates between Independents and the Presbyterian majority in parliament – in a paradigmatic way:

> That which a man may not voluntarily binde himself to doe, or to forbear to doe, without sinne: That he cannot entrust or refer unto the ordering of any other: Whatsoever (be it Parliament, Generall Councels, or Nationall Assemblies:) But all things concerning the worship and service of God, and of that nature; that a man cannot without wilfull sin, either binde himselfe to doe any thing therein contrary to his understanding and conscience: not to forbeare to doe that which his understanding and conscience bindes him to performe: therefore no man can refer matters of Religion to any others regulation. And what cannot be given, cannot be received: and then as a particular man cannot be robbed of that which he never had; so neither can a Parliament, or any other just Authority be violated in, or deprived of a power which cannot be entrusted unto them.[13]

An early liberal argument of this sort for toleration is, however, highly ambiguous. On the one hand, the claim that there is a natural right to religious and political liberty does connect the demand for toleration with a radical demand for political *justice*, that is, the basic demand for the general justification of the exercise of political power. In this perspective, toleration is not merely an 'exemption' being 'granted' to some 'non-normal' subjects, but a general rule of the way citizens treat each other within the confines of natural right. We see here the glimpse of a new, different conception of toleration, the *respect conception*, according to which democratic citizens respect each other as legal and political equals even though they differ greatly in their ethical–religious views about the good and true way of life.

---

[12] See J. Lilburne, 'Englands Birth-Right Justified' (1645), in W. Haller (ed.), *Tracts on Liberty in the Puritan Revolution* III (New York: Octagon, 1965), pp. 257–308.

[13] W. Walwyn, 'A Help to the Right Understanding of a Discourse Concerning Independency' (1644/45), in J. R. McMichel and B. Taft (eds.), *The Writings of William Walwyn* (Athens, GA: The University of Georgia Press, 1989), pp. 136–7.

On the other hand, the argument for freedom of conscience based on the theory of the 'unfree free conscience' mentioned above is not only compatible with the permission conception of toleration, it is also potentially exclusive of those persons who do not have the right form of conscience: atheists and Catholics, for example, as Locke famously argued (and with him Milton, differing from the more tolerant Levellers and Baptists such as Roger Williams). In Locke's first *Letter*, for example, it is clear that there can be no justified claim to the freedom *not* to believe in God. Indeed, we could call the fear that, without a particular religious basis, there could be no morality and no functioning state *Locke's fear*[14] (shared by many later Enlightenment thinkers such as Montesquieu, Rousseau, and Voltaire) – a fear, to be sure, still very much present in contemporary societies. Cases like *Lautsi* – and the opposition to judgments to remove crucifixes or crosses – attest to that.

To continue our more optimistic story about toleration, we thus need to turn to a different voice in the historical discourse of toleration, one that questioned Locke's fear (though not as a direct reaction to Locke): the Huguenot philosopher Pierre Bayle (writing in exile in Rotterdam).[15] In his *Pensées diverses sur la Comète* (1683)[16] he introduced the so-called 'Bayle's paradox' by saying that religion was not necessary to support morality which rested on other motives (the desire for social recognition) and insights (of natural reason) independent of religious belief, and that religious fanaticism rather than atheism was the main danger for morality and the state. He even ventured the courageous idea that a 'society of atheists' would be possible – and possibly be more peaceful than religious societies.

What is more, one of Bayle's decisive insights was that *mutual toleration* among persons with different religious beliefs could only be possible if there was an independent moral basis of respect among human beings that would rule out the exercise of religious force. In his *Commentaire philosophique sur ces paroles de Jésus-Christ 'Contrain-les d'entrer'* (1686)[17], he provides such a justification of toleration which avoids the problems

---

[14] 'The taking away of God, tho but even in thought, dissolves all'; J. Locke, *A Letter Concerning Toleration*, ed. J. Tully (Indianapolis: Hackett, 1983), p. 51.

[15] I discuss Bayle's view more extensively in my 'Pierre Bayle's Reflexive Theory of Toleration', in M. Williams and J. Waldron (eds.), *Toleration and its Limits*. Nomos XLVIII (New York University Press, 2008), pp. 78–113.

[16] P. Bayle, *Various Thoughts on the Occasion of a Comet*, trans. Robert Bartlett (Albany: State University of New York Press, 2000).

[17] P. Bayle, *Philosophical Commentary*, trans. and ed. A. G. Tannenbaum (New York: Peter Lang, 1987).

that Locke's defence of religious liberty faced. From studying Augustine's famous arguments about the possibility and productivity of *terror* in freeing men from religious error and enabling them to see the truth 'from the inside', so to speak, if properly informed,[18] Bayle already knew what Locke had to acknowledge after being confronted with Jonas Proast's critique: that although authentic and sincere beliefs could not be directly produced by outward force, there were many other indirect ways to block men on a road of error and to make them turn around.

> I readily grant that Reason and Arguments are the only proper Means, whereby to induce the Mind to assent to any Truth, which is not evident by its own Light: and that Force is very improper to be used to that end *instead* of Reason and Arguments … But notwithstanding this, if Force be used, not in stead of Reason and Arguments, i.e. not to convince by its own proper Efficacy (which it cannot do), but only to bring men to consider those Reasons and Arguments which are proper and sufficient to convince them, but which, without being forced, they would not consider: who can deny, but that *indirectly* and *at a distance*, it does some service toward bringing men to embrace that Truth, which otherwise, either through Carelesness and Negligence they would never acquaint themselves with, or through Prejudice they would reject and condemn unheard, under the notion of Error?[19]

To avoid such counterarguments to a classic defence of the freedom of conscience, Bayle argued on normative grounds that every person had a moral duty to mutually justify any exercise of force – a duty that could

---

[18] For Augustine's justification of the duty of intolerance, see esp. his letter to Vincentius (letter 93), written in 408; Augustine, *Letters*, vol. II, tr. Sister W. Parsons (New York: Fathers of the Church Inc., 1953).

[19] See J. Proast, *The Argument of the Letter Concerning Toleration, Briefly Consider'd and Answer'd*, reprint of the edition of 1690 (New York and London: Garland, 1984), pp. 4–5. For a convincing critique of Locke on the basis of Proastian considerations, see esp. J. Waldron, 'Locke, Toleration, and the Rationality of Persecution' in *Liberal Rights. Collected Papers 1981–1991* (Cambridge University Press, 1993), Chapter 4. Where I disagree with Waldron, however, is his claim that Locke did not find a plausible counterargument to Proast. For that, however, Locke had to change his position and move towards the epistemological–normative argument that we find in Bayle (in superior form). In his later letters on toleration, Locke argues that the use of religious–political force is in need of mutual justification, and that Proast's main assumption of the undeniable truth of the Church of England is unfounded. See esp. Locke, *A Second Letter Concerning Toleration*, in *The Works of John Locke* VI (Aalen: Scientia, 1963), p. 111, where he asks Proast to put forth a mutually justifiable argument 'without supposing all along your church in the right, and your religion the true; which can no more be allowed to you in this case, whatever your church or religion be, than it can to a papist or a Lutheran, a presbyterian or anabaptist; nay, no more to you, than it can be allowed to a Jew or a Mahometan'.

be seen by the means of 'natural reason'[20] – and he argued on epistemological grounds that in a case in which there was a stand-off of one religious reason versus another, there was no sufficient justification for using force on either side. And this not because Bayle was a religious sceptic (as many have thought), but because Bayle insisted on faith being *faith* and not knowledge: as long as there was no reasonably non-rejectable proof as to the truth of one religion or confession, the duty of mutual justification called for tolerance (but not for scepticism, for knowing that one's faith ultimately is faith – based on 'relative evidence'[21] – one has good reasons to regard it as true as long as it does not run against natural reason).[22] From that perspective, the claim of people like Bossuet,[23] who believed that they were in possession of the truth and therefore could legitimately exercise force – according to Augustine's interpretation of the saying *compelle intrare* (Luke 14, 15ff.) – would turn into nothing but a pure and illegitimate exercise of domination. According to Bayle, in an argument about the norms and laws that are to regulate the common life, to assume precisely what is contested, namely the truth of one church rather than another, is 'childish' and 'ridiculous';[24] if such arguments were legitimate, 'there would be no kind of crime which could not become an act of religion by this maxim.'[25] As Bayle points out, a society can only exist peacefully if there is a generally acceptable definition of right and wrong independent of struggles about the true church.[26]

---

[20] See Bayle, *Philosophical Commentary*, p. 30: '[B]ut if it's possible to have certain limitations with respect to speculative truths, I don't believe there ought to be any with regard to those practical and general principles which concern morals. I mean that all moral laws without exception, must submit to that idea of natural equity, which, as well as metaphysical light, *enlightens every man coming into the world* … I would like whoever aims at knowing distinctly this natural light with respect to morality to raise himself above his own private interest or the custom of his country, and to ask himself in general: *Is such a practice just in itself? If it were a question of introducing it in a country where it would not be in use and where he would be free to take it up or not, would one see, upon examining it impartially, that it is reasonable enough to merit being adopted?*' (Emphasis in original.)

[21] *Ibid.*, p. 93.

[22] Hence from a Baylean perspective, contrary to Brian Barry, *Justice as Impartiality* (Oxford University Press, 1995), p. 179, in matters of religion it seems quite possible and reasonable that 'certainty from the inside about some view can coherently be combined with the line that it is reasonable for others to reject that same view'.

[23] See J.-B. Bossuet, *Politics Drawn from the Very Words of Holy Scripture*, tr. and ed. P. Riley (Cambridge University Press, 1999).

[24] Bayle, *Philosophical Commentary*, p.13.   [25] *Ibid.*, p. 47.

[26] *Ibid.*, p. 85.

In his famous *Dictionaire historique and critique* (1696)[27], Bayle care-fully explained the distinction between knowledge and faith and the pos-sibility of a form of 'natural' practical reason that would lead to an insight into the duty of mutual justification. Faith was not seen, in a fideist sense, as being *against* reason but, as Bayle said, as being *beyond reason* (*dessus de la Raison*): faith was not irrational, but at the same time reason could not prove the true faith.[28] Human reason had to accept its own boundaries and finitude and the unavoidability of (what Rawls later called) 'reasonable disagreement'[29] in matters of faith. According to Bayle, those who would give up their faith because of that – because they cannot prove its truth in a demonstrative way – and would become sceptics or atheists are no good believers:

> Once again, a true Christian, well versed in the characteristics of super-natural truths and firm on the principles that are peculiar to the Gospel, will only laugh at the subtleties of the philosophers, and especially those of the Pyrrhonists. Faith will place him above the regions where the tem-pests of disputation reign ... Every Christian who allows himself to be disconcerted by the objections of the unbelievers, and to be scandalized by them, has one foot in the same grave as they do.[30]

For our story, Bayle's insights are essential. A justification of toleration such as Bayle's does avoid the pitfalls of a traditional argument for the liberty of conscience, which are (a) that the claim *credere non potest homo nisi volens* (Augustine) does not provide an argument against the sup-pression of religious errors or against religious 'guidance' because it is possible that 'mild' force can bring about sincere beliefs, and (b) that such toleration could only extend to *authentic* religious beliefs (whereas a cri-terion for such beliefs seems to be lacking), and of course only to *religious* beliefs (and not to atheists). Bayle's alternative justification also avoids, if we look at the recent history of liberal thought, the problems of the view that religious liberty as part of a wider notion of political liberty is jus-tified because personal autonomy is a precondition for the good life, for only the life 'lived from the inside', on the basis of autonomously chosen

---

[27] Pierre Bayle, *Historical and Critical Dictionary*, Selections, trans. Richard H. Popkin (Indianapolis: Hackett, 1991).

[28] '[D]ifference in opinion seems to be man's inherent infelicity, as long as his understand-ing is so limited and his heart so inordinate.' Bayle, *Philosophical Commentary*, p. 141.

[29] See J. Rawls, *Political Liberalism* (New York: Columbia University Press, 1993), pp. 54–66; C. Larmore, 'Pluralism and Reasonable Disagreement' in *The Morals of Modernity* (Cambridge University Press, 1996), Chapter 7.

[30] Bayle, *Historical and Critical Dictionary*, Third Clarification, p. 429.

values, could be good.[31] This is a plausible, though non-generalizable conception of the good life, for it is not clear whether a life lived according
to traditional values that are not chosen but simply taken over in a con-
ventional, non-critical way would be worse (i.e., subjectively less fulfilling
and objectively of a lesser ethical value) than one that is autonomously
chosen. The politically *free*, the personally *autonomous* and the ethically
good life may be three separate things.

Of course, my alternative view also calls for a certain kind of respect for
the autonomy of persons. Yet this kind of respect is not based on a particular *ethical* conception of the good, but on a *moral* notion of the person
as a reasonable being with (what I call) a *right to justification*.[32] This right
to justification is based on the recursive general principle that every norm
that is to legitimize the use of force (or generally regulate social life) claims
to be reciprocally and generally valid and therefore needs to be justifiable by reciprocally and generally non-rejectable reasons. *Reciprocity* here
means that neither party makes any claim to certain rights or resources
that are denied to others (reciprocity of content), and that neither party
projects its own reasons (values, interests, needs) onto others in arguing
for its claims (reciprocity of reasons). One must be willing to argue for
basic norms that are to be reciprocally and generally valid and binding
with reasons that are not based on contested 'higher' truths or on conceptions of the good which can reasonably be questioned and rejected.
Generality, then, means that the reasons for such norms need to be shareable among all persons affected, not just dominant parties.

I should emphasize the word 'shareable' here, for the criteria of reciprocity and generality allow for judgements as to the justifiability of
claims even if – as is to be expected – no consensus is to be found.[33] A few
brief examples: Those who argue for the equal legal respect of intimate

---

[31] See W. Kymlicka, *Multicultural Citizenship* (Oxford University Press, 1995), p. 81. For
a critique of Kymlicka's view, see R. Forst, 'Foundations of a Theory of Multicultural
Justice', *Constellations* 4 (1997), pp. 63–71 (with a reply by Kymlicka in the same issue).

[32] On this point, see R. Forst, *The Right to Justification. Elements of a Constructivist Theory
of Justice* (New York: Columbia University Press, forthcoming).

[33] I agree with J. Waldron, 'Toleration and Reasonableness' in C. McKinnon and
D. Castiglione (eds.), *The Culture of Toleration in Diverse Societies* (Manchester University
Press, 2003), pp. 13–37, that in a pluralist society there will always be contestation about
the 'compossibility' of different ideals and practices of the good. And I do not want to
suggest that I have developed what he radically doubts, a 'Kantian algebraic liberalism'
that would provide a general formula for solving such conflicts in a clearly non-rejectable
way. Yet I want to claim that with the help of the criteria of reciprocity and generality we
can plausibly identify better and worse arguments for generally valid norms in many
cases, looking at the claims and the reasons given. An argumentative 'asymmetry' (*ibid.*,

relationships between persons of the same sex may have, given the criterion of reciprocity, superior arguments as compared to those who argue on the basis of a mutually contestable, religious understanding of 'nature'. Those who want to forbid persons from wearing headscarves in schools (be they teachers or students) must be able to show how far the practice of wearing such symbols really violates basic rights and democratic principles. And those who want crucifixes to be put up in public classrooms by law need to show how far this is compatible with the equal rights of citizenship in a religiously pluralist political community. And it is questionable whether such arguments have been presented in the latter two cases.

The normative ground for this conception of toleration is the moral demand to respect each other's autonomy as a reason-giving and reason-receiving being. Whether those who are respected in that way will eventually lead an ethically better life can therefore be the object of disagreement; there must be no disagreement, however, about the duty of justification and the criteria of reciprocity and generality. This is the *normative* component of that justification of toleration, while the *epistemological* component consists of an insight into the finitude of reason: that reason is not sufficient to provide us with the one and only, ultimate answer about the truth of the good life which would show that all other ethical beliefs are false.

Most important in this context, however, is the insight that, according to this conception of toleration, to be tolerant implies the willingness and the capacity to distinguish between one's *ethical* beliefs about the true and good life and the general *moral* norms and principles one thinks every person, regardless of his or her view of the good, has to accept (or, better: cannot reciprocally and generally reject).[34] Bayle's theory clearly implies such a distinction, and looking at the history of toleration one may say

---

p. 30) of claims and reasons, then, is important for such judgments. Is the claim, to use Waldron's Rushdie-example, to be protected from blasphemous insult as strong as the claim to be protected from being threatened in life and liberty because of what you think and say? Can the first claim be generalized and supported with reciprocally valid reasons in the same way as the second? I doubt that it can. What seems to me undisputed, however, is that toleration is the attitude of those who are willing to engage in such arguments, who accept the criteria of reciprocity and generality and who accept in a given case that their arguments do not suffice to be the basis of general law. Still, given Waldron's justified doubts, it is important to add another reason for toleration connected to this: the toleration of those who see that a debate remains in a standstill and that therefore no side can show its claims and reasons to be superior. In such a case, toleration means to accept that other grounds for the regulation of a conflict have to be found, by way of compromise.

[34] On this distinction, originally drawn from J. Habermas's discourse ethics, and the difference of various 'contexts of justification' as well as of 'contexts of recognition', see R. Forst, *Contexts of Justice*, tr. J. Farrell (Berkeley: University of California Press, 2002).

that such a differentiation, in theory as well as in practice, may be the greatest achievement within the discourse of toleration. It comes, however, at a certain cost, which makes tolerance (according to the respect conception as I sketched it) into a demanding *moral–political virtue*:[35] the cost is that in the case in which you cannot present reciprocally and generally non-rejectable arguments for your ethical judgements, you have to accept that you are not justified to make these judgements the basis for generally binding legal norms.[36]

4   Toleration and democracy

Referring back to the three components of toleration, the main difference between the permission conception and the respect conception is that, according to the former, all three components are determined by the ethical views of the dominant majority or authority, while in the respect conception things look different. The *objection* may be based on one's particular ethical (or religious) views; the *acceptance*, however, will be based on a general consideration of whether the reasons for objection are good enough to be reasons for *rejection*, that is whether they are reciprocally and generally justifiable. If they turn out to be sufficient for a negative *ethical* judgement, but not for a negative *moral* judgement, the case for toleration arises: for then one has to see that one's ethical objection does not justify a moral condemnation and a rejection. This is the insight of toleration.

And this is why in a political context, toleration and democracy must be seen as components of political justice: of the imperative not to force others to live under norms and laws that cannot be adequately justified toward them. Toleration then is not just and not primarily a virtue of subjects of democratic law; it is primarily a virtue of democratic citizens as *lawmakers*. Toleration means, for example, that you come to see that even if you firmly believe that the cross is the symbol of the true faith, you also have to accept that it would be wrong to have it put up in classrooms of public schools by law. Such an insight is an insight of justice and of fairness toward minorities. Most often it does not come naturally, rather, such insights are generated in practices of social justification where the terms and relations of justification are such that minorities do have a chance to exercise what we could call the 'force toward the better

---

[35] On this point, see my 'Tolerance as a Virtue of Justice', *Philosophical Explorations* IV (2001), 193–206.

[36] Bayle himself, one should add, only saw this as a moral and civic virtue; politically, he stood in the tradition of the *politiques*, arguing for a strong sovereign like Henri IV.

argument'. So here, again, toleration is part of practices of power, but in a different way as compared to the hierarchical permission conception. The respect conception presupposes that the 'power of justification' that all those who are part of a social conflict can generate – a social and public form of power constituted by assent and agreement – is available such that minorities can develop sufficient argumentative strength to make their case heard and, in fact, effectively undeniable, if they fulfil the criterion of reciprocity and others don't – and if the public and political institutions are arranged such that this justificatory advantage becomes visible and counts. Hence a critical political theory of toleration has to focus on the *relations of justification* in a given society, that is the major discursive, formal and informal ways in which justificatory power can be generated, especially by minorities.[37]

As I already indicated, our story would be far too optimistic if we thought that historically this has become the dominant conception of toleration, which is neither true given the practices of toleration nor given the most important writings on toleration. Enlightenment thought before Kant hardly reached the height of Bayle's conception. Therefore, the general idea that the Enlightenment marked the highpoint of thinking about toleration and then also made the step *beyond toleration* by positively institutionalizing the right to religious liberty in the American and French Revolutions is mistaken. No doubt the idea of a basic right to religious liberty does take a decisive step beyond the permission conception of toleration, but it is wrong to assume that this takes one 'beyond toleration', for (a) toleration is still called for, as I said, but now on the horizontal level of citizens as authors and addressees of the law, and (b), from a critical perspective, the permission conception is still very much alive in the interpretations of what a right to religious liberty means: does it simply mean not being forced to give up one's minority religious views, or does it entail equal public and political status for minorities? In democratic states, the old absolutist permission conception is gone, but there is still a constant struggle going on between the democratic form of the permission conception and the democratic form of the respect conception. Hence, if we want to develop a genealogy of our sense and practice of toleration, both of my stories have to form a *single* one. Toleration is a dialectical concept.

---

[37] On this, see my 'First Things First. Redistribution, Recognition and Justification', *European Journal of Political Theory* 6 (2007), 291–304, and my *Justification and Critique* (Cambridge: Polity Press, forthcoming).

Chapter 3

Natural reason, religious conviction, and the justification of coercion in democratic societies

ROBERT AUDI

The present age is witnessing two sharply contrasting sociopolitical phenomena. On one side are forces that favor democracy and its characteristic accommodation of diversity in religion and other realms; on the other side are religious fundamentalisms that tend to stimulate identity politics and provide openings for clergy to influence government in far-reaching ways. This chapter will assume both that freedom of religion is an important concern for any sound democracy and that even where a majority of citizens are of the same religion, democratic societies should maintain a separation of "church" – of religious institutions – and state. Finding an appropriate separation is a perennial problem in political philosophy and legal theory. This challenge is an *institutional problem*. A related difficulty is what constitutes an appropriate balance between religious and other considerations in the political conduct of individual citizens. This is an *individual citizenship problem*. Legal theorists have written much on the former problem and, especially since the 1980s, have become concerned with the latter. I take it to be a clear case of a problem that, in part because it concerns the relation between ethics and law, needs attention from both moral philosophy and legal theory.

1   Liberty and equality as democratic ideals

Democracy is often characterized as a kind of government of, by, and for the people.[1] Much content is implicit in these three monosyllables. The "of" indicates that the people are the governed and suggests that the category of the governed includes those who govern. The "by" indicates that those

---

[1] In his Gettysburg Address, Abraham Lincoln, in honor of the fallen soldiers of the Union Army, famously expressed the resolve "that government of the people, by the people, for the people, shall not perish from the earth" (November 19, 1863).

who govern come from among the people as opposed to, say, a hereditary monarchy. The "for" is best understood as at least a rough equivalent of "for the benefit of." This gives the triad normative content. If a democracy is, minimally, a political system in which government is of, by, and for the people, we can readily see that both liberty and a certain kind of basic political equality are required. Without liberty, people cannot truly govern themselves, and they would likely be agents of others who control them. Without a kind of basic political equality, one that minimally embodies a commitment to one person, one vote, "the people" would not truly govern themselves. In most such cases only some of them would govern, and a small proportion of citizens would have disproportionately more political power than others. Liberty, including religious liberty, and basic political equality are morally cogent ideals in any case. What *degree* of religious freedom should be legally permissible and how the state should protect it are quite different matters.

Where there is liberty, there is room for pluralism. Where sociocultural life is complex, liberty virtually guarantees a pluralism in the society in question. This is not to say that *fostering* pluralism is intrinsic to a sound democratic system of government, though a case can be made for that view. My interest is in highly pluralistic democracies, which exist in much of the world today. Moreover, it is religious pluralism – including secular citizens as constituting one among the religiously plural groups – that most interests me here.

Coercion is of special concern for at least two reasons. First, it negates liberty. What we are coerced to do we do not freely do. Second, it creates inequality, in the sense that insofar as one person exercises coercive power over another, the latter is not the equal of the former. Moreover, liberty is the default position in democracies – at least in the liberal kind of interest here. Government, even more than individuals, should coercively restrict the liberty of citizens only with adequate justification. Does this also hold for residents who are non-citizens? Much of the world is now experiencing illegal immigration, and many countries have legal aliens who do not have the legal rights of citizens.[2] A full theory of the justification of governmental coercion must take account of the rights of these residents, but here it suffices to focus on citizens as the central concern of the theory of government and to suggest that, other things being equal (as admittedly they often will not be), legal residents should have the liberties of citizens.

---

[2] For discussion of this matter see J. Hagan, "Negotiating Social Membership in the Contemporary World," *Social Forces* 85 (2006), 631–42.

My earlier work contains much about the justification of coercion by governmental institutions. Here is a representative passage:

> A liberal democracy – one in which the freedom of citizens is a central concern – by its very nature resists using coercion, and prefers persuasion, as a means to achieve cooperation. What we are persuaded, by being offered reasons, to do we tend to do autonomously and to identify with; what we are compelled to do we tend to resent doing. Thus, when there must be coercion, liberal democracies try to justify it in terms of considerations – such as public safety – that any rational adult citizen will find persuasive and can identify with.[3] This is one reason why religious grounds alone are not properly considered a sufficient basis of coercion even if they happen to be shared by virtually all citizens. If rational citizens in possession of the relevant facts cannot be persuaded of the necessity of the coercion – as is common where that coercion is based on an injunction grounded in someone else's religious scripture or revelation – then from the point of view of liberal democracy, it lacks an adequate basis.[4]

In a later work I proposed a necessary condition for justified coercion. The basis of the view is that citizens' rights to freedom and to autonomy should be abridged only when restricting the former can be seen to respect the latter.[5] As in that text, I do not claim that this condition is sufficient, but at least in many cases of justified coercion, it is met.

On this surrogacy view (which I merely sketch here), coercing a person, for a particular reason, to perform an action, in a given set of circumstances, is fully justified only if at least the following three conditions hold in the circumstances (perhaps with further qualification they, or some extension of them, are also sufficient for justified coercion):

(a) Someone else (most often, fellow citizens in the cases that concern us) has a (moral) right, in the circumstances, to have this action performed by the person – certainly a feature of most cases in which a liberal democracy can reasonably coerce its citizens – or at least the

---

[3] A weaker condition would require only the capacity to understand the grounds, but I doubt that this condition would suffice. Actual identification, however, is not required; since we are not talking about ideally rational citizens, such things as confusion or prejudice can interfere.

[4] See R. Audi and N. Wolterstorff, *Religion in the Public Square: The Place of Religious Convictions in Political Debate* (Lanham, MD: Rowman & Littlefield, 1997), p. 16.

[5] On this issue see Paul J. Weithman, "John Rawls's Idea of Public Reason: Two Questions," *The Journal of Law, Philosophy and Culture* 1 (2007), p. 51, where he suggests that my view is concerned only with preserving autonomous action rather than autonomous lives. Here and on page 50 Weithman construes my view too narrowly. In any case, the notion of autonomous action is central for and prior to that of an autonomous life.

person morally ought to perform the action in the circumstances, for example to abstain from stealing from others.[6]

(b) If fully rational (hence willing to imagine a reversal of positions or roles between oneself and others) and adequately informed about the situation, the person would see that (a) holds and would, for the reason in question, say from a sense of how theft creates mistrust and chaos, or for some essentially related reason, perform the action, or at least tend to do so.[7]

(c) The action in question is both an "important" kind of conduct (as opposed to breaking a casual promise to meet for lunch) and one that may be reasonably believed to affect someone else (and perhaps not of a highly personal kind at all).[8]

Thus, it is permissible, on grounds of the general welfare, to coerce people to pay taxes only if they ought to do so in the circumstances, can see this, and would (if fully rational and adequately informed) be appropriately motivated by seeing it.

---

[6] The reason must be essentially related because otherwise the agent's hypothetical attitude will not be sufficiently connected with the coercive reason to warrant the coercion. A typical case would be this: where r is the state's reason, e.g. to protect other citizens, the related reason would be, say, to fulfill my duty not to harm others. Roughly, if the agent's reason is not r, it is something like a first-person version of r. It should also be noted that this approach does not imply that *all* moral obligation is discernible by reflection of this kind. It does seem appropriate, however, that the obligations grounding state rights of coercion should be thus discernible; and this is one reason to think that such obligations correspond to citizens' rights. The set of conditions (a)–(c) might be extensionally equivalent to conditions under which, on T. M. Scanlon's view, no one can "reasonably reject" the provision in question; there is at least an interesting resemblance. See T. M. Scanlon, *What We Owe to Each Other* (Cambridge, MA: Harvard University Press, 1998).

[7] I assume here that a *fully* rational person with certain information about others has certain altruistic desires; if rationality is understood more narrowly, my formulation must be revised (unless we may assume, as I do not, that for fully rational persons motivation to do something is entailed simply by a realization that it is one's moral obligation). The basic idea could, however, be largely preserved. I make a case for such desires in Chapter 6 of my book *The Architecture of Reason: The Structure and Substance of Rationality* (Oxford University Press, 2001).

[8] See the discussion at pages 65–6 in my book *Religious Commitment and Secular Reason* (Cambridge University Press, 2000). The point here does not deny the possibility of weakness of will or suggest a motivational internalist view on which self-addressed moral judgements or other self-addressed action-guiding judgements are intrinsically motivating. For an account of motivational internalism and many references to literature on the topic see Chapter 10 of my book *Moral Knowledge and Ethical Character* (Oxford University Press, 1997).

Two clarifications are needed immediately. First, I have been assuming that adequate information in this context must be of a kind accessible to human persons on the basis of their normal rational capacities as human beings – on the basis of *natural reason*, in a sense that will be clarified below. Second, strictly speaking, determining what counts as justified coercion must be relativized to an appropriate description of the acts in question. We may require of citizens types of acts that are determined by convention and are in that sense arbitrary. Thus, driving on the left side of the road is not intrinsically a kind of behavior we may coerce, but driving *on the side adopted by legislative convention* is.

The first passage quoted above (written earlier) has been subjected to provocative criticism by Nicholas Wolterstorff. In a recent article he says:

> Audi, so far as I can tell, holds not only that the reasons [appropriate to justify coercion] must be drawn from that freestanding neutral source ["freestanding" is Rawls's term for what is neutral "with respect to all (controversial) comprehensive doctrines"] but that for a given coercive law to be justified, everybody must believe for the same reason that it is a good thing.[9]

Two points are important here. First, my appeal to secular reasons (which I will connect with natural reasons) is not equivalent to Rawls' appeal to freestanding ones.[10] This is partly because I do not think that a "comprehensive" moral view need be inadmissibly tied to any perspective inappropriate for justification of laws.[11] Second, I have repeatedly spoken of adequate reasons in a way that leaves open whether there can be only *one* such reason for a law or public policy or even just one unified set.[12] Justificatory overdetermination – the existence of two or more independent justifications – is possible in these cases (as in other kinds); and I have indicated that religious and secular reasons can often support the same laws and policies.[13]

---

[9] See N. Wolterstorff, "The Paradoxical Role of Coercion in the Theory of Political Liberalism," *Journal of Law, Philosophy and Culture* 140 (2007).

[10] See J. Rawls, *Political Liberalism* (New York: Columbia University Press, 1995), p. 10.

[11] This is argued in Chapter 1 of *Religious Commitment and Secular Reason* and, in a different way, in "Moral Foundations of Democracy, Secular Reasons, and Liberal Neutrality Toward the Good," *Notre Dame Journal of Law, Ethics and Public Policy* 19 (2005), 197–218.

[12] Audi, *Religious Commitment and Secular Reason*, e.g. p. 87.

[13] *Ibid.*, pp. 130–3.

Another kind of question Wolterstorff raises is what we ought to do if we cannot convince others of a justification for a proposed coercive law. He says that for me "the role of citizen requires that if one fails in the attempt to inform others of one's reasons, one then ought to refrain from supporting that coercive law."[14] I have not implied this or anything as general. Failure to persuade others, even failure to inform them of one's reasons, where one has made a reasonable effort, does not entail lack of justification for supporting a coercive law. I think (and would expect Wolterstorff to agree) that there are many reasons why one might fail to persuade others (his word is "inform," but the challenge is greater given the stronger reading that seems clear in the context). It might be that the others in question are (e.g.) misinformed or plainly in the grip of manipulative rhetoric. Here, given adequate reason for the coercive position, one may in general still proceed (which is not to say one must proceed).

A very different case, however, is one in which the reasons in question are not compelling to citizens who are as informed, and as rational, in the matter as oneself. There, one characteristically is prima facie obligated not to proceed (a point to be clarified below). Any political philosophy must take account of these different cases, and this chapter is partly devoted to indicating how this should be done. Practical wisdom will be required; no simple formula suffices. One standard is that liberty is the default position: if there is no cogent case for restricting a freedom, coercion should not be used to prevent its exercise.

In the same paragraph Wolterstorff says that:

> [I]f you share with me my conviction that some proposed coercive law is a good thing, then it will not function coercively for either of us ... if everybody shares with me that conviction, then it will not function coercively for any of us.[15]

The notion of functioning coercively needs analysis. A law may function coercively for one in roughly the sense that awareness of and aversion to its sanctions is essential in motivating one's conformity to it. Call this the *psychological sense* of "functioning coercively." A law may also function coercively by imposing sanctions such that awareness of them would reduce the freedom of those within its scope if they were inclined to violate it. Call this the *structural sense*. The latter does not entail the former, since there may in fact be no one who is compelled to act accordingly: no

---

[14] Wolterstorff, "The Paradoxical Role of Coercion," p. 142.   [15] *Ibid.*

one need be tempted to violate the law, particularly if it meets sufficiently wide approval.

Consider the psychological sense first. Granted, in passing a coercive law that we consider a good thing, we (normally) do not feel coerced; we may indeed be exercising a kind of autonomy. But our approval of the law does not imply that, in conforming to it, we will not sometimes be motivated by aversion to punishment and feel compelled to conform. In the detached cool moments of legislation, we may ignore a significantly strong tendency to violate the very provisions we see to be desirable.

As to the structural sense, apparently Wolterstorff is not taking this sense into account. But surely a democracy must consider not just what it allows the people to *do freely*, but also what it makes them *free to do*. The latter is roughly the scope of liberty; the former is roughly freedom in action – *behavioral liberty*. The scope of liberty is crucial whatever the psychology of any particular population. It is a structural element in a society. Legislators – and, especially, writers of constitutional provisions – should attend to standards for citizens in general. Those who pass laws at one time may be very different in attitudes and aims from those who, later, must obey them. Sound legislation, particularly when it restricts liberty, must anticipate changes that may be brought by pluralism or even simply by the ever-present currents of historical change.[16] Those who pass coercive legislation may not feel coerced in conforming to it, and a great majority of the population may be psychologically similar. But later populations and minorities may be very different.

2 Separation of church and state as an element in democracy

I assume that an appropriate church–state separation is a protection of both religious liberty and governmental autonomy. This separation is most commonly considered in relation to restricting governmental activity toward religion. We may also take the separation to concern restricting the activities of churches toward government, but that is an aspect of church–state separation I have explored elsewhere and will not pursue here.[17] As to governmental regulation, three principles I would defend are a liberty principle that requires government to protect

---

[16] The points in this paragraph concerning psychological liberty are consistent with, though they go beyond, those Wolterstorff cites in "The Paradoxical Role of Coercion," at p. 142, as objections by Kent Greenawalt. But their exchange does not address structural freedom (liberty).

[17] See, e.g., Audi, *Religious Commitment and Secular Reason*, Chapters 2–3.

religious liberty, an equality principle requiring its equal treatment of different religions, and a neutrality principle requiring its neutrality toward religion. The equality principle implies non-establishment as ordinarily understood. If all religions had a common element and if establishing a religion built solely on this element should be possible, then a limited kind of establishment might be possible within the constraints of equality (limited in part because the common element might be major in one religion and minor in another).[18] As to the neutrality principle, it is not entailed by the other two together nor is it, so far as I know, required by the US Constitution. In political philosophy it is also more controversial.[19] Much could be said about each, but here a few clarifications must suffice.

Although liberty is the default position for a liberal democracy, it cannot be unlimited. The limitations are determined by moral considerations such as human rights, but we need not take rights as morally basic.[20] Whether we appeal to rights or not, the appropriate limitations would imply the moral wrongness of certain extreme forms of religious conduct. Such conduct, like ceremonial mutilation of children, violates reasonable standards for protecting persons. Even non-violent treatment of women and, especially, children may be justifiably prohibited by law; for example, where children are forced, under religiously protected parental powers, to marry while they are in their early to mid teens, as the State of Texas has maintained has been the case in a Mormon community raided by Texas authorities in the spring of 2008.[21]

This limitation on protection of religious liberty also illustrates the limited governmental neutrality toward religion which defenders of liberal democracy have generally considered appropriate. Proper protections of religious liberty provide for great diversity in styles of life, but prohibit (non-self-defensive) harms to other persons. Even restrictions of religious liberty that involve only standards of dress may be warranted. Consider the possibility that certain garments would be dangerous in a factory where they might catch in machinery. The questions raised recently in France concerning dress codes for students, and in Turkey, concerning

---

[18] Whether "civil religion" might be establishable within the limits of the equality and neutrality principles is considered in my paper "Natural Reason, Secularity, and Governmental Neutrality toward Religion," *Religion and Human Rights* 4, 1–20 (2009).

[19] See Wolterstorff's contribution to Audi and Wolterstorff, *Religion in the Public Square*.

[20] This is argued in my paper "Wrongs Within Rights," *Nous* 15 (2005), 11–139.

[21] "Texas Loses Court Ruling Over Taking of Children," *New York Times* (May 30, 2008).

the propriety of headscarves for women are different and more controversial.[22] We can say, however, that the mere fact that a mode of dress is not a direct harm to anyone does not imply that government has no justification for restricting it in public. The case for restraint should, other things equal, be stronger in proportion to the importance of the mode of dress for the religious citizens in question.

As these points indicate, equality must be understood to allow differential treatment provided its basis is non-religious and otherwise justified. Consider, having state holidays on Christian feast days. This may in fact advantage Christians, but may be instituted because it well serves a majority of the population, not because that majority is Christian. The governmental policy in question might equally have benefited some other religious group. To be sure, minority religious groups should, within the limits of practicability, be given comparable leave for their religious observances, at least in government employment.

Even religious freedom and governmental neutrality toward religion, then, may be limited in some ways in a morally well-grounded liberal democracy that is appropriately neutral in matters of religion. This point is probably not controversial, but there is disagreement concerning the degree to which a democracy may properly promote the practice of religion as such, provided it does not prefer one religion over another.[23] Suppose that a majority of the people want compulsory religious education in the schools. Why is this objectionable? After all, one might provide for religious children to be instructed only in their own denominations and by people approved by authorities in those denominations. For the non-religious, one might provide religious education that, being simply *about* religion, is essentially secular. Such curricular requirements might, however, benefit the religious, if only by promoting understanding of the religions studied.

Neutrality toward religion – the third standard of the partial theory of church–state separation I am defending – presents a definition problem

---

[22] France's national legislature outlawed headscarves in French schools in March of 2004. "French Senate Approves Ban on Religious Attire," *Washington Post* (March 4, 2004). The European Court of Human Rights upheld the law in Eur. Ct. H. R., *Dogru* v. *France*, 4 December 2008. The ban on headscarves at universities then in effect was held not to violate the European Convention on Human Rights, see Eur. Ct. H. R. (Grand Chamber), *Leyla Şahin* v. *Turkey*, 10 November 2005. In February 2008 the Turkish National Assembly lifted the 80-year-old ban on wearing headscarves at universities. "Ban on Head Scarves Voted Out in Turkey," *Washington Post* (February 10, 2008).

[23] For an extensive debate on the kind of religious neutrality appropriate to liberal democracy, see Audi and Wolterstorff, *Religion in the Public Square*.

even apart from the difficulty of defining "religion." Two points and two examples will help. First, governmental neutrality does not imply governmental indifference. Indeed, religious liberty is an important kind of liberty and governments should solicitously preserve it. Second, governmental neutrality toward religion does not prevent contingent circumstances from causing religious institutions to benefit from laws or policies instituted by government. The first example to follow will illustrate this.

Consider educational vouchers: certificates, which enable parents who do not want to educate their children in public schools, to use the funds that they pay, or would have paid through taxes, for public education. Their purpose is to defray the cost of private education. The practice of offering vouchers to all who qualify for them might benefit some religious groups. Some contend that the practice would weaken the public school system, thereby reducing democratic cooperation; but even supposing this to be so, it is unclear that (unless the magnitude of the effect is great) it is sufficient reason to deny parents the funding. Note too that some secular parents might support a voucher system as strongly as some religious parents and that nothing in voucher programs themselves precludes governmental requirements that citizenship be studied and its practice encouraged, both in private schools and in public ones.[24]

A second example is science education. Government may require teaching evolutionary biology in public school science – even in required science courses – despite some religious parents' contention that this infringes upon their religious liberty to raise their children with the belief in, say, creationism. To be sure, a liberal–democratic government may not properly sponsor hostility to religion; but that cannot be understood to preclude teaching, as true or highly confirmed, a theory that denies some scriptural claims. Teaching evolutionary theory as true does not imply any metaphysical claims, including any denial of the view that the physical world was created by God and remains under divine sovereignty.[25]

---

[24] There is far more to say about the status of vouchers of various kinds in relation to the three principles of church–state separation I have sketched. For an indication of special issues relating to the US Constitution and of some relevant legal literature, see A. S. Greene, "Why Vouchers Are Unconstitutional, and Why They're Not," *Notre Dame Journal of Law, Ethics and Public Policy* 13 (1999), 397–408.

[25] For discussion of this issue see K. Greenawalt, *Does God Belong in Public Schools?* (Princeton University Press, 2005) and my critical study of it, "Religion and Public Education," *Virginia Law Review* 93, 4 (2007) 1175–95. One may be reminded here of the "Lemon test": "First, the statute must have a secular legislative purpose; second, its principal or primary effect must be one that neither advances nor inhibits religion; finally, the statute must not foster 'an excessive entanglement with religion'." See *Lemon* v. *Kurtzmann* 403 US 602 (1971).

Given that for some political philosophers (such as Rawls) liberal democracy should be neutral toward "comprehensive" views of the good,[26] it should be stressed that the kind of governmental neutrality I support is not *value*-neutrality. This is evident even in relation to the kinds of moral considerations that, for any sound democracy, figure in restricting liberty. As illustrated already, these involve a notion of harm. Thus, even on a negative conception of morality, according to which its concern is only to prevent harm, we would still need an account of harms or of some still wider range of evils that can justify limitations on the freedom of citizens. For liberal democracy is clearly committed to supporting the maximal liberty that citizens can exercise without producing certain harms (or a substantial likelihood of them).[27] Thus, even if a liberal state could be neutral toward the good, it could not be neutral toward the bad. It could not be value-neutral.

There is, however, no sharp distinction between a government's restricting liberty as a way to prevent harm and its doing so as a way of promoting some good. Consider education. Compulsory education is essential to prevent the harms attendant upon ignorance. These include public health hazards and liability to political manipulation by demagogues. But education is surely one kind of good, and in practice it is impossible to provide education in a way that makes it effective in preventing harm yet is not inherently good. This is illustrated by competent teaching of history, literature and science.

3   Standards for freedom of expression vs. standards for support of laws and public policies

The liberty, equality, and neutrality principles apply to conduct in general, but so far I have been focusing on laws and public policies and on the principles of governmental conduct that are most needed for preserving a reasonable separation of church and state. These three principles apply to governmental laws and policies relating to free expression as well as to other kinds of behavior. I am assuming that liberal democracies recognize a moral right to "maximal" freedom of expression in public discourse, and that here, as in other realms of conduct, liberty is the default

---

[26] Rawls, *Political Liberalism*, p. 10.

[27] J. S. Mill's famous harm principle in *On Liberty* is a prominent example of the kind of view in question. See Mill, *On Liberty* (2nd edn.) (London: John Parker and Son, 1859) p. 101.

position. Roughly, this is to say that, in a government's regulatory activities, it is restrictions of liberty, especially of thought, expression, and free association, that the government must justify. Permitting "natural" and other liberties is not normally in need of justification.

Those engaging in free expression need not have any particular purpose in expressing themselves. More important for the purposes of this chapter, they need not aim at coercion or even persuasion. By contrast, advocacy of laws or public policies normally is intended to persuade, and most of those are also coercive. Moreover, supporting them by voting to institute them is commonly intended to require conformity on pain of legal penalty, which is a form of coercion. For coercion of others, as opposed to free expression of thoughts and feelings, there are higher standards – moral and legal. We are morally free, and should be legally free, to seek to *persuade* others to do things we ought not to *coerce* them to do.

Related to this distinction is another: it is essential to distinguish *rights* from *oughts*. There are things many of us ought to do, such as give to charity, which we nonetheless have a moral right *not* to do. No one may coerce charitable contributions or even properly assert that financially able non-contributors have violated the rights of charities. Moreover, whereas for what one morally ought to do one has a *reason*, having a right to do something does not imply having any reason to do it. The right to abstain from giving to charity is an example.

I would argue (as would many others) that given our moral rights, free expression and advocacy should be legally limited only by a harm principle, *roughly* a principle to the effect that the liberty of competent adults should be restricted only to prevent harm to other people, animals, or the environment (in that order of priority). *Ethically*, however, both free expression and advocacy – and especially advocacy of coercive laws and public policies – should meet standards higher than this very permissive legal one. The next section proposes principles expressing such higher standards.

4   Some major principles governing support of laws and public policies

Regarding the ethics of good citizenship, I have defended a standard I have termed:

The principle of secular rationale:

> citizens in a free democracy have a prima facie obligation not to advocate
> or support any law or public policy that restricts human conduct, unless

they have, and are willing to offer, adequate secular reason for this advocacy or support (e.g. for a vote).[28]

This principle has been widely misunderstood. Here are some needed qualifications of the principle and an indication of its basis.

A prima facie obligation has a degree of normative force that is in a certain way limited: the obligation is *defeasible* and may be overridden. Appeal to religious considerations could be necessary to gain sufficient support for enacting laws that will prevent Nazis from coming to power. Then one *should* appeal to them (though there are appropriate and inappropriate ways to do so). The prima facie obligation in question, like many other prima facie obligations, is compatible with a *right to act otherwise*. Here I presuppose what elsewhere I have argued for: that there are wrongs within rights. For instance, there are some things, such as giving nothing to charity, that we ought not to do even though we have a right to.[29]

A *secular reason* for an action (or a belief) is roughly one whose status as a justifier of action (or belief) does not evidentially depend on (but also does not deny) the existence of God; nor does it depend on theological considerations, or on the pronouncements of a person or institution *as* a religious authority. This notion is epistemic, roughly a matter of evidential grounding. It is not a matter of the content of reasons: a secular reason may be to the effect that preservation of governmental neutrality toward religion is desirable, and here the notion of religion figures in the content of the reason. Secular reasons for laws – say considerations of public safety – will typically *accord* with reasons that are supported by at least some major religion. Suppose we have a religious obligation to promote human flourishing in a sense requiring good health. This will generate a derivative obligation – prima facie but possibly strong – to support public safety.

An *adequate reason* (for something) is one that, in rough terms, evidentially justifies the belief, act, or other element it supports. The notion is objective but complex and non-quantitative. In many applications it is controversial, but no plausible political or legal philosophy can do without it. *Excusability* also needs comment. It can explain why someone who violates the principle of secular rationale is not *ipso facto* a "bad citizen."

---

[28] This formulation is drawn from Audi, *Religious Commitment and Secular Reason*, p. 86, though I published essentially the same version much earlier in "The Separation of Church and State and the Obligations of Citizenship," *Philosophy and Public Affairs* 18 (1989), 259–96.

[29] See Audi, "Wrongs Within Rights."

Like other failures, this one may be fully excusable. I think it often is. Special circumstances free us of blameworthiness, but they also reveal that apart from them we would have merited blame. Excusability is not a status to be aimed at, as is justification; but any theory of obligation or responsibility should take it into account.

The principle of secular rationale is non-exclusive. First, it does not rule out having *religious* reasons for legal coercion, nor imply that such reasons can never justify anything. Second, it does not even rule out having *only* religious reasons for lifting oppression or expanding liberty. It concerns coercion, not behavior of just any kind; and it accords with the idea that freedom is the default position in a liberal democracy. Largely for that reason, it is a standard whose support may appropriately come from a wide variety of considerations. Third, it does not imply that religious reasons should be "privatized." Indeed, one might quite properly indicate, publicly, that one is supporting, say, illegalizing assisted suicide, *not* from religious grounds – such as one's reverence for God's gift of life – but for secular reasons, such as protection of vulnerable patients.

This is another place where critical remarks by Wolterstorff give rise to an occasion for clarification. With my position as well as Rawls' in view, he says that "it is religious reasons that are to be excluded ... Any reason that is not shared by everybody is excluded."[30] I have already noted that adequate reasons need not be shared by everyone, but need only be in a certain way accessible to rational adults. I have also indicated why religious reasons are not the only kind in question but are nonetheless special. Insofar as non-religious reasons are similarly special, however, the principle of secular rationale may be extended to them.[31]

As to the exclusivism charge, I have just explained why the adequacy requirement provides for an important role for religious reasons. They can even be evidentially sufficient to justify the position in question and motivationally important for one's holding it, or both, even though they should not be the sole justification one has. It also seems to me that religious reasons can even be motivationally *sufficient* for properly supporting coercive conduct, since this allows that adequate secular reasons may also be motivationally sufficient.[32]

---

[30] Wolterstorff, "The Paradoxical Role of Coercion," p. 144.

[31] Audi, *Religious Commitment and Secular Reason*, pp. 100–3.

[32] The appropriate motivational role of secular and religious reasons in supporting coercive laws and public policies is discussed in detail in Audi, *Religious Commitment and Secular Reason*, pp. 96–100.

Defining religion is another problem here. Fortunately, we do not need a definition, as opposed to important criteria. Here are nine criteria features, each relevant to, though not strictly necessary for, a social institution constituting a religion or (as applied to individuals) to an individual having a religion: (1) appropriately internalized belief in one or more supernatural beings (gods); (2) observance of a distinction between sacred and profane objects; (3) ritual acts focused on those objects; (4) a moral code believed to be sanctioned by the god(s); (5) religious feelings (awe mystery, etc.) that tend to be aroused by the sacred objects and during rituals; (6) prayer and other communicative forms concerning the god(s); (7) a worldview according the individual a significant place in the universe; (8) a more or less comprehensive organization of life based on the worldview; and (9) a social organization bound together by (1)–(8).[33]

This characterization is broad, but it is better to avoid too narrow a conception of religion than to err on the side of excessive restriction of the notion. To be sure, there are dangers of excessive definitory breadth, since one might then extend privileges, such as tax exemptions and legal permissions to use certain drugs in rituals, that may burden society in certain ways. Here, however, definitory breadth seems preferable for a free society, since it means protecting liberty and equality better than would be likely on too narrow a conception.

Let me conclude this section by exploring the relation between rationality and consensus. Again it is helpful to consider something Wolterstorff says: "Rationality does not typically yield consensus. Rationality coupled with information typically leaves us disagreeing."[34] I agree that this holds in some important ethical matters. But thoughtful people do agree on a great deal when it comes to ethics, at least at the level of prima facie obligation and often on such overall judgements as that it is wrong to treat people unequally on grounds of race or ethnicity, to punish people for crimes they did not commit, and to torture people

---

[33] These features are stressed by W. P. Alston, in *Philosophy of Language* (Englewood Cliffs: Prentice-Hall, 1964), p. 88 (I have slightly revised his list) This characterization does not entail that a religion must be theistic, but theistic religions are my main concern. It is noteworthy that in *United States* v. *Seeger*, 380 US 163 (1965), the Supreme Court ruled that religious belief need not be theistic; but theistic religions raise the most important church–state issues, at least for societies like those in the Western world. For discussion of the significance of *Seeger* in relation to church–state aspects of the foundations of liberalism, see Abner S. Greene, "Uncommon Ground, a review essay on J. Rawls's *Political Liberalism* and on R. Dworkin's *Life's Dominion*," *George Washington Law Review* 3 (1994), 646–73.

[34] Wolterstorff, "The Paradoxical Role of Coercion," p. 147.

as punishment.[35] In any case, Wolterstorff refers to "information," presumably to an indefinitely large quantity but not to adequate or full information.[36] Is it obvious that fully rational persons will disagree in ethical matters when they share *all* the relevant (non-moral) information and conscientiously reflect for a long time on it? Perhaps there are special cases in which they will, such as the justifiability of capital punishment, but these are surely instances in which a case can be made for allowing freedom to be the default position.

5   Natural reason, secular reasons, and religious convictions

Some of what has been said bears on the basis and knowability of the principle of secular rationale. Regarding its basis, first, it supports liberal democracy and religious liberty; second, it helps to prevent religious strife; and third, it is needed to observe the Do-unto-others principle, since clearly rational citizens may properly resent coercion based essentially on someone else's religious convictions. It should also be noted that I could have called it *the principle of natural reasons*.[37] This would highlight both its central stress on our natural rational endowment and its continuity with certain elements in the natural law tradition as expressed in Aquinas.[38] Clearly we can take our natural endowment as God-given even if we regard the *knowledge* it makes possible – notably including moral knowledge – as attainable even without dependence on theology or religion. A religion or a theology can make moral claims and even "scientific" (factual) claims – understood roughly as claims having moral or scientific content and confirmable by moral or scientific methods. There is no good ground for holding either that such claims must be tied to the religion or theology in question for their intelligibility or their justification or that a

---

[35] I have provided a moral epistemology that supports these points in *The Good in the Right: A Theory of Intuition and Intrinsic Value* (Princeton University Press, 2004).

[36] Wolterstorff, "The Paradoxical Role of Coercion."

[37] One qualification needed here is that there are secular reasons whose normative domain is not clearly encompassed by natural reason understood as an endowment of normal persons. Consider an aesthetic reason for believing that a line of poetry detracts from the value of the poem in which it occurs. If this requires a kind of sensitivity that a rational person need not have, it cannot be treated, as can a technical reason, in terms of groundability in natural reasons of an "ordinary" kind. The kinds of secular reasons that are apparently not also natural ones, however, can be separated from the kinds that concern this chapter, which clearly are natural in the relevant sense.

[38] T. Aquinas, *Summa Theologiae*, I.II. Q. 95 a. 1; I.II. Q. 96 a. 4 (trans. Fathers of the English Dominican Province, Blackfriars edn. 1963).

religion or theology's implying unreasonable positions in these moral or scientific matters has no bearing on assessing it, particularly in its bearing on sociopolitical life.[39]

In speaking of natural reason, I refer to a general human capacity for apprehending and responding to grounds for belief and for action. It is customary to speak of human reason in relation to both the theoretical realm, in which we must regulate belief, and the practical realm, in which we must regulate action (practice, in a broad sense). Theoretical rationality embodies an appropriate responsiveness to the grounds for belief, which may be broadly conceived as truth-indicators. Practical rationality embodies an appropriate responsiveness to grounds for action, grounds that may be broadly conceived as goodness-indicators. A person who is rational in an overall way – globally rational – must have both kinds of rationality and a significant degree of integration between them.

On the side of theoretical reason we must include not only responsiveness to sensory experience, memory, and introspective consciousness – for instance a consonance between perceptual experiences and observational beliefs – but also minimal capacities in logic, inductive as well as deductive, and some minimal intuitive capacities. The latter are manifested at least in understanding self-evident propositions. Those include certain propositions in the domain of practical reason, say that if grasping a smoking-hot skillet will cause one excruciating pain, then one has reason not to do this. This is not the place to summarize my overall theory of rationality (developed elsewhere[40]), but what has been said should help to clarify the basic conception of natural reason.

Aquinas spoke of "natural reason, whereby we discern what is good and what is bad."[41] Related to this, he affirms, as the first precept of natural law, that *"good is to be done and promoted, and evil is to be avoided* ... so that all the things which the practical reason apprehends as man's good belong to the precepts of the natural law under the form of things to be done or avoided."[42] Earlier in the same article he indicated that the

---

[39] For an informative discussion of Thomistic natural law theory that confirms this (e.g. by countenancing self-evident moral principles) see G. Grisez, J. Boyle and J. Finnis, "Practical Principles, Moral Truth, and Ultimate Ends," *American Journal of Jurisprudence* (1987), 99–151.

[40] See Audi, *The Architecture of Reason.*

[41] D'Aquinas, Summa, I.II. Q. 91 a. 2.

[42] *Ibid.* at I.II. Q. 94 a. 2 (emphasis in original).

precepts of the natural law are "self-evident principles," and in Q. 91, Art. 3 he said that:

> [J]ust as in the speculative reason, from [*naturally known*] indemonstrable principles we draw the conclusions of the various sciences ... so too it is from the precepts of the natural law ... that the human reason needs to proceed to the more particular determinations of certain matters.[43]

Particularly given his notion of the self-evident as having "its predicate contained in the notion of the subject"[44] – which implies that self-evident propositions are knowable "in themselves" – it would seem to be a mistake to take his notion of knowability by natural reason to imply epistemic dependence on any religious source, such as revelation – a point entirely consistent with his taking natural reason to be God-given and, in that way, ontically dependent on God.

Might there, however, be a reason that is both secular *and* adequate to support what it is supposed to support, yet not natural? One might argue for this as follows. Imagine a reason that is highly technical, say a consideration understandable only by highly trained chemists – for instance that having chemical constitution *c* is a reason to consider an effluent toxic. This is not apprehensible by (unaided) natural reason even supplemented by common-sense knowledge. One might say of such technical reasons, however, that they are *groundable* in natural reasons, on the assumption that there is an appropriate inferential route by which they may be reached from natural reasons. The route begins with common-sense observations; these may be taken together with theoretical developments that apply and reapply natural reason; and the destination is the technical propositions in question. The technical reasons in question, then, are indirectly accessible to natural reason given the kind of process I am sketching.

To be sure, that a highly reliable chemist has testified that a chemical being in an effluent is a reason to consider it toxic *is* a natural reason to think it toxic. The deliverances of natural reason carry with them the kind of presumption of credibility that Thomas Reid emphasized in describing our dependence on testimony.[45] Moreover, that a person is reliable on certain topics can (at least for non-theological matters) be known or

---

[43] *Ibid.* at I.II. Q. 91 a. 3 (emphasis added).

[44] *Ibid.* at I.II. Q. 94 a. 2.

[45] Among his "first principles" Reid includes a principle of credulity with one of veracity. Speaking of God as intending that "we should be social creatures" and as implanting "in our natures two principles that tally with each other," he says:
> The first of these principles is, a propensity to speak truth ... Truth is always uppermost, and is the natural issue of the mind ... Another original principle ... is a disposition to confide in the veracity of others, and to believe what they tell us. This is

evidenced by natural reason. That such a person's testimony is a reason to believe the person's attestation is also thus apprehensible. Once again, however, it should be stressed that the notion of the natural that I am employing is epistemic, not ontic. Such reasons are not epistemically dependent (roughly, evidentially dependent) on religious experience, religious authority, or revelation, but this does not imply the metaphysical proposition that we could apprehend them without divine creation or concurrence. (Recall St. Anselm's appeal to pure reason in his famous ontological argument and Descartes' appeal to the "light of nature" in his *Meditations*.[46])

Natural reason in the sense in question is plausibly considered an endowment of normal adults who have the kind of understanding of a natural language appropriate to functioning in civil society. Given this level, I believe the prima facie obligation to have natural reasons is not in general unfulfillable.

6 Natural reasons and religious identity

In the light of what has been said here, we can address a challenge to the principle of secular rationale presented in a wide-ranging paper by Habermas that contains important points about the relation between religion and democracy.[47] Habermas maintains that the "demand [of the principle of secular rationale] is countered by the objection that many religious citizens would not be able to undertake such an artificial division … without jeopardizing their existence as pious persons … A devout person pursues her daily rounds by *drawing* on belief."[48]

To appraise this objection, we should consider the suggestion that the distinction between the religious and the secular is artificial and the idea that religious citizens make it jeopardizes their identity. Regarding the first, without denying that there are borderline cases, I want to stress

  the counterpart to the former; and, as that may be called *the principle of veracity*, we shall … call this *the principle of credulity*.
  (T. Reid, "An Inquiry into the Human Mind on the Principles of Common Sense" in *Inquiry and Essays*, ed. R. Beanblossom and K. Lehrer [Indianapolis: Hackett, 1983], pp. 94–5.)

[46] See St. Anselm, *Monologion*, Prologue, trans. S. Harrison, paras. 65, 71, in *The Major Works*, ed. B. Davis and G. C. Evans (Oxford and New York: Oxford University Press, 1998); and R. Descartes, *Meditations on First Philosophy*, trans. and ed. J. Cottingham (Cambridge University Press, 1996), p. 18.

[47] J. Habermas, "Religion in the Public Square," *European Journal of Philosophy* 1 (2006), 1–25.

[48] See *ibid.*, p. 8.

that there are many clear ones. It should help to think in terms of natural rather than secular reasons, though the relevant natural reasons are all in fact secular. Public health rationales for inoculations are clearly secular; the view that duty to God requires opening school days with prayer is clearly religious. Requiring inclusion of evolutionary biology in the high school science curriculum on the ground that it is respected and considered scientifically central by the vast majority of biological scientists is a secular rationale. By contrast, *some* rationales for requiring that creationism be included are clearly not secular, for instance the premise that respect for God's sovereignty requires the endorsement of teaching the Genesis account of creation. I grant, however, a case can be made for the secularity of the contention that intellectual responsibility and respect for religious perspectives requires, in such a science curriculum, *recognizing* creationism (or intelligent design) as possible accounts of the origin of the human species. This contention, to be sure, involves the *concept* of religion, but makes no appeal to any religious truth or authority. The notion of a natural reason does not preclude religious concepts from figuring in its *content*; it is epistemically, not contentually, independent of religion and theology.

Regarding the jeopardized-identity idea, why would trying to make the kind of distinction in question threaten a devout person's identity? The principle of secular rationale does not imply that religious reasons are not *good*, nor even that secular ones are better in terms of truth-conduciveness. It is also put forward with the specific understanding that religious people can *view* the former as generally better reasons and can be motivated more (or wholly) by them. The principle posits a prima facie obligation to have adequate secular reasons for supporting institutional coercion; it does not preclude religious reasons.

It may help to consider the power of the Golden Rule: any normal adult can understand, on the basis of natural reason, the revulsion to being compelled to do something (such as kneel and pray) on the basis of someone *else's* religious convictions. If we can rationally want others to abstain from coercing us on the basis of their religious reasons, we can understand religious reasons well enough to be guided by the principle of secular rationale.

It is interesting to note that Habermas himself suggests that "religious citizens must develop an epistemic stance toward the priority that secular reasons enjoy in the political arena."[49] This injunction presupposes

---

[49] *Ibid.*, p. 14.

the conceptual abilities needed for the principle of secular rationale. One could not reliably follow it without ability to identify secular reasons and to compare them with other kinds. But suppose we also assume what Habermas calls a "requirement of [secular] translation" – that "[t]he truth content of religious contributions can only enter into the institutional practice of deliberation and decision-making if the necessary translation [of 'convictions in a religious language'] already occurs in ... the political public sphere."[50] This requirement implies not only that in general educated religious citizens can *understand* secular discourse, but also that they can find an appropriately strong *correspondence* between the two. The second implication is stronger than any implication of the principle of secular rationale. Both points, however, support the conclusion that the suggestion of the principle of secular rationale's jeopardizing identity is at best exaggerated.

7   Religious reasons and rational disagreement

I have already stressed the important role the principle of secular rationale – of natural reasons – leaves open for religious reasons. I now want to stress a principle I have more recently introduced as a complementary companion to the secular rationale principle:
The principle of religious rationale:

> Religious citizens in a liberal democracy "have a prima facie obligation not to advocate or support any law or public policy that restricts human conduct, unless they have, and are willing to offer, adequate religious reason for this advocacy or support."[51]

The underlying idea is that the ethics of good citizenship calls on religious citizens to constrain their coercion by seeking a rationale from their own religious perspective. This is a perspective it would be hypocritical or worse for a religious citizen to ignore in such a weighty matter. I take that to be a point defensible both on ethical grounds and from at least the

---

[50] *Ibid.*, p. 10. It should be noted that Habermas rarely if ever uses "translation" in the sense requiring synonymy and indeed works with more than one notion of translation. For clarification of at least three notions see T. M. Schmidt, "The Semantic Contents of Religious Beliefs and their Secular Translation. Jürgen Habermas' Concept of Religious Experience" in *Religion: Immediate Expierence and the Mediacy of Research*, ed. by Hans-Günter Heimbrock and Christopher Scholtz (Göttingen: Vandenhoeck & Ruprecht, 2007), pp. 175–188.

[51] This principle first appeared in print in my paper "Religiously Grounded Morality and the Integration of Religious and Political Conduct," *Wake Forest University Law Review* 36, 2 (2001), 251–77.

majority of religious perspectives – including some from which the principle of secular rationale would be rejected.

The ethics of citizenship in a pluralistic democracy must take account not only of actual disagreement between citizens but of the possibility of *rational* disagreement between "epistemic peers" relative to the matter in question: roughly, persons who are (in the matter(s) in question) equally rational, possessed of the same relevant evidence, and equally conscientious in assessing that evidence. Rational disagreement between epistemic peers can occur not just inter-religiously – between people who differ in religion (or one or more of whom is not religious at all)-but also intra-religiously. To be sure, if we think that a disagreement is with an epistemic peer and we wish to retain our position, we should seek new evidence for it, or at least to discover a basis for thinking the disputant is not as rational or as conscientious in appraising the issue. But the most reasonable conclusion may be that there is epistemic parity between us and, for that reason, the disagreement cannot be readily resolved in one's favor. To many conscientious citizens this may seem to be how things stand on the permissibility of assisted suicide, capital punishment, or abortion.

What is the appropriate response to persistent disagreement with an apparent epistemic peer? One response is skepticism: we might conclude that neither party is justified. There could be a difference in the disputants' conflicting justifications that one simply cannot discover. However, should we always suppose both that this is so, and that our own view is preferable? A quite different response to persisting disagreement with an apparent epistemic peer is humility: minimally, concluding that we might be mistaken or at least less justified than our peer. Humility is a response that would tend to prevent taking one's view as a basis for establishing coercive laws or public policies, and in that way it gives some support to the idea that in liberal democracies liberty is the default position. With all this in mind, I propose a *principle of rational disagreement*:

> The justification of coercion in a given instance is inversely proportional to the strength of the case for epistemic parity among disputants who disagree on whether coercion in that instance is warranted.

The idea is roughly that X's justification for coercing Y to A for reason(s) R is weaker in proportion to the strength of the case for the parity of X and Y regarding their disagreement on whether R constitutes adequate reason to require Y to A (where X takes the affirmative view and Y the negative). This principle is supported, as are other elements in my view, by considerations of reciprocity. It is certainly in the spirit of "Do unto others as you would have them do unto you."[52]

The principle of rational disagreement is a useful adjunct to the principle of secular rationale (or natural reasons) but is not essential to the appropriate employment of the latter. The principle of rational disagreement also helps to nourish a kind of humility and respect for others' views that is a desirable element in democratic societies of any kind. The principle does not specify *how* weak the justification for coercion becomes as the case for parity becomes stronger. I suggest that the need for toleration becomes dominant if the case is conclusive. This is in good part because the justification for coercion in a given instance approaches zero as the strength of the case for epistemic parity among disputants who disagree on whether the relevant coercion in that instance is warranted approaches conclusiveness. In this light, we can formulate a more specific principle applicable both to governmental and to individual action:

The principle of toleration:

> If it is not reasonable for proponents of coercion in a given matter to consider themselves epistemically superior to supporters of the corresponding liberty, then in that matter the former have a prima facie obligation to tolerate rather than coerce.

In practice, the effectiveness of this principle depends on the conscientiousness of those who would coerce. If unconscientious, they would readily think it reasonable to take defenders of the liberty in question to be less than epistemic peers in the relevant matter. If conscientious, they would tend to resist this view.

8   The place of religious considerations in public discourse

I have distinguished standards for ethically justifiable advocacy from standards for ethically justifiable free expression. I have also suggested that, as the principles I have proposed indicate, the ethics of citizenship places stronger constraints on the former than on the latter. Let me conclude with some comments on some of the standards for religious expression. These are in effect standards for *non*-privatization. The uses of religious language are unlimited: think not just of advocacy and persuasion, but of self-expression, self-description, and providing information. I may need to tell you my religious position to say, in any depth, who I am.

---

[52] Matthew 7:12.

The position I have been presenting sharply contrasts with Judge Michael McConnell's view that "the 'principle of secular rationale' rests on a false distinction between generally accessible reasons and religious ideas ... and that there is no convincing constitutional or philosophical reason that democratic deliberation should be secular."[53] Consider the separable points here in turn.

First, I make no claim that all religious ideas are inaccessible, on the basis of natural reason, to normal adult citizens; indeed, some correspond to ethical principles understandable through natural reason. But religious experience and sheer religious authority may, in the thinking of some people, figure as grounds of reasons, and there we either do not have accessibility in a relevant sense or do not have a basis in natural reason for either belief or action.

Second, that a reason figures in deliberation, even importantly, is compatible with its being restricted in the moderate way the principle of secular rationale requires. That principle does not preclude even overtly religious reasons from playing a role in such deliberation; its force is instead to constrain that role in a way that is defensible from many religious perspectives as well as from a secular point of view.

Third, given these points, there is no justification for speaking of epistemic "pre-screening devices like the principle of secular rationale."[54] Religious reasons are not implied to be inadmissible in political discourse, inappropriate as possible evidences, or epistemically deficient. The point is that, by themselves, they should not be taken to justify coercion by law or public policy in democratic societies. There are many reasons for this, but the point is most easily seen to be plausible in the light of reflection on the Do-unto-others principle.

A further point is needed to indicate another reason why McConnell's critical remarks do not undermine the principle of secular rationale. In criticizing Rawls's view (and by implication, mine) he says, "[a]bolitionists and civil rights leaders ... advanced religious arguments to bring about a more just society, and they defined justice by reference to their religious commitments."[55] I have stressed that the principle of secular rationale applies to coercion, not liberalizations.[56] Indeed, the prima facie

---

[53] M. W. McConnell, "'Secular Reason and the Misguided Attempt to Exclude Religious Arguments from Democratic Deliberation'", *Journal of Law, Philosophy, and Culture* 2 (2007), pp. 159–74.

[54] *Ibid.*, p. 169.   [55] *Ibid.*, p. 165.

[56] See Audi, *Religious Commitment and Secular Reason*, p. 88.

obligation it posits can be overridden if religious considerations are the only kind strong enough to prevent the rise of a tyrant.[57]

One reason why liberalization (as lifting restrictions of freedom) differs from coercion in the range of appropriate reasons supporting it is that freedom is the default position in liberal democracy and may properly be supported by a wider variety of reasons than those needed to justify coercion. Coercion of adult citizens must be justified by such natural reasons as that certain liberties would be harmful; liberalization can be justified by simply showing the lack of adequate natural reasons for coercion, and, arguably, may be properly supported by conscientiously held personal reasons that include religious ones. This is not to say that appeal to religious reasons favoring liberalization is always evidentially adequate or otherwise desirable; it may be not only unneeded but intellectually weak, misleading, or even divisive. Still, where religious reasons for liberalization, say for lifting oppression, are combined with secular ones, this may have the good effect of enhancing both justification and motivation to act accordingly and of indicating an important case in which the two kinds of reasons coincide in their implications for law or public policy.

Fifth, even where we seek to enhance liberty, we could still be injudicious in the *way* we appeal to religious considerations, even where doing so is in itself unobjectionable or even desirable. Doing it in a sectarian way, as where we appeal to a controversial clerical authority, may invite those with competing religious views to enter the discussion in such a way that avoidable trouble, and perhaps serious strife, will ensue. To be sure, there are apparently "comprehensive reasons" (in Rawls's sense), such as the value of a Kantian kind of autonomy in human life, that are shared by all the religious traditions likely to be represented in a democratic state. But, even where such commonality exists, noting it may lead to people's bringing into public discourse religious arguments that divide them.

Sixth, it is important to see that, in claiming that the abolition and civil rights leaders "defined justice by reference to their own religious convictions," McConnell goes further than proposing the admissibility of religious reasons as a basis of laws. Perhaps some of the people in question did subscribe to such definitions, but justifying claims about justice is one thing, and defining the notion of justice is another. It is quite possible to work with a definition of *justice* – such as "equal treatment of

[57] Ibid.

persons" – that is not intrinsically theological even though one *accepts* it on theological grounds. McConnell is not explicitly distinguishing the *conception* of justice possessed by a person and the person's *concept* of justice. The former often does not adequately reflect the latter, and different people may fail to see that they share a concept; for, owing to their different conceptions, they have conflicting beliefs, and would frame different definitions of the relevant terms. One case of this occurs where the concept is of a kind, such as the concept of justice, that belongs to natural reason. Even if a major reason I have for caring about justice is religious, and even if most of my paradigms of just actions come from religious literature, I may have the same egalitarian or meritarian concept of justice as a secular citizen. The conception (or the associated theory) many have in using a concept, then, may be substantially religious even if the concept is not intrinsically religious and they share it with secular peers. Sometimes, though not always, seeing the distinction in question can be a basis for agreement – or at least as much agreement as the principle of secular rationale requires.

So far, I have largely left open some matters of judgement that deserve brief comment before I conclude this chapter. What are some of the *standards* of good citizenship for the sociopolitical use of religious discourse? One is simply judiciousness. Will what we say be illuminating or alienating, consensus-building or divisive, clarifying or obfuscating? There are myriad considerations here, of both ethics and prudence. A second consideration is a spirit of reciprocity, based partly on a sense of universal standards available to all rational, minimally educated adults. An appeal to a Biblical narrative, for instance, can be clarifying with regard to such secular questions as whether prosperous nations are obligated to give more than they do to poor ones. Consider also the Do-unto-others principle. The *wording* is biblical; the *content* is a call for reciprocity, even universalizability. Both are standards that, in some form, are also central in any plausible secular ethics.

There is, then, no conflict between being religious and adhering to both the principle of secular rationale and that of religious rationale. A desirable integration is most likely to be well reasoned and stable if it is supported by a *theoethical equilibrium*: roughly, a rational integration between religious and religiously grounded deliverances and insights concerning moral matters and, on the other hand, secular ethical considerations. There are theological reasons, at least from the point of view of *natural* theology, for thinking that a high degree of such integration is possible at least for those who conceive God as omniscient, omnipotent, and omnibenevolent.[58] Religious citizens who achieve theoethical equilibrium will typically have *both* natural and religious reasons for their standards governing freedom and coercion.

I close with the suggestion that public discourse in a liberal democracy is best served by citizens having, and, in a wide range of important matters, using, an appropriate *civic voice*.[59] Such a voice is a matter of intonation and manifest respect for others. Our voice is not determined by the content of what we say but by *how* we say it, which is in turn partly a matter of *why* we say it. Our voice may reflect religious elements; but in citizens adhering to the principle of secular rationale – of natural reasons – it will also indicate a respect for standards that, simply as rational persons, we do or can have in common, and should take as a basis for setting the proper limits on our liberty. If these standards are not implicit in our religious commitments, they are at least likely to be standards by which we can conscientiously argue against coercive laws or policies based on someone else's religious convictions.

The relation between religion and politics is of great importance in the current global climate. Religion is often a powerful force in politics, culture, and most other realms. In many Western societies where the influence of religion has waned among the more educated citizens, its influence among immigrants has grown. Whatever its sociocultural role, as we strive to support democratic government, we must find a sound and credible theory of the standards that should structure governmental relations toward both institutional religion and religious individuals. I have defended three principles toward this end: one calling for governmental protection of religious liberty, the second requiring government to treat different religions equally, and the third requiring governmental neutrality toward religion. These standards do not, however, speak to the ethics of citizenship as regards individuals. For that case I have defended a principle of secular rationale – of natural reasons – aimed at enhancing cooperation in pluralistic societies while respecting the importance of

---

[58] This is argued in Chapter 5 of *Religious Commitment and Secular Reason*, where I have acknowledged that the case is not uncontroversial.

[59] The concept of civic voice is clarified in Chapter 6 of *Religious Commitment and Secular Reason*, with special reference to the importance of secular motivation as typically an influence on one's voice: our motivation for what we say commonly influences our voice as much as the content of what we say. Any content may be voiced in importantly different ways, and some of the differences are highly significant for the quality and harmony of civic discourse.

religious perspectives and convictions that may often divide people. This principle is combinable with a counterpart principle of religious rationale, which calls on religious citizens to seek adequate religious reasons before supporting coercive laws or public policies. Both principles are supported by the proposed principles of rational disagreement and toleration, which call on all of us to abstain from coercion where apparent epistemic peers argue for liberty. All of these principles support positing a prima facie obligation to respect liberty and to support its restriction only for the kinds of reasons that can be both respected and shared by rational, adequately informed citizens regardless of their religious position. At the same time, the principles provide for religious reasons to shape inquiry, to figure in deliberation, and to guide the discourse of religious citizens when they speak or, especially, advocate policies, in the public sphere. The proper role of religious reasons in attempts to justify coercion is limited, but this is, in the long run, as much a protection of religious liberty as of the freedom rights of all citizens irrespective of their religious convictions.[60]

[60] Earlier versions of this chapter were presented in the 2008 Conference on Religion in the Public Sphere held at the European University Institute (May 22–23, 2008) and in the Center for Law, Philosophy and Culture at the Catholic University of America (September 25, 2008), and at the University of Cologne (in a lecture series October 20–24, 2008), the University of Oxford Jurisprudence Discussion Group (May 22, 2008) and the University College London–Oxford Law Colloquium (October 29, 2008). A longer version appeared in (and is reprinted from) the *Journal of Law, Philosophy and Culture* (2011). For helpful discussions of drafts I am grateful to audiences on those occasions and to Roger Crisp, John Finnis, Rainer Forst, Rae Langton, George Letsas, Paolo Monti, Andreas Speer, Nicos Stavrulos, and William Wagner.

4

The 'other' citizens: religion in a multicultural Europe

MALEIHA MALIK

Introduction

Britain marked the two-hundred-year anniversary of the abolition of the slave trade in March 2007 with a ceremony at Westminster Abbey. The Queen and Tony Blair were among those attending the commemoration. The ceremony, however, was interrupted by a 39-year-old man named Tony Agbetu who demanded that the Queen should apologise for her ancestors' role in supporting the slave trade. 'You should be ashamed', shouted Tony Agbetu as he ran in front of the altar at Westminster Abbey. 'We should not be here – this is an insult to us', he said. 'I want all the Christians who are Africans to walk out.'[1]

Tony Agbetu was from an organisation called Ligali, whose official aim is to 'challenge the misrepresentation of African people and culture in the British media'.[2] Ligali's remit includes not only economic, social and political equality but also 'cultural' justice on behalf of the African community. Tony Agbetu's challenge to Britain's official memory of its relationship with slavery, and his act of interrupting a national ceremony in Westminster Abbey in the presence of the Queen and the Prime Minister, was not merely about slavery. This dramatic interruption of the British national celebration of the abolition of slavery is a useful point of entry into an enquiry about religion in the European public sphere. Tony Agbetu's protest illustrates an important shift towards the 'politics of recognition' that has taken place in European liberal democracies. The claims of individuals (like Tony Agbetu) and groups (such as Ligali) are no longer limited to economic, social and political equality. These

---

[1] See the report of the event 'Protestor Disrupts Slavery Commemoration', *The Guardian*, 27 March 2007.

[2] For details about Ligali see www.ligali.org (last accessed 10 August 2011).

individuals and groups now also argue for 'cultural accommodation' and 'recognition' as part of their political claim to be treated as full citizens in European liberal democracies.

Of course, a paradigm for analysing this topic is 'postcolonial' studies. I discuss some of these ideas, but my aim in this chapter is the more modest one of using Tony Agbetu's political protest as a point of entry to discuss two themes which are often considered separately but which I relate to each other. The first theme has to do with the increasing importance of religion in the European public sphere in the specific context of the increasing religious and cultural diversity that has resulted from migration after the Second World War. The second set of issues arises from the fact that many of these new migrants are former 'colonial subjects' who have been rapidly transformed into 'equal citizens' of liberal democracies in the last sixty years. Both these themes emerge from Tony Agbetu's protest. At first sight, Tony Agbetu's claim is made as a Christian to other Christians. Yet it is also clear that his religion maps onto other related social categories such as race and culture because his appeal is to 'all the Christians *who are Africans*' to walk out. This is a dramatic illustration of my first argument: that an analysis of religion in the European public sphere has to be understood in the context of increasing racial and cultural diversity. My second argument is linked to Tony Agbetu's insistence that there should be an apology for Britain's involvement in the slave trade. I suggest that one consequence of increasing racial and cultural diversity is that the history of European empire is not a matter of past 'melancholia' but rather it continues to shape political debates in the present.[3] I discuss these issues in the first two sections of the chapter, before uniting them in a third section which explores their relevance for analysing two contemporary controversies: Islamic headscarves and the sharia debate.

1   'Religion' in the European public sphere

There is now a well-established academic and popular literature discussing the impact of demographic changes – and non-European migration into Europe – on racial or ethnic diversity. Although there has been some discussion about the impact of these changes on 'religion', this analysis has been skewed in favour of a discussion of Muslims or Islam. This

---

[3] For a detailed discussion of the connection between 'multiculturalism' and the history of empire, see P. Gilroy, *After Empire: Melancholia or Convivial Culture?* (London: Routledge, 2004).

assumption, that the presence of non-Christian minorities in Europe is a 'new' phenomenon, ignores the presence – and precedent – of religious minorities such as Jews. There needs to be greater attention to the way in which certain stories – and fantasies – that are told about a past homogenous Christian Europe have unfairly excluded some religious groups.

Nevertheless, migration into Europe since the Second World War does bring new challenges. Most obviously, the non-European cultures with whom colonial states had contact in the past were geographically distant from the European metropole. Now, both Europeans and their 'others' from non-Western cultures inhabit the same geographical, temporal and spatial sphere. Moreover, in the past it was possible to argue that non-Europeans should be subject to a different system of political and legal rights to European citizens. Now, those who have full citizenship in a European nation state can – and do – claim rights as equal citizens. Even if there are still cultural or religious differences that mark out some individuals or groups as non-Western, the contemporary context is one in which the geographical and political distance between Europeans and 'others' has been significantly reduced. Claims by minority religious groups – for the public accommodation of their private religious identity – cause special difficulties because they challenge the liberal secular settlement. Non-Christian religions are unlikely to have developed sophisticated responses to European secularism in a way that has been achieved by majority or well-established religious minorities.[4] The public sphere will often be structured in a way that favours religious minorities so that those who are often seeking the accommodation of religious needs will be newer religious minorities.[5]

Moreover, as the protest of Tony Agbetu illustrates, even Christians who are from racial, ethnic and cultural minorities will face forms of exclusion from the European public sphere. Religion, therefore, needs

---

[4] T. Asad's work discusses the argument that secularism emerges out of a particular historical experience that may make it more hospitable to religions such as Christianity who have participated in that process. See for example: T. Asad, *Formations of the Secular: Christianity, Islam and Modernity* (Stanford University Press, 2003), Introduction and Chapters 1 and 6.

[5] See for example R. McCrea's analysis of EU law and public policy. McCrea concludes that a religious presence in the public sphere has been identified by the Union as particularly threatening to the liberal democracy in contrast to its ready acceptance of the public roles of culturally and historically entrenched Christian denominations in many member states. See R. McCrea, 'Limitations on Religion in a Liberal Democratic Polity: Christianity and Islam in the Public Order of the European Union', *LSE Legal Studies Working Paper*, 18 (2007).

to be categorised within a wider frame than 'religion and belief'. Tony Agbetu, for example, was a Christian. His claim to be 'excluded' from the national ceremony in Westminster Abbey was not just a claim based on religion. Rather, a range of other overlapping factors are also relevant to understanding why he felt excluded, as well as understanding his political protest. Race as a 'biological' construct is now widely accepted as an inappropriate paradigm for discussions of racism as a 'social' problem. Although difference based on 'colour' or visible ethnic difference remains a crucial way in which individuals and social groups become racialised, there is an increasing recognition that racism also includes other criteria. This new wider form of racism is concerned with visible markers of biological difference such as colour, but it also concerns itself with cultural racism as one way in which individuals and groups are racialised. Etienne Balibar develops this concept through an analogy with anti-Semitism and concludes cultural racism also concerns itself with 'signs of a deep psychology, as signs of a spiritual inheritance rather than a biological heredity'. Balibar also writes that this wider definition is more appropriate to capture the range of harm caused by 'racism in the era of "decolonisation" which is based on the movement of peoples from the former colonies into Western Europe'.[6]

The issue of cultural racism and postcolonialism is not just a peripheral adjunct to discussions of religion in the European public sphere. Traditional liberal political theory is not silent on the issue of the place of 'native' and colonial peoples to definitions of the political community. As Bhikhu Parekh notes, classical liberal theorists such as Locke and Mill had no difficulty in justifying English colonialism: they categorised members of different non-European cultures as lacking in individuals and 'backward'. These writers saw no reason to respect the integrity of these cultures or to see them as including a valid way of life or value. It followed, therefore, that there were no serious obstacles to dismantling these cultures, denying them territorial integrity and making them subject to an external European 'civilising' mission.[7] James Tully has also noted the relationship between colonialism and traditional liberal constitutionalism. Tully argues that many of the assumptions that underlie modern constitutionalism, and particularly its bias against non-European

---

[6] For a general discussion of cultural racism see T. Modood, *Multicultural Politics: Racism, Ethnicity and Muslims in Britain* (Edinburgh University Press, 2005), Chapter 1; and for the quotation from E. Balibar, see pp. 27–28.

[7] B. Parekh, *Rethinking Multiculturalism: Cultural Diversity and Political Theory* (London: Palgrave Macmillan, 2006), pp. 38–49.

cultures, were formed during the age of European imperialism, which makes them inhospitable to claims of cultural accommodation. Tully proposes alternative constitutional frameworks and conventions that open up a dialogic process between all citizens and which, he argues, is a form of constitutionalism that can accommodate cultural diversity in liberal democracies.[8]

2 Europe's 'other' citizens

Parekh and Tully both identify liberalism's failure to properly address the issue of non-Western cultures – as well as cultural diversity – at the level of liberal political and constitutional theory. The issue, however, also has important practical implications. For example, one reading of the European Court of Human Rights (ECtHR) case law on Islamic headscarves supports the view that European legal institutions are implicated in recreating cultural and religious homogeneity at the cost of safeguarding the individual right to religious freedom.[9] The recent call for 'Sharia Courts' by British Muslims provides another example that illustrates the point that postcolonial history and memory have an impact on politics and law. South Asian Muslims had a history of making claims against the British colonial authorities for separate family law courts. Contemporary claims by British South Asian Muslims, who insist that a system of separate family law is important to their individual and religious autonomy, need to be understood in that context.

In both the public debates about headscarves as well as sharia courts, non-Western religious difference is converted into 'barbarism' and a threat to liberal values. The process through which cultural racism maps onto ideas of civilisation that render certain religious practices – for example the Islamic headscarf – as barbaric, reactionary or intrinsically incompatible with modernity can be traced through an analysis of the history of ideas of classical evolutionism.[10] George W. Stocking Jr. has identified the way in which ideas of civilisation in mid eighteenth-century and nineteenth-century British, French and German thought are influenced by 'ethnological' thinking about human races. These

---

[8] J. Tully, *Strange Multiplicity: Constitutionalism In An Age of Diversity* (Cambridge University Press, 1995), esp. Chapters 1–3.

[9] See C. Evans, 'The "Islamic Scarf" in the European Court of Human Rights', *Melbourne Journal of International Law* 7(1) (2006), 52.

[10] For further details of this analysis see M. Malik, 'Feminism and its "Other": Female Autonomy in an Age of Difference', *Cardozo Law Review* 30(6) (2009), 2613–28.

Victorian origins of contemporary thought on human, social and cultural evolution remain significant for our present analysis. One aspect that Stocking identifies is the way in which ideas of progress of human beings mapped onto changes in the ideas of the origin of man, which were in turn influenced by changes in the religious meaning of human development. Stocking states: 'The religious assumptions that had provided the underlying basis of ethnological explanation were now among the major phenomenon to be explained. Conversely, the psychic unity of man was no longer a conclusion supporting the single origin of mankind but rather a premise for establishing the human invention of cultural forms.'[11] This fragmentation in the idea of a single religious origin for man also had a temporal consequence, because within this paradigm, which was an 'evolutionary context', it was increasingly the case that 'contemporary savages no longer stood on the margins of history as the degenerate offshoots, waifs and strays of mankind. For better or for worse, they were incorporated into the main movement of civilisation.' Stocking concludes that:

> Although united in origin with the rest of mankind, their assumed inferiority of culture and capacity now reduced them to the status of missing links in the evolutionary chain. Their cultural forms, although at the centre of anthropological attention, had still only a subordinate interest. One studied these forms not for themselves, or in terms of the meaning they might have to the people who created them, but in order to cast light on the processes by which the ape had developed into the British gentleman.[12]

This comparative method used the fact of cultural difference between European and non-European cultures as a way of affirming their superiority, as well as reaffirming binaries between civilisation and barbarianism.

Stocking also demonstrates that within this process the 'position of women' became a measure of civilisation. Yet the way in which the fact of comparison between European and non-European cultures operated to confirm the superiority of European self-belief and confidence in their 'civilisational values' often remains obscure in the debates about feminism and women's rights. There is an assumption that a concept such as autonomy has a universal appeal that can free itself from the ideas of evolutionism that have distorted the analysis of what is 'civilised' rather than 'barbaric'. Placing the analysis within the wider context of

---

[11] G. W. Stocking Jr., *Victorian Anthropology* (New York: The Free Press, 1987), p. 184.
[12] *Ibid.*, p. 185.

evolutionary thinking about civilisations that maps on to a comparison between Western and non-Western cultures is one challenge to this universalism.

In her analysis of the relationship between Orientalism and feminism, Meyda Yegenoglu uncovers a similar process through which non-Western religious difference is deemed to be inferior. She argues that one way in which Western feminism's universalist foundations are secured is by denying the context from which the Western subject is analysing (or comparing herself to) the non-Western subject.[13] Her analysis suggests that Western feminism re-enacts the errors of orientalist thoughts at a fundamental level because 'the Western subject (irrespective of the gender identity of the person who represents the Orient) occupies not only the position of the colonial, but also a masculine subject position.'[14] For Yegenoglu, this insight is important, because it allows us to understand that Western concepts of female autonomy (and the self more generally) achieve the goal of autonomy through a process of interaction with, as well as exclusion of, its non-Western 'Other'.[15]

3   The 'uncivilised modern': Islamic headscarves and the 'sharia debate'

The analysis of writers such as Stocking and Yegenoglu assists in understanding how 'cultural' and 'religious' difference is constructed to create hierarchies so that the West becomes associated with civilisation and women's equality, whilst other cultures and religions are assumed to be at an 'earlier' stage of development. Stocking's analysis, for example, suggests that evolutionary forms of analysis encourage us to place cultural and religious differences on a linear temporal scale for comparison that treats 'difference' as part of the same process of development rather than as indicative of plural life forms. This process supports assumptions that visible signs of cultural or religious difference – for example the headscarf or an adherence to religious ethical or legal norms – are the unfinished project of modernity. Where individuals fail to adapt themselves to this linear timescale of what is deemed to constitute 'civilised modern' conduct, the response is to try to reimpose this linear timescale by imposing solutions that require the elimination of the difference (e.g. a

---

[13] M. Yegenoglu, *Colonial Fantasies: Towards a Feminist Reading of Orientalism* (Cambridge University Press, 1998), Chapter 4.
[14] *Ibid.*, p. 59.   [15] *Ibid.*, p. 11.

ban on the Islamic headscarf or religious tribunals) through processes of assimilation.

Yet, there are alternative approaches to cultural and religious difference that can avoid or minimise the risk of cultural racism or of reproducing orientalist errors. A large part of the challenge is to avoid constructing cultural or religious difference in linear evolutionary terms that places it as pre-modern in comparison to the West.[16] Once these legacies of orientalism and colonialism are identified and minimised, it is more likely that the analysis of situations such as the Islamic headscarf or sharia tribunals is reasonable and constructive. In the next section, I want to discuss Islamic headscarves and sharia courts to examine whether it is possible to develop a more reasonable and constructive analysis that avoids the wholesale rejection of these minority religious practices.

A   The Islamic headscarf

In the context of the Islamic headscarf cases this means taking seriously the choices of individual women rather than using blanket stereotypes in which the headscarf becomes a signifier for two inherently contradictory symbols: on the one hand, the aggressive nature of Islam and Muslims; and simultaneously, a symbol of the oppression by Islam of Muslim women, thus replicating the 'postcolonial' fantasies about the Orient discussed by Meyda Yegenoglu. The paradoxical nature of the ECtHR's analysis of the Islamic headscarf has been noticed by Carolyn Evans, who concludes that in cases such as *Leyla Şahin*[17] (and also *Dahlab*[18]) the Court 'relied on two contradictory stereotypes of Muslim women as the essential basis for the decisions … they also demonstrate the extent to which the Court was prepared to rely on government assertions about Islam and the wearing of headscarves – assertions that were not substantiated by any evidence or reasoning'.[19]

---

[16] See for example, U. S. Mehta, *Liberalism and Empire: A Study in Nineteenth-Century British Liberal Thought* (University of Chicago Press, 1999), Introduction and Conclusion. See also M. Malik, 'The Branch on Which We Sit: Multiculturalism, Minority Women and Family Law' in A. Diduck and K. O'Donovan (eds.), *Feminist Perspectives on Family Law* (Routledge, 2006), pp. 221–3.

[17] *Leyla Şahin* v. *Turkey*, Application No. 44774/98, (2005).

[18] *Dahlab* v. *Switzerland*, Application No. 42393/98, (2001).

[19] Evans 'The "Islamic Scarf"', p. 54. For a discussion of the way in which these stereotypes may be operating outside the law in the contemporary social sphere, see for example V. Amiraux, 'Speaking as a Muslim' in G. Jonker and V. Amiraux (eds.), *Politics of Visibility: Young Muslims in European Public Spaces* (London: Transaction Publishers, 2006), p. 25.

The political and legal analysis of 'religious difference' in relation to practices such as the Islamic headscarf needs to move beyond these orientalist and postcolonial stereotypes. An example of a more sophisticated approach that avoids these errors can be found in the reasoning of Lady Hale in the *Shabina Begum* case, which endorses a more complex analysis of the headscarf as a matter of individual choice.[20] Lady Hale emphasised the importance of taking into account the full context of reasons as to why a young adolescent woman may adopt the headscarf. She also pointed to the need to provide some 'personal space' within which young Muslim girls can adjust themselves to changes in their body and appearance.[21] Lady Hale acknowledged that some feminists, such as Sahgal and Yuval Davis, 'go on to point out that, "One of the paradoxes is that ... women collude, seek comfort and even at times gain empowerment from the spaces allocated to them by fundamentalist movements".' However, Lady Hale firmly rejected these arguments and made the following explicit statement confirming that gender equality should prioritise an individual woman's autonomy: 'If a woman freely chooses to adopt a way of life for herself, it is not for others, including other women who have chosen differently, to criticise or prevent her.'[22]

B Muslim 'sharia' law

The debate about accommodating Muslim family law that followed the speech of the Archbishop of Canterbury (Archbishop Rowan Williams) also illustrates the way in which stereotypes about non-Western culture continue to influence contemporary analysis of religion. Archbishop Williams had suggested that there may be some useful role for 'multicultural jurisdictions' which devolve some decision-making in areas such as family matters back to religious communities.[23] His speech was met with a vigorous denunciation throughout the British media. The public hysteria that followed this incident confirmed the difficulty of having a reasonable public discussion about accommodating Muslim religious norms in an atmosphere in which Islam and Muslims are routinely demonised

---

[20] *Shabina Begum* v. *Denbigh Schools* [2006] UKHL 15, per Lady Hale, para. 96.

[21] *R* v. *Headteacher and Governors of Denbigh High School* (*ex parte* Shabina Begum) [2006] UKHL 15, para. 93.

[22] *Ibid.*, per Lady Brenda Hale at para. 96, p. 39.

[23] See the 'Archbishop's Lecture – Civil and Religious Law in England: A Religious Perspective', 7 February 2008, available at www.archbishopofcanterbury.org (last accessed 10 August 2011).

in public debates.[24] The overreaction to proposals to accommodate British Muslim family norms also echoed the Canadian experience.[25] In many instances, the 'rejecters' deployed stereotypes about 'oppressed Muslim women'.[26] This is not to say that there is not an important issue about addressing risks of harm to women and girls from any move towards sharia (or indeed any religious) arbitration. As I argue below, there need to be important limits and safeguards to address these risks. Nevertheless, what is noteworthy about the debates about sharia law and Islam is the way in which 'orientalist' stereotypes are deployed in contemporary debates.[27]

Yet Archbishop Williams' central claim that Muslim legal and ethical norms – the sharia – were already guiding the conduct of British Muslims is self-evident. Presenting state law and minority religious norms as two strictly separate systems of norms fails to take into account the intermediary spaces where individuals often apply a hybrid mixture of norms to guide their conduct or to settle disputes. Once these alternative spaces are analysed, it becomes clear that many Muslims are using alternative forums (which are usually associated with local mosque formation) for advice, consultation and dispute resolution. These Muslim community organisations – often labelled 'Sharia Councils' – are alternative forums for dispute resolution which apply Muslim legal and ethical principles, as well as cultural norms of local communities. Sharia Councils usually focus on family law issues, for example marriage and divorce, although they also provide advice in areas such as contract and inheritance. They also provide advice and assistance on Muslim family law to members of the Muslim community, solicitors and in some situations the judiciary. The three main functions of the Sharia Council are: first, reconciliation and mediation; second, issuing Muslim divorce certificates; and third, producing expert opinion reports on Muslim family law and practice.[28] As Samia Bano has noted, Sharia Councils are closely linked to diasporic

---

[24] See J. Petre and A. Porter, 'Archbishop Williams Sparks Sharia Law Row', *The Daily Telegraph*, 8 February 2008.

[25] N. Bakht, 'Were Muslim Barbarians Really Knocking on the Gates of Ontario?: The Religious Arbitration Controversy – Another Perspective' (Ottawa, 2007, on file with the author).

[26] See for example the 'One Law for All' Campaign, at www.onelawforall.org.uk/ (last accessed 17 August 2011).

[27] For a detailed analysis of this process see S. Fernandez, 'The Crusade Over the Bodies of Women' in M. Malik (ed.), *Anti-Muslim Prejudice in the West, Past and Present* (2009), 43(1) *Patterns of Prejudice*).

[28] S. Bano, 'Muslim Family Justice and Human Rights: The Experience of British Muslim Women', *Journal of Comparative Law* 38 (2007), 45.

transnational networks that cut across the national and international space. Many of the members who give 'opinions' in the Sharia Councils often have links with countries of origin of Muslims such as Pakistan and Bangladesh. They represent diverse and varied 'schools of thought' within Islam. They can also be understood as part of the process through which Muslims use a hybrid range of sources (their religious and cultural norms as well as state law) to guide decision-making and conduct. Moreover, the common assumption that Sharia Councils are 'forced' upon Muslim women, who are reluctant users of these systems, fails to reflect a more complex picture: Muslim women are often willing and active users of these forums, and they are seeking the reform rather than abolition of this form of Muslim family justice.[29]

The public hysteria that greeted Archbishop Williams' speech failed to reflect these complexities. Moreover, it failed to properly scrutinise whether some religious ethical and legal norms can be legitimately accommodated in ways that strengthen liberal democracies. Two examples of how religious norms may be accommodated can usefully make these abstract points more concrete: a discussion of Islamic mortgages reveals the considerable benefits of accommodation of Islamic legal norms; whilst the case of separate family law tribunals illustrates the risks of the vulnerability of Muslim women.[30]

The first example illustrates the way in which multicultural accommodation can work successfully. In the UK, the Finance Act 2003 abolished an excessive and double stamp duty on mortgages that comply with the Islamic law (Sharia) norms prohibiting the charging of interest. As most UK mortgages involve the house buyer borrowing money, the regime of a double stamp duty on those mortgages that complied with Islamic law was a significant barrier to the development of more widespread home finance for Muslims. The abolition of this penalty by the Treasury has laid the foundation for cheaper mortgages for those Muslims who are unable to buy normal financial products because their faith prohibits it.

This legal change could have short-term results in terms of greater financial stability through making home ownership easier for British Muslims. It should make the mortgage market operate in a fair and accessible way. There are also longer term and more subtle benefits. These

---

[29] *Ibid.* See also S. N. Shah-Kazemi, 'Untying the Knot: Muslim Women, Divorce and the Shariah', Report of the Nuffield Foundation (London: Nuffield Foundation, 2001).

[30] For a detailed analysis see M. Malik, *Muslim Legal Norms and the Integration of European Muslims*, Robert Schuman Centre for Advanced Studies (RSCAS Policy Papers, 2009).

types of modest concessions can yield considerable and magnified political benefits for minorities. Such moves have the potential to reduce the
gap between the experiences of Muslims in their daily and practical lives
and their experience of mainstream legal and political institutions. This
in turn can encourage the meaningful identification of minorities such as
British Muslims with mainstream political and legal institutions.

The issue of accommodating Muslim family law, however, raises a different range of issues because of the spectre that this may entail harm
to women through 'multicultural vulnerability'.[31] This term refers to the
risk faced by certain individuals within a minority group whose rights
as citizens are compromised by the grant of public recognition to traditional rules and practices. The prospect of 'multicultural vulnerability'
becomes most obvious in the area of family law. At first sight the grant
of separate jurisdiction to traditional groups in areas of family law seems
unproblematic. The response of some liberal democracies has been to
make exactly this concession to its racial, cultural and religious minorities. A noteworthy example was Canada, where Ontario's Arbitration
Act 1991 permitted the use of alternative dispute resolution procedures
to resolve personal disputes in areas as diverse as wills, inheritance, marriage, remarriage and spousal support. The legislation allowed individuals to resolve civil disputes within their own faith community, providing
all affected parties gave their consent to the process and the outcomes
respect Canadian law and human rights codes. Muslim groups in Ontario
had indicated a wish to set up a system of Muslim personal law tribunals (comprising retired judges, religious scholars, private arbitrators and
lawyers) that would govern some aspects of family law. More recently,
this strategy of accommodation was criticised with the result that there
were restrictions on the use of religious arbitration.[32] There is some limited evidence that some British Muslims would welcome this option. The
Guardian/ICM poll (November 2004) based on a survey of 500 British
Muslims found that a clear majority want Islamic law introduced into this
country in civil cases relating to their own community. Some 61 per cent
wanted Islamic courts – operating on sharia principles – 'so long as the
penalties did not contravene British law'.

Although existing research cannot confirm the number or nature of
all the systems of applying Muslim legal norms – for example Sharia

---

[31] See A. Shachar, *Multicultural Jurisdictions: Cultural Differences and Women's Rights*
(Cambridge University Press, 2001).
[32] See Bakht, 'Were Muslim Barbarians Really Knocking on the Gates of Ontario?'

Councils and Muslim Family Arbitration – it is clear that there is significant use of these informal forms of dispute resolution within Muslim communities, particularly in the context of family law. Although some bodies such as the Muslim Arbitration Tribunal are increasingly centralising their procedures and services,[33] the councils are not unified under one system and there is no 'common procedure' that governs their approach to dispute resolution. The decisions of these tribunals are subject to national law and they cannot be automatically enforced through the domestic state legal system. All members of the Muslim community retain the right to refer to an English court at any point in the proceedings, and any agreement that falls within the definition of an arbitration agreement can also be reviewed if there is evidence of pressure, duress or coercion.

Sharia law is not a part of English or Scottish law in a formal way, but provided that these rules and tribunals do not contravene any legal provisions they are free to operate. These councils deal with contractual matters and personal law such as inheritance, as well as family law matters such as divorce. The parties have to consent to the decisions of these councils, which only have powers to make recommendations to the parties. These councils are wholly dependent on the consent of the parties to enable the resolution of the dispute because these bodies do not have any enforcement powers.

In the specific context of Muslim family law, there is no recognition of Muslim marriages and divorces in English law. For Muslim marriages to be recognised as legally valid they have to conform with the terms of the Marriages Act 1949, which would require that the places where the marriage is carried out (e.g. a mosque) is registered. Most of the cases that are dealt with by Sharia Councils and the Muslim Arbitration Tribunals concern the dissolution of marriage where a woman seeks a religious declaration that her marriage has been dissolved and that she is divorced.[34] In these cases, if the woman or the parties jointly want any agreements relating to the division of matrimonial property or children to be recognised by English authorities, they have to submit a consent order to an English court. These consent orders are scrutinised to ensure that they comply with English family law principles, to safeguard the rights of the parties and especially women and children.

---

[33] See www.matribunal.com/ (last accessed 10 August 2011).

[34] Bano, 'Muslim Family Justice and Human Rights', p. 45. See also Shah-Kazemi, 'Untying the Knot'.

Alternatively, the parties using Sharia Council or Muslim dispute resolution can sign an agreement under the Arbitration Act 1996 which allows
them to authorise a third party to resolve their dispute. This applies to civil
law disputes. It is worth pointing out that the Arbitration Act 1996 specifies that decisions of arbitrators that are illegal or contrary to public policy
are not enforceable. It is also worth noting that there has been use of this
civil arbitration mechanism by British Jews, whose 'rabbinical court' –
the Beth Din – deals with the granting of divorce and the dissolution
of the religious limb of Jewish marriages. In this context, the problem
of a refusal of a recalcitrant spouse to grant a religious divorce has been
addressed through specific statutory provisions, so that the Matrimonial
Causes Act – as amended by the Divorce (Religious Marriages) Act 2002 –
enables a court to require the dissolution of a religious marriage before
granting a divorce. This provision can be used in the context of Jewish
divorces. Muslims can also apply for recognition – and therefore protection – under this legislative provision, although they have not yet registered to use this facility.

From the perspective of religious autonomy and the accommodation
of minorities there are clear advantages to such a move. Family law governs some of the most private and intimate aspects of who we are and
it relates to our personal identity in the most profound way. It therefore
seems appropriate to allow citizens in a liberal democracy to reach an
agreement about the rules that will govern these aspects of their life. If
all persons, and women in particular, freely choose to be governed by a
traditional justice system – the argument goes – then there seem to be no
conclusive reasons why the state should not respect these choices. This
is at first sight an attractive argument. However, this analysis moves too
swiftly from free choice to a separate system of family law. Most significantly, such a quick analysis pays insufficient attention to the myriad of
ways in which granting control over family law to a traditional culture or
religion has the potential for causing harm to vulnerable group members
such as women.

We should ask ourselves why traditional groups always give priority
to gaining control over family law issues. The answer should not surprise
us. Women and family law become a focus – sometimes an obsession –
for traditional groups concerned with the preservation and transmis-
sion of their culture or religion because they recreate collective identity
by reproducing and socialising future members of the group. Therefore,
controlling with whom and on what terms they should undertake their
childbearing and child rearing functions becomes an issue not only for

individual women, their partners and families but also for the wider community. From this perspective, it becomes a critical matter that women should enter into their most intimate relationships and functions in a way that preserves the membership boundaries and identity of the whole community. For these reasons, the control of women – especially in the areas such as sexuality, marriage, divorce and in relation to their children – is a recurring feature of traditional cultural and religious communities. Women are also often given the status of passing on the particular collective history of the tradition and its social, cultural and religious norms to the next generation. Women become a public symbol of the group as a whole. This explains why traditional communities focus on family law when they demand accommodation. These groups insist that they, rather than the state, should have exclusive jurisdiction in these key areas.

One of the most powerful arguments for multiculturalism is that there are power hierarchies between minority groups, majorities and the state that should be renegotiated. However, this recognition of external hierarchies should not blind us to the fact that there are also power hierarchies within groups. These internal inequalities of power may cause vulnerable individuals such as women to bear a disproportionate cost of any policy of accommodation of cultural or religious practices. These costs can include entering into a marriage without the right to divorce; inadequate financial compensation in the case of divorce; giving up the right to custody over children; restriction on the right to education, employment or participation in the public sphere; giving up the right of control over their own bodies and reproductive systems. It is often argued that many women choose to remain members of a group despite the fact that traditional rules and practices undermine their interests. 'They have a right to exit but they freely choose to remain' is often the response to any challenge. But this 'right to exit' argument is not a realistic solution to the problem of oppression within groups. It offers an ad hoc and extreme option to what is often a systematic and structural problem within traditional cultures and religions. It puts the burden of resolving these conflicts on individual women and relieves the state (which has conceded jurisdiction in this area to the group) of responsibility for the protection of the fundamental rights of its citizens. Most significantly, the 'right to exit' argument suggests that an individual woman at risk from a harmful practice should be the one to abandon her group membership, her family and community. The complexity of the choices that women face in these circumstances makes it more likely that they will continue to consent to practices despite the fact that they experience harm. This internalisation of harmful practices is exactly what exacerbates women's vulnerability in these contexts. In the case of Muslim women the 'right to exit' argument is rendered yet more problematic by the fact that this 'exit' is also from a faith community. The stark fact is that emotional attachment, economic circumstances and religious commitment makes the 'exit' not only an unrealistic but also a tragic choice for many Muslim women.

The previous discussion confirms that traditional cultures and religions cannot claim to be immune from interventions and criticism where they harm their members. The accommodation of Muslim family law in Britain along the lines developed in Ontario is certainly a debate worth having. Such a move has the potential for a greater coalescence between the most intimate experiences of British Muslims in their daily private lives and their experience of normative political and legal institutions. Where there is evidence of coercion or a risk of harm the state must be willing to protect individual Muslims despite the religious or cultural claims of their community. There need to be procedures which ensure that women are fully informed about the nature and consequences of their choices. Any discussion about special family law tribunals must take seriously the risks that such a strategy poses for vulnerable individuals such as women.

It is often argued that women who choose Muslim arbitration forums are subject to pressure and that these forums should be prohibited. However, two leading researchers on Muslim family arbitration have concluded that these forums fulfill an important need for Muslim women.[35] Muslim women want to continue to have access to these forums, although they want to see important 'internal' reforms. It may also be necessary to require a more explicit articulation of the need for consent and the limits of arbitration in those cases where women choose to use these forums. If it is correct that there is real demand for these forums from women themselves, this suggests that a strategy of abolition is unlikely to be successful, and it speaks instead to the need for reform and training to transform these forums into a more 'user-friendly' environment for women.

There may be several options for reform in this context. One option would be to prohibit these forms of alternative dispute resolution (sharia tribunals) altogether. This would tackle the problem of any coercion. However, if it is true – as suggested by the research – that women are using these tribunals because of a pressing need – and out of choice – then a

---

[35] Bano, 'Muslim Family Justice and Human Rights', p. 45.

blanket prohibition is likely to result in the informal use of these tribunals, thereby increasing Muslim women's vulnerability. The present approach of allowing these tribunals to operate as another form of arbitration is also not ideal because it does not take into account the specific risk to women of being 'conciliated' back into violent or coercive relationships. One solution would be to accept that human rights law provides the minimum floor which binds all the parties in this context and which justifies state intervention to secure the rights of women. This may require training of staff, inspection and procedures to ensure that women are fully informed about the nature and consequences of their choices. Marion Boyd's proposals in Ontario recommended the use of alternative dispute resolution in these contexts, but they also set out other recommendations and safeguards. Boyd's report, released in December 2004, came after meeting with more than two hundred people and receiving almost forty submissions. Boyd made forty-six recommendations, including: regulations to ensure proper record keeping, mandating written decisions, and training of arbitrators; imposing a duty on arbitrators to ensure that parties understand their rights and are participating voluntarily; providing for greater oversight and accountability, including empowering courts to set aside arbitral awards for various reasons including unconscionability, inadequate financial disclosure or if a party did not understand the nature or consequences of the arbitration agreement; public education and community development; expanded appeal possibilities; and further policy analysis to determine whether additional safeguards are required.

At present, there is no evidence that the UK government is willing to allocate the resources that would be necessary to provide these safeguards. Any discussion about special family law tribunals must take seriously the risks that such a strategy poses for vulnerable individuals such as women. Bypassing mainstream family law procedures and safeguards in favour of traditional forms of justice in special tribunals is a serious decision which deserves sober reflection. An additional advantage of an approach that permits some recourse to these tribunals, but which regulates them to meet safeguards, is that the social group is encouraged to reform its practices from within. This may provide a more effective way of transforming social group norms that may harm women, as well as empowering women within these communities to demand and initiate change without abandoning their group membership.[36]

---

[36] See Shachar, *Multicultural Jurisdictions*.

Two recent cases in the UK courts also illustrate an approach towards sharia law and the accommodation of Muslim legal norms that avoids wholescale condemnation whilst at the same time safeguarding public policy. The first case – *KC and NNC* v. *City of Westminster Social and Community Services Department*[37] – concerned the legal validity of an Islamic marriage ceremony, which took place on the phone between a British man based in Britain who was mentally disabled (through substantial intellectual impairment and autism), and a Bangladeshi woman who was based in Bangladesh. On behalf of the bridegroom it was argued that Islamic ideas of 'welfare' supported the practice of marrying those who were mentally ill so that their partners could provide them with 'care'. Owing to the bridegroom's incapacity, the marriage was held to be invalid despite the fact that it may be valid in Bangladesh and by some interpretations of sharia law. The Court of Appeal relied on the principles of public policy to assert its inherent jurisdictions and to declare that the marriage was void. Significantly, the Court of Appeal limited its decision to this particular set of facts which focused on the mental incapacity of the bridegroom to give consent, rather than declaring that all 'telephone' marriages were illegal. Moreover, the basis of the decision was public policy rather than a blanket refusal to apply sharia law. There was not, therefore, the type of reference to sharia law as incompatible with democracy or rule of law that was a feature of the European Court of Human Rights decision in *Refah Partisi*.[38] This suggests that there is some scope for applying the principle of 'severance' in relation to the use of sharia law or Muslim legal norms in English law. For example, the courts will be able to consider the norm that is being applied, to evaluate it against public policy principles and reach an overall conclusion about its applicability in a British context. This would allow courts to make decisions about which parts of sharia law can apply because they are compatible with English law and public policy, whilst refusing to apply those parts of the religious norms that contravene law or public policy.

The second case where sharia law has been considered is the House of Lords decision in *EM (Lebanon) (Fc) (Appellant) (Fc)* v. *Secretary of State For The Home Department Appellate Committee*.[39] In this case the appellant was a woman who came to Britain from Lebanon. Her son

---

[37] [2008] EWCA Civ 198.
[38] Eur. Ct. H. R. (Grand Chamber), *Refah Partisi (The Welfare Party) and others* v. *Turkey*, 13 February 2003.
[39] [2008] UKHL 64.

had reached the age of seven when, under the system that regulates the custody of a child of that age under sharia law in Lebanon, his physical custody would pass by force of law to his father or another male member of his family. Any attempt by her to retain custody of him in Lebanon would be bound to fail because the law dictates that a mother has no right to the custody of her child after that age. She may or may not be allowed what has been described as visitation. That would give her access to her son during supervised visits to a place where she could see him. But under no circumstances would his custody remain with her. Therefore, the close relationship that exists between mother and child up to the age of custodial transfer could not survive under that system of law where, as in this situation, the parents of the child are longer living together when the child reaches that age. The House of Lords concluded that in this situation there was a real risk that the very essence of the family life that mother and child had shared together up to that date would be destroyed or nullified. The House of Lords observed that this system of child custody under these sharia law rules was not compatible with the European Convention on Human Rights standards, which require the mutual enjoyment by parent and child of each other's company as a fundamental element of family life. A second feature of these custodial rules was that they discriminated between mothers and fathers, which would contravene the principle of non-discrimination on the ground of gender.

In *EM*, the House of Lords decided to allow the woman leave to remain and relied on Article 8 of the European Convention on Human Rights, which guarantees right to privacy and family life. Significantly, both Lord Bingham and Lord Carswell made it clear that they were not passing judgment more widely on the status of sharia law. The House of Lords observed that in deciding this appeal on the basis of the right to privacy and family life (Article 8 of the European Convention on Human Rights) they were applying British domestic law as well as the common values of the states who are members of the Council of Europe. Lord Bingham and Lord Carswell also made it clear that they were not passing judgment on the law or institutions of any other state. Nor were they setting out to make comparisons, favourable or unfavourable, with sharia law, which prevails in many countries, reflecting the religious and cultural tradition of those countries. This approach reinforces the view that British courts are not willing to undertake wholesale and blanket condemnations of sharia law or Muslim legal norms, but that they are willing to consider the impact of these rules on a case-by-case basis, as well as scrutinising the public policy implications of permitting the application of these norms. This pragmatic and incremental approach – which focuses on the impact of Muslim legal rules on individuals, enshrined constitutional and human rights values, as well as public policy – is in sharp contrast to the wholesale condemnation of the sharia by the European Court of Human Rights in the *Refah Partisi* decision.[40]

Conclusion

The increasing presence of postcolonial subjects raises questions about how the cultural and religious practices of these European citizens can be accommodated. European and national political and legal institutions grant of formal rights through provisions such as the right to religious freedom (Article 9 of the European Convention on Human Rights) or religious equality (EU Employment Equality Directive). Yet the legacy of colonialism, as well as contemporary cultural racism, results in a distorted analysis that deems some non-Western religions to be 'barbaric' or 'backward' in comparison with Western norms. This poses a serious challenge for an analysis of religion in European states. The examples discussed – Islamic headscarves and the sharia law debate – confirm the complexity of accommodating the claims of minority religions in liberal democracies. In the Islamic headscarf cases, deeply entrenched stereotypes – drawing on orientalist and colonial assumptions – about 'oppressed' Muslim women serve to undermine female autonomy. In the sharia debate, the wholescale rejection of the sharia prevented a more constructive public debate about whether, and how, it could be accommodated in liberal democracies. For example, the Treasury's accommodation of the needs of British Muslims for mortgages is a salutary reminder that an imaginative and sensitive response to a real practical problem can sometimes yield more promising results than abstract definitions of multiculturalism and citizenship. The introduction of a separate system of family law for Muslims highlights a different point because it suggests in some cases there may be good reasons to limit the accommodation of a religious minority where there is a real potential for harm to vulnerable individuals.

The institutional context of increasing cultural and religious diversity in the European public sphere is critically important. The debate about accommodating religious minorities and legal norms, and the resulting negotiation between the majorities and minorities, needs to be carried

---

[40] *Refah Partisi (The Welfare Party) and others* v. *Turkey.*

out within mainstream EU and national institutions. Civic society and the media are also important actors within this process. This procedure is likely to ensure the broadest range of participation in public debate and political negotiations. Points of difference and friction between majorities and minorities, or religious groups and the state, can often act as a catalyst towards a stable form of integration. In some cases we must be satisfied with an outcome that is a patient and resigned modus vivendi. More optimistically, this technique also has some potential to redeem the worst excesses of multicultural politics: to generate a deeper and more meaningful identification with European and national institutions for the majority and minority, in a joint enterprise, that creates and sustains a coherent political community rather than a plethora of self-interested splinter groups.

Of course, inclusive political debate and participatory democracy is essential for accommodating religious minorities in European liberal democracies. There is also an important role for a public debate about the extent to which present structures of power in European nation states are based on the exploitation and persecution of non-Western people.[41] By challenging the official version of the stories about history, national origin and power, individuals such as Tony Agbetu open up a wider debate in contemporary diverse liberal democracies. The Cambridge historian Quentin Skinner recently summarised this relationship between history, power and exclusion by concluding:

> It stems from the fact that all communities tell stories about themselves, about the distinctive nature of their formation and achievements. These stories can have a powerful role in constituting our identities, and so in defining and sustaining our common life. But they are also subject to endless manipulation, for it will always be in the interests of the powerful – rulers and opinion-formers alike – that certain stories should be remembered, and in certain ways, and that other stories should be forgotten. That being so, it is I think part of the moral importance of historical study that historians should be ready to engage with these stories and take a critical stance towards them. The role, you might say, is that of bearing witness, ensuring that the stories which define and sustain us are as little as possible imposed upon us in such a way that particular groups or ideals are misleadingly praised, or misleadingly blamed, or unjustly omitted from the record altogether.[42]

---

[41] For a discussion, see D. Bell, 'Agonistic Democracy and the Politics of Memory', *Constellations* 15(1) (2008), 148.

[42] Q. Skinner, 'The place of history in public life', *History and Policy, Policy Paper* 35, (November 2005), available at www.historyandpolicy.org/archive/policy-paper-35.html (last accessed 10 August 2011).

Tony Agbetu's challenge to Britain's official memory of its relationship with slavery, and his act of interrupting a national religious ceremony in Westminster Abbey in the presence of the Queen and the Prime Minister, was not merely about slavery. This act is also a point of entry into a more profound enquiry – of the way in which those who exercise political power over citizens also have at their disposal the means to manipulate what it means to 'be European'.

5

Islam and the public sphere: public reason or public imagination?

CHIARA BOTTICI AND BENOIT CHALLAND

In 2008 the Archbishop of Canterbury posed the problem of the possibility of accommodating some elements of the sharia inside England's legal system.[1] The idea that Islamic jurisprudence could formally co-exist next to civil laws in England provoked passionate reactions and indignation on the part of different sectors of the public sphere. Outraged reactions accused him of calling for a formal and general adoption of sharia law and many called for his resignation.[2]

As this example shows, there seem to be good reasons to raise the question 'does Islam represent a challenge for the European public sphere?' The aim of this contribution is to address such a question in a twofold way. On the one hand, it aims at situating the question by asking why we raise this question in the first place. As we will see, in order to answer such a meta-question one must look more closely at the complex background within which European citizens deliberate: within this background, we will look at both the role of public reason and that of public imagination. In the current setting, the European public sphere is structured in such a way as to privilege some religions (mainly Christianity) over others (notably Islam) (section 1).

On the other hand, we also aim to provide a more constructive answer, by addressing the question at a more general and philosophical level. If the first part of this chapter looks at the role of Islam within the European public sphere by taking the latter to mean a palpable and living reality, the following sections explore such a relationship by looking at the European public sphere as it could be. The underlining assumption is that the way

---

[1] For the full speech, see www.archbishopofcanterbury.org/1575 (last accessed 17 August 2011).

[2] For reactions in British media, see, e.g. www.timesonline.co.uk/tol/comment/faith/article3328024.ece (last accessed 17 August 2011).

in which the contemporary European public sphere works may not match the standards set by the ideal of it. Within this second perspective on the public sphere, we will distinguish between two conceptions: a more general one, where 'public' is opposed to 'private' and a more restricted one where 'public' is opposed to what is 'secret' and 'closed'. By drawing from its own ideals of *maslahah* and *istislah*, understood respectively as the common good and the technique of deliberation aimed at determining it, Islamic philosophy of law has the resources to generate a lively public sphere on its own (section 2).

However, if we take the more restricted conception of the public sphere, as a third sphere between the state and the economy where *democratic* citizens meet to deliberate as *equals*, then a tension between Islam's claim to the equality of the believers and the reality of an institutionalised religion where this is never realised in practice emerges. But, in this sense, the challenge is not only on the side of Islam, but also on that of all the revealed religions of the Book (section 3).

1 Public reason and public imagination: from Rawls to Hollywood

Before starting any theoretical enterprise, it is always a helpful exercise to raise the preliminary question of why we are formulating this question in such a way and precisely at this point in space and time. This does not mean aiming at jumping out of ourselves, but simply to situate the question, by trying to investigate both its explicit and implicit presuppositions. As we will see, the question we are dealing with complicates in meaning when read in the light of the assumptions and absences that it reveals within itself.

Let us start from the latter: absences. Why Islam, and not another religion? Why not Buddhism or Judaism? As we have already suggested there seem to be prima facie good reasons to raise the question with reference to Islam. Together with the Archbishop of Canterbury's case, other examples, such as that of the protest against the Danish cartoons or the so-called 'Muslim headscarves' seem to point to a tension between Islam and the European public sphere. Yet recent studies have shown that there are relatively few demands from Muslim groups in Western Europe. For instance, on the basis of their quantitative analysis of collective claims-making, Statham, Koopmans, Giugni and Passy conclude that 'scholars have mistakenly raised the high prominence of a few cases, such as Rushdie, to general theories about the integrative capacity of the liberal national state, leading to exaggeration'.[3] Similarly, Rivera, while studying violent reactions against Islam in France and Italy, notes the 'hypertrophied symbolic reaction' in spite of actually few problematic situations.[4]

What lies at the basis of such a discrepancy between the reality and the way in which we perceive it? To answer such a question, one needs to look at the way in which both public reason and public imagination actually work within the European public sphere. European citizens do not deliberate in the social, historical and imaginative vacuum. Reason can provide arguments about matters of common concerns, but it often relies on imagination when it comes to implementing them. This is the reason why, if we want to get a realistic picture of the way in which the contemporary European public sphere works, we need to take into account a variety of forces operating within it.

The European public sphere has historically been shaped by a series of images and stereotypes about Islam that do not cease to exercise their influence today. One just needs to think of how the geographical space where Islam rose to prominence in the seventh and eighth centuries (the 'Orient') has historically served to define the 'West', the 'Occident'. This is what Edward Said tried to convey with his notion of 'Orientalism', the attitude to represent all that is depicted as part of the 'Orient' as the reverse of the Occident, and vice versa.[5] The West does not exist without imagining the East and, in the representation of the East as opposed to the West, Islam played a crucial role.

Take the notion of 'oriental despotism' discussed by many European thinkers: they assumed that such a system had to be despotic because they imagined that it had to have the same oppressive force on society that European rulers had, and therefore overlooked the fact that 'oriental' rulers had a much lighter impact on societies, their functions being much more limited than those of their 'western' counterparts.[6] The influence of this *topos*, together with similar ones such as the 'modern' versus 'barbaric' dichotomy, on the way in which Europe has thought of itself as a political and social system is such that certain authors have claimed that

---

[3] P. Statham, R. Koopmans, M. Giugni and F. Passy, 'Resilient or Adaptable Islam?. Multiculturalism, Religion and Migrants' Claims-Making for Group Demands in Britain, the Netherlands and France', *Ethnicities* 5(4) (2005), 452.

[4] A. M. Rivera, *La guerra dei simboli* (Bari: Edizioni Dedalo, 2006), p. 16, (transl. ours).

[5] E. Said, *Orientalism* (London: Routledge, 1978).

[6] S. Eisenstadt, 'Concluding Remarks: Public Sphere, Civil Society, and Political Dynamics in Islamic Societies' in M. Hoexter, S. N. Eisenstadt and N. Levtzion (eds.), *The Public Sphere in Muslim Societies* (Albany: State University of New York Press, 2002), pp. 139–61.

Orientalism, as a discipline, contributed to the emergence of the field of Western sociology,[7] and that Islam has functioned as a 'constitutive outsider' to modernity and to secularity.[8]

More recently, within the post-9/11 political context, all those *topoi* have been revived and given further emotional appeal. The terrorist attacks against the Twin Towers and in Europe have indeed largely been framed within the idea of a civilisational clash between Islam and the West.[9] This means that instead of presenting these events as the result of the actions of single individual human beings acting out of a more or less complex series of motivations, both US and European media largely presented them as a clash between civilisations. The result is that the idea of a clash between Islam and the West has become one of the most powerful political myths of our time.[10]

A political myth is a process of elaboration of a common narrative, which grants significance to the political conditions and experiences of a social group.[11] As narratives that provide significance to the world we live in, political myths have a threefold function: cognitive, practical and aesthetical. Political myths are *cognitive* schemata for the mapping of the social and political world. By reducing the complexity of the world, they enable people to come to terms with the multifaceted character of their experience. But they also have a *practical* function: they are mapping devices through which people orient themselves in the world and *act* within it. Their practical impact in turn depends on what we can call their *aesthetical* force, that is, the fact that people are prompted to act because they *feel* they are part of a political drama.

Even in the abstract formulations of philosophy there can be a space for the work of such a myth. Public reason goes at times hand in hand with public imagination. For instance, John Rawls' attempt to propose a normatively desirable and practically viable set of laws of peoples has not been immune from it. One of the most original aspects of his theory is precisely his attempt to include in the society of peoples even peoples who

---

[7] G. Stauth, *Islam und Westlicher Rationalismus: Der Beitrag des Orientalismus zur Entstehung der Soziologie* (Frankfurt: Campus, 1993).

[8] S. Bracke and N. Fadil, 'Islam and Secular Modernity under Western Eyes: A Genealogy of a Constitutive Relationship', *Working Paper* (5/2008, Robert Schuman Centre, Florence: European University Institute), p. 2.

[9] E. Abrahamian, 'The US Media, Huntington and September 11', *Third World Quarterly* 24(3) (2003), 529–44.

[10] For this analysis of the myth of a clash between Islam and the West, see C. Bottici and B. Challand, *The Myth of the Clash of Civilizations* (London: Routledge, 2010).

[11] C. Bottici, *A Philosophy of Political Myth* (Cambridge University Press, 2007), p. 179.

cannot be labelled as 'just'. To this aim, he proposes an imagined example of a non-liberal people, which he calls 'Kazanistan'.[12] This mental experiment, which is apparently neutral as such, and is even aimed at admitting this hypothetical non-liberal people into the society of peoples, is a potential site for the work of the myth of the clash between civilisations. How can it be so? In the first place, its name 'Kazanistan' is not so innocent, because it cannot but recall in the readers' mind countries with similar names – the name being apparently a fusion between 'Afghanistan' and 'Kazakhstan', two Muslim majority countries.

Furthermore, the fact that the 'imagined' Kazanistan is a Muslim country is not left to the imagination of the readers, given that Rawls says it explicitly in the *Introduction* of his book.[13] Why, however, should it be assumed that a non-liberal people have to be Muslim? Even if the general argument of the book is that a clash between the imagined Muslim country and the 'liberal democratic peoples' is not unavoidable, still the very construction of such a mental experiment recalls some of the *topoi* of the Orientalist literature about Muslim countries – first, the idea that a Muslim country cannot be 'liberal' in Rawls' sense, that it cannot be democratic but allows in the best case a consultation hierarchy,[14] that it will not separate the state from the church and can at best enable the toleration of religious minorities, and that, as most Muslim rulers, rulers of Kazanistan are likely to have sought empire.[15] To summarise, by characterising it in such a way, Rawls more or less implicitly suggests that a Muslim country can at best be 'decent'.[16]

Intellectual discourses could never have produced a political myth without the further work that took place at the more subconscious level. Together with books and intellectual discourses circulating in the European public sphere, we should therefore also look at other public opinion sources. Particularly helpful is looking at what we can call *icons* of a political myth, that is at those images that by means of a synecdoche can recall the whole myth.[17] Among the icons of the myth of a clash between Islam and the West that circulated in the European public sphere in the last decades, particularly powerful are those that are transmitted in the mass media, be they Hollywood films, newspaper articles or school textbooks. In his survey of

---

[12] J. Rawls, *The Law of Peoples* (Cambridge, MA: Harvard University Press, 1999), pp. 75–8.
[13] *Ibid.*, p. 5.   [14] *Ibid.*, p. 77.   [15] *Ibid.*, p. 76
[16] *Ibid.* Rawls' example of Kazanistan conveys a widespread view that Muslim countries are unruly, or not easily democratic, and his observations remain only a footnote.
[17] Bottici, *A Philosophy of Political Myth*.

Hollywood films, Jack Shaheen[18] has shown that, out of 1,000 films that have Arabs or Muslim characters, 12 were 'positive' depictions, 52 'even-handed' and the rest of more than 900 were 'negative'. Here Arabs and Muslims (most of the times conflated with one another) appear mainly through stereotypes such as that of the camel-riding barbaric Bedouin, the rich and stupid sheikh who exercises his violence on western women or, finally, that of mad terrorist and airplane hijacker. By playing on the registers of fear or derision, according to the different context, such icons are transmitted in a subconscious way. This explains the primacy effect of political myth: by slipping into our social unconscious since childhood such images can come to deeply influence our most basic perceptions of the world, and become thus difficult to dismantle afterwards.

Among the material particularly relevant for children and youth in general are school textbooks. The study of nearly 100 French, German and Italian textbooks published between 1950 to date suggests that the representation of Islam is increasingly tied to the fate of Europe in terms of opposing collective identity and political trajectories. This interlink is best shown by two types of material: maps and images. The former shows that, in the first two or three decades of its inception, the construction of a European space was delimited and visualised in terms of the 'other' embodied by the Eastern European communist threat, while now the most common representation of Europe is that of a cultural space defined by its Christian origins and, as such, opposed to that of Islam.[19] When coming to the second type of material, the analysis of images associated with Islam shows a gendered opposition between Europe and contemporary Islam: the Islamic civilisation is most often illustrated through images of women who are systematically veiled, oppressed and without a voice and agency, while Muslim men are most often depicted as fanatical, violent and dangerous. In such representations one could perceive the projection of a paternalising Europe that has to redeem and save Muslim women from barbarism.[20]

---

[18] J. Shaheen, *Reel Bad Arabs. How Hollywood Vilifies a People* (New York: Olive Branch Press, 2003).

[19] B. Challand, 'The Sequences of Europe. Creating the European Self in History Textbooks (1950–2005)', *Contexts: The Journal of Educational Media, Memory, and Society*, vol. 2, (New York: Berghahn Books, 2009).

[20] B. Challand, 'Islam and Europe, Islam in Europe: A Gender-Based Reading of the Visual Representations of Islam in French, Italian and German Textbooks' in G. Jonker and S. Thobani (eds.), *Recasting the Image of The Other: Muslims in European Textbooks* (London: I. B. Tauris, 2009); see also L. Abu-Lughod, 'The Muslim Woman: The Power of Images and the Danger of Pity', *Eurozine* (2006).

This already suggests that all these icons do not only have a powerful cognitive and aesthetical force, but also a relevant practical impact. The icon of the veiled and oppressed women has largely served as a justification for the wars waged in the name of the 'war on terror' (especially in Afghanistan). Politicians' explicit discourses, such as the reference to the icon of the crusade or the Italian Prime Minister Berlusconi's statement on 26 September 2001 that 'we should be conscious of the superiority of our civilisation', only reinforce the work of a political myth that is done at another level. Indeed, as Geisser observed in his analysis of the emergence of a new Islamophobia in France, the sources of the mediatic Islamophobia are not so much explicit statements about the evils of Islam. At least in France, it is rather the case that journalists are very cautious in their statements and at times explicitly deny the paradigm of the clash. The sources of what he calls the 'mediatic Islamophobia' are the insistence on the 'securitarian ideology', that is the continual assertion of the need for more security, and the parallel – only at times related to the former – 'mediatic diabolization of Muslims'. As he observes, 'the mediatic portrayal of Muslim-ness is mostly constrained by the prism of a radical and conflictual Otherness; it largely plays on the repertoire of threat, when not straightforwardly of a catastrophe.'[21]

To conclude on this point, an analysis of all those sources, in particular visual ones, shows that the narrative of a clash between Islam and the West has worked and still is working as a powerful political myth, that is, as a narrative on the basis of which people perceive the world, act and feel about it. As a consequence it contributed deeply to the shaping of European public opinion. The European public sphere is not only made by rational and autonomous individuals that deliberate on matters of public concern in the vacuum, but also by social actors who deliberate on the same issues by drawing from both public reason and public imagination.

2   Islam and the ideal of the public sphere

What we have described so far is the tension existing between Islam and the way in which it is perceived by the contemporary European public sphere. The fact that the latter currently works in that specific way does not yet say anything on the relationship between Islam and the public sphere as an ideal. The task of the next two sections is to analyse such a

---

[21] V. Geisser, *La nouvelle islamophobie* (Paris: La Découverte, 2003), pp. 23–5.

relationship between Islam and the ideal of the public sphere at a more general and philosophical level. In order to do so, we will distinguish between two conceptions. According to the more general meaning of the term, *public* sphere denotes a sphere that is opposed to the *private* one. The public sphere in this sense includes all that is not part of the private sphere, the sphere that concerns the citizens in their personal and familial everyday affairs. Parts of the public sphere thus understood are media, associations, fora but also formal political bodies such as parliaments, commissions, courts.

In a more restricted sense, the *public* sphere denotes a space in-between that of the economy and the state, where citizens meet to discuss and deliberate on matters of common concerns. In this more restricted sense, the term has been introduced to the debate by Habermas and the discussion that took place in the 1990s after the translation into English of his *Habilitation* dissertation on the modern structural transformation of the public sphere. Parliaments and other organs of the state are not part of the public sphere thus understood, as this is by definition the site where a critical scrutiny on government is exercised.

Let us start from the more general meaning, where 'public' is simply opposed to 'private'. Bobbio defined the conceptual couple of 'public' and 'private' as one of the great dichotomies of our political vocabulary. By great dichotomy he means a distinction between two concepts that is able to divide a universe of discourse in two spheres, jointly exhaustive, because all the items of such universe are part of it, and reciprocally exclusive, because what is part of the one side cannot simultaneously be part of the other.[22] The division established thereby must also be total, because every item must be potentially included, and principal because other dichotomy will tend to converge into it.[23]

The conceptual couple of public/private entered the Western political vocabulary relatively early in history. Already in two very much commented upon passages from the *Corpus Iuris* we find a definition of the public and private law as respectively '*quod ad statum rei romanae spectat*' and '*quod ad singolorum utilitatem*'.[24] What therefore distinguishes the public from the private is the *utilitas* of the community as different from that of singular human beings. Cicero also makes a similar point in his famous definition of the *res publica*, when he says that it is a *res* of the *populus*, where by *populus* one does not mean a simple aggregation

---

[22] N. Bobbio, *Stato, governo, società. Per una teoria generale della politica* (Turin: Einaudi, 1985), p. 4, (trans. ours).

[23] *Ibid.*, p. 4, (trans. ours).   [24] *Institutiones*, I, 1, 4; *Digesto*, I, I, 1, 2.

of individuals but rather a society held together by the *utilitatis comunione*.[25] The dichotomy of 'public' versus 'private' has thereafter become so influential in the Western political and juridical vocabulary that a neo-Kantian philosopher of law claimed it as an a priori and transcendental category.[26] Although the meanings and boundaries of such dichotomy have been very much contested in recent times,[27] the conceptual couple did not cease to exercise its influence.

If we take this meaning of the public sphere as generally opposed to the private one, then no a priori tension between it and Islam emerges. In this sense, as we will see, Islam is even better equipped than other religions to support the ideal of a common public sphere. The Islamic public sphere is based on the traditional notions of *maslahah*, or common good, and the related concept of *istislah*, understood as the technique of deliberation to determine the common good. They are both jurisprudential and theological concepts which go back to the origins of Islamic philosophy of law.[28] The concept of *maslahah* points to the necessity to distinguish between what is the mere personal interest and the common good, whilst its correlate concept of *istislah* points to a technique of deliberation aimed at reaching a decision on what constitutes in each circumstances the common good.[29] What is most important is the fact that *istislah* is defined in opposition to the interpretative approaches exclusively based on the scriptural sources and has therefore been interpreted as a form of *phronesis*.[30] The concept of *maslahah* can therefore be compared to that of

[25] Cicero, *De re publica, De legibus*, English transl. C. Walker Keyes, (Cambridge, MA: Harvard University Press; London: W. Heinemann, 1977), I, 41, 48.

[26] G. Radbruch, *Rechtsphilosophie* (Leipzig: Quelle und Meyer, 1932), pp. 122–7.

[27] The dichotomy is contested: for feminists, this dichotomy perpetuates the domination of males by relegating women in the private sphere, whilst others pointed to the impossibility of maintaining such a dichotomy in a context of pluralism of worldviews. See S. I. Ben and G. Gaus (eds.), *Public and Private in Social Life* (London: Croom Helm, 1983), and I. Honohan, 'Dealing with Difference: The Republican Public Private Distinction,' in M. Baghramian and A. Ingram (eds.), *Pluralism: The Philosophy and Politics of Diversity* (London: Routledge, 2000).

[28] A. Salvatore, 'The Exit from a Westphalian Framing of Political Space and the Emergence of a Transnational Islamic Public', *Theory, Culture & Society* 24(4) (2007), 45–52; S. Eisenstadt, 'Public Spheres and Political Dynamics in Historical and Modern Muslim Societies' in J. Arnason, A. Salvatore and G. Stauth (eds.), 'Islam in Process. Historical and Civilizational Perspectives', *Yearbook of the Sociology of Islam* 7 (Bielefeld: Transcript, 2006), pp. 306–18.

[29] For a discussion of the place of *maslahah, istislah* and *istihsan* in Islamic jurisprudence, see the detailed entry 'Maslahah' in J. L. Esposito (ed.), *The Oxford Encyclopedia of the Modern Islamic World*, vol. 3 (Oxford University Press, 1995), p. 63.

[30] A. Salvatore, *The Public Sphere: Liberal Modernity, Catholicism, Islam* (New York and Basingstoke: Palgrave Macmillan, 2007), p. 195.

res publica in as far as both denote a common good or public interest that cannot be reduced to the mere sum of individual single goods, but at the same time is distinguished from it in as far as it is directly applicable to legal reasoning through its correlate concept of *istislah*.

As Salvatore observed, the idea of *maslahah*, while incorporating several layers of traditional legacies, ranging from Greek philosophy, through the influence of Judaism and Christianity, to Roman law itself, has been the object of systematic reflections particularly from the eleventh century onwards.[31] The idea of an Islamic public sphere therefore has a long-standing tradition. It is in particular the Maliki school, one of the four canonical Sunni legal schools, that more consistently upheld the centrality of *maslahah*. Although the concept has been rejected by the Hanbali legal school of jurisprudence (which is better known under its modern description of Wahhabism, the most conservative interpretative school of Islamic jurisprudence[32]), it kept exercising its power over centuries. The Islamic public sphere is therefore not only conceptually possible but also a palpable living reality, which goes far back in time.[33] In particular, since the Middle Ages Islamic civilisation has been congenial to the nourishing of a common public sphere that goes beyond Westphalian boundaries, so that we can speak of a tradition of a genuinely *transnational* public Islam.[34] On a sociological level, this is partly due to its economy, based as much on commerce as on a wide non-profit sector (the religious endowments, for example), and partly to the role of the *ulama*. The latter are religious scholars formally independent from political power who, as guardians of the common good (*maslahah*) and of the moral order of the *umma*, the community of all believers, played a crucial role in the creation of a public sphere and, at times, in the critique of rulers.[35]

---

[31] *Ibid.* pp. 156–8.
[32] There are four schools of jurisprudence in the Sunni world (Hanafi, Maliki, Shafi'i and Hanbali). Except for the Hanbali, all Sunni and Shiite schools of jurisprudence grant space to *maslahah* as a founding basis of legal reasoning. See the entries 'Law: Sunni Schools of Law' in Esposito, *Oxford Encyclopedia of the Modern Islamic World*, vol. 2, pp. 456–62 and vol. 3, p. 63.
[33] Salvatore, *The Public Sphere*; Salvatore, 'The Exit from a Westphalian Framing of a Political Space'; Hoexter, Eisenstadt and Levtzion (eds.), *The Public Sphere in Muslim Societies.*
[34] Salvatore, 'The Exit from a Westphalian Framing of a Political Space', p. 51.
[35] S. Eisenstadt, 'Public Spheres and Political Dynamics'; N. Eisenstadt, 'The Public Sphere in Muslim Societies' in N. Goele and L. Amman (eds.), *Islam in Public: Turkey, Iran and Europe* (Istanbul Bilgi University Press, 2006), pp. 443–60.

Drawing from such a tradition, the notion of *maslahah* is still increasingly invoked for supporting the flourishing of an Islamic public sphere. For instance, it has been used in the critique of delegitimised post-colonial regimes. Since most of such autocratic regimes do not lend public spaces for political criticism, the religious language appears as a natural alternative in which to express opposition to them. This reinforces the transformation of Islam as a faith into a source for a public Islam. Such opposition at times takes the aggressive connotation of an Islamist project. But it is not necessarily so. The Islamic public sphere is also the site for a *critical* discourse[36] which reflects Muslim reformist views of traditional notions denoting justice and a participative commitment to community welfare like *maslahah*.

If with the term 'public' sphere, we understand simply the sphere that is opposed to the private one, then we must recognise that part of the Islamic public sphere thus understood are very different actors and social practices which go from the creation of forum to critically debate issues of public concern to veiling at schools and terrorist attacks. As Goele among others pointed out, both in Muslim homelands and in European countries of immigration, Muslim actors seek to make their religious difference visible in the public sphere through very different practices such as food taboos (*halal* meat, alcohol prohibition), veiling and the construction of mosques.[37] Islam is thus carried to the forefront of public life by the political claims and daily practices of Muslim migrants, urban youth, Islamic intellectuals and pious middle classes. Still, as Ayubi underlines, if Islam 'stresses above all the *collective* enforcement of *public* morals' (and therefore induces pious Muslims to intervene in the public sphere), this should not be mistaken with an orientalist and essentialist claim that Islam is by definition a *political* religion.[38]

On a legal level, the implementation of the discourse on *maslahah* does not coincide with the administrative apparatus of a territorial state. The normative basis lies rather in the myriad sites of meta-legal orientation and advice that through the vehicle of advisory legal opinions (*fatwas*) or even in more informal shapes proliferate in the press, electronic media and particularly on the Internet. This new model does not supersede the residual

---

[36] S. Buck-Morss, *Thinking Past Terror: Islam and Critical Theory on the Left* (London and New York: Verso Books, 2003).

[37] N. Goele, 'Islamic Visibilities and Public Sphere' in N. Goele and L. Amman (eds.), *Islam in Public: Turkey, Iran and Europe* (Istanbul Bilgi University Press, 2006), pp. 3–43.

[38] N. Ayubi, 'Rethinking the Public/Private Dichotomy: Radical Islamism and Civil Society in the Middle East', *Contention* 4(3) (1995), 81 (his emphasis).

territorial and administrative spaces of religious institutions (such as al-Azhar for Sunni Muslims, or Qom for the Shi'ites), but it greatly contributes to redefine Islamic normativity and to a renewal of the understanding of the sharia as a legal practice. Indeed, the understanding of the latter has become more contested than ever. European Muslims in particular are in the vanguard of this process of contestation and redefinition.[39]

We touch here on an important point. If there is no a priori tension between Islam and the normative ideal of a public sphere, there might be a tension between the concrete reality of a movement that is genuinely transnational and the boundaries of the European Union that, however contested they might be, find a concrete and formal definition in the boundaries of its member states. This, however, is a tension that recurs within the concept of a *European* public sphere itself. In a contest of economic, political and cultural globalisation, what is specifically *European* in the European public sphere? In as far as this does not simply include formal political bodies such as the European institutions, but also media, associations and networks that are transnational in scope, it becomes difficult to draw clear-cut boundaries.

But the boundaries of the specifically European public sphere are not the only ones that become porous and contested in a globalising world. Indeed, it is the very distinction between 'public' and 'private' that is called into question. Already in the 1980s Bobbio observed that the great dichotomy of public/private is tackled in the contemporary world by the double process of privatisation of the public and publicisation of the private.[40] In his view, the latter found its most concrete expression in the welfare state and more generally in any policy of public intervention in the economy.[41] As an example of the opposite process of 'privatisation of the public' he mentioned the emergence of contractual relationships, which are typical of the private sphere, in public formal affairs such as the trade unions' labour contracts and the contract among different parties for the coalitions of government.[42] Another example that we may add is the so-called Islamic finance, that is, a set of financial regulations governing economic exchanges which are defined on the bases of Islamic principles.[43] Even if

[39] Salvatore, 'The Exit from a Westphalian Framing of a Political Space'; A. Caeiro 'Transnational Ulama, European Fatwas, and Islamic Authority' in M. van Bruinessen and S. Allievi (eds.), *Production and Dissemination of Islamic Knowledge in Western Europe* (London: Routledge, 2006).

[40] Bobbio, *Stato, governo, società*, pp. 16–17.

[41] *Ibid.*   [42] *Ibid.*

[43] R. Wilson, 'Islamic Finance in Europe', European University Institute, *Policy paper RSCAS PP*, 2 (Florence: Robert Schuman Centre, 2007).

such practices emerged in Muslim-majority countries (Saudi Arabia in particular after the economic boom generated by the increase of oil prices in the 1970s), it is now widely practised by the largest European corporate banking resorts, yet this Islamisation of the market does not create any sense of disagreement in public debates.[44]

Today we have reached a further stage in both such processes. On the one hand, in the epoch of a general neo-liberal consensus, the public is reduced to the mere sum of private interests, quite often those of big corporations and lobbies. On the other, such a privatisation of public affairs goes together with an increased influence of the public within the private sphere. It is revealing that issues that once used to be mentioned as exemplary of a sphere that cannot be ruled by state power, such as changing the sex of individuals,[45] is now subject to a great deal of legislation. The possibility of intervention on the ultimate questions of life and death that the state and other formal apparatuses today have is incomparably greater than in the past. Not by chance did the need for new categories such as that of bio-law emerge. In an age when the political is conceived in terms of contractual relationships once limited to the private sphere and when, by contrast, typically private issues such as the sex of individuals are regulated through the instrument of law, it seems to be difficult to maintain the public versus private dichotomy. The questioning of such a dichotomy is therefore not only limited to Western societies, but is a process linked to political and economic globalisation on the one hand and to the new possibilities of interventions in private life opened by bio-technologies on the other.

3   The democratic public sphere: publicity and equality

Together with the concept of the public sphere as opposed to the private, there exists also a more restricted and specific meaning. In a more limited meaning of the concept, the 'public' is not opposed to the 'private' but rather to what is 'secret' and 'closed'. Although this second meaning of

---

[44] On Islam and market, see also P. Haenni, *L'Islam de marché: L'autre révolution conservatrice* (Paris: Seuil, 2005).

[45] A famous aphorism on the limits that nature itself sets the political power, which Dicey borrowed from a eighteenth century writer and made famous, reads as follows: 'It is a fundamental principle with English lawyers, that a Parliament can do everything but make a woman a man, and a man a woman'; A. V. Dicey, *Introduction to the Study of the Law of the Constitution* (London: ECS Wade, Macmillan, 1959), p. 43. Today such limits are more contested than ever.

the term also goes far back in the past, it is in the work of Habermas, and the discussion that followed it, that it was given the central place that it currently enjoys in contemporary debate.[46]

In Habermas' account, the public sphere is a body of individuals joined together to discuss matters of public concern or common interest as equals. This idea had its momentum in early modern Europe through the formation of the bourgeois public sphere, which aimed to mediate between the society and the state by holding the state accountable to society via publicity. In fact, as Fraser observed, this bourgeois public sphere operated through exclusionary mechanisms that systematically excluded women and the lower social strata. If we take into account what certain revisionist historiography has shown about those exclusionary mechanisms, we can hardly deny that the modern public sphere was a 'masculinist ideological notion that functioned to legitimate an emergent form of class rule'.[47] Habermas recognises that his normative ideal was never fully realised (in particular the access to the public sphere has never been so open as he claimed), but he still sees in his reconstruction of the early modern bourgeois society the closest historical manifestation to such an ideal.[48]

In this view, the public sphere is the 'theatre in modern societies in which political participation is enacted through the medium of talk', and therefore also 'an institutionalized arena of discursive interaction'.[49] In other words, it is the communicative engine of democratic politics. The problem, however, for Habermas, as well as for his critics, has been that of elaborating a viable model of the public sphere which is adapted to the conditions of welfare state mass democracy, in which society is increasingly intertwined with the state, and publicity, in the sense of the critical scrutiny of the state, gave way to a public sphere understood as a platform for advertising and for the manufacture of public opinion.[50] In this more restricted meaning of the term, the public sphere denotes, therefore, a 'third sphere' between that of the economy and the bureaucratic state,[51] which is in principle accessible to everybody

---

[46] N. Fraser, 'Rethinking the Public Sphere: A Contribution to the Critique of Actually Existing Democracy', *Social Text* 25–26 (1990), 56–80.

[47] *Ibid.*, p. 62.

[48] J. Habermas, *The Structural Transformation of the Public Sphere: An Inquiry into a Category of Bourgeois Society* (Cambridge: Polity Press, 1989).

[49] Fraser, 'Rethinking the Public Sphere', p. 57.

[50] Habermas, *The Structural Transformation of the Public Sphere*; Fraser, 'Rethinking the Public Sphere'.

[51] M. Somers, 'What's Political or Cultural about Political Culture and the Public Sphere?', *Sociological Theory* 13(2) (1995), 113–44.

and where citizens as equals meet to discuss and deliberate on issues of public concern. While according to the broader meaning of the term part of the public sphere is all that is not included in the private one (including formal institutions such as governments and parliaments), the more restricted meaning of the term excludes the state with its apparatuses. Indeed, if the public sphere is the site where the state can be rendered accountable to society through publicity, then it must be by definition autonomous from the state. In this sense, the concept of the public sphere tends to turn into that of a specifically *democratic* public sphere as it is for its democratic potential that such a concept has been given so much attention.[52] This view of the *public* sphere as opposed to the 'secret' and 'closed' one rests on two fundamental presuppositions: publicity and equality. Let us discuss each of them separately and see how Islam relates to them.

In the first place, the public sphere thus understood denotes a space that is public in the sense of open and visible. Kant defined publicity (*Öffentlichkeit*) in this sense as the 'transcendental formula of public law' to denote the fact that maxims of actions which cannot stand the test of publicity (*Öffentlichkeit*) thus understood are illegitimate. No public law could exist without respecting such a formula.[53] Take as an example the maxim 'I will sign that contract but will not respect it if that proves to be contrary to my interest'. Obviously such a maxim of action would destroy itself in the light of its full publicity. Terrorist organisations such as Al-Qa'eda are therefore excluded from such a concept of the public sphere in as far as their action cannot stand the maxim of publicity thus defined.

The question remains, however, of whether Islam is in principle contrary to such a principle. Is there something intrinsic to the Islamic faith which renders it recalcitrant to publicity thus understood? If we consider the Islamic tradition of thought on *maslahah* and *istislah*, the answer must be negative. The idea of *maslahah* and, in particular, of the correlate concept of *istislah*, understood as a technique of legal reasoning on the common good, is that of a common good that must be deliberated upon in public and which trumps other legal reasoning techniques not adapted to the modern lifestyle.[54] And the public we are talking about is a genuinely

---

[52] Goele, 'Islamic Visibilities and Public Sphere'; C. Calhoun, 'Introduction' in C. Calhoun (ed.), *Habermas and the Public Sphere* (Cambridge MA: MIT Press, 1990).

[53] I. Kant, *Perpetual Peace: A Philosophical Sketch*, trans H. B. Nisbet, in *Political Writings* (Cambridge University Press, 1991), p. 126.

[54] Esposito, *Oxford Encyclopedia of the Modern Islamic World*, vol. 3, pp. 63f.

transnational one. As Salvatore observes, the normative legitimacy of a transnational Islamic public can be measured at a level comparable to the politically expansive radius of Habermas' communicative action.[55]

The current hypertrophy of various Islamic movements, especially in Western Asia,[56] is the best proof of this congeniality of Islam to the ideal of a publicity: as there is little space for democratic participation, since most of the regimes under control, at least until the wave of revolts in 2011, are one-party systems and the political economy is under the tight control of only a few, the only public space (as it was the case in Poland and East Germany in the 1970s and 1980s) where people can meet, discuss and possibly think of collective actions is the place of worship. This situation, together with the appeal of the ideal of *maslahah*, contributed to turning mosques into a privileged place to aggregate collective claims and project them onto the public. The radicality of certain Islamist challenges can be best explained as a proportionate reaction to ferocious authoritarian states in which fundamentalist groups act.[57] As Eisenstadt observes, contemporary Islam is taken between two poles of a continuum ranging from a politics of pluralist opening (Western Asia has always been a place with highly fragmented groups of population[58] thereby forcing a sort of peaceful coexistence between and recognition of minorities and interfaith politics) and a 'Jacobin fundamentalist tendency' of anti-pluralism.[59]

More complicated is the relationship between Islam and the presupposition of equality. On a purely conceptual level, all Muslims should be equally guaranteed access to the public sphere. This is partly a consequence of the already mentioned strong concept of the common good (*maslahah*), which should inspire the conduct of the community of all believers (*umma*), and partly of the idea that all Muslims are equal in the face of God. Eisenstadt, for instance, strongly emphasises how the Islamic ideal of the equality of Muslims in front of God makes Islam particularly

---

[55] Salvatore, 'The Exit from a Westphalian Framing of a Political Space', p. 51. On the need to rethink the notion of public sphere beyond its Westphalian framework, see also N. Fraser, 'Transnationalizing the Public Sphere. On the Legitimacy and Efficacy of Public Opinion in a Post-Westphalian World' *Theory, Culture and Society* 24(4) (2007), 7–30.

[56] We will follow here Halliday's terminology to avoid the Eurocentric description of 'Middle East'. See F. Halliday, *The Middle East in International Relations: Power, Politics and Ideology* (Cambridge University Press, 2005).

[57] Ayubi, 'Rethinking the Public/Private Dichotomy', p. 79.

[58] S. Abdelaziz, 'The Role of Islam in the Public Square. Guidance or Governance?', *ISIM Papers* (Amsterdam University Press, 2005), p. 5.

[59] N. Eisenstadt, 'The Public Sphere in Muslim Societies', p. 458.

congenial to the development of a strong public sphere.[60] To such a claim for formal equality, we may add the important fact that the Muslim duty of solidarity (in particular through the practice of *zakaat*, almsgiving, one of the five pillars of Islam) is aimed at alleviating the more material social and economic inequalities.

According to such an interpretation, the Islamic public should be a public of equals. However, in practice this is far from being the case. And the reasons for this are not accidental. Not just within all historical manifestations of the Islamic faith, but for all the three monotheisms, equality in the face of God remained an ideal that was never fully realised. In the first place, this is due to the fact that all these religions generated clerical hierarchies within them. This is particularly clear if we look at the position of women within such hierarchies: in all institutionalised expressions of the three great monotheist religions of the book *women* are relegated to inferior positions and it is *men* who control the means of religious interpretations. The battle of Islamic feminism, which is also done through the means of the Islamic public sphere, is yet far from obtaining an equal position of men and women, and, in particular, an equal access to the official means for interpretation.

With regards to gender, not just Islam but the three monotheistic religions of the book are still unable to generate a public of fully equal members. The general problem is that a public of equals in the face of God is by definition a public of equals in the face of an absolute Other. If this is perfectly compatible with the broader conception of the public sphere analysed above, it can hardly be reconciled with the idea of a specifically democratic public sphere. The tension between religion and democracy derives from the fact that a presupposition of the latter being that of the full equality of its citizens.

The most tangible sign of such a tension is perhaps the different evolutionary pace of religion and democracies. While the latter follow the needs that each time emerge within the society itself, the former is much slower in doing so. A polity which does not respond to the principle of autonomy according to which the people are obliged to follow only the law they have given to themselves is not a democracy. The principle of autonomy, however differently understood, always implies the idea of self-rule. As a consequence, a democratic society inspired by such a principle cannot but follow the relatively rapid evolutionary rhythm of the society.

---

[60] S. Eisenstadt, 'Public Spheres and Political Dynamics', pp. 306–18.

On the contrary, in all revealed religions of the book, the law that is revealed as the will of God is by definition the law of an Other. The monotheistic law is therefore given by definition not in an autonomous, but in a heteronymous way.[61] Here lies the main root of the tension we are exploring. Dispute may arise with regard to the interpretations of the will of God, but two substantially differing interpretations are not admitted: they can at best generate another faith. To say 'so it is written, this is the will of God' amounts to saying 'you cannot imagine it otherwise'.[62] For instance, an interpretation of the will of Allah which says that Mohammed was not a prophet would be immediately stigmatised as a heresy. The ensemble of the possible interpretations accumulated over time usually crystallise into a canon or a tradition that can hardly be subverted in a sudden and radical way. This happens only at times of revolutionary events, mainly resulting in the creation of another faith (as was the case for the Reformation). As a result, the evolutionary rhythm is usually much slower than that of democratic polities.

This is again clearly reflected in the inferior position of women. The question of their role is not just a marginal issue in as far as denying that full equality between men and women amounts to denying the principle of full equality *tout court*. Whilst in democratic polities women are universally given full equality to men, in all revealed religions they are still relegated to inferior positions (for instance they are not admitted in the highest ranks of the clergy). To conclude on this point, if Islam has some specific resources to empower the idea of a democratic public sphere, it is on the other hand also disempowering because of the importance of the idea of an absolute Otherness. The challenge is not therefore on the side of Islam alone, but on that of all the monotheistic religions of the book.[63]

---

[61] C. Castoriadis, 'Institution de la société et religion' in C. Castoriadis, *Domaines de l'homme. Carrefour du labyrinthe* (Paris: Seuil, 1986), pp. 455–81.

[62] C. Bottici, 'The Politics of Imagination and the Public Role of Religion' in *Philosophy and Social Criticism* 35(8) (2009), 985–1005.

[63] The transnational dimension (and liminality) of contemporary Islam in search of a possible constitutive contribution to a European public sphere can be both an advantage and a disadvantage in reaching the democratic pluralistic end of the continuum described by N. Eisenstadt ('The Public Sphere in Muslim Societies', p. 458): if access to new media has 'played a significant role in fragmenting and contesting political religious authority' (A. Salvatore and D. F. Eickelman (eds.), *Public Islam and the Common Good* (Leiden; Boston: Brill, 2004), p. 9) opening thus new venues of participation for Muslims, other militant groups have also favoured the radicalisation of other groups in the destructive politics of identity (thus creating false impressions that the problem is with Islam, the religion).

Conclusions

There is nothing intrinsic to Islam that represents a challenge for the European public sphere. With its ideals of the common good (*maslahah*) and the technique of rational deliberation aimed at determining it (*istislah*), Islam could rather sustain the flourishing of a lively public sphere. If there is a challenge, this is to the specifically democratic potential of the public sphere and it is not from Islam, but from all monotheistic religions as such. Whatever solution one can find to such a challenge, it will have to take into consideration not just the power of public reason but also that of public imagination.

This was already clear in the discussion raised by the Archbishop's proposal to include some elements of the sharia in the English legal system with which we began. His speech was much more nuanced than how it has been perceived. In the first place, he started by highlighting that the very term sharia is largely misunderstood (sharia is a method of law rather than a single complete and final system[64]) and that 'as a matter of fact certain provisions of sharia are already recognised in [England's] society and ... law'.[65] But in the minds of Europeans, the very term sharia immediately evoked images of oppression and despotism. It worked like an electric spark that set people's imagination and fears aflame.

This also explains why it is rarely said that the talk which explored 'the limits of a unitary and secular legal system in the presence of an increasingly plural (including religiously plural) society'[66] was not exclusively limited to sharia, but also addressed possible Christian and Jewish contributions to a form of legal pluralism. The outrage crystallised on the sharia because at work there were not only individuals who deliberate in a purely rational way, but also human beings who cannot resist the power of the myth of a clash between Islam and the West.

---

[64] See the entry 'Sharia' in J. L. Esposito *Oxford Dictionary of Islam* (Oxford University Press, 2003).

[65] For a response of some of the accusations levelled against the Archbishop, see www.archbishopofcanterbury.org/1581 (last accessed 17 August 2011).

[66] *Ibid.*

PART II

6

Law v. religion

LORENZO ZUCCA

Introduction

On 1 January 2009 the Vatican reformed its system of legal sources. The Lateran pacts of 1929 established that Italian laws will be automatically transposed as valid laws of the Vatican state. From now on, the Vatican is not automatically transposing Italian laws. It will check them one by one in order to establish whether or not Italian laws are in conflict with Catholic moral principles. The most important aspect of this constitutional revolution is the acknowledgment of an open conflict between secular laws and religious principles. Once the existence of a conflict is established, the next question is to ask how to solve these conflicts and, even more crucially, who is to solve them. From this viewpoint, the Vatican aims at becoming the final adjudicator of the more pressing moral and political problems. Abortion, euthanasia, stem cell research and many other problems would be ultimately and authoritatively adjudicated by the Vatican.

It is necessary to stress at this point that there is a clear difference between a theoretical authority and a practical authority. A theoretical authority tells us what we should believe in; a practical authority tells us how to behave. The Vatican aims at regaining its status as theoretical authority in moral matters. But it also aims at becoming a practical authority in situations of conflict by claiming that its moral high ground should take priority over the legal compromise. The confusion between theoretical and practical conflicts should be resisted. To begin with, the search for the truth of theoretical authorities should not be burdened by local compromises imposed by the resolution of practical conflicts. Also, practical conflicts require different skills than theoretical conflicts: they are more about outcomes rather than premises. Finally, someone's absolute moral conviction may even be an obstacle to the resolution of a practical conflict that would satisfy individual with incompatible worldviews.

Law's business is to solve practical conflicts. It guides our behaviour in the public sphere and regulates our relationships. Practical conflicts can be very varied. They can be about how to keep a promise in economic transactions or how to guarantee privacy in a world in which communication is virtually limitless. The former is the realm of contract law and the latter is the realm of constitutional law. There are infinite examples, as any law attempts to give guidance under circumstances of conflicting interests. Religion, however, is not interested in every field of law (although this varies according to each religion). Religion is interested in the big moral problem of today's society. Its natural field of intervention is constitutional law at the level of principles, in particular those principles embedded in constitutional rights. Of course it also deals with family law issues, and at times with criminal law problems. But constitutional rights penetrate any field of law, and they are more open to arguments from morality.

The conflict between law and religion is all pervasive in the area of practical conflicts. But there is in the literature a lot of confusion about what that conflict is really about. The language of conflict is often abused and overused. Commentators talk about conflicts of rules, principles, values and even conflict of identities or clashes of civilizations. In order to avoid such an unstable and vast terminology, I deliberately place my analysis within precise boundaries. The conflicts I am interested in here are practical conflicts, that is those conflicts that deal with the issue of how to behave under certain circumstances. The core case of practical conflict is when a norm states an obligation to do something and another norm states an obligation not to do that very thing. A classical example is the religious norm that makes it obligatory to wear the Islamic scarf and the (French) secular norm that makes it obligatory not to wear the Islamic scarf in public schools. The gist of the conflict between law and religion can be identified with a conflict of obligations stemming from a range of different norms.

There are two main strategies that have characterized the management of practical conflicts between law and religion in secular democracies. The first strategy concerns the scope of law and religion. Modern secular states sharply distinguish between the public and the private sphere. Law rules in the public sphere, whereas religion does so in private assuming that an individual is a believer. This strategy has the advantage of simplicity. But the problem is that religion is advocating a growing place in the public sphere and the secular state does not seem to be armed with strong enough arguments to prevent that from happening. Moreover, simplicity is not synonymous with accuracy: religion has always played a role in the public sphere, but it often was considered as complementary and therefore never opposed. The rise of new religious demands that are at odds with secular laws, make the distinction between private and public spheres more obsolete.

The second strategy deals with the stringency of legal or religious obligations. This requires from the adjudicator a difficult evaluation of the importance of obligations within constitutional frameworks. Sometimes legal obligations will be deemed as paramount and a religious minority will have to yield to that. So for example, Jehovah's Witnesses' refusal of blood transfusions is overridden when it risks jeopardizing one's life. At other times, religious obligations can be recognized as paramount and therefore justify exemptions to existing legal regimes. For example, the obligation not to carry knives is overridden by the Sikh religious obligation to carry their ceremonial knife. In few cases the conflict is persistent as law and religion fail to successfully justify the priority of one obligation over another. Examples of this situation are many, but the most debated conflict involves the obligations stemming from the so-called right to life and its application to beginning- and end-of-life cases.

This chapter will explore the varieties of practical conflicts between law and religion, starting from the central idea that the core case of conflict is that between obligations stemming from legal or religious norms. The first section will ask the question: what are the conflicts between law and religion? Following on from that interrogation, it will be necessary to establish how to deal with those conflicts. This will be the central question of the second section.

1   The varieties of conflicts

At the core of conflicts between law and religion are obligations. But of course each obligation originates in a different norm. We can build a typology by focusing on the norms that ground conflicting obligations. The most general distinction to draw at this point is that between norms that belong to the same normative system and norms that belong to different normative systems. We therefore have conflicts from within and conflicts from without. An example of the former is the conflict between rights; an example of the latter is the conflict between domestic and foreign norms that requires a sophisticated adjudication based on conflict of laws.

A second helpful distinction may be that between duty-imposing and power-conferring norms. It is easy to understand how duty-imposing norms may be in conflict since they prescribe specific behaviours that at times are not jointly performable. For example, the right to free speech makes it possible to utter speech that may be injurious. But the right to be

Table 6.1

	Duty-imposing norms	Power-conferring norms
Within the system	e.g. Conflict of Rights	e.g. authority of arbitration tribunal
Outside the system	e.g. Conflict of Laws	e.g. ultimate authority between church and state

protected against racial or religious hatred makes that speech impermissible in principle. It is more difficult at first to see why power-conferring norms could give rise to a conflict between law and religion. However, if we accept that there are conflicts between duty-imposing norms, then the next step is to ask who will adjudicate those conflicts. If the adjudicator is a religious institution working as an arbitrator according to the laws of the country, then this arbitrator is likely to reach decisions that impose obligations in conflict with obligations imposed by ordinary laws. For example, the Muslim Arbitration Tribunal may well reach a decision that recognizes *talaq* divorce as permissible, while legal norms clearly prohibit it. In this case, the source of the conflict is the power-conferring norm granting authority to the institution, but the actual conflict is still between duty-imposing norms.

A   Fundamental rights and the conflict between law and religion

Fundamental Rights are the main source of duty-imposing norms leading to conflicts between law and religion. One of the reasons for this is that fundamental rights lack a clear secular foundation. Disagreement between religious and non-religious people about the foundation of fundamental rights is endless and all pervasive. A concept like dignity, for example, is very much open to arguments from both sides. The stakes are very high as the interpretation of such a concept is radically different if its foundation is god-based rather than human-based. A god-based conception of dignity would be very static and would essentially prescribe what is not permissible to do to humans. A human-based conception of dignity would be very dynamic and would essentially prescribe what is permissible to do to humans. The lack of foundation makes it impossible to establish a harmonious heaven of values underpinning fundamental rights. If we do not agree on what are the most important properties of fundamental rights that make them so central to our legal political system, we will have great trouble in ranking those rights when they prescribe incompatible behaviours. As a consequence, we will be compelled to accept that any system of fundamental rights is underpinned by a value pluralist realm of values.

Another reason for rights to be conducive to conflicts is their indeterminacy. Rights are cast in very broad and imprecise language that yields very little guidance as to the right way of articulating their claims under specific circumstances. This means that an extensive work of interpretation is necessary. It also means that the label of rights justifies almost any claim as long as one learns to use the language to one's own advantage. Religious groups are appealing to rights more frequently in order to claim exemptions or privileges. Many secular people see this as a misuse of rights that are regarded as Trojan horses for religious people to encroach upon public policies. The truth is that fundamental rights are indeterminate and offer everyone the possibility of making claims that are merely self-interested. What are, then, these conflicts of rights involving law and religion?

Even if Art. 9 of the European Convention on Human Rights (ECHR) specifically protects religious freedom, the European regime of religion depends on a range of rights spanning from Art. 2 ECHR to Arts. 8, 10, 11 and 14. Religion has a strong interest in policing the boundaries of life (Art. 2), which conflicts with a secular interest in furthering individual autonomy (Art. 8). Also, religious expression can be protected as any other form of expression (Art. 10); more often than not, religion claims that other expression ridiculing or offending religion should be limited; see for example the Muhammad cartoon saga. In addition, religion has a considerable interest in being able to assemble if not associate for political purposes (Art. 11). This is not always easy to accept and often conflicts with secular norms of the constitution, as was the case in Turkey with the *Refah Partisi* case. Finally, religion claims to be able to organize itself according to its norms; this creates a problem if those norms discriminate on sexual or gender basis (Art. 14). In what follows I will give some egregious examples of conflicts between obligations stemming from fundamental rights.

(i) Art. 2 v. Art. 8

The scope of the value of life is bitterly contested. Some believe that to value one's life includes the recognition of one's ability to decide when to end that life. In most cases this is not very difficult as suicide is always possible. But in some exceptional cases some patients are stuck with their ill body and unable to carry out alone the ultimate act of their life. The question is whether we should allow them to do so by assisting them in their last informed decision to quit their lives.

Religious institutions and religious people want to resist this suggestion. They claim that our life is not our property as it has been granted by God, who is the only one in control of matters of life and death. Nonreligious people disagree with the idea that God is the ultimate adjudicator. But they are uncertain as to whether we should assist people in dying. When they do think so, they generally rely on the value of individual autonomy, which must allow for a room of decisional privacy on the part of the individual. Life is theirs and they certainly cherish it. But if for some reason they become detached from their life and only think about limiting the pain life protracts, then they should be given a chance to end their life.

The leading European case in this area is *Pretty*.[1] Mrs Pretty had a motor neurone disease which paralyzed her completely. In addition, her disease was slowly, but surely, killing her. She asked the Director of Public Prosecution (DPP) for her husband to be excused had he accepted to assist her suicide. The DPP rejected her request, arguing that prohibition of killing cannot be excused. She then embarked on the judicial route which took her to Strasbourg. The ECtHR examined her arguments under Arts. 2, 3, 8, 9 and 14 of the ECHR. In particular, the Court examined her claim that the right to life includes a right to die, and rejected it. It also examined her claim that her right to privacy covers her right to decide on how to die. The ECtHR also rejected this claim, arguing that the blanket ban imposed by the law was not disproportionate as it responded to a very pressing social need (namely, the protection of vulnerable people who could be pressurized into accepting an earlier death).

Interestingly, the Catholic Bishops' Conference of England and Wales filed a brief with the intent of keeping the ban:

> They emphasised that it was a fundamental tenet of the Catholic faith that human life was a gift from God received in trust. Actions with the purpose of killing oneself or another, even with consent, reflected a damaging misunderstanding of the human worth. Suicide and euthanasia were therefore outside the range of morally acceptable options in dealing with human suffering and dying. These fundamental truths were also

---

[1] Eur. Ct. H. R., *Pretty v. the UK*, 29 April 2002.

recognised by other faiths and by modern pluralist and secular societies, as shown by Article 1 of the Universal Declaration of Human Rights (December 1948) and the provisions of the European Convention on Human Rights, in particular in Articles 2 and 3 thereof.[2]

The Catholic Bishops' Conference claimed controversially that suicide and euthanasia were outside the range of morally acceptable options. Even more controversially, they argued that modern pluralist and secular societies recognize those fundamental truths. If anything, when talking about euthanasia we locate ourselves at the core of moral conflicts between deeply held values. And by definition, modern pluralist societies are open as to the definition of the value of life and disagreement is great.

(ii)   Art. 9 v. rights of others

In Europe the leading case is *Kokkinakis* v. *Greece*.[3] This is also the first case dealing with freedom of religion at the ECtHR. Kokkinakis was a Greek Jehovah's Witness. He was sent to jail several times for acts of proselytism. On 2 March 1986 Kokkinakis and his wife visited the house of Mr Kyriakis, a Greek Orthodox priest, with the intent of presenting their views and distributing some religious materials. Shortly after their visit the police were called and Kokkinakis and his wife were arrested, prosecuted and convicted for proselytism. Before the ECtHR they claimed that the ban on proselytism was a breach of their fundamental right to religious freedom.

The problem is that the ban on proselytism is said to be compatible with the Greek Constitution – which establishes the Orthodox religion as the religion of the state – as it is meant to preserve a degree of religious coexistence and it applies indiscriminately against all religious groups. The apparent conflict faced by Greek courts now was that between freedom of religion and the principle of an established church. Greek courts unanimously held that the ban on proselytism was perfectly consistent with freedom of religion. The plaintiff challenged the latter claim. The ECtHR found that this interference with religious freedom was disproportionate. In this case, the tension between freedom of religion and the prohibition of proselytism is made worse by the constitutional establishment of one religion. A secular state, in this case, has a better claim for religious pluralism as it aims to protect equally all different religions. Moreover, secularism should not be about polarizing the society.

---

[2] *Ibid.*, para. 29.   [3] Eur. Ct. H. R., *Kokkinakis* v. *Greece*, 25 May 1993.

However, secularism may polarize a society when it boils down to a normative position that rides roughshod over societal views. A good illustration of this issue is the *Leyla Şahin* case.[4] Leyla was a student of medicine at Ankara University. She was compelled to move to Vienna to continue her studies after her local university turned the screw on the scarf ban. She nonetheless decided to challenge the decision of the university to ban headscarves in public places on the ground that it violated her freedom of religion.

The Turkish Constitutional Court (TCC) held that the principle of secularism was of constitutional rank; it pointed out that secularism makes religious freedom possible by severing individual religious consciences from political interference:[5] so far so good. But the constitutional court made a mistake: when considering freedom to manifest one's religion in public, it argued that religious dress can be held to be incompatible with the principle of secularism. In other words, the constitutional court saw a conflict where there was none. It believed that secularism mandated absolute religious neutrality in the public sphere. By holding this, it actually undermined the very idea that secularism is there to support religious freedom including freedom to manifest one's own religion in public. Secularism understood in such a rigid way is incompatible with other principles. Moreover, it is hard to square with religious practices in Turkey. If the society is predominantly Muslim, it is not desirable nor is it feasible to prohibit any form of religious display.

The Turkish Constitutional Court took an extreme view of the principle of secularism, one that divides and polarizes the society instead of creating the conditions for cohabitation. It is surprising to note that the ECtHR paid lip service towards this highly problematic understanding of secularism. It simply afforded a great margin of appreciation to the Turkish institutions. But to do so neither supported secularism nor did it support freedom of religion. Yet it ascertained a political conflict, whereby the principle of secularism clashes with the principle of freedom of religion.

(iii)   Art. 10 v. Art. 10

Free speech and religion give rise to a second important conflict. In a democratic society free speech is often portrayed as paramount. However, its scope was recently questioned when free speech was stretched to

---

[4] Eur. Ct. H. R. (Grand Chamber), *Leyla Şahin v. Turkey*, 10 November 2005.
[5] *Ibid.*, para. 39.

protect religious insult and offense. The tension is that between the right to free speech and the right not to be offended in one's own religion.

In Europe, where free speech and secularism play a paramount role, there is a presumption in favour of liberty. However, courts do draw a line; the ECtHR, for example, confronted the issue of blasphemy in its seminal case *Otto-Preminger-Institut* v. *Austria*.[6] The case concerned a film that portrayed the holy Christian family in highly derogatory terms. The ECtHR had to decide whether the administrative sanction preventing the screening of the movie was in breach of Art. 10 of the convention or whether it was justified on grounds of protection of religious feelings. Strasbourg argued that the administrative sanction was justified as the film risked provoking a strong reaction within a prevalently Christian population.

Critics of this decision argue that there is no tension between free speech and the right not to be offended in one's own religion because the latter is not a right properly speaking. If there is a right not to be offended, or harmed, by other people's words, this must apply to any feeling, not only religious ones. We can be offended as football supporters, political partisans and so on. But there is nothing special about religion that warrants an ad hoc protection. This may be true on political grounds: it is hard to find a precise political reason why religion should be specially protected.

Perhaps it is just a change in social circumstances. Critics of the protection of religion claim that societies rush too quickly to regulate new social phenomena without paying enough attention to the underlying principles that would offer a solution if properly understood and interpreted. Even if they accept that hate speech should somehow be regulated, they contend that there is no authority that can police the line between free speech and hate speech effectively. This is open to disagreement.

(iv) Art. 11 v. secularism

The conflict is at its peak when it involves political parties. The role of religion in politics is often ambiguous. Christian parties are a traditional feature of European political systems. But what would be the legal status of Islamic parties? Are they all to be banned because they promote sharia law and Islamic values? Or should we distinguish between moderate and authoritarian parties? It would seem logical to allow for the representation of European Muslims through political parties provided

---

[6] Eur. Ct. H. R., *Otto-Preminger-Institut* v. *Austria*, 20 September 1994, *Serie* A, 295.

that they respect the basic conditions of political orders: democracy, fundamental rights and rule of law. Against this background, it is somehow perplexing to observe a string of cases coming from Turkey and dealing with the dissolution of Islamic parties. The leading case is *Refah Partisi*.[7]

The conflict at stake in these cases is that between the principle of secularism and the principle of free association. The most obvious problem concerns the articulation of these principles in more precise directives. The trouble is that the task of articulating these principles is in the hands of the TCC, which clearly represents, and is composed of, the members of the secularist elite. This means in other words that secularism will always be interpreted as being at odds with the association of political parties of religious inspiration. But what are the arguments for the dissolution?

In *Refah Partisi* (Welfare Party), the case against the party was brought sometime after its constitution. In fact, Refah already had one year in government with a coalition of other parties. The opponents to Refah contested that in its manifesto the party did not rule out the possibility of resorting to violence as a means of political action. Moreover, Refah advocated in its manifesto the establishment of plural legal systems whereby secular people would be subject to secular law and religious people would be subject to religious law, at least in the fields of private and criminal law. The latter claim was held to be at odds with the secular constitution that mandates the principle of one secular law for the whole society. The former issue was more generally held to be at odds with the integrity and safety of the constitutional order.

However, in the one year of Refah Partisi's governmental experience there was no immediate sign of its willingness to either resort to violence or to push forward a plural legal system. There was, so to say, a gap between its deeds and its words that did not exactly warrant an action against the party. Nevertheless, opponents to Refah seized the first opportunity to ask the TCC for its dissolution. Based on a mere exegesis of Refah's manifesto, the TCC reached the conclusion that the party endangered the secular constitutional order and therefore had to be dissolved.

The case was referred to the ECtHR, where plaintiffs claimed that their right to political association had been unduly limited. In a rather controversial decision, the Grand Chamber of the ECtHR followed

---

[7] Eur. Ct. H. R. (Grand Chamber), *Refah Partisi (The Welfare Party) and others* v. *Turkey*, 13 February 2003.

once again Pilate's way. After considering the legitimacy and proportionality of the interference on the party's right to political association, the ECtHR decided to leave to Turkey a large margin of appreciation when deciding the conformity of a political association to its secular constitution.

The story does not stop there. Refah's politicians, including the present prime minister, created a new party with similar aims but a more moderate style. The outcome was the AK party (AKP), which is now the ruling party in the country and has produced the prime minister and the president. The morale of the story is that a party's dissolution on grounds that are not shared by the whole society does not entail the curtailment of an association's political life. To the contrary, it may even lead it to success, as happened for AKP. Undeterred by this development, some opponents of AKP asked the TCC to step in again and also dissolve the present ruling party. In a recent decision the TCC reached an odd compromise by which the AKP is maintained in power but the public funding it receives is halved. This time the TCC was under too much pressure both from within and from outside. And it is arguable that the way in which the conflict between secularism and political association was dealt with in Refah's case did not serve as a good precedent. Secularism is still very much regarded by part of the elite as an article of faith that cannot accommodate a religious party. Perhaps there is something wrong with the way in which the conflict has been presented. Perhaps it should not be regarded as an absolute principle unable to yield to political compromise. There is an area of conflict where absolute lines are drawn even more firmly.

B Power-conferring norms and the conflict between law and religion

Power-conferring norms confer power to an institution or a designated person to adjudicate a number of disputes. In Europe the unequivocal principle is that legal disputes must be adjudicated by ordinary courts according to ordinary laws. There are, however, some exceptions which fall under the generic name of alternative dispute resolution. These include mediation, conciliation and arbitration. The last is a particularly interesting case in the context of conflict between law and religion, as some European countries give the possibility to parties to have some of their disputes solved by an arbitrator who applies religious laws. In the UK, for example, there exist Jewish courts, of which the London Beth Din is a prominent example,[8] and since 2007 there has been a Muslim Arbitration Tribunal (MAT) that applies sharia law in a few selected areas:

> The Muslim Arbitration Tribunal (MAT) was established in 2007 to pro-vide a viable alternative for the Muslim community seeking to resolve disputes in accordance with Islamic Sacred Law and without having to resort to costly and time consuming litigation. The establishment of MAT is an important and significant step towards providing the Muslim com-munity with a real opportunity to self determine disputes in accordance with Islamic Sacred Law.[9]

These methods of alternative dispute resolution raise possible conflicts between secular laws and religious principles. If religious principles were incompatible with secular laws, then the decision of the arbitrator enfor-cing those principles would be regarded as a way of smuggling in the legal system obligations that are incompatible with legal norms. But the prin-ciples of sharia law are generally not in conflict with the requirements of the law in Europe, as stressed by Lord Phillips, Lord Chief Justice.[10] The Archbishop of Canterbury raised a similar point in his speech at the High Court on 7 February 2008. His point was that individual personal con-duct based on the principles of sharia law need not be in conflict with the laws of England. In certain carefully defined legal matters such as 'aspects of marital law, the regulation of financial transactions and authorised structures of mediation and conflict resolution',[11] it would be desirable to give the choice of jurisdiction to the parties.

Where conflicts are possible is at the level of sanctions for non-compliance with sharia law. European legal systems uniformly prohibit severe physical punishment, which is sometimes prescribed under some interpretations of sharia law. It is clear that those sanctions would be banned from any European jurisdiction. This does not exclude more sub-stantive conflicts between European laws and sharia law.

C   Conflict of laws and conflicts between law and religion

Ordinary courts are facing a growing number of cases in which two rules of different legal systems clash. Strictly speaking these are clear examples

---

[8]   www.theus.org.uk/the_united_synagogue/the_london_beth_din/about_us/ (last accessed 11 August 2011).

[9]   www.matribunal.com/index.html (last accessed 11 August 2011).

[10] Speech by Lord Phillips, 'Equality Before the Law' delivered at the East London Muslim Centre on 3 July 2008.

[11] *Ecclesiastical Law Journal* 10 (2008): 262–82.

of legal conflicts: they involve two valid rules which prescribe incompatible behaviours; and we have to choose between the two, thereby putting one rule to the side. For example, rules in conflict may concern family law and have religious roots: can we recognize polygamy? What is the legal status of *talaq* divorce?[12]

In principle European legal systems strictly prohibit polygamy. So if a second marriage takes place in Europe, it is customarily annulled. But what if the marriage has already taken place in another country where polygamy is allowed? In this case the conflict of rules is the following:

- Rule 1 says polygamy is strictly prohibited.
- Rule 2 says it is not the case that polygamy is prohibited.

When courts deal with problems of private international law, rule 2 is a potential candidate for incorporation in the legal system of the litigation for the purpose of the adjudication of the present case. The judge will have to apply rules of conflict establishing which rule applies. In France, for example, the judge recognized that a polygamous relationship could yield some legal consequences such as the payment of children's benefits.

Talaq divorce is another feature of sharia law. When the husband pronounces for three times the word *talaq*, the marriage is deemed to be dissolved. As a matter of principle, *talaq* divorce is considered to be against the law in most European countries. However, some courts recognize that it has some validity if *talaq* divorce took place abroad and both parties can be present to confirm this fact before a judge. Once again the conflict between two rules is quite explicit in theory. In practice, there is some accommodation which becomes more and more necessary as our societies welcome a growing number of immigrants.

D   The church–state relationship and conflict between law and religion

Norms that regulate the relationship between church and state may also give rise to conflicts between law and religion, in particular when there is a privileged relation as is the case between the Vatican state and Italy. This is an interesting case as it has implications at three levels. First, it concerns the mutual independence of two normative systems: Italian laws

---

[12] Pascale Fournier, *Muslim Marriages in Western Countries* (Aldershot: Ashgate, 2008).

and Vatican laws. Second, it is about the relationship between two sovereign states. Third, it is about the separation between church and state. The Vatican would like to free itself from these institutional burdens and focus on its status as an authoritative moral voice at the global level. The trouble is that in order to exercise effective authority, one has to take into account institutional and other contingent burdens in order to reach the best possible compromise.

The aim of this exercise is to establish an autonomous body of laws, a *Corpus Vaticanum*, which would be firmly rooted in objective moral principles. Needless to say objective moral principles of the Catholic Church would take absolute priority over conflicting laws of the Italian, and of any other, state or international organization. The Vatican has recently refused to approve a United Nations declaration decriminalizing homosexuality. The *Corpus Vaticanum*, albeit limited in dimension, aspires to offer a unique voice in the sphere of comparative law and a unique understanding of law at the global level.

In the words of Jose Maria Serrano Ruiz, the architect of this reform, the Vatican intends to become the ideal city state, a model for other states from a normative viewpoint. His main arguments for breaking free from Italian laws are three. First, Italian laws are too many and a simplification is required. Second, Italian laws, as are any other secular laws, are too unstable. The Vatican is instead committed to Aquinas' ideal of *lex rationis ordinatio*, which requires a stable framework of concepts and values for the law. Third, there is a growing number of conflicts between Italian (or any other secular) laws and non-negotiable principles of the Catholic Church. The Vatican, given its privileged position as an independent state, clearly wants to become the ultimate authority on moral aspects of the law. It aims to become an exemplary and universal authority on the resolution of conflicts between secular laws and religious principles.

There are a number of difficult conflicts between law and religion. To deal with them, secular states have to rethink their secular commitment afresh and articulate new responses to old problems. In what follows I do not attempt to provide detailed guidance on how to cope with those conflicts. To do so would be well beyond the realm of this chapter. Instead, I focus on two main issues that make the decisions of the secular states more difficult. On the one hand, the fact of pluralism makes it very hard for the secular state to square all the competing claims. This is why a common framework is needed. On the other, the widespread fear of Islam creates a phobic environment that is not conducive to sound policies regarding the relationship between law and religion in European societies.

2   How to deal with conflicts between law and religion?

Secularism in Europe is weak. Mainly this is because it does not offer principled accommodation between law and religion. Instead, it simply yields to shabby compromises based on contingent and local reasons. Secular Europeans are confident that they do not need to argue for their case as history has already decreed the victory of their side. So when religion asks for recognition, secular people make concessions according to their own interpretation of the local and contingent relations between the church and the state. Secular confidence, however, is a double-edged sword for at least two reasons. First, it simply assumes, without arguing for, the superiority of secular reasons over any other religious reasons. It thereby excludes any possibility of exchange and mutual understanding. Second, it breeds a sentiment of fear towards new religious creeds that are not part of the local practices and are thereby regarded as irrational and unacceptable. The phobia engendered by this attitude clouds judgement and makes it impossible to treat any religious claim in an open and rational way.

A   A marketplace of religions

European societies are characterized by a growing pluralism. Individuals have not only increasingly varied religious backgrounds, but also racial and cultural backgrounds. The challenge is to devise a framework within which individuals and groups enjoy the maximum level of liberty and equal rights. The fact of pluralism also means that conflicts between different worldviews will highlight even more strongly disagreement over the interpretation of basic values and fundamental rights. Even if disagreement is part and parcel of our constitutional regimes, this should not let one lose sight of the fact that liberty and equality are and should be paramount when a person is called to adjudicate a conflict between obligations that concern him. The way in which religions adjudicate conflicts is also important and should have a role in public debate. But no religion should have a monopoly on the adjudication of conflicts, and law should prevent this from happening. In order to achieve these ambitious aims, law should set up a marketplace of religions.

A marketplace of religions is a way of carving out a place of religion in the public sphere. Religions bring out in public their comprehensive views and suggest how those views would influence the decision of some conflicts of obligations. Believers and non-believers will be free to follow the guidance of any religion. They will also be free to disregard it and follow instead the guidance provided by secular laws. It is essential to stress that the marketplace of religion has internal and external limits. Internally, competition between religions must be enhanced. As a result, no church can be allowed to have a monopoly within a state. Externally, the marketplace of religion is subordinated by the marketplace of democracy. The relationship between the two will be a key element of an improved European secular philosophy. In a nutshell, the authority of the law stemming from the marketplace of democracy should be regarded as giving a default position and act as a last resort in case of unrelenting disagreement.

(i)   Internal limits

The principle of equality between religions and other systems of thought is central in the understanding of the legal framework, with the exception of a situation of deadlock between two comprehensive views, in which case a secular comprehensive view will have to be preferred as it is a last resort, default position. The principle of equality entails that in the marketplace of religions there cannot be an institution that enjoys a monopolistic position, especially in matters of conflicts of obligations. Religious monopolies can be de jure or de facto. Both of them should be regulated away so that religious pluralism can truly flourish within the legal framework.

De jure monopolies can at times be very blatant. Any constitution that recognizes an established church or a privileged relation between the state and a church suffers from a presumption of de jure monopoly. So for example, the Greek Constitution that recognizes the Greek Orthodox Church as the established church and allows a preferential legal treatment is under a strong presumption of de jure monopoly of one religion and risks affecting the possibility of an open society where religious pluralism can thrive. From this viewpoint, the *Kokkinakis* case rightly insisted that the crime of proselytism could only be defined in the narrowest manner in order not to affect freedom of religion.

There should be a presumption of de jure monopoly also when a constitution entrenches a strong and aggressive secular principle such as *laïcité*, as is the case in France and Turkey. The presumption is confirmed if *laïcité* is interpreted in such a way as to exclude religious comprehensive views from participating in public life. It was therefore wrong for the French state to ban altogether the Islamic scarf from public schools. And it was wrong for the Turkish Constitutional Court to ban the Islamic Party, Refah Partisi, from political life. Now it should be possible to distinguish between a situation in which secularism occupies a position of de jure monopoly to the total exclusion of religious voices in the public sphere and the situation in which secularism is a default position that makes the marketplace of religions possible.

De facto monopoly can also hamper the chances of construing a legal framework in which liberty and equality for all religious people and groups is guaranteed and protected. De facto monopoly is met when one church exercises a very strong influence on political and civil society. Few would object to the idea that the Catholic Church exercises a very strong influence in Italy or in Spain. In Italy, the most recent occurrence of such interference is the instance I described above. Italian laws will hereafter be evaluated according to the moral yardstick of the Catholic Church. Other examples could be multiplied. A notable one concerns the presence of religion in the public square. Any central square in Italy is dominated by a church. This is often equated much too quickly with the idea that other religions have to ask permission from the Catholic Church if they wish to manifest themselves in those places. A recent example concerned a pro-Palestinian demonstration that ended up in Milan's central square at the time of prayer for Muslim people. They therefore proceeded to pray in front of the Catholic cathedral, and this provoked an outrage in the society. But if there was no de facto monopoly of one religion in Italy, then there would not be an assumption that the Catholic Church controls the most public of all places: the central square of the city.

The marketplace of religions therefore imposes internal limits to all the participants and in particular to the religions playing monopolistic roles in European states. It is not enough to expect from those religions top-down tolerant attitudes vis-à-vis the other religious movements. The marketplace of religion should be free from arbitrary domination. This does not mean that religious pluralism will be entrenched in this way; it simply means that the possibility of religious pluralism should always be preserved.

(ii)   External limits

My suggestion that law should make religious freedom and equality possible assumes that law is the ultimate authority, and the last resort, for the adjudication of conflicting obligations. The idea of a marketplace of religions gives a greater place to religion in public life by providing a framework within which religions and other comprehensive views can express their voices and recommendations as how best to solve those conflicts while respecting diverging opinions. When agreement as to a local or alternative method for the resolution of conflicts is impossible, then the law should step in and provide the answer itself. In order to do so, the law cannot rely on its pretended neutrality but has to rely itself on a comprehensive view that is meant to be inclusive of religious and non-religious people.

Conflicts of obligations stemming from legal, moral and religious norms take place at different levels and between different agents. Constitutions and international treaties can at best provide a general framework, and a last resort method, for adjudicating those conflicts. The point of those frameworks is to guarantee liberty and equality for religious and non-religious people. Conflicts can take place at three different levels. First, conflicts of obligations can be the object of resolution of an individual decision. Second, conflicts of obligations can be between two members of the same community who share the same comprehensive views. Third, conflicts of obligations can be between two members of the same community whose comprehensive views differ.

A strong legal framework will enhance liberty in the following ways. First, when an individual is required to reach a decision between conflicting obligations, he is in principle free to decide according to his own self-imposed values or according the best interpretation of his religion. So for example, when a woman has to decide whether to abort or not, she will have to be allowed to follow her own judgement or the judgement of the religion to which she belongs. When a conflict of obligations takes place between two different persons who happen to share the same comprehensive views, then a strong legal framework oriented in favour of liberty should give them the opportunity to have their disagreement decided by an adjudicator applying the principles that belong to their comprehensive views. So for example, two Muslim people who disagree on the best way to apply a financial regulation they agreed, should have the freedom to opt for an adjudicator who is trained in sharia-based finance law. Finally, when two individuals whose comprehensive views differ have to resort to an external adjudicator in order to deal with a conflict of obligations, they should be free to opt for an arbitrator close to their interests. In these three cases the law does not pre-empt the solution of the conflict. Crucially, however, it creates a framework without which the liberty of each of those individuals would be radically limited.

Moreover, the law provides a last resort for the adjudication of those conflicts. If in any of those cases disagreement persists and a solution cannot be found, then the law through its constitutional principles and institutions should provide a last resort for adjudicating the conflict in a way that prevents polarization between different individuals and groups belonging to one society. At times, this will be possible through a carefully reasoned opinion. Other times, a choice will have to be made in favour of one comprehensive view over another. In the latter cases, preference will be given for the situation that enhances the principle of liberty protected by the legal framework. So for instance, if disagreement is raging between religious and non-religious people over the issue of the beginning and end of life for the purpose of adjudicating matters of abortion and euthanasia, the legal framework will have to prioritize permissibility over impermissibility.

Some may argue that to recognize a public marketplace of religions amounts to unduly legitimizing some religious norms and institutions, thereby entrenching discrimination towards vulnerable people within religious groups. For example, vulnerable women could be pressurized into agreeing to resolve their disputes before religious arbitration tribunals. Needless to say, putting pressure on anyone would be in itself punishable by ordinary law. But the point here is different. The alternative to a marketplace of religions is a black market of religions where religious norms are strictly applied in private away from the scrutinizing eye of the public. Women would equally be discriminated against and denied any access to justice be it ordinary or based on an alternative dispute resolution. Given this bleak picture, I have no doubt about choosing the marketplace of religions, which recognizes a great place for religions in the public sphere in exchange for a greater responsibility in justifying the legitimacy of religious norms within secular frameworks.

B   A phobia-free polity

The fact of (Islamo)phobia seems to me well established. People associated with Islam are readily caricatured and portrayed as irrational and violent, if not as terrorists. Their rights are therefore interpreted in a biased and limited way. I believe that robust secularism should provide a phobia-free environment where decisions about rights and duties of people can be reached under normal circumstances.

Conflicts of obligations are a good starting point for mutual knowledge. Some of the great issues of the beginning and end of life cannot be explained away by any secular or religious philosophy. Instead, each position should be pushed to articulate as much as possible its own reasons in a way that everyone can grasp and follow. This is the hard problem of public reason, a form of reason that speaks to everyone without discrimination. Is public reason possible given that it requires burdensome processes of translation for some people? Is it desirable, given that there is always something lost in translation from religious argument to public reason?

Mutual knowledge is costly, difficult and by any means imperfect. But it is also necessary and unavoidable. Secular people simply cannot afford to assume that their reasons are better and superior to any other religious view just because they believe their history shows that this is the case. Secular philosophy must constantly rearticulate the reasons for which it is better to live under a secular framework rather than a religious one. Moreover, secular philosophy should also accept that at times, in order to make communication possible between religious and non-religious people, it will have to sacrifice something of value. Secular reason is not the same thing as public reason. To move from one to another it is necessary to leave outside of the public realm some aspects of the secular comprehensive view.

Mutual knowledge inevitably leads to an interrogation of oneself. It is only when we compare our fundamental values with someone else that we can appreciate their strength and scope. When we are confronted with the way in which someone solves her own conflict of obligation, we are pushed to reflect about the way in which we would ourselves solve that conflict. In turn, this triggers the most fruitful interrogation on what we really stand for if we stand for anything. Thus, sharia law should not be a taboo, something unknown and offensive. Many members of the communities in which we live follow some of the precepts of sharia law and this does not prevent them from being good citizens at the same time. It is interesting to confront the way in which they solve some of the conflicts mentioned above so as to understand whether our fundamental values really differ so much as we believe they do. Some people who firmly reject any process of mutual knowledge would be surprised by how much their principles overlap with those of sharia law.

Even more importantly, any genuine mutual exchange would push each of us and our communities to articulate in the best possible way the fundamental tenets of European secular philosophies. Mutual knowledge can be beneficial in two ways. When agreement between apparently incompatible positions is found, then mutual acceptance is much easier. When disagreement is confirmed, each one of us is pushed to find a possible way out of the stalemate. The process of conflict pushes us toward more knowledge and in particular self-knowledge. Why do Europeans cherish their secular positions? It is not enough to state that that is a matter of fact and that secularism is a static commandment written in stone.

Robust secularism is necessary in order to guarantee coexistence between religious and non-religious people as well as between people of different religious creeds.

(i) The necessity of robust secularism

Secularism must be robust in many ways. First it must be robust as opposed to weak secularism that accepts too many shabby compromises: it should be a clear practical authority. Second, it must be robust in the articulation of its own fundamental tenets: it should be a clear theoretical authority. Third, secularism must be robust but not aggressive. It cannot impose solutions but only propose them. It cannot use the force of violence, but only the force of reason. Finally, secularism must be robust in order to guarantee an environment free from fears and phobias; this is the last point I want to discuss here and I will do so with reference to the conflict between free speech and the right not to be offended in one's religious beliefs.

Free speech is often regarded as a paramount concern of liberal democracies. In an age of Muhammad cartoons, one feels more compelled to pay greater attention to this problem. It does not mean that a genuine conflict exists. The case is presented as follows:

1. Free speech permits injurious and offensive statements.
2. Injurious and offensive statements against one religion are not permitted.

This case appears very difficult at first. However, to test this in a real context we can have a look at the way in which the Racial and Religious Hatred Act 2006 deals with the balance between free speech and the right to be screened from hatred. In section 29 J, after having defined what amounts to expression and behaviour that stirs up religious hatred, the Act states:

> Nothing in this Part shall be read or given effect in a way which prohibits or restricts discussion, criticism or expressions of antipathy, dislike, ridicule, insult or abuse of particular religions or the beliefs or practices of their adherents, or of any other belief system or the beliefs or practices of its adherents, or proselytising or urging adherents of a different religion or belief system to cease practising their religion or belief system.

The UK Racial and Religious Hatred Act 2006 defines away the conflict by setting what I call a presumption of priority. Free speech still sets the tone for the context in which we express ourselves. We presume that our words are free even when we want to criticize or ridicule another religion. The Act nonetheless carves out an egregious exception, which concerns behaviour and expression that intends to stir up religious hatred. How do we know what falls in the latter category? This will be part of a longer story that has to unfold in future years and concerns the relationship between various groups in a society. The best we can do is to avoid prefacing that relationship as a conflict.

What is possible to stress at this point, however, is the following. Fundamental rights adjudication tends to polarize positions in two opposite camps with two discrete arguments that are somehow decontextualized. But if we stop and think about the value of free speech, for example, it is clear that everyone has an interest in a background environment free of phobias and prejudices. If thoughts and beliefs are exchanged in a phobia-ridden environment, then the quality of expression is bound to be low and partisan. If, on the contrary, free exchange of ideas happen in an environment conducive to mutual understanding, then the overall quality of expression will be much higher. If we keep in mind this overall goal, then individual expression of hatred will somehow be permissible and yet immediately relegated to the dustbin of thoughts by the vast majority of people. Unfortunately, when we are living in a hysteric environment, expressions of hatred are only likely to raise the heat and lower the light.

Conclusion

The possibility of conflict between law and religion is actual and present. It must be thoroughly examined and understood before jumping at any normative conclusion as to how to solve those conflicts. As a matter of fact, some of the conflicts will not be solvable in a way that does not involve sacrifices for either religious or non-religious people. A religion that claims exclusive truth cannot possibly reach a compromise on issues that involve the denial of those very truths. Yet practical conflicts call for constant compromises. In order to avoid confusion it will be necessary to distinguish sharply between theoretical conflicts between comprehensive views on what to believe and practical conflicts between those views on how to behave. If conflicts can be freely allowed at the theoretical level, there must be a cutting point at the practical one. The cutting point does not have to follow orthodox lines between the public and the private sphere. A bigger role for religion in the public sphere can be allowed, but it also has to be strictly regulated.

At the theoretical level, the best we can do is to promote mutual knowledge in order to understand why compromises cannot be accepted on comprehensive grounds. To know more about the way in which religions deal with general issues of morality can equally help everyone push their own boundaries in order to find better solutions. Theoretical conflicts should be welcome as they provide a constant engine for finding better and more articulated responses to common present problems and challenges. Disagreement at the theoretical level can only be beneficial if it is a spur to further thinking.

At the practical level, however, conflicts are not tolerable if they push different groups of a society in totally different directions, thereby giving rise to an unbridgeable gap or excessive polarization. Here again it is necessary to distinguish between micro- and macro-management of conflicts. At the micro-level, it is desirable to leave individuals and groups free to decide how to behave by following one of the possible solutions based on comprehensive views of a religion or of any other system of thought. At the macro-level, however, secular law must necessarily set out what happens if religious and non-religious comprehensive views are unable to give guidance locally on how to behave in cases of conflicts of obligations.

Europe is blessed and cursed with the fact of pluralism. Each European should realize that the fundamental values in which she believes are at the same time sacred and fragile. Liberty and equality, to take but one example, are the outcome of many centuries of struggle and yet can be lost and compromised away very quickly. By deciding where one stands on conflict of values, one reaffirms and ranks those values. It is a particularly difficult exercise which needs to be carried out under the best possible cognitive conditions. If we let fear and suspicion guide those fundamental decisions, we would simply jettison our values. In particular, we would jettison our very premise of value pluralism. European societies must rise to that challenge and show that they can cope with disagreement and difference better than they do at the moment.

7

Unveiling the limits of tolerance: comparing the treatment of majority and minority religious symbols in the public sphere

SUSANNA MANCINI AND MICHEL ROSENFELD

1 The constitutional treatment of religion: the challenge of strong religion and fundamentalisms

Globalization poses two daunting challenges to traditional approaches to reconciling constitutionalism and religion. First, large-scale migration makes constitutional democracies much more religiously diverse, leading to confrontations between newly arrived religions that are at significant odds with prevailing mores and well-entrenched religions established in the country of immigration. Moreover, intensification of religious fanaticism and fundamentalism – including that behind global terrorism – are presumed a direct reaction to dislocations and inequities associated with globalization[1].

Second, the concurrent process of globalization and privatization has led to a blurring of the line between the public sphere and the private sphere. Religion has become "deprivatized," in a trend started in the 1980s in countries as different as Iran, Poland, Brazil and the United States,[2] thus not only seeking a much increased role in the public sphere but also in the political arena. Consequently, reconciliation of constitutionalism and religion through adherence to secularism in the public place becomes increasingly difficult and contested.

The revival of religion in pluralist and multicultural settings steeped in identity politics seriously challenges the legitimacy of the dominant conception of constitutionalism anchored in the principle of secularism. Theoretically, there is a radical challenge to the essential tenets

---

[1] G. Borradori, *Philosophy in a Time of Terror: Dialogues with Jürgen Habermas and Jacques Derrida* (Chicago University Press, 2003).
[2] J. Casanova, *Public Religions in the Modern World* (Chicago University Press, 1994).

that animate the project of the Enlightenment: a clear-cut distinction between faith and reason; commitment to entrusting the public sphere to the rule of reason; and promotion of equal liberty for all. Moreover, certain practices associated with the Enlightenment project may have often been inconsistent, but its theoretical foundations have been steadfast throughout. For example, a political actor can be motivated by his religious faith and yet his political actions would remain consistent with secularism so long as he sought to influence and persuade other political actors through arguments deriving from public reason.[3] Indeed, certain contemporary religions are compatible with such use of public reason, but others are not. Fundamentalist religions often seem incompatible with the rule of public reason, and in the context of the revival of religion, even certain non-fundamentalist religions may find it unduly constraining.

Concurrently, a radical postmodern philosophical attack has been launched against a key Enlightenment tenet, namely the cleavage between the realm of reason and that of faith.[4] The postmodern challenge builds on the "disenchantment of reason" associated with the perception that reason as the means to the implantation of a universally justified rational order gives way to purely instrumental reason – that is a use of reason for purposes of advancing the narrow interests of the powerful, fostering colonialism and neo-colonialism, exacerbating disparities in wealth, and so on.[5] The reduction of reason to instrumental reason turns the means of the Enlightenment against its ends, and particularly against the pursuit of liberty and equality for all.

As instrumental reason spreads, alienated social actors tend to retreat to individualist isolation in futile opposition to an increasingly oppressive and meaningless social reality.[6] This produces a fragmentation of competing postmodern visions fueled by subjectivism stemming from disenchanted individualist isolation.[7] In this postmodern setting, all

---

[3] See J. Rawls, *Political Liberalism* (New York: Columbia University Press, 1993).

[4] M. Rosenfeld, "A Pluralist Critique of the Constitutional Treatment of Religion" in András Sajó and Sholomo Avineri (eds), *The Law of Religious Identity. Models for Post-Communism* (The Hague: Kluwer Law International, 1999) pp. 39–40.

[5] J. Habermas, "Conceptions of Modernity: A Look Back at Two Traditions" in J. Habermas, *The Postnational Constellation: Political Essays* (Cambridge: Polity Press, 2001), pp. 130, 138–40.

[6] *Ibid.*, p. 140.

[7] See J. Habermas, "The Postnational Constellation and the Future of Democracy" in J. Habermas, *The Postnational Constellation: Political Essays* (Cambridge: Polity Press, 2001), pp. 58, 88.

competing discourses and conceptions of the good emerge as ultimately purely subjective and equivalent, thus negating any priority to secularism, modernism, reason or Enlightenment values.[8] Accordingly, the Enlightenment project is full of contradictions and irrationalism, and passion and subjectivism are frequently prone to overcome the rule of reason. As the line between reason and the irrational blurs and the private and public spheres collapse into one another, the foundations that lend support to the nexus between constitutionalism and secularism seem increasingly precarious.

These developments have huge theoretical and practical implications that are closely linked to one another. For those both religious and secular who wish to avert the implantation of religious hegemonies or of war among religions, it is imperative to rethink how a new viable nexus between constitutionalism and religious pluralism may be theoretically grounded and practically implemented. Under current constitutional practice, there are essentially five different models for managing the relationship between the state and religion. These are:

1. the militant secularist model bent on keeping religion completely out of the public sphere (e.g., French and Turkish *laïcité*);
2. the agnostic secularist model which seeks to maintain a neutral stance among religions but does not shy away from favoring religion over atheism and other non-religious perspectives (this is close to current American constitutional jurisprudence);
3. the confessional secular model, which incorporates elements of the polity's mainstream majority religion, primarily for identitarian purposes, and projects them as part of the polity's constitutional secularism rather than as inextricably linked to the country's main religion (e.g., Italy's or Bavaria's adoption of the crucifix as a secular symbol of national identity);
4. the official religion with institutionalized tolerance for minority religions model (e.g. the United Kingdom, Scandinavian countries, Greece);
5. and the *millet*-based model in which high priority is given to collective self-government by each religious community within the polity (e.g., Israel).

[8] For a discussion of the contrast between Derrida's and Habermas' understanding of the historical deployment of the Enlightenment project, see M. Rosenfeld, "Derrida's Ethical Turn and America: Looking Back from the Crossroads of Global Terrorism and the Enlightenment," *Cardozo Law Review* (2005), 815, 826–31, 836–7.

All of these models have serious shortcomings. The militant secularist model, purportedly neutral toward religion, often seems downright hostile to it and, particularly, to minority denominations. Think of the French law of March 17, 2004, which prohibits "the wearing of symbols or clothing by which students conspicuously manifest a religious appearance" in all state schools.[9] This law is neutrally worded and therefore theoretically applicable to all symbols, including Christian ones. Controversies, however, have arisen exclusively in relation to the right of pupils belonging to religious minorities to wear symbols such as the veil, the *kippah*, and the turban, which, unlike the small crucifixes usually worn by Christians, are by nature conspicuous. The agnostic secular model, though arguably open to all religions, puts those who do not embrace a religious conception of the good at a disadvantage. In the confessional secularism model the state privileges the "national religious inheritance" as a key element of civic cohesion, thus granting preferential treatment to the "historical national religion" and mere tolerance to all others. This is potentially doubly problematic: on the one hand, it excludes minority religions and non-religious ideologies from the mainstream in such a way as to cut off or diminish the role of the latter in the building of national identity; on the other hand, if adherents to the majority religion are divided among the culturally attached and the deeply religiously committed to it, the latter may object to attempts to "secularize" sacred symbols. The Italian and German controversies over the display of the crucifix in public schools are good examples of this phenomenon. The official national religion model is explicit about privileging the country's majority religion, but seems prone to insufficient tolerance of minority religions and of non-practicing members of the official religion. Thus, Greece, which operates under this model, is the only European Union country to ban proselytism in its constitution.[10] Finally, the *millet* system is unsatisfactory too in that it tends unduly to disadvantage non-conformists or dissidents within recognized religious communities, and to thwart secular initiatives such as the polity-wide pursuit of gender-based equality.

This chapter focuses on key current questions through a comparative analysis of the treatment of displays of religious symbols in public places. These questions include: whether, assuming commitment to pluralism, multiculturalism and religious and non-religious comprehensive

---

[9] Law No. 2004–228 of March 15, 2004, Journal Officiel de la République Française [JO][Official Gazette of France], March 17, 2004, p. 5190.

[10] See Art. 13, para. 2, Greek Constitution, 1975

views, there may be ways to improve on existing models or to replace them with better suited ones given the new religious and political realities; and whether tolerance can be redeployed to boost pluralism while avoiding irreconcilable conflicts between religious fundamentalism and secularism.

The place of religious symbols in public spaces provides a particularly good case study in as much as conflicts over such symbols constitute a direct challenge to the legitimacy of the dominant conception of constitutionalism as inextricably linked to secularism. In a pluralistic society, religious symbols play a key role in identity-related dynamics. Moreover, globalization, large-scale migration and the aftermath of September 11, 2001 have dramatically increased the quest for social cohesion and strong collective identities. Religious symbols figure prominently in this quest because they evoke absolute, and therefore reassuring, truths, although they can easily turn into catalyzers of aggression, to the extent that they generate blind fixations and unquestioned adherences.[11] Religious symbols at once unite and divide, thus setting barriers between self and other. Majorities and minorities seek shelter in religious symbols, as a reflex against the increasing difficulty they experience in finding a common core of shared civic values. Moreover, a comparative analysis of the reactions of courts and legislators confronted with such conflicts reveals a tendency to counter or minimize pluralism, rather than to seek a reasonable accommodation of the different religions within the polity.

Furthermore, conflicts over religious symbols lead to blurring of the line between secularism and religion. Whether in conflicts over majority (e.g. the crucifix) or over minority (e.g. the Islamic veil) symbols, courts and legislators often secularize the meaning of religious symbols and interpret it consistent with the sensibilities, prejudices and identitarian claims of the majority. On the one hand, the religious significance of majority (Christian) symbols is watered down and presented in "cultural" terms as indicia of the historical and cultural dimensions of national identity only incidentally linked to a particular religion. On the other hand, minority, and, particularly Islamic, symbols are cast as expressions of cultural and political values and practices at odds with liberal and democratic ones. As a practical consequence of this trend, crucifixes may be displayed in public schools because secularized Christianity becomes a structural element

---

[11] L. L. Vallauri, "Simboli e Realizzazione" in E. Dieni, A. Ferrari and V. Pacillo (eds.), *Symbolon/Diabolon: Simboli, Religioni, diritti nell'Europa multiculturale* (Bologna: Il Mulino, 2005), p. 14.

of Western constitutional identity, while the wearing of Islamic symbols is banned or restricted because they are portrayed as portents of illiberal and undemocratic values.

2 Religious tolerance and cultural Christianity

From a constitutional standpoint, the modern state steeped in the normative order issuing from the Enlightenment should at once be neutral regarding religion, by neither favoring it nor disfavoring it within its public sphere, and be equally protective of its citizens' freedom *of* and *from* religion within the private sphere. Many constitutions reflect this dual constitutional prescription. Thus, the US Constitution's "Establishment Clause" prohibits the state from adopting, preferring or endorsing a religion whereas its "Free Exercise Clause" enjoins the state from interfering with the religious freedom of its citizens.[12] Article 1 of the French Constitution specifies the secular character of the Republic and the duty of the state to respect all beliefs.[13] Other constitutions only contain a free exercise clause, but implicitly embed the principle of separation in the founding principles of the system. This is the case in Italy where in the absence of any explicit constitutional provision, the Constitutional Court's jurisprudence[14] has instituted secularism (*laicità*) as a fundamental principle of the Italian legal system, prescribing state "equidistance and impartiality with respect to different faiths ... in order to protect freedom of religion in a context of religious and cultural pluralism."[15] The United Kingdom, in contrast, has an official church, but also a high degree of accommodation for minority religions yielding a model of "inclusive multiculturalism." In Germany there is no strict separation between church and state and the constitution of the each *Land* regulates the role of religion in the public sphere according to its dominant religious tradition. All *Länder* constitutions, however, protect religious freedom and prohibit discrimination on the ground of religion.

---

[12] US Constitution Amend. I, 1791.

[13] Art. 1, French Constitution, 1958.

[14] Corte cost., April 11, 1989, n.203, available at www.giurcost.org/decisioni/1989/0203s-89.html (last accessed September 5, 2011).

[15] Corte cost., July 1, 2002, n.327; Corte cost., November 13, 2000, n.508; Corte cost., October 11, 1997, n.329; Corte cost., September 30, 1996, n.334; Corte cost., November 29, 1993, n.421; Corte cost., April 19, 1993, n.195; Corte cost., January 11, 1989, n.13; Corte cost., May 23, 1990, n.259; Corte cost., April 11, 1989, n.203. All of these cases are available at the Constitutional Court's website www.cortecostituzionale.it/actionGiurisprudenza.do (last accessed September 5, 2011).

In all the above cases the constitutional handling of the relationship between religion and the state draws on the Enlightenment but remains far short of its ideals. This is hardly surprising given the wide gap between Enlightenment ideals and how they have actually fared since they were launched in the eighteenth century. A telling example of this is provided by contemporary constitutional jurisprudence regarding the relationship between religion and the state. Secularization and the transition to liberalism resulted in a state model no longer endorsing a conception of the good related to a particular religion, but that put in question the powers of integration of a secularized society. The nation state with its emphasis on a distinct national identity anchored in a common history, language, tradition and culture displaced religious belief as the source of integration of the polity, but that did not preclude religion's persistent survival as an implicit mainstay engrained in the secular nation's tradition and culture. And because of Europe's overwhelmingly Christian heritage, repression of the latter quite naturally prompted its return as (Christian) culture and tradition.[16]

Conflicts over religious symbols provide a particularly salient example of how the entanglement between national identity and the polity's Christian heritage actually shapes the understanding of religious tolerance and informs the interpretation of religious rights. To illustrate this, we will first analyze the type of conflict that arises when a religious symbol deriving from the majority religion is used as a component of the "public language" of identity by state authorities. We will then turn to the kind of conflict that arises when the individual right to wear religious symbols and clothing is sought to be limited in the name of other rights and principles that bear equal constitutional value. In principle, this second type of conflict may arise equally in relation to the majority religion and to minority ones. Comparative analysis will demonstrate, however, that controversies have almost exclusively concerned minority symbols, chief among them the Islamic headscarf.

3   The putative neutrality of Christianity and the desecration of majority symbols

The display of Christian symbols in state schools has been challenged in many countries, including the United States, Switzerland, Germany and

---

[16] See D. Augenstein, *A European Culture of Religious Tolerance*, European University Institute Working Paper LAW 2008/04, p. 7.

Italy. The Italian and Bavarian judgments on the display of the crucifix are particularly clear examples of the blurring of the line between religion and secularism.

In 2005 Italian administrative courts ruled on the legitimacy of the display of the crucifix in state schools,[17] and concluded that "[t]he crucifix … may be legitimately displayed in the public schools because it does not clash with the principle of secularism, but, on the contrary, it actually affirms it."[18] Much to the disbelief of most constitutional law scholars stands the assertion that secularism has been achieved in Italy thanks to the founding Christian values. Accordingly, it would be paradoxical to exclude a Christian symbol from the public domain because of the principle of secularism, which is supposed to be actually rooted in Christianity.

According to these courts, the crucifix does not have a univocal religious significance, but several that are context dependent. In a church it has a religious significance, but in a school it also embodies social and cultural values widely shared even among non-believers. In the public schools the crucifix is a religious symbol for believers, but it also evokes the fundamental state values that constitute the basis of the Italian legal order for all citizens. The crucifix, therefore, has an important educative function regardless of the religion of the schoolchildren.

Earlier, in 1991, the Bavarian Supreme Court had similarly reasoned:

> [w]ith the representation of the cross as the icon of the suffering and Lordship of Jesus Christ … the plaintiffs who reject such a representation are confronted with a religious worldview in which the formative power of Christian beliefs is affirmed. However, they are not thereby brought into a constitutionally unacceptable religious–philosophical conflict. Representations of the cross confronted in this fashion … are … not the expression of a conviction of a belief bound to a specific confession. They are an essential object of the general Christian–occidental tradition and common property of the Christian–occidental cultural circle.[19]

---

[17] The crucifix is listed in the "furnishing of all classrooms" of public schools in two royal decrees that date back to the 1920s (Art. 19 of the royal decree n. 1297 of April 26, 1928 and Art. 118 of the royal decree n. 965 of April 30, 1924) The two royal decrees had been enacted by the fascist government before the 1948 Constitution came into force. These decrees are administrative law sources, and thus the Constitutional Court cannot review them, as it may only review primary sources originating in the legislature.

[18] TAR Veneto, Mar. 17, 2005, n.1110, para. 16.1.

[19] Bayerischer Verwaltungsgerichtshof [BayVGH] [Bavarian Higher Administrative Court] June 3, 1991, p. 122; Bayerische Verwaltungsblatter [BayVBl] pp. 751–4, (FRG), reprinted in *Neue Zeitschrift fuer Verwaltungsrechts [New Journal of Administrative Law]*, Issue 11, 1991, p. 1099.

It follows that the placing of a crucifix in classrooms of state schools does not injure the basic rights (to negative freedom) of pupils and parents who, on religious or philosophical grounds, reject such representation.

A liberal democracy cannot plausibly impose an *obligation* to display the crucifix in public schools, without weakening or neutralizing its religious significance. The Italian and Bavarian courts accordingly had to proceed to disarticulate the semantic significance of the crucifix.[20] Thus, the crucifix loses its specific (religious) value and becomes a general symbol of civilization and culture, available for free use by the state to meet the needs of the political community. Such an instrumental use of religion is not only inappropriate from a secular political and ethical point of view, but it also prompts government interference in church matters contrary to the principle of state neutrality or equidistance. This was actually stressed in the German Federal Constitutional Court's 1995 judgment prohibiting the display of the cross in Bavarian state schools on the ground that the pressure to learn "under the cross" is in conflict with the neutrality of the state in religious matters.[21] Moreover, according to the Court,[22] not considering the crucifix as a religious symbol connected with a specific religion violates the religious autonomy of Christians and actually produces a desecration of the crucifix itself. A similar argument is found in Justice Brennan's dissenting opinion in the US Supreme Court decision in *Lynch* v. *Donnelly*[23] where the Court's majority concluded that the city of Pawtucket, RI, had not violated the Establishment Clause by including a crèche in its annual Christmas display. However, in Brennan's view:

> The crèche has been relegated to the role of a neutral harbinger of the holiday season, useful for commercial purposes, but devoid of any inherent meaning and incapable of enhancing the religious tenor of a display of which it is an integral part. The import of the Court's decision is to encourage use of the crèche in a ... setting where Christians feel constrained in acknowledging its symbolic meaning and non-Christians feel alienated by its presence. Surely, this is a misuse of a sacred symbol.[24]

---

[20] A. Morelli, "Simboli, religioni e valori negli ordinamenti democratici" in E. Dieni, *I simboli religiosi tra diritto e culture* (Milan: A. Giuffrè, 2006) [hereinafter *I simboli religiosi*), p. 85.

[21] Bundesverfassungsgericht [BVerfG] [Federal Constitutional Court] May 16, 1995 (*Kruzifix-Urteil*), 93 Entscheidungen des Bundesverfassungsgerichts [BVerfGE] 1 (FRG), available at www.kirchen.net/upload/1232_Kreuz.pdf (last accessed September 5, 2011).

[22] *Kruzifix-Urteil*, 93 BVerfGE 1.

[23] *Lynch* v. *Donnelly*, 465 U.S. 668 (1984).

[24] *Lynch* v. *Donnelly* [465 U.S. 668, 728].

Another recurrent element in the "crucifix cases" is the supposed universal character of Christianity *as opposed* to the parochial nature of other denominations. Although neither the Italian nor the Bavarian challenges to the display of the crucifix were brought by Muslims, the two judgments rely explicitly on a comparison between Christianity and Islam, concluding that whereas the former is rooted in the state's democratic values, the latter is incompatible with them. Thus Christianity, *unlike other religions*, is presumed inherently inclusive of the tolerance and freedom that are pillars of the secular state. According to the Italian court, there is "a perceptible affinity ... between the essential core of Christianity" and that "of the Italian Constitution." The Court does admit that "during history, many incrustations were settled on the two cores, and especially on Christianity,"[25] but nonetheless, harmony between the two endures because "despite the Inquisition, anti-Semitism and the Crusades" it is "easy" (!) to recognize the most profound core of Christianity in the "principles of dignity, tolerance and religious freedom and therefore in the very foundation of a secular state."[26] Moreover, the display of the crucifix does not discriminate between Christians and non-Christians, because "exclusion of infidels is common to all religions except Christianity, which considers faith in the omniscient secondary to charity, that is to say respect for the others." It follows that "the rejection by a Christian of those who do not believe implies the radical denial of Christianity itself, a substantial abjuration, which is not the case in other religions."[27] Which "other religions" the judge refers to is no mystery as the judgment refers to "the problematic relationship between certain states and the *Islamic* religion."[28] The Court also refers explicitly to the two principal preoccupations that cause Westerners sleeplessness after 9/11: the clash of civilizations and the threat of Islamic fundamentalism. According to the Court, globalization and large-scale migration make it "indispensable to reaffirm, even symbolically, our identity (through the display of the crucifix), in order to avoid a clash of civilizations." Consistent with this, the Court emphasizes that the crucifix – which embodies the value of tolerance – must be displayed in public schools, in order to teach "*non European pupils* ... to reject all forms of *fundamentalism*."[29]

In the Bavarian case the Court draws the contrast even more starkly. Its judgment explicitly differentiates between the approved display of the crucifix and "cases in which the teacher ... through the wearing of

---

[25] TAR Veneto, Mar. 17, 2005, n.1110, para. 11.7.
[26] *Ibid.*, para. 11.6.   [27] *Ibid.*, para. 13.3.
[28] *Ibid.*, para. 10.1, emphasis added.   [29] *Ibid.*, emphasis added.

attention-drawing clothing (Baghwan)... which unambiguously indicates a specific religious or philosophical conviction, impermissibly impairs the basic right to negative religious freedom of pupil and parent."[30]

A similar belief in the universal nature of Christianity, but not of other religions, was recently expressed by US Supreme Court Justice Antonin Scalia, during the oral argument in the case of *Salazar* v. *Buono*,[31] a case dealing with the constitutionality of the display in a military cemetery of an eight-foot-high Christian cross, originally erected as a memorial to soldiers killed in war. Justice Scalia defined as an "outrageous conclusion" the observation made by the plaintiff's attorney, that "the only war dead that that cross honours are the Christian war dead." Stating that "the cross is the most common symbol of the resting place of the dead," Scalia asked "What would you have them erect? – A cross – some conglomerate of a cross, a Star of David, and you know a Moslem half moon and star?"[32]

The attorney's reaction ("I have been in Jewish cemeteries. There is never a cross on a tombstone of a Jew"[33]) apparently provoked a burst of laughter in the Courtroom,[34] but Scalia's comment remains troubling.

In many constitutional democracies, the notion of secularism as equidistance by the state in relation to the different faiths is increasingly under attack. It Italy, for example, not only the Vatican, but also leading political players suggest that a "new" understanding of secularism is needed, a "positive" or "healthy" one to counter the relativistic wave that Western democracies are supposedly currently experiencing. "Positive" secularism does not place all denominations on an equal footing: it calls for the state to recognize that the "national religious inheritance" is not just one among several denominations, but rather a key component of civic cohesion.[35] This seeks to justify preferential treatment for the "historical national religion" and mere tolerance for the rest.[36]

This "positive" understanding of secularism is by no means "new." Gustavo Zagrebelsky defines it as a "pale reincarnation of the past, a sort of 'semi-secularism' that represents what remains of the old dream of the 'Christian Republic', and is based on the opposite of the Westphalian principle: *cuius religio, eius et regio*."[37] The result is a "new form of alliance between religion and public power, where the ethical force of the first one upholds the political force of the latter and vice versa."[38]

---

[30] *Neue Juristiche Wochenschrift*, 38 (1995), p. 1101.

[31] *Ken L. Salazar et al.* v. *Frank Buono*, No. 08–472, October 7, 2009, oral argument.

[32] *Ibid.*, p. 39.   [33] *Ibid.*   [34] *Ibid.*

[35] G. Zagrebelsky, *Stato e Chiesa. Cittadini e cattolici, Passato e Presente*, Issue 73, 2008, p. 16.

[36] *Ibid.*, p. 17.   [37] *Ibid.*, p. 18.   [38] *Ibid.*, p. 19.

The crucifix cases mesh with this "new" understanding of secularism, which can be characterized as "post-secular"[39] or "confessional" secularism. Judges do not contest the viability of secularism, but they interpret it in a way that makes it compatible with granting privileges to Christianity, thus denying any clear-cut distinction between the realm of faith and that of reason, and refusing to confine the public sphere to the latter realm.

4   Unveiling the limits of tolerance: Islam as the irreconcilable "other"

There is a striking contrast between the treatment of Christian symbols and those belonging to religious minorities, particularly in the context of public schools. Surprisingly, in spite of significant variations in their country's management of the relationship between religion and the state, German, British and French cases all subject Islamic symbols to a process of semantic disarticulation resulting in interpretation according to majoritarian cultural parameters. The mechanism is analogous to the one applied by the Italian and Bavarian judges in the crucifix cases analyzed above. Unlike in the latter, however, the conclusion in cases involving Islamic symbols is that these (or certain variants of them) cannot be legitimately displayed because they are associated with beliefs and behavior that contradict the essential values that state schools must promote. Among such values, gender equality, characterized as a singularly Western value, plays a key role.

The same pattern emerges in the European Court of Human Rights' "veil jurisprudence." In adjudicating the legitimacy of bans on wearing the veil, the ECtHR, while formally relying on the doctrine of the margin of appreciation, consistently interprets the *hijab* as a religious symbol which cannot be reconciled with Western values. Thus, the Court not only grants wide deference to national authorities in determining the significance of the veil, but it also makes the value judgment, concluding that wearing the *hijab* can be legitimately prohibited because it objectively endangers democratic values.

A   Germany

Five German *Länder* have adopted laws that prohibit Islamic symbols but specifically permit Christian ones in public schools

---

[39]   *Ibid.*

(Baden-Württemberg,[40] Saarland,[41] Hesse,[42] Bavaria[43] and North Rhine-Westphalia[44]). These laws constitute a direct reaction to a Constitutional Court judgment concerning the wearing of the veil by a teacher.[45] That teacher was refused a permanent civil servant post in a primary school in the conservative *Land* of Baden-Württemberg because she insisted on wearing the veil, which prompted the conclusion that she had a "lack of personal aptitude." The Constitutional Court ruled that German *Länder* had the right to ban teachers from wearing the veil as long as they passed specific laws on the matter, which prompted the *Länder* with the strongest Catholic traditions to adopt specific laws on the issue. The law enacted in Baden-Württemberg in 2004 prohibits teachers from "exercis[ing] political, religious, ideological or similar manifestations," particularly if they constitute "a demonstration against human dignity, non discrimination." However, the "exhibition of Christian and occidental educational and cultural values and traditions does not contradict" such prohibition. Human Rights Watch interviewed officials from the Baden-Württemberg Ministry of Education, Youth and Sport, who confirmed that Christian clothing and display were deliberately exempted by the legislature and that nuns' habits, the cross, and the *kippah* are permitted.[46] The law adopted in Saarland affirms that the "[s]chool has to teach and educate pupils on the basis of Christian educational and cultural values." The Hessian law bans all civil servants including public school teachers, from wearing religious clothing and symbols that may jeopardize the "neutrality of the administration and state" or endanger the "political and religious peace" in the state. To determine what is banned under this law, the "humanist- and Christian-influenced Western tradition of the Land of Hesse has to be taken into due account."

[40] Gesetz zur Änderung des Schulgesetzes, April 1, 2004, and Gesetz zur Änderung des Kindergartengesetzes, February 14, 2006.
[41] Gesetz Nr. 1555 zur Änderung des Gesetzes zur Ordnung des Schulwesens im Saarland (Schulordnungsgesetz), June 23, 2004. In the explanation to the draft law, it is stated that the regulation is not limited to headscarves; however, the wearing of Christian and Jewish symbols remains possible.
[42] Gesetz zur Sicherung der staatlichen Neutralität, October 18, 2004.
[43] Gesetz zur Änderung des Bayerischen Gesetzes über das Erziehungs- und Unterrichtswesen, November 23, 2004.
[44] Erstes Gesetz zur Änderung des Schulgesetzes für das Land Nordrhein-Westfalen, June 13, 2006.
[45] Ludin, Bundesverfassungericht, September 24, 2003, 2BvR, 1436/02.
[46] Human Rights Watch, "Discrimination in the Name of Neutrality. Headscarf Bans for Teachers and Civil Servants in Germany," p. 26, available at www.hrw.org/reports/2009/02/26/discrimination-name-neutrality-0 (last accessed August 11, 2011).

In Bavaria nuns' habits are allowed[47] because, as a ministry official stated, a nun's habit is not a political symbol, while a headscarf can also be a political symbol conflicting with the equality of women.[48]

The governing parties introducing the draft laws in the North Rhine-Westphalia parliament emphasized the importance of the "Christian Western and European tradition," arguing that it is "not a breach of the neutrality requirement if a teacher commits to this tradition."[49] It follows that "the nun's habit and Jewish *kippah* remain permissible."[50]

B   *The United Kingdom*

The United Kingdom has not adopted any general regulation concerning the wearing of religious symbols and clothing by teachers and pupils. Schools have different rules and the Islamic headscarf is commonly worn in British state schools. One particularly thorny case, however, directly questioned the basis of religious tolerance and revealed a number of ambiguities regarding the British inclusive multicultural model. The case decided by the House of Lords in 2005 concerned the uniform policy of a maintained secondary community school. With about 79% of its pupils being Muslim, the school offered three uniform options. The dress code was decided after consultation with parents, students, staff and the imams of the three local mosques. All agreed that one of the options, the *shalwar kameez*, satisfied Islamic requirements of modest dress for Muslim girls. However, Shabina Begum, a Bengali pupil who had worn the *shalwar kameez* without complaint for two years, claimed the right to wear a long coat-like garment (*jilbab*), which alone met her religious requirements of concealing the contours of the female body, as was required for maturing girls, more than the *shalwar kameez* was able to do. Her claim was rejected and she never returned to school. The House of Lords upheld the school's uniform policy.[51]

"The substance of its majority position – It has been argued – may be summarized as follows: the head teacher is clearly a good and sensible head teacher, the dress code was drawn up in a reasonable way after wide consultation, schools are entitled to have dress codes, and therefore we

---

[47] Human Rights Watch, "Discrimination in the Name of Neutrality," p. 26.

[48] *Ibid.*   [49] *Ibid.* p. 28.   [50] *Ibid.*

[51] *Regina (Shabina Begum)* v. *Governors of Denbigh High Sch.* [2006] UKHL 15, [2007] 1 AC 100 (H.L.) (appeal taken from Eng.).

feel no inclination to interfere." Added by Baroness Hale is the proposition (paraphrased here) "and she is a child, whose religious views may be taken less seriously than those of an adult, and for whom schools should provide a place of protection from undue religious pressure from family and community."[52]

Many children are likely to encounter similar pressure within a number of religious communities, including fundamentalist Christians and orthodox Jews. Moreover, pressuring children to comply with religious duties is regarded as normal in mainstream religion. No judge has ever ruled that it is illegitimate for a Catholic family to impose on its children attendance at Sunday Mass, even if they would prefer to spend the day differently. When it comes to Islam, however, judges and legislators seem to feel a greater necessity to protect children's rights. There is a final disturbing element in the *Begum* case, which is expressed in the concern that allowing the *jilbab* would create two categories of Muslims within the school, which might lead to conflict, threatening the harmony and good functioning of the school as a whole. Their Lordship are certainly aware that in the many-sided Islamic world, there exist more than two categories of Muslims and that the idea that a head teacher, three local imams and a group of parents from Luton are entitled to vouch for the preferences and the needs of *all* Muslims is rather absurd. However, the Court seems to embrace this reductive version of Islam, where there is no room for diversity or for minorities within minorities: in short a watered-down version of Islam that seems less foreboding.

C   France

In July 2003, after the French courts had struggled for over a decade over the right of Muslim schoolgirls to wear the veil, President Chirac set up an investigative committee, with the task to reflect on the application of the principle of secularism. The commission, chaired by Bernard Stasi, the French state's ombudsman, interviewed representatives from different groups: political and religious leaders, school principals, social and civil

---

[52] G. Davies, "(Not Yet) Taking Rights Seriously: The House of Lords in *Begum* v. *Headteacher and Governors of Denbigh High School*," Human Rights & Human Welfare, Working Paper No. 37, 2006, available at www.ssrn.com/abstract=945319 (last accessed August 11, 2011).

rights groups. In December 2003 it issued a report,[53] which eventually led to the introduction of the law of 2004 which prohibits the display of religious symbols in state schools. Moreover, in order to clear the field of all ambiguities concerning what symbols the law was meant to target, after the law's enactment the Minister of Education issued a decree according to which "[t]he prohibited signs and dress are those by which the wearer is immediately recognizable in terms of his or her religion, such as the *Islamic veil*, whatever its name, the *kippah* or a crucifix of *manifestly exaggerated dimensions*."[54]

It had been estimated that less than one percent of the Muslim students in France had actually worn the veil. In particular, a total of 1,256 *foulards* were reported in France's public schools at the start of the 2003–04 school year. Only twenty of these cases were judged "difficult" by school officials.[55]

Five years after the enactment of the "veil law," after suffering a heavy electoral defeat in the regional elections, French President Sarkozy launched a campaign against the *burqa/niqab* type of veil. In September 2010 the French parliament adopted a new law making it illegal to wear full-face veils in public.[56] The statistics of the Interior Ministry indicate that the number of women who wear the *burqa* in France is no more than 1,900.[57]

In preparation of the enactment of the "burqa law," the French National Assembly drafted a report,[58] which is in many ways analogous to that released by the Stasi Commission. In the view of the latter, the ban of religious symbols was necessary to maintain public order, as "wearing an ostensibly religious symbol … suffices to disrupt the tranquillity of the life of the school."[59] The relationship between the presence of the symbols

---

[53] Commission de reflexion sur l'application du principe de laïcité dans la republique, "Rapport au president de la republique," available at www.lesrapports.ladocumentation-francaise.fr/BRP/034000725/0000.pdf (last accessed August 11, 2011).

[54] Circulaire Nr. 2004–084 of May 18, 2004, Journal Officiel de la Republique Française [JO] [Official Gazette of France], May 22, 2004, emphasis added.

[55] Elaine R. Thomas, "Keeping Identity at a Distance: Explaining France's New Legal Restrictions on the Islamic Headscarf," *Ethnic & Racial Studies* 29 (2006), 237, 239.

[56] Law n. 2010–1192 of October 11, 2010 (Journal Officiel, October 12, 2010). The Conseil Constitutionnel upheld the constitutionality of this law, stipulating only that the ban should not apply to public places of worship; judgement n. 613 DC of October 7, 2010.

[57] Assemblée nationale, "Rapport d'information n. 2262, au nom de la mission d'information sur la pratique du port du voile intégral sur le territoire national," January 26, 2010, p. 28. [hereinafter Rapport 2262], available at: www.assemblee-nationale.fr/13/rap-info/i2262.asp (last accessed September 5, 2011).

[58] Rapport 2262.

[59] Commission de reflexion sur l'application du principe de laïcité dans la republique, "Rapport au president de la republique," p. 41.

and the disruption of school studies, however, is far from clear. The Stasi Commission referred to a number of practices (all associated with Islam), such as "course and examination interruptions to pray or fast," the refusal by schoolgirls to engage in sporting activities and the objections by pupils to "entire sections of courses in history or earth science,"[60] which certainly have a disruptive potential, but are neither caused nor aggravated by the use of the veil. The Commission also viewed Islamic headscarves as a threat to public order because they are associated with communitarianism.[61] The report mentions the difficult socio-economic situations of the *banlieue* inhabited by "many nationalities" (unemployment, poor school attendance etc.) and the risk that "communitarian groups with politics based on religion exploit this actual social unrest in order to mobilize activists."[62]

A similar pattern used by the drafters of the new proposed resolution on the *burqa* heavily relies on unproven assumptions and on the dialectic of the clash of civilizations. According to it, "The evidence we have gathered during our hearings show also the difficulties and the deep unease felt by people who every day are in contact with the public ... Barbarity is growing. Violence and threats are frequent ... This is not acceptable, and each time such an attack takes place, it is our living together based on the Spirit of Enlightenment that is violated."[63] The language of this passage – and in particular the juxtaposition of "barbarity" and the "Enlightenment" – is a clear assertion of the incommensurability of "Occident" and "Orient." Moreover, the only nexus between these "barbarities" and the full veil is the assumption that the latter is worn by subjugated women, whose husbands recur to violence in order to maintain control over them – an assumption contradicted by all available data.[64] The proposed resolution, however, heavily relies on the said assumption: "We know that this degrading garment goes hand in hand with the submission of women to their spouses, to the men in their family, with the denial of their citizenship."[65] Again, the nexus between poverty, segregation, communitarianism and the use of the veil is not clear. All the two reports suggest is that the use of the veil is imposed on women who live in the *banlieue* by communitarian groups without producing any hard data as support. Hence, just like in

---

[60] *Ibid.*   [61] *Ibid.*, pp. 45–6.   [62] *Ibid.*

[63] Rapport 2262, p. 14.

[64] See the research done by anthropologist John Bowen, a world authority in comparative social studies of Islam at: *Student Life*, www.studlife.com/news/2009/09/25/france-asks-anthropologist-to-testify-on-burqa-debate/ (last accessed August 11, 2011).

[65] *Ibid.*

the German, British and the European Court of Human Rights cases, the argument that Muslim women are often not autonomous agents within their culture, and that they must therefore be protected by state authorities in order to advance gender equality, remains a totally unproven, and a heavily paternalistic, assumption.

D   The European Court of Human Rights

The ECtHR has also dealt with the "Islamic veil issue." In all cases, it has held the ban on the veil to be consistent with the Convention. The main argument throughout has been that states are best placed for determining when interference with religious freedom becomes necessary in a democratic society, thus justifying the grant of a wide margin of appreciation.

In the past, the ECtHR had often legitimized the interference by states with certain rights, and in particular free speech, in order to protect the cultural/religious sensitiveness of the (Christian) majority. In several cases, the Court upheld measures against dissemination of ideas in order to protect morals as defined by the majority culture.[66] Thus, for example, in *Otto-Preminger Institut* v. *Austria*[67] the Court stated that those who exercise freedom of expression relating to religious beliefs and opinions may have an obligation "to avoid as far as possible expressions that are gratuitously offensive to others, and thus an infringement of their rights, and which therefore do not contribute to any form of public debate capable of furthering progress in human affairs."[68]

The ECtHR further specified:

> [The Austrian courts found the film objected to] to be an abusive attack on the Roman Catholic religion according to the conception of the Tyrolean public … The Court cannot disregard the fact that the Roman Catholic religion is the religion of the overwhelming majority on Tyroleans. In seizing the film, the Austrian authorities acted to ensure religious peace in the region … [and did not] overstep[] their margin of appreciation.[69]

In all the cases involved, the application of the doctrine of the margin of appreciation resulted in the protection of the collective religious and cultural freedom of the majority. Just as in the "Bavarian Crucifix Order," the

---

[66] Eur. Ct. H. R., *Müller and Others* v. *Switzerland*, April 28, 1988, *Serie* A 212; Eur. Ct. H. R., *Wingrove* v. *United Kingdom*, November 25, 1996.
[67] Eur. Ct. H. R., *Otto-Preminger-Institut* v. *Austria*, September 20, 1994, *Serie* A 295.
[68] *Ibid.*, para. 49.
[69] *Ibid.*, para. 36. But see *ibid.*, p. 60 (Palm, Pekkanen, and Makarczyk, JJ, dissenting).

ECtHR balancing approach resulted in an extra guarantee of protection to cultural homogeneity and in a denial of rights to individuals belonging to ideological minorities.

The Court also relied on the doctrine of the margin of appreciation in *Dahlab* v. *Switzerland*,[70] but in that case did not end up on the side of religion as it decided that prohibiting women from wearing a headscarf in the capacity of teacher at state schools did not amount to interference with their right to freedom of religion. According to the Court, "in displaying a powerful religious attribute on the school premises … the appellant may have interfered with the religious beliefs of her pupils."[71] In addition, the Court emphasized:

> It must also be acknowledged that it is difficult to reconcile the wearing of a headscarf with the principle of gender equality, which is a fundamental value of our society enshrined in a specific provision of the Federal Constitution and must be taken into account by schools.[72]

Moreover, the Court feared that the appellant's attitude could provoke reactions and conflicts:

> [A]llowing headscarves to be worn would result in the acceptance of garments that are powerful symbols of other faiths, such as soutanes or kippas.[73]

With this, the Court sanctioned a clear double standard, as it did not question the fact that "the principle of proportionality has led the cantonal government to allow teachers to wear discreet religious symbols at school, such as small pieces of jewellery."[74] In short, it is now compatible with the Convention for teachers to wear "discreet" crucifixes, but not "conspicuous" veils.

In two cases decided on December 4, 2008 – *Dogru* v. *France*[75] and *Kervanci* v. *France*[76] – the ECtHR decided that the expulsion of two veiled pupils from state schools did not violate the Convention. The Court noted that in France the principle of secularism is fundamental and that states must be granted a wide margin of appreciation regarding the relationship

---

[70] Eur. Ct. H. R. (2nd section), *Dahlab .v Switzerland*, February 15, 2001.
[71] *Ibid.* (quoting the Federal Court of Switzerland).
[72] *Ibid.* (quoting the Federal Court of Switzerland) (internal citations omitted).
[73] *Ibid.* (quoting the Federal Court of Switzerland).
[74] *Ibid.* (quoting the Federal Court of Switzerland).
[75] Eur. Ct. H. R., *Dogru* v. *France*, December 4, 2008.
[76] Eur. Ct. H. R., *Kervanci* v. *France*, App. No. 31645/04 (Eur. Ct. H. R. 2008) (no English translation available).

between the state and religious denominations. The Court went on to stress that in France, as in Turkey or Switzerland, secularism is a constitutional principle, and a founding principle of the Republic, to which the entire population adheres and the *protection* of which appears to be of prime importance, in particular in schools. Accordingly, "an attitude which fails to respect that principle will not necessarily be accepted as being covered by the freedom to manifest one's religion and will not enjoy the protection of Article 9 of the Convention." Said differently, the Court legitimated France's adoption of preventive measures in order to protect a fundamental constitutional value (secularism) from mere *attitudes* that fail to respect it. It is worth noting that the *attitude* in question in *Dogru* is the refusal of an 11-year-old to remove her headscarf during sports class.

In contrast to the trend established in Western European cases, the margin of appreciation has been applied by the Court in the Turkish veil case, *Şahin* v. *Turkey*,[77] in order to legitimize the interference with the religious freedom of the majority. The Court considered the Turkish notion of secularism – which is shaped as a militant democracy clause and meant to protect the Kemalist regime *from Islam* – to be consistent with the values underpinning the Convention.[78] Thus, the Court accepted that, in protecting the principle of secularism, the state may impose certain limitations on individual rights. The Court observed that "the principle of secularism ... is the paramount consideration underlying the ban on the wearing of religious symbols in universities,"[79] and accordingly:

> when examining the question of the Islamic scarf in the Turkish context, there must be borne in mind the impact which wearing such a symbol, which is presented or perceived as a compulsory religious duty, may have on those who choose not to wear it ... Imposing limitations on freedom in this sphere may, therefore, be regarded as meeting a pressing social need ... especially since ... this religious symbol has taken on political significance in Turkey in recent years.[80]

The Court went on to stress that "democracy does not simply mean that the views of the majority must always prevail: a balance must be achieved which ensures the fair and proper treatment of people from minorities and avoids any abuse of a dominant position. Pluralism and democracy must be based on dialogue."[81] And this led the Court to the conclusion that Turkey, in imposing the scarf ban, did not overstep its margin of appreciation.[82]

---

[77] Eur. Ct. H. R., (Grand Chamber), *Leyla Şahin* v. *Turkey*, November 10, 2005.
[78] *Ibid.*, para. 114.   [79] *Ibid.*, para. 116.   [80] *Ibid.*, para. 115.   [81] *Ibid.*, para. 108.
[82] *Ibid.*, para. 122. But see *ibid.*, p. 99 (Tulkens, J., dissenting).

It is curious that the Court used the margin of appreciation doctrine to protect *minorities* when the majority religion happens to be Islam. If we read this together with the legitimization of Turkey's militant anti-Islamic notion of secularism and with the statement in *Dahlab* that the veil cannot be reconciled with certain fundamental principles, the Court seems to imply a certain degree of incompatibility between Islam and liberal democracy (something that is explicitly stated in the case of *Refah Partisi*).[83] In contrast, all the cases, such as *Otto-Preminger*, in which the Court protected the sensibilities of mainstream Christianity, suggest that the latter is fully compatible with democracy and with the values that underlie the Convention. In sum, Christianity and Christian values can be defended even at the expense of trampling on fundamental individual freedoms, because the ECtHR does not perceive them as conflicting with the core values of the Convention system. Islam, on the other hand, even when it is the religion of the vast majority, can be restrictively regulated on the ground that it threatens the democratic basis of the state.

This trend was confirmed by the decision in *Lautsi* v. *Italy*,[84] which settled the Italian crucifix controversy discussed above. Using the margin of appreciation, the Court concluded that the mandatory display of crucifixes in Italian state school does not violate religious freedom and the parents' right to educate children according to their beliefs. This decision is particularly incoherent on several grounds; chief among them is that it stands the margin of appreciation doctrine on its head. The margin of appreciation presumes deference to a country's authoritative determination that a particular practice is consistent with the Convention. However, as the ECtHR acknowledges, Italian courts are divided over the legitimacy of the display of the crucifix. Hence, the Court took sides in a domestic dispute among courts, embracing the Catholic position. Second, the Court purports to distinguish the crucifix from the headscarf, on account that the first is an "essentially passive symbol" and the latter a "powerful" one. Indeed, Christ did suffer passively on the cross, but to imply that representing his suffering is much less likely to have an

---

[83] Eur. Ct. H. R. (Grand Chamber), *Refah Partisi (The Welfare Party) and others* v. *Turkey*, February 13, 2003.

[84] Eur. Ct. H. R. (GC) Application no. 30814/06, March 18, 2011. The Chamber had previously held Italy in violation of the Convention: Eur. Ct. H. R. (2nd section), *Lautsi* v. *Italy*, November 3, 2009. On this decision see S. Mancini, "The Crucifix Rage: Supranational Constitutionalism Bumps against the Counter-Majoritarian Difficulty," *European Constitutional Law Review* 6 (2010), 6–27.

impact on children than the wearing of a mere piece of cloth on a teacher's head defies all logic.

5   The lesson of religious symbols: the religious as secular and the secular as religious

Given the "disenchantment of reason" and the consequent retreat from modernism, postmodern subjectivism and the revival of religion, including the spread of religious fundamentalism,[85] loom as two sides of the same coin as they seek to fill the void left by the retreat of reason. Religion, accordingly, becomes "de-relativized" at the same time that it becomes "deprivatized," and as a corollary, secularism falls off its modernist pedestal and becomes akin to one more religion. Or more precisely, religion (gauged from within) finds more room to project its truth as absolute, while secularism viewed from the outside can be more readily cast as yet one more (false) religion. This, moreover, transforms the conflict between faith and reason into one among competing faiths. For example, in the 1980s Protestant fundamentalist parents brought cases before the US federal courts, in which they sought condemnation of the curriculum of the public schools attended by their children as unconstitutionally imposing the "religion" of "secular humanism" in violation of the Establishment Clause.[86] The courts rejected these claims, but in so doing did little to debunk the logic of the complaining parents.

Since fundamentalists regard their religion as the absolute truth that accounts for everything to the last detail, any utterance at odds with their religious truth strikes them as issuing from another (false) religion. A mere statement in a literary text read during English class to the effect that "nature is powerful and beautiful in its mysterious ways," which would strike an average contemporary reader as innocuous and devoid of significant religious connotation, would hence be doubly offensive to fundamentalist parents like those who brought suit. First, the statement in question is contrary to these parents' religion, which asserts that nature

---

[85]   A distinction must be drawn between religious fundamentalism as a religious matter and as a politico-constitutional matter. From a purely religious standpoint, a "fundamentalist" is someone who takes holy texts literally; from a politico-constitutional standpoint, in contrast, a "religious fundamentalist" is one who considers his or her religion as the exclusive and absolute truth and who insists that the state be ruled pursuant to the dictates of the true religion.

[86]   See *Smith* v. *Bd. of Sch. Comm'rs*, 827 F.2d 684 (11th Cir. 1987); *Grove* v. *Mead Sch. Dist. No. 354*, 753 F.2d 1528 (9th Cir. 1985).

can in no way be considered as being independent from the will of God. And second, in requiring these parents' children to read such statements, the school is spreading a false religion that denies the existence of God or at least his omnipresence and omnipotence.

This conflict between the visions of fundamentalist Protestants and US federal judges in the 1980s may seem arcane and no more than an isolated instance, pitting a handful of religious fanatics against the secular establishment committed to reason, constitutionalism and religious freedom for all. Upon closer scrutiny, and particularly as set against the case on religious symbols discussed above, however, the conflict in question looms as emblematic of the current predicament.

The comparative analysis of religious symbols-related conflicts has revealed that these are often characterized in terms of a sharp antagonism between Islam and the Christian "West." As emphasized above, majority symbols are legitimized as representing cultural values that are universally shared by the citizenry, in spite of the presence of minorities, and particularly Muslims who are cast as "the other."

In relation to minority symbols, when the contest is over the Islamic headscarf, judges and legislators restrict or ban its display either as incompatible with certain core principles of a democratic system (frequently gender equality) or with democracy *tout court*. The relevant cases openly rely on this dichotomy between Islam and Christianity to prescribe restrictive regulation of manifestations of Islamic religion and culture in the public sphere.

The French case seems different at first, but ultimately falls within the same pattern. In France it is not secularized Christianity, but militant secularism that is used to incorporate the forcibly shared, dominant values. Indeed, French secularism assumes the characteristics of a majority religion. The French State does not confine itself to ensuring the peaceful co-existence of all religions and non-religious perspectives, but becomes a party in the conflicts among them. The State identifies itself with one (the secular, majoritarian) conception and forcibly extends it to all groups and individuals. The secular republic requires a secular attitude from its citizens.[87]

The ideological use of secularism suggests the existence of a community of destiny, unified not by a common ethnic origin, but rather by the will of the French *philosophes*, which finds its natural expression in a secular

---

[87] J. W. Scott, "Veiled Politics," *The Chronicle Review*, November 23, 2007, at B10, available at www.chronicle.com/ (last accessed August 11, 2011).

state culture. Secularism, however, goes hand in hand with a Christian outlook, being the product of the historical process of separation between European states and Christian churches. Even in its French militant version, therefore, it ends up preferring the (secularized) Christian majority. In sum, both "militant secularism" and "secularized religion" are used by public authorities in order to protect cultural and religious homogeneity. While in the other cases secularism is watered down, in France the admission of Christian symbols in spite of secularism has the effect of diluting religion while preserving homogeneity. Both the compulsion to learn "under the cross" and that to learn bareheaded testify to the existence of a homogeneous collective identity and of outsiders who either accept to share, even symbolically, the values of the majority, or face exclusion from the public sphere.

6   The ideal conditions

As our analysis of religious symbols-related conflicts has demonstrated, none of the types of constitutional treatment of religion actually in force in contemporary democratic polities fully conforms to the dictates of the Enlightenment. Given the number and variety of experiences involved, it seems most unlikely that any entirely successful alternative is looming over the horizon. It seems useful, accordingly, to inquire into the ideal conditions that would be best suited to allow for the optimal relationship between secularism and religion, consistent with full realization of the objects set by the Enlightenment project. These ideal conditions could provide a workable counterfactual[88] yielding a baseline against which to assess existing arrangements and furnishing adequate criteria for determining whether existing models of constitutional regulation might be perfectible, or whether the Enlightenment project is ultimately doomed to failure (at least as it pertains to the handling of religion).

Establishing the ideal conditions in question would depend above all on achieving the following essentials: first, setting a clear and workable divide between faith and reason; second, elaborating a conception of secularism that is truly *areligious* in that it neither favors nor disadvantages any religion or the non-religious; third, instituting a public

---

[88] A counterfactual is a constructed model that is contrary to fact but bears sufficient connections to relevant factual orderings to furnish workable criteria of perfectibility or appropriate standards for purposes of critique. See M. Rosenfeld, *Just Interpretations: Law Between Ethics and Politics* (Berkeley: University of California Press,1998), p. 124.

sphere clearly and firmly delimited from the private sphere and entirely amenable to the rule of a religious secularism; and fourth, populating the private sphere with religions and non-religious ideologies susceptible of being veritably treated equally – that is of benefiting from *substantive* as opposed to merely formal equal treatment[89] – and amenable to confining their expression and activities within the precincts of the private sphere.

The first of the four essentials clearly seems the easiest to achieve in theory and to set in motion as a fruitful counterfactual. This can be done by drawing the line between what is amenable to the methods of scientific inquiry or of empirical verification, on the one hand, and that which is not, such as religious beliefs or metaphysical convictions, on the other. At a counterfactual level at least, this line can be consistently and systematically maintained, but not so under actual historical circumstances. Moreover, strict adherence to this divide would not only exclude religion from the public sphere, but also morals and even arguably certain political claims. Take, for instance, Kant's famous moral claim that we ought to treat all fellow humans as ends and not as means. This claim is certainly not susceptible to empirical or scientific validation or falsification.

One may object that Kantian morality (and Kant himself) appeal to public reason, that is to "reasons accessible to all, irrespective of their religious belief,"[90] and Kantian morality is therefore clearly within the realm of reason as conceived by the foremost philosopher of the Enlightenment. This is an undeniable historical fact, but one can still defend the narrower conception of reason carved out to be consistent with our counterfactual as being better suited for purposes of constructing ideal conditions. As a matter of fact, one can plausibly accuse Kantian morality of being ultimately an expression merely of the "religion" of "secular humanism." Not only are the claims made by Kantian morality beyond any factual verification, but also, unlike the propositions of logic, they need not be accepted as valid by anyone who makes proper use of her rational capabilities. By drawing the line narrowly, the counterfactual would exclude some claims that would be acceptable under a Kantian or Rawlsian conception of public reason, but would also protect against endless discussion and blurring

---

[89] For example, in a polity comprised of Christians, Jews and Muslims, a legal prohibition of male circumcision would treat all three religions equally from a formal, but not from a substantive, standpoint. This is because whereas Judaism and Islam prescribe male circumcision, Christianity does not.

[90] See A. Sajó, "Constitutionalism and Secularism: The Need for Public Reason," *Cardozo Law Review* 30 (2009), 2401.

and against the constant danger of unleashing interminable slippery slopes.[91]

The second among four essentials, namely a version of secularism that is areligious and that neither favors nor disfavors any religion or the non-religious looms as impossible to achieve. This is because one cannot rely on the epistemological distinction between what falls within the purview of science and what does not to craft a secularism that could qualify as areligious. Indeed, acting in conformity with science may readily qualify as anti-religious from the standpoint of at least some religions. For example, state-mandated vaccination of the entire population to prevent a deadly epidemic would be justified pursuant to universally accepted standards of contemporary medical science and yet at the same time counter a particular religion's prescription of any medical intervention as being against the will of God. The latter religion need not question the effectiveness of the vaccine, as that may be irrelevant in terms of the belief in the divine proscription to which it feels compelled to adhere.

In view of the preceding observations, no plausible conception of secularism emerges as *inherently* areligious, even as a purely counterfactual matter. This does not mean that the second essential must be dropped, but it does require that it be coordinated in a relational manner with the third and fourth essentials. Indeed, for secularism to be able to count as being areligious, it need not avoid conflict with all religions, but only with those with a presence within the relevant polity.

The characteristics of the third essential, a public sphere clearly distinguishable from the private sphere and amenable to exclusive rule under the precepts of areligious secularism, readily emerge in light of the previous discussion. From a counterfactual perspective, the divide between the public and the private sphere should track the counterfactual divide between reason and faith that informs the first essential. The public sphere should be exclusively confined to the realm of reason; the private sphere, on the other hand, would be equally amenable to the realm of faith and to that of reason. However, since even under the best of circumstances there would seem to be relatively little chance that adherents to all

---

[91] This counterfactual achievement does not imply, of course, anything similar at the factual level. There is a crucial difference between the realm of science and that of morals. What *counts* as science – as opposed to its relevance, utility or desirability – can be systematically determined in accordance with a set of established standards open to all. Because of this, to determine whether an assertion does belong to the realm of science (or empirical observation or logic) does not involve any act of faith in the sense that any assertion to validity in morals does.

different ideologies within a given polity would agree to characterize its public sphere as areligious, the ideal public sphere should be as reduced in scope as possible.

The fourth essential is that religions and non-religious ideologies being relegated to the private sphere be susceptible of substantive equal treatment within the confines of that sphere. For this to be possible, even counterfactually, it is necessary that no religion involved claim an entitlement in accordance with its own religious norms to priority or exclusivity with respect to other religions or non-religious ideologies within the polity, or to a stake in that polity's public sphere. Fundamentalist religions would obviously squarely negate any possibility of coming close to achieving the counterfactual requirements in question, as would any religion that requires intervention into the public sphere.

Before shifting from the counterfactual to the actual historical record concerning the relationship between secularism and religion, two further points warrant brief mention. The first of these is that certain political ideologies are better suited than others for purposes of approximating the counterfactual; the second, as already alluded to above, that some religions and some types of religion are more suited than others with the same purposes in mind.

The three principal political ideologies that are consistent with contemporary constitutional democracy and the ideals of the Enlightenment are liberalism, republicanism and communitarianism.[92] Some of these – and even some versions of the same one[93] – carve out a larger and more intrusive role in the public sphere than others. Moreover, some allow for greater autonomy of religious communities than others.

Concerning the second point mentioned above, it is obvious that some religions seem more inherently compatible with areligious secularism than others. Thus, a merely contemplative religion is obviously compatible with areligious secularism whereas an aggressively proselytizing one is definitely not. Moreover, beyond these extremes, certain combinations of religions within a polity may be more amenable to approximation to areligious secularism than others. Furthermore, of the three major Western religions, as indicated by the jurisprudence on religious symbols, Christianity seems much better suited to secularism than Islam or Judaism. This is due, in important part, to Christianity's commitment to

---

[92] For a comparison of these three ideologies from a pluralist perspective, see Rosenfeld, *Just Interpretations*, pp. 217–24.

[93] For example, libertarian liberalism calls for a more limited public sphere than its egalitarian counterpart.

the separation between the realm of God and that of Cesar as opposed to Islam's and Judaism's all-encompassing approaches requiring that religious rule extend over both the public and the political sphere. Because of this key difference, the counterfactual construct pointing to ideal conditions would be better off embracing Christianity rather than its two major Western counterparts in order to yield the best possible approximation of areligious secularism. But that would create a paradox. If the pursuit of areligious secularism leads to a preference for Christianity, would that not undermine the whole project by lifting Christianity above Islam and Judaism?

Based on the preceding analysis, the counterfactual elaborated above does not provide a pristine model that many would be eager to emulate. On the one hand, this counterfactual contains features that are undesirable or impossible to approximate. It provides a sharp and sustainable divide between reason and faith, but the idea that Kantian morals should be barred from the public sphere for the same reason as fundamentalist religion seems highly unattractive. On the other hand, even at the counterfactual level, the model in question is remarkably tenuous as it provides a conception of areligious secularism that cannot stand on its own. Finally, even if the counterfactual does not automatically favor Christianity – and there is a good argument that it does not, but that it is rather only open to certain liberal versions of many religions, such as liberal Protestantism, Reform Judaism, and so on – it would require suppression of a large number of religious ideologies with large followings in most contemporary constitutional democracies.

7   Beyond the present predicament: can and should the Enlightenment project be salvaged?

The preceding discussion suggests that it would be unproductive to seek ever greater approximation of the above elaborated ideal counterfactual. Does that mean that the Enlightenment project must be completely abandoned when it comes to the constitutional treatment of religion? And even assuming that it need not, should it be abandoned?

The Enlightenment project has not become futile, but it ought to be transformed and reoriented. The divide between reason and faith need not be abandoned, but it must be conceived as much more fluid and uncertain, and it must be redeployed to address current threats to core Enlightenment values as opposed to those of the past. In the eighteenth century it was organized religion that was the Enlightenment's fiercest adversary; today, it is fundamentalist and strong religions, with more moderate and more liberal religions often barely, if at all, at odds with scientific reason. One possibility, therefore, is to switch to a situational and relational approach.

The distinction between the public and the private sphere may no longer be useful for present purposes, but it might be fruitfully replaced by reliance on the contrast between *intra*-communal and *inter*-communal relationships. Broadly speaking, all those who share the same religious ideology[94] can be said to belong to a single religious community. Consistent with this, moreover, dealings within a single religious community are "intra-communal," whereas those involving two or more religious communities, or a religious and a secular community, or those that purport to transcend the bounds of all relevant religious communities, are "inter-communal."

The attractiveness of framing relationships in terms of the distinction between the intra-communal and the inter-communal is enhanced given that the citizen of a typical contemporary constitutional democracy is bound to become immersed in a number of different communities at once and to have to negotiate conflicts and tensions that arise as a result. A German-speaking Swiss Catholic feminist woman, for example, belongs to the Swiss nation, to one of its four main linguistic groups, to one of its two dominant religions, and to one socio-political group with particular aims and views regarding women's equality and gender-based relationships. Depending on the circumstances, the woman in question may focus more on her national identity than her linguistic group identity, or vice versa. On some occasions, her Catholicism may be in tension or conflict with her feminism. Because of that, she may decide to live with a certain amount of dissonance and inconsistency unless her various commitments become so incompatible that she must withdraw from some of the communities to which she belongs.

What is crucial for our purposes is that this single individual must constantly shift from intra-communal to inter-communal perspectives in the management of her multiple allegiances. Moreover, the kinds of operations that take place at the individual level can also be carried out at the collective level by various groups within the polity and the polity itself as the group of the whole. Except in cases of clear incompatibility, the dynamic between intra-communal and inter-communal dealings should

---

[94] We emphasize "religious ideology" rather than "religion" in order to allow for the characterization of different sects or denominations to be treated as different communities.

afford numerous possibilities for peaceful coexistence within a constitutional order among proponents of numerous and diverse religious and secular ideologies.

The dynamic between intra-communal and inter-communal dealings can also be helpful in reconfiguring secularism in light of the futility of pursuing a neutral areligious ideal and of the seemingly inevitable links between secularism and religion revealed in the course of retracing the history of the various actual incarnations of the concept. Functionally, secularism should promote peaceful and productive inter-communal relationships within the polity combined with guaranteeing maximum room for intra-communal autonomy consistent with preserving the integrity of the space needed for inter-communal exchanges. Substantively, on the other hand, secularism would draw on two distinct sources of identity. In part, secularism would draw on that which makes possible and facilitates inter-communal coordination and cooperation among religious ideologies, and among the latter and non-religious ones. What would be encompassed within this rubric would vary from one setting to the next, depending on the religions, history and cultures involved. In any case, incorporation of elements drawn from religion or religious culture would be entirely permissible. The criterion of validity for such elements derived from religion would not depend on how close or removed they may be from religion itself, but on whether they advance or hinder the smooth functioning of the requisite channels of inter-communal exchange.

In part also, secularism would draw on another source of identity, rooted in the traditional Enlightenment conception of the term. In contrast to the first source of identity, which could be characterized as secularism's inter-communal identity, this second source could be regarded as secularism's intra-communal identity, or in other words, as secularism's conception of itself as a separate and distinct ideology. Indeed, in all contemporary constitutional democracies, there are certain citizens who are secular rather than religious, who put science ahead of faith, and who believe that the pursuit of liberal liberty and equality for all should trump any divine prescription to the contrary. These "intra-communal" secularists have as much a right to have a place at the inter-communal table as do the proponents of the various religious ideologies.

Secularism's inter-communal identity is contextually dependent on the actual ideologies involved, whereas its intra-communal identity is self-contained, as one can easily imagine a well-functioning, self-enclosed, homogeneous, secular society cut off from all religion. In actuality, however, the gap between these two identities is likely to prove far less stark for three principal reasons. First, intra-communal secularism must figure in the elaboration of its inter-communal counterpart to the extent that the secularist ideology is present in the relevant polity. Second, given the tendency to develop plural identities and multi-group memberships, elements of the secularist ideology are bound to slip into intra-communal precincts of competing ideologies. Thus, some liberal religions are quite compatible with commitment to liberal liberty and equality for all. Moreover, some adherents of non-liberal religions may nonetheless embrace certain secular values and cope with the tensions involved through compartmentalization. And, third, by the same token, proponents of intra-communal secularism need not shut the door to religion, and may in fact embrace religion without contradiction so long as they adhere to the primacy of the secular outlook.

From the standpoint of traditional Enlightenment values, secularism occupied a privileged place and the acceptance of religion was conditioned on compatibility with deployment of the secular project. In the context of the present reconfiguration of secularism, however, no such clear answers readily emerge. Secularism and the constitutional order it fosters are inherently tolerant of diversity, but why prefer secularism's tolerance over other kinds of tolerance or even over intolerant ideologies once one concedes that secularism as such is but one intra-communal ideology among many?

This last query forces one to focus on the larger question of whether the Enlightenment project is worth preserving at this point in time, or whether it would be preferable to abandon it in favor of a more suitable alternative. And, given the recent inroads of postmodernism and derelativized religion as well as the continuing progression of the disenchantment of reason, no readily available or obvious all-encompassing answer could be offered with confidence.

One can advance, however, two more modest answers. The first one is somewhat circular, but may nonetheless carry significant weight among proponents of constitutional democracy. Constitutionalism requires secularism (in some form) and they both go hand in hand with certain core Enlightenment values. Constitutionalism may thrive with a reconfigured on redeployed Enlightenment project, but it cannot survive the complete abandonment of the latter. Therefore, if for no other reason, the Enlightenment project ought to be preserved for the sake of constitutionalism.

The second answer is that contemporary polities are typically multiethnic, multicultural and religiously diverse, and that secularism, at least in its inter-communal dimension, provides the best means to preserve the peace and to maintain the good functioning of such pluralistic societies. This second answer may be buttressed by either a lesser evil prudential argument or a more positive normative argument deriving from a pluralistic conception of the good. The former argument is predicated on the conviction that unless a stand-off among competing ideologies is maintained, a serious threat to the public order would ensue. The latter more positive argument relies, for its part, on the premise that pluralism is good and worthy of pursuit because it multiplies and enhances every person's opportunities for self-realization and self-fulfillment.

The preceding discussion leaves one with a vexing lingering question. The version of the Enlightenment project needed for the legitimation and operation of contemporary reconfigured secularism is dramatically more modest, less assertive, and less encompassing than that which emerged in the Age of the Enlightenment. Is that due to the ravages of postmodernism and derelativized religion? Or, is it rather due to the fact that much of the Enlightenment project has met with success and has become quietly internalized and subconsciously stored in the public psyche of contemporary constitutional democracies?

Both the preceding theoretical discussion and the prior analysis of the constitutional jurisprudence regarding religious symbols point to one distinct conclusion. The reconceived principle of secularism and the Enlightenment values it relies upon loom as indispensable to peaceful coexistence within our increasingly multi-ethnic, multicultural and multi-religious polities. This reconceived secularism is above all pluralist, and although it may not be able to set itself fully apart from religion – and even from some religions more than others – or from seeping into the inner walls of discrete religious communities, it is the best hope for harmonizing (as best as possible) intra-communal and inter-communal dealings. Pluralist secularism's principal creed is that no intra-communal truth is entitled to command inter-communal acceptance. This, in turn, commands a broad and generous conception of tolerance and of acceptance of the other. In terms of religious symbols, this translates into refraining from official imposition of majority ones and greater acceptance of minority ones as long as they are not proven to pose a threat to the survival of pluralist secularism itself – a very high threshold indeed.

8

Objective, critical and pluralistic? Religious education and human rights in the European public sphere

IAN LEIGH

Few subjects are as fraught with difficulty for legislators and officials as education concerning religion in state schools. With the exception of some militant atheists there is a general acceptance that religious education is an appropriate and, in the view of some, essential topic for inclusion in the school curriculum. There the consensus ends, however. The rationale for religious education, the implications for the content of the syllabus and way in which it is delivered, the role of religious bodies in such education, the treatment of minority religions and the question of exemption for certain pupils are all fiercely contested.

While these debates are not new, there have been major recent developments in the human rights jurisprudence concerning religious education in state schools in Europe. The *Folgerø* judgment, in which the Grand Chamber of the European Court of Human Rights divided 9:8 concerning the compatibility of religious education in Norway, is perhaps the most important on this issue for the past twenty years.[1] It has been closely followed by *Zengin* v. *Turkey* – a similar challenge to religious education in Turkish schools.[2] These decisions are of intrinsic interest and

I am grateful to participants in the workshop on 'Religion in the European Public Sphere: A Secular Dilemma' at the European University Institute on 30–31 May 2008, and especially Camil Ungureanu and Lorenzo Zucca and to two anonymous referees, for comments on an earlier draft. After completion of this chapter the European Court of Human Rights gave judgment in *Grzelak* v. *Poland* Appl. No. 7710/02 (15 June 2010) and *Appel-Irrgang and others* v. *Germany* Appl. No. 45216/07 (20 October 2009). These are discussed in I. Leigh, 'The European Court of Human Rights and Religious Neutrality' in M. Evans, T. Modood and J. Rivers (eds.), *Religion in a Liberal State* (forthcoming).

[1] Eur. Ct. H. R. (Grand Chamber), *Folgerø and others* v. *Norway*, 29 June 2007.
[2] Eur. Ct. H. R. (Former 2nd section), *Hasan and Eylem Zengin* v. *Turkey*, 9 October 2007.

raise some important questions. Can a state with an established church or in which there is a clear majority religion justifiably reflect these facts in its arrangements for religious education in schools? What provisions should be made for minority religions? In a liberal society should parents be permitted to opt out of religious education, thereby insulating their children from understanding part of the cultural heritage and other religions? Conversely, if an opt-out is not permitted, then does this entail that the religious education delivered must be such that it does not violate parents' rights?

In this chapter I deal first with some of the major controversies about the rationale of religious education, before moving on to consider statements of purpose made by international bodies such as the Council of Europe and the Organisation for Security and Cooperation in Europe (OSCE).[3] Against that background a critique is undertaken of the reasoning of the European Court of Human Rights in the *Folgerø* and *Zengin* decisions concerning religious education and the right to exemption.

1   The rationale for religious education in public schools

There are five major types of approach that typify attitudes towards religious education by the state.[4]

The first is often termed a *confessional* approach, that is religious education (or, in the older terminology, 'religious instruction') has the official objective of instilling or developing religious beliefs in the pupil. Historically this was the dominant approach within Europe, although in practice most European states have abandoned a confessional approach to religious education in recent decades.[5] The confessional approach was

---

[3] Especially the OSCE Office of Democratic Institutions and Human Rights, *Toledo Guiding Principles on Teaching about Religion and Beliefs in Public Schools* (Warsaw, 2007) (referred to below as the '*Toledo Guiding Principles*'), available at www.osce.org/odihr/29154 (last accessed 17 August 2011).

[4] See further R. Ahdar and I. Leigh, *Religious Freedom in the Liberal State* (Oxford University Press, 2005), Chapter 8. For a different scheme of classification (into confessional and varieties of non-confessional religious education) see I. Plevsner, 'Promoting Tolerance Through Religious Education' in T. Lindholm, W. Cole Durham and B. Tahzlb-Lie (eds.), *Facilitating Freedom of Religion or Belief: A Deskbook* (Leiden: Martinus Nijhoff Publishers, 2004).

[5] For example, in the UK the Millar Report, *Moral and Religious Education in Scottish Schools* (1971), disclaimed any confessional aspirations for religious education. Recent accounts of European practice include: E. Kuyk, R. Jensen, D. Lankshear, E. Löh Manna and P. Schreiner (eds.), *Religious Education in Europe* (Oslo: IKO – ICCS, 2007); and R. Jackson, S. Miedema, W. Weisse and J.-P. Willaime (eds.), *Religion and Education in Europe* (Münster: Waxmann, 2007).

often associated with a formal link between an established religion and the state or at least with societies with a clear majority religion. Religious minorities might be accommodated through provisions enabling pupils to opt out or to have alternative religious education lessons in their own religious tradition. A confessional approach is retained in a minority of European countries: in Irish primary schools, for example, pupils are prepared in school hours for taking the sacrament for the first time, although a parental opt-out (arguably ineffective) is available.[6] The confessional approach is open to the objection of liberals that it offends against the principle of neutrality between conceptions of the good and is coercive. It could be said that confessional religious education risks offending the principle of voluntariness in matters of religion since teachers are in authority over pupils and this position should not be misused. Moreover, in some instances a confessional approach could be overbearing and amount to religious indoctrination.

Some of these perceived defects may be corrected by a stance of state *neutrality* in religious education in which the school's task is to present the major religions without any preference and without the objective of instilling belief in any of them. The neutral approach is consistent with classical liberalism. John Stuart Mill, for example, argued that there could be no objection to religious education in schools confined to facts about religions, that is the content of key beliefs and doctrines, and learning about significant figures, events and practices of observants.[7] In a modern variant of this approach Bruce Ackerman claims that liberal schools should be neutral with regard to the choices children might make and provide them with the wide 'range of cultural materials' they may find useful in developing their own moral ideas and patterns of life.[8] Although the neutrality approach better protects the position of minorities, nevertheless some religious groups may question whether true neutrality is possible

---

[6] See A. Mawhinney, 'The Opt-Out Clause: Imperfect Protection for the Right of Freedom of Education in Schools', *Education Law Journal* 1 (2006), 5–16; and A. Mawhinney, 'Freedom of Religion in the Irish primary school system: a failure to protect human rights?', *Legal Studies* 27 (2007), 379. For more general discussion of the compatibility of Irish education with constitutional provisions guaranteeing religious freedom, see R. O'Connell, 'Theories of Religious Education in Ireland', *Journal of Law and Religion* 14 (1999–2000), 433.

[7] J. S. Mill, *On Liberty* (1959) in D. Spitz, *The Annotated Text of On Liberty* (New York: Norton, 1975), p. 99.

[8] B. Ackerman, *Social Justice in the Liberal State* (New Haven: Yale University Press, 1980), pp. 155–6.

and object to the implicit pluralism towards religions or to specific non-confessional pedagogical approaches towards religious education.

This may especially be the case where a curriculum adopts a thematic style that compares issues across religions (for example, festivals, worship, food, prayer and so on); this may fail to convey an overall sense of each religion, studied in its own right or of the experience of belief as such.[9] Alternatively, teachers of religious education commonly employ a phenomenological approach. Without attempting to instil religious belief, this nevertheless goes beyond the simple communication of information about religions and takes an 'insider's perspective' or empathetic approach.[10] The objective is to enable pupils to understand what it is like for a believer to participate in the religious experiences or practices of a particular belief, for example, by visiting a place of worship or talking to believers from a particular faith group. The phenomenological approach may, however, cause difficulties where children or the families they come from have a settled set of beliefs (whether religious or humanist), which make it difficult or even offensive to them to learn about practices associated with other religions.

In contrast to neutrality some theorists espousing *civic liberalism* argue that the overriding purpose of education should be to develop a child's capacity for autonomous choices as future citizens of the liberal state. From this Levinson, for example, concludes that schools should be 'common' (that is, equally accessible to all segments of the population), should not reflect 'socially divisive' conceptions of the good, and should be 'detached' (from parental and family religious backgrounds).[11] Levinson accepts that this need not result in sanitising religion from schools in all circumstances.[12] It is plain, nevertheless, that countries such as France, which treat pupils as public beings once they enter the school gate and confine religion to the private realm, may find it much easier to fulfil these conditions than will those that permit schools with a religious ethos or allow religious dress or an act of worship within school time.

---

[9] The academic or phenomenological approaches described may equally be used where the overriding objective is a form of civic liberalism. For discussion of different approaches, see *Toledo Guiding Principles*, Chapter 3.

[10] *Ibid.*, p. 47.

[11] M. Levinson, *The Demands of Liberal Education* (Oxford University Press, 1999), esp. Chapter 5.

[12] She claims, for example, that 'until recently' (writing in 1999, noting the emergence of a significant Muslim minority) that religion in the UK was not socially divisive and so religiously affiliated schools were unproblematic: *ibid.*, p. 158.

Stephen Macedo similarly argues for the place of schools in promoting a transformative civic liberalism, that is one that through public education shapes its future citizens so that they are 'willing to support its fundamental institutions and principles and take part in defining those principles'.[13] This, he contends, takes priority over accommodating diversity or multiculturalism. Accordingly, like Levinson, he is critical of some of the legal concessions, such as exemption from classes or exercises, made to the religious sensibilities of parents.[14] It is clear then that a positively liberal education based on these premises would potentially cut across a number of commonly accepted beliefs and practices reflected in constitutional and human rights guarantees and designed to protect family interests in religious upbringing.[15] Religious groups may object to the explicit pluralism and perceive it as actively hostile to or undermining religious education within the family or religious group from which children are drawn.

A *separatist* approach attempts to avoid these pitfalls by maintaining a strict separation between the state and religious groups – leaving religious education to the latter and to parents, outside state schools. All religious groups are treated equally in the sense that they are equidistant from the classroom. Although consistent with a certain strand of liberal tradition, separatism disavows the opportunities that *civic liberalism* sees in religious education for instilling lessons in mutual toleration and citizenship. In societies divided on religious lines segregation may be reinforced by a separatist approach. Withdrawal of state engagement in religious education entails that some children (from outside religious groups or with unconcerned parents) will receive no religious education and others, at best, will only learn about their own religious tradition or – at worst – may be uncritically indoctrinated in misperceptions or stereotypes of other religions. Moreover the absence of religious education from the curriculum does not necessarily connote religious neutrality: religious parents and pupils may claim that its omission sends a powerful message of the relative

---

[13] See S. Macedo, *Diversity and Distrust: Civic Education in a Multicultural Democracy* (Cambridge, MA: Harvard University Press, 2000), p. 164.

[14] *Ibid.*, Chapter 6.

[15] Levinson accepts that reversal of US Supreme Court authority in *Pierce* v. *Society of Sisters* 268 US 510 (1925) and *Wisconsin* v. *Yoder* 406 US 205 (1972) would be entailed. See Levinson, *The Demands of Liberal Education*, p. 162. To that we can add denunciation of Article 18.4 of the International Covenant on Civil and Political Rights and of Article 2 of the First Protocol to the European Convention on Human Rights.

official (un)importance of religion compared to other subjects on the curriculum.[16]

All four approaches considered so far are relatively benign in their treatment of religions, even if religionists may on occasion perceive them to be less so. By contrast a *secularist* approach attempts to actively counter what it sees as the negative effects of religious belief by promoting a form of official secular humanism in state education. Such an approach represents a non-neutral comprehensive ideology which is actively hostile to religion. Whether or not accompanied by other forms of state repression of religious liberty (as in some former Communist countries and contemporary China and Central Asian republics), *secularism* nevertheless attempts to undercut the societal influence of religions in the longer term by inoculating children against the virus.

In practice the dominant models of religious education on offer in contemporary Europe are what I have labelled neutrality, civic liberalism and separatism. Of course these only approximate to the precise pattern of religious education in any particular country and some national systems contain elements of more than one model. Although neither confessional nor secularist approaches are widespread, that does not prevent some parents from complaining of indoctrination and others objecting to what they see as an educational environment or method of teaching that is actively hostile to religious faith.

As we have seen, despite the move way from confessional approaches there are several reasons for liberals to embrace religious education within state schools. Arguably, some minimum of religious education is necessary to fulfil one commonly stated liberal goal for education – training for citizenship – since religion has played an important historical part in shaping present-day culture and is an important aspect of contemporary society. On the same basis, learning about the religious beliefs of others may be a foundation for promoting the liberal virtue of toleration. It can, for example, combat ignorance among pupils of the beliefs of those from other religious backgrounds. Increasing awareness and knowledge of a range of religious beliefs may, on one the hand, help to reduce mutual intolerance and, on the other, help to validate and integrate as citizens pupils from minority religious groups. Aspirations like these represent the modern European orthodoxy – as can be seen from pronouncements from

---

[16] In view of the general attitude of the European Court of Human Rights towards Protocol 1 Article 2, however, parental dissatisfaction with the epistemic absence of God is unlikely to translate into a cogent human rights claim.

the Council of Europe Parliamentary Assembly and the Organisation for Security and Cooperation in Europe.

2 Practical and human rights implications

The Organisation for Security and Cooperation in Europe has recently produced a detailed set of guidelines: *Toledo Guiding Principles on Teaching about Religion and Beliefs in Public Schools*.[17] Against the back-cloth of increasingly visible religious diversity and conflict in Europe these principles are premised on the belief that religious education is a vital tool for the elimination of prejudice, intolerance and discrimination. They therefore attempt to lay the practical foundations for greater mutual understanding and respect between religious groups.

The *Toledo Guiding Principles* are intended to offer 'practical guidance for preparing curricula for teaching about religions and beliefs' and pre-ferred procedures for assuring fairness in the development of curricula', while abjuring any ambition to impose a standard curriculum or any par-ticular pedagogical approach.[18] As such they also address the training of teachers in delivering religious education[19] and the treatment of pupils from diverse religious backgrounds.

It is now generally accepted that state schools should not be involved in confessional religious education. The OSCE summarise current ortho-doxy in their 2007 guidelines:

> The starting point is the understanding that teaching about religions and beliefs is not devotionally and denominationally oriented. It strives for student awareness of religions and beliefs, but does not press for student acceptance of any of them; it sponsors study about religions and beliefs, not their practice; it may expose students to a diversity of religious and non-religious views, but does not impose any particular view; it educates about religions and beliefs without promoting or denigrating any of them; it informs students about various religions and beliefs, it does not seek to conform or convert students to any particular religion or belief.[20]

Likewise, the Parliamentary Assembly of the Council of Europe in 2005 reaffirmed the contemporary importance of religious education on a non-confessional basis:

> Knowledge of religions is an integral part of knowledge of the history of mankind and civilisations. It is altogether distinct from belief in a specific

---

[17] See *Toledo Guiding Principles*.   [18] *Ibid.*, p. 10.   [19] *Ibid.*, Chapter 4.
[20] *Ibid.*, p. 21.

religion and its observance. Even countries where one religion predominates should teach about the origins of all religions rather than favour a single one or encourage proselytising.[21]

However, the Parliamentary Assembly goes further:

> By teaching children the history and philosophy of the main religions with restraint and objectivity and with respect for the values of the European Convention on Human Rights, it will effectively combat fanaticism. Understanding the history of political conflicts in the name of religion is essential.[22]

Overall the Parliamentary Assembly seems to be predominantly neutral in its approach to religious education, although there are also clear undertones of a mild form of civic liberalism present here.

Much the same can be said of the OSCE *Toledo Guiding Principles*: while falling short of advocating that states provide religious education, they stress the opportunities presented for education about the importance of freedom of religious belief, promoting mutual toleration between different religious groups and the importance of religion as a cultural factor.[23]

Wisely, however, the OSCE does not fall into the trap of confusing neutrality and religious indifference. It recognises, for example, that the fact that a teacher is religiously committed should not debar them delivering religious education provided they are able to perform in a professional manner, including demonstrating respect for human rights. This is an important elaboration, bearing in mind the recurring references to 'objectivity' and 'neutrality' in religious education that appear throughout international human rights documents and jurisprudence.

Although objectivity and neutrality may be slippery concepts when applied to religion, there is a consensus about what is unacceptable – religious indoctrination. In a key passage in its judgment in the Danish sex education case *Kjeldsen Busk Masden and Pedersen*, the European Court of Human Rights stated concerning Article 2 of the First Protocol of the Convention (the right to respect for parents' religious and philosophical convictions in education):

> The State ... must take care that information or knowledge included in the curriculum is conveyed in an objective, critical and pluralistic

---

[21] Recommendation 1720 on Religion and Education, Council of Europe Parliamentary Assembly, 4 October 2005, para. 8.

[22] Recommendation 1720 on Religion and Education, Council of Europe Parliamentary Assembly, 4 October 2005, para. 7.

[23] *Toledo Guiding Principles*, pp. 13–14.

manner. The State is forbidden to pursue an aim of indoctrination that might not be considered as respecting parents' religious and philosophical convictions.[24]

Unfortunately this is a somewhat circular formulation and it leaves unclear whether a failure to communicate information objectively, critically and pluralistically always violates the right.[25]

The legal literature from North America distinguishes between education *about* religion, which judges in Canada certainly, and to some extent in the United States, have regarded as acceptable, and *religious indoctrination* which has been treated as unconstitutional. The former is perceived as academic, whereas the latter has the goal of conversion or instilling religious belief in the child. In a leading Canadian decision, the *Elgin County* case,[26] the Ontario Court of Appeal argued that:

> State-authorized religious indoctrination amounts to the imposition of majoritarian religious beliefs on minorities ... It creates a direct burden on religious minorities and non-believers who do not adhere to majoritarian beliefs.[27]

The UN Human Rights Committee in General Comment 22 has employed a comparable distinction between 'objective and neutral' school instruction concerning religions in general and *instruction in* a particular religion. The latter, it argues, raises human rights concerns under Article 18 of the International Covenant on Civil and Political Rights (freedom of thought, conscience and religion) 'unless provision is made for non-discriminatory exemptions or alternatives that would accommodate the wishes of parents and guardians'.[28]

Although the European Court of Human Rights, the Ontario Court of Appeal and the UN Human Rights Committee are all using similar terminology, there is an underdeveloped but potentially important

---

[24] Eur. Ct. H. R., *Kjeldsen Busk Masden and Pedersen* v. *Denmark*, 7 December 1976, para. 53.

[25] See P. Taylor, *Freedom of Religion: UN and European Rights Law and Practice* (Cambridge University Press, 2005), p. 168. At pp. 169–70 Taylor points out that in the Convention context 'indoctrination' should for reasons of consistency be taken to invoke violation of the *child's* Article 9 right by violating the *forum internum*, as well the *parent's* right to respect for their religious and philosophical convictions. My criticism (below) of the Court's more interventionist use of Article 2 Protocol 1 is that it is applied to state conduct that would not ordinarily be said to violate Article 9(1) in this way.

[26] *Canadian Civil Liberties Assoc.* v. *Ontario (Minister of Education)* (1990) 65 DLR (4th) 1 (Ont. CA).

[27] *Ibid.*, pp. 23–4.

[28] General Comment 22, para. 6. See also *Hartikainen* v. *Finland*, UN Human Rights Committee 40/78.

difference in their use of it. The court in *Elgin County* equated all state confessional religious education with impermissible indoctrination, whereas for the Human Rights Committee the effect is different – it is suspect and requires special protections for those wishing to opt out. As will be seen in the next section, the European Court of Human Rights jurisprudence also follows the latter approach but its most recent pronouncements may have the effect of moving towards the *Elgin County* position.

Moreover, the distinction between indoctrination and education masks a crucial ambiguity, concerning the purpose of the acceptable category – education *about* religion. As we have seen, neutral and civic libertarian approaches, notwithstanding that they are techniques of education *about religion*, nonetheless raise distinct problems of religious liberty. Even the most 'objective' treatments of religion in the classroom are likely to be found as objectionable by some parents of religious or atheist conviction.

These questions are closely connected to the safety valve frequently found within national educational systems for such parental concerns – exemption or opt-out provisions. Such exemptions are usually regarded as an enlightened concession to freedom of conscience. They can be seen as undesirable, however. If the purpose of educating pupils about a number of religions is so that they are aware of key beliefs that different groups within their society hold and are able to assess their cultural and historical importance, it is questionable whether parents or pupils should be able, by opting out, to avoid learning about religions other than their own. The case against allowing such avoidance rests, then, on the need for awareness of other's beliefs in order to live as a good citizen and the place of understanding in the promotion of toleration. The OSCE's *Toledo Guiding Principles* make the point:

> Where programmes for teaching about religions and beliefs are well-designed, and are clearly not aimed at supporting any particular religious or non-religious understanding of the world, the need for opt-outs may be minimal or non-existent.[29]

On the other hand, religious groups with a less detached view may argue that exposure to beliefs that they see as erroneous or worse carries a risk of harming the spiritual development of their children.[30] Muslim parents,

---

[29] *Toledo Guiding Principles*, p. 70. And see *ibid.*, p. 72.

[30] It has been held in the US that even where religious education has a secular purpose, the free exercise of religion requires an opt-out provision for children who claim that attendance violates their freedom of conscience: *Crockett* v. *Sorenson*, 568 F. Supp. 1422 (1983). For an example of (unsuccessful) parental objection by 'fundamentalist Christians' to

for example, may regard religious education as an attempt to convert their children to Christianity and withdraw their children.[31] It is not unimaginable that a staunch atheist might similarly object to his or her children being taught about what they see as superstitions – as the *Folgerø* litigation from Norway, discussed below, demonstrates.

3   The approach of the European Court of Human Rights

In *Folgerø* v. *Norway*[32] a challenge was brought by a group of humanist parents to the arrangements for religious education in Norwegian state schools. Norway had introduced a compulsory course on 'Christian Knowledge and Religious and Ethical Education' (or KRL) in 1997 which was designed to provide a general introduction to Christianity (which occupied around 55 per cent of the teaching) and to other major world religions and outlooks, including non-religious life stances. The parents objected to the failure to allow a total exemption from the course. The state contended, however, that a total exemption would defeat the objectives of promoting dialogue among pupils from various faiths, and of providing all pupils with a basic knowledge of the religions covered in the course. Successive challenges brought by the parents before the Norwegian Courts failed. Both the European Court of Human Rights and the UN Human Rights Committee,[33] to which a similar complaint was brought, concluded, however, that the course was insufficiently objective not to require the possibility of an exemption and that the partial opt-out scheme established by Norway did not prevent violations of the claimants' right to have their children educated in accordance with their religious and philosophical convictions. The judgment of the Grand Chamber of the European Court of Human Rights is noteworthy for the serious division that it produced over fundamental questions: the Court ruled by a

---

exposure of their children to other beliefs: *Mozert* v. *Hawkins County Board of Education* 827 F. 2d. 1058 (1987).

[31] Open Society Institute, *Muslims in the UK: Policies for Engaged Citizens* (Budapest: Open Society Institute, 2005), p. 158.

[32] Eur. Ct. H. R. (Grand Chamber), *Folgerø and others* v. *Norway*, 29 June 2007.

[33] *Leirvåg* v. *Norway*, UN Human Rights Committee, CCPR/C/_/D/_1155/2003, Communication No. 1155/2003, 23 November 2004, available at www.unhchr.ch/tbs/doc.nsf/(Symbol)/6187ce3dc0091758c1256f7000526973?Opendocument (last accessed 12 August 2011).The Human Rights Committee ruled that there was a violation of the right of parents to secure the religious and moral education of their children in conformity with their convictions under Art. 18.4 of the International Covenant on Civil and Political Rights.

majority of 9:8 that there had been a violation of Protocol 1 Article 2 of the Convention (the right of parents to have their children educated in accordance with their religious and philosophical convictions).

The majority applied the standard of whether the syllabus was critical, objective and pluralistic in its treatment of religions. They found that:

> notwithstanding the many laudable legislative purposes stated in connection with the introduction of the KRL subject in the ordinary primary and lower secondary schools, it does not appear that the respondent State took sufficient care that information and knowledge included in the curriculum be conveyed in an objective, critical and pluralistic manner for the purposes of Article 2 of Protocol No. 1.[34]

Pluralism and objectivity did not require that equal treatment be given to all religions and philosophies. The Grand Chamber found that it was within the margin of appreciation of the Norwegian government to adopt a syllabus that devoted greater attention to Christianity than to other religions.[35] This did not *in itself* constitute a departure from the necessary principles of pluralism and objectivity amounting indoctrination.

However, on closer analysis the curriculum was unbalanced to the extent that it raised concerns: there was a clear difference in the depth of knowledge required concerning Christianity as compared to other religions, which in the majority's view undermined the objective of 'understanding, respect and the ability to maintain dialogue between people with different perceptions of beliefs and convictions'.[36] The syllabus had to be understood in the context of the so-called 'Christian object clause' which provided:

> The object of primary and lower secondary education shall be, in agreement and cooperation with the home, to help give pupils a Christian and moral upbringing, to develop their mental and physical abilities, and to give them good general knowledge so that they may become useful and independent human beings at home and in society. [37]

Nor could the injunction to teachers under the syllabus to follow a 'uniform pedagogical approach in respect of the different religions and philosophies' compensate for this.

This part of the Grand Chamber's judgment is striking for the depth of detailed analysis which probes specific matters concerning the delivery of the curriculum. These might have been thought to be well within

---

[34] *Folgerø v. Norway,* para. 102.   [35] *Ibid.,* para. 89.   [36] *Ibid.,* para. 95.
[37] Section 1–2(1) of the Education Act 1998.

the state's margin of appreciation. Although ostensibly applying all three criteria of 'critical, objective and pluralistic', in practice the majority's adverse reaction to the extent to which Christianity predominated in effect led it to give much less weight to the requirements within the syllabus for delivery in an objective and pluralistic manner. This perhaps illustrates the difficulty in assessing criteria that are mixed, with some more easily measurable (e.g. the proportion of time devoted to specific religions) than others. There is a contrast with the emphasis of the OSCE *Toledo Guiding Principles* upon ensuring fairness in *procedural* matters of curriculum design and delivery.

Nevertheless, the overall approach jars with the majority's initial starting point of the margin of appreciation. The majority of the Grand Chamber acknowledged that:

> the setting and planning of the curriculum fall in principle within the competence of the Contracting States. This mainly involves questions of expediency on which it is not for the Court to rule and whose solution may legitimately vary according to the country and the era.[38]

Presumably it would be open to Convention states to have no religious education in state schools and to leave this matter entirely to faith groups, on the one hand. In Albania, France[39] and the former Yugoslav Republic of Macedonia it is not taught at all and in Slovenia only in last years of state education. This would nevertheless be contrary to the recommendations of the Parliamentary Assembly of the Council of Europe.[40]

In twenty-five of the member states of the Council of Europe religious education is a compulsory subject, whereas it is available on an optional basis in a further eighteen states.[41] In the light of this it cannot be said that European states have a common mind that religious education is necessary for citizenship, or historical or cultural awareness, despite pronouncements of the Council of Europe Parliamentary Assembly stressing its importance.

Nevertheless where a state does decide that some knowledge about religion is an essential part of citizenship and cultural education and

---

[38] *Folgerø* v. *Norway*, para. 84.
[39] Except in the Alsace and Moselle regions. See *Zengin* v. *Turkey*, paras. 30–32.
[40] Recommendation 1720 on Religion and Education, Council of Europe Parliamentary Assembly 4 (October 2005).
[41] Andorra, Armenia, Azerbaijan, Bulgaria, Croatia, Spain, Estonia, Georgia, Hungary, Italy, Latvia, Moldova, Poland, Portugal, the Czech Republic, Romania, Russia and Ukraine: *Zengin* v. *Turkey*, para. 33.

therefore adopts a compulsory syllabus that permits no exemptions, there is no violation of the Convention, provided the syllabus passes the 'critical, objective, and pluralistic' test. As the majority of the Grand Chamber recognised in *Folgerø*, Protocol 1 Article 2:

> does not embody any right for parents that their child be kept ignorant about religion and philosophy in their education.[42]

Indeed, the former European Commission of Human Rights found in a case from Sweden that it is a legitimate aim of public policy for the government to seek to ensure all children receive sufficient factual religious knowledge, even if the consequence is that an exemption available to minority religions is denied to the children of atheists who would not otherwise receive adequate alternative religious education.[43]

In terms of active challenges to religious education arising from Protocol 1 Article 2 it is those states where the subject is part of the regular curriculum, then, that are of particular interest. Of these the subject is truly compulsory (in the sense of an absolute requirement on at least some pupils to attend) in only Finland, Greece, Norway, Sweden and Turkey. The remaining twenty countries are divided equally into those where pupils may opt out of religious education[44] and those where they may choose a substitute lesson.[45]

Given this very wide range of potentially compatible approaches, the judgment of the majority of the Grand Chamber appears to excessively interfere in matters of national discretion. This is all the more regrettable since the judgment also gives little concrete guidance to states like Norway – that undoubtedly comprise the bulk of the Council of Europe – in which one religious group (Christianity, in practice) predominates, about how to chart the fine line between reflecting the religious background, history and culture of the society without oppressing children from minority backgrounds. There was no suggestion, for example, that the Norwegian syllabus crossed into the forbidden domain of 'indoctrination'. Rather,

---

[42] *Folgerø* v *Norway*, para. 89.
[43] Eur. Comm. H. R., *Angeleni* v. *Sweden*, 3 December 1986, *Decisions and Reports* 51, p. 41. The Commission found that the Swedish policy of exempting from religious education only pupils of other religious persuasions and not atheists did not violate Article 14. See also Eur. Comm. H. R., *Zénon Bernard* v. *Luxembourg*, 8 September 1993, *Decisions and Reports* 75, p. 57. Contrast *Crockett* v. *Sorenson*.
[44] Austria, Cyprus, Denmark, Ireland, Iceland, Liechtenstein, Malta, Monaco, San Marino and the United Kingdom: *Zengin* v. *Turkey*, para. 31.
[45] Germany, Belgium, Bosnia and Herzegovina, Lithuania, Luxembourg, the Netherlands, Serbia, Slovakia and Switzerland: *Zengin* v. *Turkey*, para. 32.

the majority of the European Court of Human Rights appear to apply a more demanding threshold test in which a perceived imbalance or lack of objectivity in the treatment of different religions necessitates provision of a full opt-out.[46]

As a consequence of the European Court of Human Rights' willingness to examine these issues in detail and its failure to articulate clear principles, there now arises the prospect of a series of cases challenging syllabuses in different European countries entailing fact-sensitive analysis of the context, the legal provisions and the specific syllabus by the Court. This is an unfortunate likely by-product of the Grand Chamber's approach. In fact *Folgerø* has already been followed by a further decision in October 2007 (considered below) in which the European Court of Human Rights ruled unanimously that Turkey's system of religious education violated the rights of a parent from the Alevi stream of Islam.[47] Challenges in other states are likely to follow.

The availability of a partial exemption did not save the curriculum from inconsistency with the Convention in *Folgerø*. The majority found that to utilise the exemption would be burdensome to parents in practice (since they would need to keep a close interest in the subject-matter of lessons). Moreover, the requirement to give reasonable grounds when applying for exemption could be construed as making an application conditional on disclosure of the 'intimate aspects' of the parents' beliefs, contrary to Articles 8 and possibly 9. While opt-out provisions must clearly be effective to have any value, the turn towards treating them as of no effect if there is some cost to using them is a regrettable move in the direction of the North American approach. The Canadian courts especially have tended to discount such exemptions if there is a risk that the child will be made to feel different or stigmatised,[48] rather than regarding the use of an opt-out as an opportunity to celebrate religious diversity as a dimension of pluralism. International human rights law does not provide that exercise of religious liberty should be free of personal cost or embarrassment, however. If this approach is questionable, another aspect of the majority's treatment in *Folgerø* of the partial opt-out is more convincing. The majority of the Grand Chamber argued that to allow pupils to be

---

[46] By contrast the *Toledo Guiding Principles*, p. 69, seem to take a more restrictive view of the necessity for full opt-outs, referring to instances where the teaching amounts to teaching *of* (rather than about) a religion.

[47] *Zengin* v. *Turkey*.

[48] *Zylberberg* v. *Sudbury Board of Education* (1988) 52 DLR (4th) 577 (Ont. CA); *Canadian Civil Liberties Assoc.* v. *Ontario (Minister of Education)* (1990) 65 DLR (4th) 1 (Ont. CA).

exempted from active participation (for example in prayers and singing) but nonetheless to require them to be present in class while the remainder participated substantially diminished the value of the exemption.

The finding of a violation of Protocol 1 Article 2 would appear to leave the Norwegian government and like-minded states with a range of unattractive options.

A full exemption could be granted to parents to excuse their children's participation in religious education. However, as the Court has pointed out previously, such exemptions inevitably create administrative and practical difficulties for schools.[49] The grant of a full exemption from religious education could also be an unfortunate precedent since many knowledge-based subjects cause conflicts of conscience for particular groups (e.g. sex education, information technology, the teaching of evolution, and so on). To offer exemption from all these would risk fracturing the education system and undermining the state's competence to decide what education best prepares children for life in society.

In practice, where parents are dissatisfied with state schooling for religious or other reasons, they have the option of sending their children to a private school in accordance with their convictions.[50] There are some limits to the distinctive path that such schools may take imposed by the Convention (for example, with regard to corporal punishment[51]), but, nevertheless, private schooling represents a viable alternative, particularly where, as in Norway, there is a substantial state subsidy (85 per cent of the costs of private education are borne by the state). Despite this facility the majority of the Grand Chamber concluded that the existence of private schools did not absolve Norway from 'its obligation to safeguard pluralism in State schools which are open to everyone'.[52] Bearing in mind the realistic alternatives open to minority groups that found that partial exemption did not sufficiently accommodate their convictions, the Court's interpretation of this obligation comes close to imposing impossible demands on the state in a plural society. At the very least, as I argue

---

[49] Eur. Ct. H. R., *Kjeldsen, Busk and Pedersen* v. *Denmark*, 7 December 1976, Series A no. 23, para. 53.

[50] Interestingly, the Norwegian government provided evidence that thirty-one private Christian schools had been established since the introduction of the new syllabus, suggesting perhaps that some of these parents were dissatisfied with state schooling but had exercised the option of exit, rather than partial exemption.

[51] Eur. Ct. H. R., *Costello-Roberts* v. *UK*, 25 March 1993; *R* v. *Secretary of State for Education and Employment ex p. Williamson* [2005] UKHL 15; [2005] 2 WLR 590.

[52] *Folgerø* v. *Norway*, para. 101.

below, the judgment appears to prescribe by implication a particular pattern of religious education where the Convention text allows for a spectrum of possible approaches.

Earlier Convention jurisprudence was undoubtedly more accommodating of state diversity and gave stronger recognition to the difficulties that states face in balancing the need for a common curriculum on the one hand and the sensitivities of parental and pupils' consciences on the other, as can be seen by brief reference to two decisions of the former European Commission of Human Rights.

In *Angeleni* v. *Sweden*[53] a challenge was brought by atheist parents to the arrangements for religious education in their daughter's school. The school had refused to give exemption from the classes since under Swedish law only adherents of other religious groups were so entitled, provided there were equivalent arrangements outside school for religious knowledge classes. The Commission found that the Swedish policy of exempting only pupils of other religious persuasions and not atheists did *not* violate Article 14 taken in conjunction with Article 9. Although it did discriminate according to religion, there was an objective and reasonable justification: the government's policy that all children should receive sufficient factual religious knowledge was a legitimate objective.

In another decision, *Zénon Bernard* v. *Luxembourg*,[54] decided under Article 2 Protocol 1, the Commission concluded that there was an objective and reasonable justification for difference in approach to exemption claims by non-religious pupils compared to some religious groups. Luxembourg law required pupils to take either a course in religious and moral education or the secular alternative moral and social education. Only pupils from a religion whose adherents did not give lessons during school hours could be exempted. This policy was intended to minimise the disruption from exemption claims, while accommodating religious objections and preferences. In the Commission's view the difference in treatment of religious and non-religious parents and pupils was justified by reason of the government's obligation to respect religious and philosophical convictions of parents from minority religions. There was no requirement to either 'level up' (to give a general right of exemption) or to 'level down' (to remove the differential treatment).

---

[53] Eur. Comm. H. R., *Angeleni* v. *Sweden*, 3 December 1986, *Decisions and Reports* (DR) 51, p. 41.

[54] Eur. Comm. H. R., *Zénon Bernard* v. *Luxembourg*, 8 September 1993, DR 75, p. 57.

Compared to these two earlier decisions the majority approach in *Folgerø* is more restrictive. In *Angeleni* v. *Sweden* and *Zénon Bernard* v. *Luxembourg* the Commission accepted that a state policy of requiring children from atheist families to attend religious education classes could in some circumstances be justified, despite differential treatment compared to other minority groups. Full exemption was not required. The Commission in both instances accepted that there was no indoctrination and did not engage in close scrutiny of the curriculum in terms of balanced content of the kind employed by the majority of the Court in *Folgerø*.

Apart from the full exemption route, the implicit alternative open to Norway in order to comply with the *Folgerø* judgment would be to weaken the predominant attention given to Christianity in the syllabus. As the Norwegian government and the joint dissenting opinion pointed out, however, the syllabus was devised for a society in which there is a state church to which 86 per cent of the population belong. The Court's earlier jurisprudence states clearly that the presence of an established religion does not of itself violate the right to freedom of belief and religion of non-members.[55] Although the Convention certainly does not require a separation of church and state on the US model (there is no establishment clause and a number of European states – Norway included – in fact have established religions), one could not say that it prevents it either. As Rex Ahdar and I have argued, this aspect of the European position can be termed 'weak establishment' and is clearly distinguishable from the US establishment clause approach.[56] It is commonplace to find that the existence of a state-endorsed religion is reflected also in the education system. In Norway's case the footprint of these arrangements was the so-called 'Christian objects clause'. Nevertheless, Norway had clearly abandoned a 'confessional' approach to religious education in 1969 and it was no part of the schools' role to propagate religious belief; the role of the education sector was quite distinct from that of faith groups and parents in this regard. Bearing that in mind, it is not clear what further symbolic

---

[55] Eur. Ct. H. R., *Darby* v. *Sweden* (1991), 13 July 1989, para. 45. Likewise the UN Human Rights Committee has acknowledged in General Comment 22 that it is possible for there to be a state religion without necessarily impairing of the rights of non-adherents under Arts. 18 and 27 ICCPR: UN Human Rights Committee, *General Comment No. 22 (48), The Right to Freedom of Thought, Conscience, and Religion (Article 18)*, (Forty-Eighth Session, 1993) UN Doc. CCPR/C/21 Rev. 1/Add. 4 (1993), reprinted in UN Doc. HRI/GEN/1/Rev. 8 at 194 (2006), para. 9.

[56] Ahdar and Leigh, *Religious Freedom in the Liberal State*, Chapter 5.

dilution of statements concerning the purpose of education would achieve in practice.

Nor is it obvious that a respect for human rights requires such a move. Education cannot take place in a spiritual and moral vacuum: it is inevitable that there will be an implicit worldview, whether or not this is enshrined in legislation. Of course, it could be argued that pluralism itself should occupy this place of honour. Only the most comprehensive of liberals would argue, however, that this solution would make religious education significantly more 'objective' than that adopted in Norway. Moreover, there is no legal basis in the European Convention to argue that it requires a strong state endorsement of pluralism (i.e. as a type of confessional state religion or philosophy) of this kind. To be sure there are a number of pronouncements from the European Court of Human Rights extolling the virtue of pluralism in a weak sense,[57] but none of them goes so far as to compel a particular pattern of state–religion arrangements.

The minority opinion, by contrast, recognises greater discretion for a state to give preference to the historic majority religion:

> The notion of pluralism embodied in these provisions should not prevent a democratically elected political majority from giving official recognition to a particular religious denomination and subjecting it to public funding, regulation and control. Conferring a particular public status on one denomination does not in itself prejudge the State's respect for parents' religious and philosophical convictions in the education of their children, nor does it affect their exercise of freedom of thought, conscience and religion.[58]

Whereas the majority had emphasised the predominance of Christianity in the syllabus, the minority stressed that the duty on teachers to present all religions and philosophies from the standpoint of their particular characteristics applied equally. Differences in the treatment of religions were quantitative rather than qualitative and these differences were within the margin of appreciation, having regard to the place of Christianity as the state religion in Norway and to Norwegian history.[59] In any event the

---

[57] For example in *Zengin* v. *Turkey* at para. 69 the Court opined that: 'in a democratic society, only pluralism in education can enable pupils to develop a critical mind with regard to religious matters in the context of freedom of thought, conscience and religion.' See also A. Nieuwenhuis, 'The Concept of Pluralism in the Case-Law of the European Court of Human Rights', *European Constitutional Law Review* 3 (2007), 367.

[58] *Folgerø* v. *Norway*, Joint Dissenting Opinion, p. 51.

[59] *Ibid.*, p. 52.

dissenting judges noted that other religions made up roughly half the subject matter of the curriculum.

The minority also disagreed concerning the partial exemption provisions, finding them not to be excessively burdensome or intrusive,[60] and that to allow exemption by observation fell within the national margin of appreciation. Exemption by observation, they pointed out, was in accordance with the distinction between transmitting knowledge about a religion while exempting the activity itself. This view gives stronger emphasis to the state's assessment that knowledge of religion was a necessary part of education. Indeed the majority of the Court had also recognised that Protocol 1 Article 2: 'does not embody any right for parents that their child be kept ignorant about religion and philosophy in their education'.[61]

The new assertiveness of the European Court of Human Rights does not only affect those countries with an established religion. Even a secular state with a clear religious majority may be found to have failed to respect the Convention rights in education, as *Zengin* v. *Turkey* shows.[62] The key issue in this instance was not the legal favouritism given to one religion. Rather, it was the way in which the religious education syllabus was implemented, which the Court found was insufficiently critically objective and pluralistic. Although the Court found[63] that the 'intentions' behind the syllabus for the 'religious culture and ethics' course (which referred to secularism, freedom of thought and religion, and fostering toleration) were compatible with the principles of pluralism and objectivity enshrined in Protocol 1 Article 2, the execution of the course nonetheless violated these. The portrayal of Islam was limited to the Sunni understanding and gave no recognition to the Alevi faith until the ninth grade.[64] Moreover, exemption from the course appeared to be only available to parents of children who identified themselves as Christian or Jewish.

Zengin confirms the impression that the Court is now prepared to engage in systematic and probing analysis, including of the proportions of time devoted in the classroom to each religion and the specific exercises undertaken. This showed that only fifteen pages of the relevant coursebook were devoted to other religions in general and that the Alevi stream of Islam received virtually no acknowledgement. Both the exercises to be undertaken by the pupils and the general approach were entirely from

---

[60] See also Eur. Comm. H. R., *C.J., J.J. and E.J.* v. *Poland*, 16 January 1996, DR 84, p. 46, holding no violation of Articles 8 or 9 despite the applicant's claim that their daughter had been stigmatised by reason of claiming exemption from religious education classes.
[61] *Folgerø* v. *Norway*, para. 89.   [62] *Zengin* v. *Turkey*.
[63] *Ibid.*, para. 59.   [64] *Ibid.*, para. 67.

the Sunni perspective. Such detailed scrutiny shows that the European Court of Human Rights does not take assertions that the objective of religious education is to instil cultural knowledge or to foster toleration at face value.

At one level this is commendable, since it is plainly possible for there to be a gap between aspiration and delivery in the classroom or, more cynically, for high-sounding statements to be inserted as a bureaucratic exercise in Convention-proofing. At another level, however, the Court's approach is problematic. It is plainly impractical for the Strasbourg judges metaphorically to watch over the shoulders of every religious education teacher in Europe. Even if this were possible, it would be highly undesirable because the margin of appreciation recognises a variety of approaches to state religion relations within Europe to education.

The decision also demonstrates the dangers of making provision according to religious labels and failing to provide for minority variations. (Non-Muslims were not required to attend the classes in religious culture and ethics in Turkish schools, but no equivalent conscience provisions were available to minority Muslim groups.) It is plain that the European Court of Human Rights now has considerable unease with educational systems in which the state officials apply religious or denominational labels to pupils that affect their entitlements. This disquiet goes beyond the assertion that it is impermissible under the Convention for a state to set itself up as the arbiter of religious truth.[65] It extends also to anything that in effect requires pupils or parents to identify their religious affiliation to the state in order to claim legal benefits.[66]

This is a new development – the earlier jurisprudence does not support the idea that religious liberty embraces religious privacy,[67] although some authors have criticised it for that reason.[68] The protection for conscience as an aspect of privacy is on the one hand a positive development, since Article 8 tends to be taken far more seriously in the Court's jurisprudence

---

[65] Eur. Ct. H. R., *Moscow Branch of the Salvation Army* v. *Russia*, 5 October 2006, para. 92.

[66] In another recent decision the European Court of Human rights in *Alexandridis* v. *Greece*, 21 February 2008, held that the procedure by which an advocate could opt to make a 'solemn declaration' rather than swearing an oath on the Gospels violated Article 9 by requiring the advocate in effect to reveal his religious affiliation.

[67] Contrast *C.J., J.J. and E.J.* v. *Poland*, p. 46. The Commission did not raise any objection to requirements that pupils disclose their religion in order to claim exemptions in either Eur. Comm. H. R., *Angeleni* v. *Sweden*, 3 December 1986, *Decisions and Reports* (DR) 51, p. 41 or Eur. Comm. H. R., *Zénon Bernard* v. *Luxembourg*, 8 September 1993, DR 75, p. 57.

[68] C. Evans, *Freedom of Religion under the European Convention on Human Rights* (Oxford University Press, 2001), p. 96.

than Article 9. On the other hand this can also be construed as an unfortunate regression to the era in the Court's jurisprudence when it determined what were essentially religious liberty cases on other rights rather than under Article 9.[69] The implication would appear to be that in order to satisfy this interpretation of the Convention, opt-out provisions must not require a declaration of particular religious affiliation (or none). In view of that, it is hard to see how differential exemptions of the kind that the Convention organs have in the past accepted could now be maintained in practice. This new approach also contradicts the threshold requirement that the Court itself applies to religious liberty claims: claimants are required under the Article 9 jurisprudence to demonstrate their beliefs reach a certain level of cogency[70] and claimants who do no more than to baldly assert that their religious or other beliefs have been violated tend to get short shrift.[71]

Conclusion

Religious education is an area in which religious, historical, cultural and constitutional differences among European states are easily apparent. It is also a touchstone for disputes among liberals and between them and others both about the purpose of education and the limits of freedom of conscience. As most European states have moved away from a confessional approach to religious education in which the purpose was to promote religious belief, tensions have begun to appear.

Although the importance of religious education in building tolerant, plural European societies is widely acknowledged, there is scope for considerable difference of opinion over what this entails in practice – in particular between civic liberalism and neutral and separatist approaches. A civic liberal approach stresses the role of state education in forming autonomous adults by giving them capacity to make choices, including religious ones. Under a neutral approach it is the school's task to present

---

[69] Eur. Comm. H. R., *Tsavachidis* v. *Greece*, 4 March 1997 (systematic surveillance of Jehovah's Witnesses by Greek secret police determined under Art. 8 rather than Art. 9); Eur. Ct. H. R., *Riera Blume and others* v. *Spain*, 21 September 1999 (forcible 'de-programming' of members of religious sect dealt with under Art. 5); see Evans, *Freedom of Religion under the European Convention on Human Rights*, p. 79.

[70] Eur. Ct. H. R., *Campbell and Cosans* v. *the United Kingdom*, 25 February 1982, Series A no. 48, pp. 16–18, paras. 25 and 27; and Eur. Ct. H. R., *Valsamis* v. *Greece*, 18 December 1996, *Reports of Judgments and Decisions* 1996–VI, pp. 2323–4, paras. 36–7.

[71] Eur. Comm. H. R., *X* v. *Federal Republic of Germany*, 5 July 1977.

pupils with information concerning religions without any preference and without the objective of instilling belief in any of them. A separatist approach, by contrast, implies state disengagement and leaves religious education to religions themselves. These approaches can have very different practical implications for religious education and for opt-out provisions. Although a mix of these arguments commonly feature in policy and jurisprudence, there is little agreement or conformity of European practice on these questions, once one goes beyond the widely shared view that a state should not take on responsibility for confessional religious education.

All this would suggest a minimal role for human rights law, limited to the role of a safety net in clear cases of indoctrination or religious coercion, but without the broader ambition of endorsing any one pattern for religious education. The OSCE, for example, while recognising the need to comply with human rights commitments, concedes that the manner of giving effect to them will be contingent on local factors.[72] By contrast the European Court of Human Rights, while paying lip service to the margin of appreciation, has embarked on a pattern of detailed scrutiny of religious education in the name of objectivity and neutrality that is anything but plural in its outcome. In view of the current diverse nature of religious education in Europe, a more modest and less interventionist approach from Strasbourg would be appropriate.

---

[72] See especially *Toledo Guiding Principles*, pp. 33–4.

9

Religion and (in)equality in
the European framework

AILEEN MCCOLGAN

Introduction

The role of religion in the public sphere has become of increasing interest to those concerned with discrimination/equality, with the expansion
of EU and domestic anti-discrimination legislation beyond the sphere of
employment and to cover new grounds such as sexual orientation and
religion.

Religious individuals and organisations have benefited from recent anti-
discrimination legislation in the EU and UK: Council Directive 2000/78
prohibiting discrimination on grounds of religion in the employment context.[1] More recently, the Commission has proposed a new directive that
would, like the UK legislation, extend the prohibition on religious-based
discrimination into education, social protection and social advantages
and access to goods and services.[2] But protections against discrimination
on other grounds have also been resisted by some religious individuals
and collectives as incompatible with freedom of religion and the asserted
equality rights of religious individuals and bodies.[3]

The question that I want to address here is the extent to which religious collectives should be exempted from rules of general application.
The rules that concern me are, for the most part, rules that prohibit discrimination on grounds including (but not limited to) gender and sexual

---

[1] The UK Equality Act 2006, Part 2.
[2] Proposal for a Council Directive on implementing the principle of equal treatment
between persons irrespective of religion or belief, disability, age or sexual orientation,
COM/2008/0426 final.
[3] See for example 'Gay adoption regulations "sinister", hits at religious freedom, bishop says'
Catholic Online, www.catholic.org, 20.2.07 (last accessed 12 August 2011). See also House
of Lords debates 24.11.97, col. 801 and *Re Christian Institute and others* [2007] NIQB 66
[2008] IRLR 36.

orientation. I want to consider the extent to which freedom of religion ought to be regarded as 'trumping' equality claims and, in light of the conclusions drawn on this, the acceptable role of religious organisations in the public domain (in particular, in the delivery of public goods and services). I will consider only equality claims which might arise external to the religious organisations (for example, on the part of those who seek or are provided with services from them) rather than potential *internal* claims to equality by members of the group; constraints of space prevent me from addressing the interesting question whether and to what extent the denial of equality *amongst* members should impact upon the entitlement of the religious group to engage in the public sphere.[4] The issue that I will focus on here is the engagement of religious organisations in the sphere outside the immediately religious, that is, in the delivery of the kinds of functions which can be delivered by non-religious organisations (residential, transport and other services including, but not limited to, functions which (whether accepted as 'public' or not by the courts)[5] are or have been significantly delivered by the state, or are paid for out of the public purse.[6] Among these functions are those related to education, health, social care, fostering and adoption.

Religious engagement in the public sphere is common in some European states. In Germany, for example, religions recognised as 'corporations in public law' (which include the Roman Catholic Church, the Evangelical (Protestant) Church, the Central Council of Jews in Germany, the Greek and Russian Orthodox Churches and the Seventh Day Adventists) are entitled to the proceeds of an income tax surcharge on members.[7] Religious corporations run numerous hospitals, nursing homes, counselling services and day care centres funded largely by the state.[8] The engagement of religious organisations in the running of

---

[4] It does seem to me, however, that much of what I conclude below may be similarly applicable to the participation in the public sphere of collectives whose discriminatory behaviour is internal only, at least where that participation carries with it public subsidy or funding in any form.

[5] See *YL* v. *Birmingham* [2008] 1 AC 95.

[6] This a significantly wider approach to 'public' than that adopted by the House of Lords in *YL*; *ibid*.

[7] Currently in the region of 9 per cent.

[8] On 22.03.08 *Newsweek* reported that 'The two main churches divvy up €18.5 billion in subsidies and a government-collected "church tax", including €3.5 billion for religious instruction in the schools. (The far-smaller Jewish community gets a lesser sum.) On top of that, the government doles out an additional €45 billion to church-run hospitals, nursing homes and other social services.'

hospitals (around a third of the total in Germany are Christian) has obvious implications for the provision of contraception, abortion, gender-assignment services and sexual health services, and it has been reported that the prevalence of discrimination on grounds of religion in relation to appointments to hospital staff serves significantly to reduce access to medical careers to non-Christians.[9] The National Secular Society website reported in June 2006 the decision of a German court in May 2006 that a woman dismissed from her job in a Catholic hospital after leaving the Church should be denied benefits on the basis that she had lost her job 'deliberately or with wanton negligence'.[10]

The apparent impunity with which religious bodies find themselves free to discriminate in relation to their employees in Germany perhaps raises questions as to the implementation there of the requirements of Council Directive 2000/78/EC. The question here, however, is whether and to what extent European law should permit such organisations to discriminate in relation to the provision of services.

Clashes might be expected to arise most regularly in connection with claims against discrimination on grounds of sex, sexual orientation or even religion (that is, the religion of the 'outside' individual pitted against the religious collective). They could, however, also arise in connection with other protected grounds. Clashes between religious freedom and race equality are possible at least in theory, for example, since a number of predominantly US-based 'Christian' churches, including the 'Christian Knights of the Ku Klux Klan', 'Aryan Nations' and a variety of other churches within the 'Christian Identity' movement, advocate white supremacism and anti-semitism. Historically the Church of Jesus Christ of the Latter Day Saints (the Mormon Church) regarded blackness as the 'mark of Cain' and discouraged interracial sexual contact, only allowing African American men full membership in 1978.[11]

1   Existing and proposed religious exemptions: European law

Council Directive 2000/43/EC (the Race Directive) is of wide material scope, regulating discrimination on grounds of 'racial or ethnic origin' in relation to employment (broadly defined to include, inter alia, vocational

---

[9]   See www.commentisfree.guardian.co.uk/anna_bawden/2007/11/wards_of_god.html (last accessed 19 May 2010).

[10] www.secularism.org.uk/losingyourreligioncanalsomeanlos.html (last accessed 19 May 2010), reporting a decision of the Civil Court of the Rheinland and Palatinate.

[11] See, too, *R (E)* v. *JFS* [2010] 2 WLR 153.

training and guidance etc., access to self-employment and occupation and trade union involvement as well as working conditions and dismissal); social protection, including social security and healthcare; social advantages; education and 'access to and supply of goods and services which are available to the public, including housing'.[12] Council Directive 2000/78/ EC, which regulates discrimination on grounds of sexual orientation, religion or belief, disability and age, applies only in relation to employment, broadly defined as above. Directive 2004/113/EC, also adopted under Article 13 TEC, extended the prohibition on sex discrimination beyond the boundaries of employment and social security for the first time to apply 'within the limits of the powers conferred upon the Community', to the supply of 'goods and services, which are available to the public irrespective of the person concerned as regards both the public and private sectors, including public bodies, and which are offered outside the area of private and family life and the transactions carried out in this context', although it does not apply 'to the content of media and advertising nor to education'.[13] And the proposed new directive on equal treatment would regulate discrimination on grounds of sexual orientation, religion or belief, age and disability 'within the limits of the powers conferred upon the Community ... [by] all persons, as regards both the public and private sectors', including public bodies, in relation to '(a) Social protection, including social security and healthcare; (b) Social advantages; (c) Education; (d) Access to and supply of goods and other services which are available to the public, including housing'.[14] Article 3 of the proposed directive provides, however, that the prohibitions on discrimination in access to goods 'apply to individuals only insofar as they are performing a professional or commercial activity'; that 'Member States may provide for differences in treatment in access to educational institutions based on religion or belief'; and that the directive is 'without prejudice to national laws on marital or family status and reproductive rights', [or to] 'national legislation ensuring the secular nature of the State, State institutions or bodies, or education, or concerning the status and activities of churches and other organisations based on religion or belief'. The exceptions provided by the proposed directive appear to have wide application in cases of potential conflict between religion/belief and sexual orientation.

---

[12] Council Directive 2000/43/EC (the Race Directive), Article 3.

[13] *Ibid.*, Article 3.

[14] Proposal for a Council Directive on implementing the principle of equal treatment between persons irrespective of religion or belief, disability, age or sexual orientation, COM/2008/0426 final.

2   Religious freedom

There is clearly ample scope for conflict between those concerned, on the one hand, with the freedom of religious individuals and collectives to adhere to their religious principles and the demand to be free from discrimination on grounds, in particular, of sexual orientation, gender and religion. A number of existing and proposed EC provisions applicable to some such conflicts have been set out above. In order to assess them, and to begin to consider the appropriate nature and extent of such exemptions, it is useful to consider the right to religious freedom as it is guaranteed by the European Convention on Human Rights (ECHR).

Article 9 of the Convention, which guarantees freedom of religion (and which, the European Court of Human Rights has accepted, is applicable to religious organisations as well as individuals[15]), provides that:

1. Everyone has the right to freedom of thought, conscience and religion; this right includes freedom to change his religion or belief, and freedom, either alone or in community with others and in public or private, to manifest his religion or belief, in worship, teaching, practice and observance.
2. Freedom to manifest one's religion or beliefs shall be subject only to such limitations as are prescribed by law and are necessary in a democratic society in the interests of public safety, for the protection of public order, health or morals, or the protection of the rights and freedoms of others.

'The right to freedom of thought, conscience and religion ... includ[ing] freedom to change [one's] religion or belief' is one of the very few unqualified rights recognised by the European Convention. Any direct interference with this 'psychic' or 'internal' individual freedom will breach Article 9 regardless of its aims and without consideration of any competing interests or rights: religious freedom trumps. The right to manifest one's 'religion or belief, in worship, teaching, practice and observance' is not unqualified, although this right has been stated by the European Court of Human Rights to be 'one of the foundations of a "democratic society" within the meaning of the Convention [which] ... in its religious dimension, [is] one of the most vital elements that go to make up the

15 See for example *Jewish Liturgical Association Cha'are Shalom Ve Tsedek* v. *France* 9 BHRC 27.

identity of believers and their conception of life [and] is also a precious asset for atheists, agnostics, sceptics and the unconcerned'.

A   Direct 'internal' interferences

The jurisprudence of the European Court of Human Rights, in common with that of the US Courts under the First Amendment to the US Constitution,[16] is robust where it concerns direct interferences by the state with what are perceived as the internal affairs of religious organisations. Among the cases in which the European Court has protected religious collectives from direct 'internal' interference by the state is *Metropolitan Church of Bessarabia* v. *Moldova*, in which the Court ruled that the respondent state had breached Article 9 by refusing to recognise the applicant church (an autonomous orthodox church) as a religious organisation separate from the Metropolitan Church of Moldova.[17] The latter was affiliated to the Russian Orthodox Church whereas the Metropolitan Church of Bessarabia, which had almost one million members, was affiliated to the Romanian Orthodox Church. The state took the view that the case involved an ecclesiastical conflict within the Orthodox Church that could be resolved only by the Romanian and Russian Orthodox Churches. Perhaps ironically, this desire to be 'hands-off' in relation to what was regarded as an internal matter had the result that those who regarded themselves as constituting the applicant church were unable to function as a church. They were not entitled to meet in order to practise their religion, their priests were not permitted to conduct religious services and, the church not having legal personality, it was not entitled to judicial protection of its assets.

In the view of the European Court, the interference with the applicant church's Article 9 rights was at least arguably prescribed by law in pursuit of a legitimate aim: the preservation of the young State of Moldova in the face of alleged pressures to reunite the Moldovan region of Bessarabia with Romania (the territory which now comprised Moldova having been repeatedly passed between Romanian and Russian control). The

---

[16]   The First Amendment provides that 'Congress shall make no law respecting an establishment of religion, or prohibiting the free exercise thereof; or abridging the freedom of speech, or of the press; or the right of the people peaceably to assemble, and to petition the Government for a redress of grievances'. *Kokkinakis* v. *Greece* (1994) 17 EHRR 397, para. 31.

[17]   Eur. Ct. H. R. (1st section), *Metropolitan Church of Bessarabia* v. *Moldova*, 13 December 2001. See similarly Eur. Ct. H. R. (Grand Chamber), *Hasan and Chaush* v. *Bulgaria*, 26 October 2000.

population of Moldova was 'ethnically and linguistically varied', but the majority were Orthodox Christians and it was the view of the state that recognition of the Moldovan Orthodox Church was a unifying factor, whereas the recognition of the applicant church would 'revive old Russo-Romanian rivalries within the population, thus endangering social stability and even Moldova's territorial integrity'. The Court went on, however, to rule that the interference was not 'necessary in a democratic society'. The role of the state in 'exercising its regulatory power in this sphere and in its relations with the various religions, denominations and beliefs' was, in the view of the Court, to 'remain neutral and impartial':

> What is at stake here is the preservation of pluralism and the proper functioning of democracy, one of the principle [*sic*] characteristics of which is the possibility it offers of resolving a country's problems through dialogue, without recourse to violence, even when they are irksome. Accordingly, the role of the authorities in such circumstances is not to remove the cause of tension by eliminating pluralism, but to ensure that the competing groups tolerate each other.

As mentioned above, the very reason put forward by the state for refusing registration to the applicant church, founded in 1992, was its desire not to interfere with what it (the state) saw as the internal affairs of a single church (the Metropolitan Church of Moldova, of which the government regarded the applicant to be a 'schismatic group'). Both the applicant church and the Metropolitan Church of Moldova claimed to be the successor of the (former) Metropolitan Church of Bessarabia, which had existed until 1944.[18] It is the case that recognition of the (new) Metropolitan Church of Bessarabia would have had repercussions for the Metropolitan Church of Moldova in terms, for example, of loss of parishioners and (it appears) church property.[19] Similarly, the schism within the worldwide Anglican church about the ordination of gay priests has implications for property rights (see further below). But any interference with the Moldovan Orthodox Church that would have resulted from state recognition of the Bessarabian Orthodox church would have been of this indirect form, rather than the very direct restrictions imposed on the latter church and its adherents by the refusal of recognition. An analogy can be drawn with freedom of association: whereas the refusal to allow a person or group to

---

[18] Until 1940 Bessarabia had been an 'administrative unit' of Moldova.

[19] Some of the breaches of Article 9 complained of involved expulsion by the Metropolitan Church of Moldova from parishes that had chosen to transfer (presumably with property) to the applicant church.

disassociate from another unit may enhance what might be regarded as the positive right of the latter to associate with its reluctant peer, it has a more immediate impact on the person or group forbidden to dissociate from unwanted colleagues and, assuming exclusive allegiance is required, prevented from associating with their companions of choice.

Judicial unwillingness to interfere directly in the 'internal' affairs of religious organisations is not limited to these types of cases. In the UK, *R v. Chief Rabbi, ex parte Wachmann* concerned a claim by a rabbi for judicial review of the decision of the Chief Rabbi of England and Wales that he was 'no longer religiously and morally fit to occupy his position as rabbi' following an investigation into allegations of adultery with a member of his congregation.[20] The English High Court ruled that the decision of the Chief Rabbi was not amenable to judicial review. According to Simon Brown J, as he then was, 'the court would never be prepared to rule on questions of Jewish law' and the claimant could not rely instead on the principles of natural justice given the difficulties inherent in 'separat[ing] out procedural complaints from consideration of substantive principles of Jewish law which may underlie them':

> That consideration apart, the court is hardly in a position to regulate what is essentially a religious function – the determination whether someone is morally and religiously fit to carry out the spiritual and pastoral duties of his office. The court must inevitably be wary of entering so self-evidently sensitive an area, straying across the well-recognised divide between church and state.
>
> One cannot, therefore, escape the conclusion that if judicial review lies here, then one way or another this secular court must inevitably be drawn into adjudicating upon matters intimate to a religious community.[21]

Judicial preference for state abstention from what could be characterised as interference in the internal affairs of religious organisations is also manifest in cases in which questions of religious doctrine are entangled with disputes, for example, over property-related matters. Such reticence is founded on a recognition of the limits of jurisdictional competence of the secular courts: as Justice William Brennan put it for the US Supreme Court in *Presbyterian Church* v. *Hull Church* (1969), a case involving a property dispute between two Presbyterian factions:

---

[20] *R v. Chief Rabbi, ex parte Wachmann* [1992] 1 WLR 1036.
[21] *Ibid.* Though see *Percy v. Board of National Mission of the Church of Scotland* [2005] UKHL 73, [2006] 2 AC 28 in which the House of Lords allowed a sex discrimination complaint by a woman minister. It should be noted that no doctrinal issue was pleaded in that case.

First Amendment values are plainly jeopardized when church property litigation is made to turn on the resolution by civil courts of controversies over religious doctrine and practice. If civil courts undertake to resolve such controversies in order to adjudicate the property dispute, the hazards are ever present of inhibiting the free development of religious doctrine and of implicating secular interests in matters of purely ecclesiastical concern.[22]

The Supreme Court there accepted that the courts could determine some property disputes, but demanded that they do so 'without resolving underlying controversies over religious doctrine'. An example of where this is possible is provided by US litigation arising out of the schism in the worldwide Anglican church over the issue of gay clergy. The Episcopal Church in Virginia took legal action in February 2007 seeking possession of the property of eleven conservative parishes that had chosen to leave the Episcopal Church and affiliate with the Anglican Church of Nigeria. In June 2010 Virginia's Supreme Court ruled that the dispute was not governed by Virginia's 'Division Statute', which provides that congregations may depart from their denominations with their property on the basis of a majority vote, as long as the property is not encumbered. This legislation was ruled constitutional by a Circuit Court in June 2008 but the Supreme Court ruled that the congregations had joined a different church – the Convocation of Anglicans in North America, established by the Anglican Church of Nigeria, rather than a different branch of the Episcopal Church or the Diocese of Virginia.

B   Indirect interference

It is evident from the case law above that conflicts arising within and between religious organisations give rise to significant difficulties for any state that seeks to regulate religious collectives while avoiding breaches of Article 9 of the Convention. The judicial approach in the cases considered above, which comes close to an unqualified prohibition, can be defended in part by drawing an analogy between the internal affairs of religious organisations and the internal (psychic) beliefs of an individual. This is not to say that 'human' rights must be applied to collectives, whether religious or other. But Article 9 protects the right to manifest religion or

---

[22] *Presbyterian Church* v. *Hull Church* 393 US 440 (1969). See also *Maryland and Virginia Eldership of the Churches of God* v. *Church of God at Sharpsburg, Inc* 396 US 367 (1970).

belief 'either alone or in community with others', and direct interference by the state in the internal functioning of a religious collective (by, for example, selecting leaders or imposing doctrinal rules) risks interfering with individuals' beliefs by purporting to instruct them on the correct content of those beliefs, if such content is to conform with the doctrine of their chosen (interfered with) religion.[23]

It is arguable, then, that the relatively strict approach to what might be classified as 'direct collective' interference is required by Article 9 even if that provision is regarded as concerned primarily with individual (human) rights. But here I want to consider the Article 9 case law relating to *indirect* interferences with religious beliefs. Such indirect interferences arise when the religious individual ventures out into the public space: when, for example, an observant Jew wishes to work in a job which is organised on the basis of a Christian calendar (preventing exit in time for the beginning of Sabbath in winter), or a hijab-wearing woman works in a context in which religious display is forbidden. The case law on this type of indirect interference tends to feature individuals rather than collectives, because it is individuals who feel the force of rules such as those mentioned above.[24] What is noteworthy here is the lack of concern shown by the European Commission and Court of Human Rights towards constraints imposed upon religious individuals in their engagement with the wider world, even where those constraints have prevented them from reconciling their religious convictions with their occupational or educational ambitions.

An early example of this is to be found in the Commission's decision in *Ahmad* v. *UK*,[25] which involved an attempt by a teacher to demand accommodation of his obligation to attend religious worship on a Friday

---

[23] Somewhat different questions arise where, as in Britain, the church is established. The Act of Supremacy 1558, which was declaratory of the common law, provides (section 8) that: 'suche jurisdictions privileges superiorities and preheminences spirituall and ecclesisticall, as by any spirituall or ecclesiasticall power or aucthorite hathe heretofore bene or may lawfully be exercised or used for the visitacion of the ecclesiasticall state and persons, and for reformacion order and correcion of the same and of all maner of errours scismes abuses offences contemptes and enormities, shall for ever by aucthorite of this present Parliament be united and annexed to the imperiall crowne of this realme.' It may be that the state in England is so intertwined with Anglicanism as to render inappropriate the characterisation of (for example) the role of the Queen (acting through the executive or Parliament) as *interference* from the outside, rather than an integral aspect of the internal functioning of the Anglican Church.

[24] Challenges are, however, brought by organisations on behalf of their members: *Jewish Liturgical Association Cha'are Shalom Ve Tsedek* v. *France* 9 BHRC 27.

[25] Eur. Comm. H. R., *Ahmad* v. *UK* (1982) 4 EHRR 126.

by his employers. The Commission, remarking that he 'remained free to resign if and when he found that his teaching obligations conflicted with his religious duties', dismissed his claim as 'manifestly ill-founded'. A similar decision was reached in *Stedman* v. *UK*,[26] in which the Christian applicant challenged the unilateral imposition on her of an obligation to work on Sundays. The Commission informed Ms Stedman that she 'was dismissed for failing to agree to work certain hours rather than for her religious belief as such and was free to resign and did in effect resign from her employment'.

In these early cases the Commission refused even to acknowledge that the applicants' rights had been interfered with, as it did in *Karaduman* v. *Turkey* in which a Muslim woman challenged a refusal to let her graduate from university unless she was photographed without her headscarf. According to the Commission: 'by choosing to pursue her higher education in a secular university a student submits to those university rules, which may make the freedom of students to manifest their religion subject to restrictions as to place and manner intended to ensure harmonious coexistence between students of different beliefs.'[27] More recently, although the European Court of Human Rights has become more willing to accept that restrictions with which members of particular religious groups find it difficult in practice to comply can amount to 'interference' with the religious beliefs of individual applicants, it has been quick to find that the restrictions are justified for the purposes of Article 9(2). In *Dahlab* v. *Switzerland*, for example, the Court rejected as manifestly unfounded an Article 9 challenge to a headscarf ban imposed on a Muslim primary school teacher.[28] The Court thought it 'very difficult to assess the impact that a powerful external symbol such as the wearing of a headscarf may have on the freedom of conscience and religion of very young children', expressed concern that 'the wearing of a headscarf might have some kind of proselytising effect, seeing that it appears to be imposed on women by a precept which is laid down in the Koran and which ... is hard to square with the principle of gender equality' and concluded that it was 'difficult to reconcile the wearing of an Islamic headscarf with the message of tolerance, respect for others

[26] Eur. Comm. H. R., *Stedman* v. *UK* (1997) 23 EHRR CD.
[27] *Karaduman* v. *Turkey* (1993) 74 DR 93, 108. See also the majority view in *Copsey* v. *WWB Devon Clays Ltd* [2005] ICR 1789 and the views of Lords Scott, Hoffmann and Bingham in *R (Begum)* v. *Headteacher and Governors of Denbigh High School* [2007] 1 AC 1000.
[28] Eur. Ct. H. R. (2nd section), *Dahlab* v. *Switzerland*, 15 February 2001.

and, above all, equality and non-discrimination that all teachers in a democratic society must convey to their pupils'.[29]

The justification in *Dahlab* rested significantly on the fact that the applicant was a teacher of young children. In the more recent decision of *Şahin* v. *Turkey*,[30] however, the Grand Chamber upheld a complete headscarf ban imposed by a Turkish university, agreeing with the fourth section[31] that the principles of secularism and gender equality, on which it accepted that the ban was based, justified the interference with the applicant's Article 9 rights. The fourth section had expressed concern about the impact of the headscarf 'presented or perceived as a compulsory religious duty ... on those who choose not to wear it' in Turkey: 'a country in which the majority of the population, while professing a strong attachment to the rights of women and a secular way of life, adhere to the Islamic faith.'[32] The Grand Chamber went so far as to suggest that, given the diversity of approaches across Europe on the issue, the extent and form of regulations concerning the wearing of religious symbols in educational institutions 'must inevitably be left up to a point to the state concerned, as it will depend on the domestic context concerned'[33] and suggested that '[a]n attitude which fails to respect th[e] principle [of secularism] will not necessarily be accepted as being covered by the freedom to manifest one's religion and will not enjoy the protection of art 9 of the convention'.[34] Judge Tulkens, in dissent, suggested that, in characterising the headscarf as a 'powerful external symbol', which 'appeared to be imposed on women by a religious precept that was hard to reconcile with the principle of gender equality', the majority went beyond as the proper role of the Court in 'determine[ing] in a general and abstract way the signification of wearing the headscarf [and] impos[ing] its viewpoint on the applicant'.

---

[29] See also *Jewish Liturgical Association Cha'are Shalom Ve Tsedek* v. *France* 9 BHRC 27 in which the Court accepted that there would have been an interference with the applicant's religious freedom if the slaughter rules of which the association complained had prevented them from obtaining religiously acceptable meat. In the event, since they were able to obtain the meat from Belgium, the Court ruled that no interference had occurred.

[30] Eur. Ct. H. R. (Grand Chamber), *Leyla Şahin* v. *Turkey*, 10 November 2005.

[31] Eur. Ct. H. R. (Fourth Section), *Şahin* v. *Turkey*, 29 June 2004.

[32] *Ibid.*, para. 108.

[33] Eur. Ct. H. R. (Grand Chamber), *Leyla Şahin* v. *Turkey*, 10 November 2005., para. 109, citing *Gorzelik* v. *Poland* (2004) 38 EHRR 4, para. 67 and *Murphy* v. *Ireland* (2004) 38 EHRR 13, para. 73.

[34] *Ibid.*, para. 114, citing Eur. Ct. H. R. (Grand Chamber), *Refah Partisi (The Welfare Party) and others* v. *Turkey*, 13 February 2003, para, 93.

C Problematising the boundaries: conflicts of conscience

It is not my intention here to take issue with the approach of the European Court to Article 9 individual accommodation cases given the concerns I express as to the protection of religious belief. It is important, however, to acknowledge the limits of the protection afforded to religious believers by Article 9 of the Convention. The distinction drawn by Article 9 between the *holding* and the *manifestation* of religious beliefs was mentioned above, where it was noted that the right to freedom of thought, belief and conscience is unqualified. But it should be noted that individual accommodation cases, cast here as involving *indirect* interferences with religion, can in practice involve interferences with belief as well as its manifestation.[35]

An individual's beliefs, religious or other, may demand action that is not regarded as a matter of personal choice in circumstances in which conflict with externally imposed rules cannot be avoided. Examples of this type of conflict might arise, for Jehovah's Witnesses, in connection with their avoidance of blood products: while individuals are unlikely to be required themselves to undergo treatment with such substances, they may well be prevented by law from withholding such treatment from their children. Some Mormons regard polygamy as mandatory for anyone who wishes to enter the highest level of heaven, thus setting up conflicts with prohibitions on bigamy. While it may be possible to avoid head-on collision with the law by keeping second and subsequent 'marriages' informal (that is, not legally recognised), Mormon parents in some communities regard themselves as bound to provide under-age girl children for 'marriage' to community elders.[36] Jehovah's Witnesses for the most part find military service incompatible with their religious beliefs, while many Jews regard male circumcision and many Christians proselytism as mandatory.[37]

---

[35] This has been recognised by the US Supreme Court, e.g. in *Wisconsin* v. *Yoder* [1972] 406 US 205, though only to the extent of recognising that interference with *action* as distinct from *belief* could require justification from the state under the first Amendment: see G. Moens, 'The Action-Belief Dichotomy and Freedom of Religion', *Sydney Law Review* 12 (1989–90), 195, 207–10 and, for discussion of the case generally, W. Galston, 'Two Concepts of Liberalism', *Ethics* 105 (1995).

[36] According to CNN, 16 September 2007, one of the witnesses in the trial in Utah of sect leader Warren Jeffs testified that she was 'trying to preserve her "eternal salvation" when she obeyed a command by polygamist sect leader Warren Jeffs to marry her cousin at age 14'.

[37] Though there is a debate in reform Judaism about the religious necessity for circumcision, which is based on Genesis 17: 'Thus shall my covenant be marked in your flesh as an everlasting pact ... And if any male who is uncircumcised fails to circumcise the flesh of his foreskin, that person shall be cut off from his kin; he has broken my covenant.'

Where such 'beliefs in action' are prohibited by the state, the individual must choose whether to comply with religious or state-imposed obligations in the event that accommodation (for example by withdrawal from the public sphere in the case of prescriptions on religious dress) is impossible or impracticable. The action of the state in (for example) overriding parental refusal of blood transfusions for children, demanding involvement in military service, prohibiting polygamy or the adoption of a particular dress code or male circumcision, is not an overt interference in the *holding* of religious beliefs: the *belief* that male circumcision, the avoidance of blood products, pacifism or compliance with a dress code is mandatory is not itself proscribed. But those *beliefs* are manifestly interfered with when the individual is prevented from acting in accordance with them, at least in circumstances where this generates a crisis of conscience because of the absence of a choice to avoid, at whatever cost, the circumstances of conflict (by, for example, studying or working elsewhere) or an implied '*force majeure*' clause in the religious doctrine. [38]

The decisions in *Ahmad, Stedman, Karaduman, Dahlab* and *Şahin* all involved applicants who could avoid acting contrary to their religious beliefs albeit at some cost to themselves, and in the case of *Karaduman* at significant cost (since it meant forgoing much of the benefit of the degree for which she had studied). But even where applicants have had no such 'outs', the ECtHR has rejected claims based on failures to accommodate. The Court has to date, for example, rejected Article 9-based challenges to compulsory military service even where no option was provided to conscientious objectors. [39] The extent and duration of such punishment is controlled by decisions such as those in *Thlimmenos* v. *Greece* and *Ülke* v. *Turkey,* in which the Court found breaches of Articles 14 and 3 respectively arising from arbitrary and manifestly excessive punishment of

---

[38] Another, at least arguably, is the determination of Amish parents in the *Wisconsin* v. *Yoder* case that their children leave state education at 14; the Amish view being that state education beyond this age would (Moens, 'The Action-Belief Dichotomy and Freedom of Religion', p. 207) 'threaten their way of life and violate their religious beliefs'.

[39] Note that Article 4, which prohibits 'forced or compulsory labour', exempts military service from this prohibition. In Eur. Comm. H. R., *Peters* v. *the Netherlands*, 30 November 1994; Eur. Comm. H. R., *Heudens* v. *Belgium*, 22 May 1995; and Eur. Comm. H. R., *Valsamis* v. *Greece* (1997) 24 EHRR 294, the European Commission rejected Art. 9-based challenges to mandatory military service itself. Note, however, that in Eur. Ct. H. R., *Bayatyan* v. *Armenia* (appl. no. 23459/03), the Court ruled admissible a challenge to mandatory military service. The decision in *Bayatyan* was reached in December 2006 and the matter has yet to receive full consideration by the Court.

refusal to serve,[40] but to date no direct challenge has succeeded. Similarly, while proselytism is a religious duty for many,[41] Article 9 protects only those forms of proselytism regarded as 'proper'.[42]

3   'Indirect' interferences and religious collectives

The next question that arises concerns the extent to which what might be classified as a 'robust' approach to Article 9 challenges by individual applicants who seek to have their religious views accommodated ought to be applied where the beliefs of religious collectives are at issue. In one sense the issues considered above – prohibitions on the use of blood products, requirements to undergo female genital mutilation or to utilise corporal punishment, for example- can be characterised as collective matters insofar as the individuals upon whom they impact are generally members of religious collectives from whose teachings they derive their individual understandings of their religious obligations. But the 'collective' cases in which I am particularly interested here are those in which the religious collective demands that it be allowed to operate as a collective with exemptions from the normal rules concerning, for example, non-discrimination on grounds of sexual orientation, gender or religion itself. Thus, for example, a church-run home for the elderly might wish to refuse accommodation to a same-sex couple, a Muslim school to exclude a pregnant schoolgirl, or a Catholic organisation to be exempted from rules prohibiting sexual orientation discrimination in the provision of adoption or fostering services or requiring it, as a supplier of education or medical services, to provide the full range of sex education or reproductive health care (including, for example, contraception and/or abortion).

The question is whether religious organisations ought to be permitted to discriminate in circumstances such that other bodies would not be, where that discrimination is said to be required as a matter of religious doctrine or belief. Such organisations might regard themselves as bound in conscience to discriminate, and may pray in aid of Articles 9 and 10 of the European Convention on Human Rights. We saw above that Article 9

---

[40] Respectively Eur. Ct. H. R., *Thlimmenos* v. *Greece* (2001) 31 EHRR 15 and *Ülke* v. *Turkey* application no 39437/98.

[41] Matthew's last verses report Jesus' command to 'Go to all the nations and make disciples. Baptize them and teach them my commands.' 'Bearing Christian Witness' is, according to the 1956 World Council of Churches' report, 'an essential mission and a responsibility of every Christian and every Church'.

[42] Eur. Ct. H. R., *Kokkinakis* v. *Greece*, 25 May 1993.

jurisprudence provides scant support for any demands for accommodation on the part of religious individuals. Is there any reason in principle why a different approach should be adopted to religious collectives? It seems clear that *direct* intrusion into the internal affairs of such organisations (such as, for example, demanding the acceptance of women or gay men as ministers[43]) would breach Article 9 as it is currently interpreted. But what of restrictions placed on churches and other religious organisations in terms of their engagement in the public sphere, where those restrictions arise from generally applicable rules, adherence with which would create doctrinal or similar difficulties for those bodies?[44] Is there sufficient reason to adopt a different approach to religious collectives in this context than that which has been applied consistently to individuals who have attempted to rely on Article 9 of the European Convention to achieve a reconciliation between their religious beliefs and obligations and their wider public engagement?

4   The value and cost of religion

A number of different arguments may be made for according special treatment of this sort to organisations. Communitarians will argue that individual identity is shaped with cultural communities that, by virtue of this, have some kind of claim to continued existence.[45] Michael Sandel and Charles Taylor, for example, discuss the centrality of family, religious and other ties to the development of the self.[46] Margalit and Raz similarly emphasise the significance of 'group culture' to the acquisition of identity,[47] advocating respect for claims to self-determination on the part of groups which are characterised by 'a common character and culture that encompass many, varied and important aspects of life'.[48] As they acknowledge, '[s]ome religious groups meet our conditions, as do social

---

[43]   At least in the case of a church lacking the kind of institutional links with the state that the Anglican Church has.

[44]   I consider here only those cases in which the religious organisations wish to discriminate in that context rather than (for example) having internally discriminatory rules as regards appointment to the ministry etc.

[45]   These arguments are frequently made in relation to 'ethnic' communities but could equally well apply to 'communities' identified by reference to religious belief.

[46]   See for example Charles Taylor, 'Atomism', in *Philosophy and the Human Sciences: Philosophical Papers 2* (Cambridge University Press, 1985); Michael Sandel, *Liberalism and the Limits of Justice* (Cambridge University Press, 1981).

[47]   A. Margalit and J. Raz, 'National Self-Determination' in Will Kymlicka (ed.), *The Rights of Minority Cultures* (Oxford University Press, 1995), p. 79.

[48]   *Ibid.*, pp. 82–5.

classes, and some racial groups'.[49] Will Kymlicka's modified liberalism also assumes the importance of 'culture' in determining 'the context of choice':[50] creating cultural narratives by reference to which 'we decide how to lead our lives by situating ourselves within [these] narratives, by adopting roles that have struck us as worthwhile, as ones worth living'.[51]

Recognition of the importance of community and culture is not problematic from an equality perspective; indeed it has long been a feminist complaint that the characterisation of persons as autonomous individuals is one that is particularly problematic for women given their disproportionate share of caring tasks.[52] But Jeremy Waldron criticises Kymlicka's assumption that the cultural embeddedness of choice requires 'one cultural framework in which each available option is assigned a meaning', positing instead the view that 'meaningful options may come to us as items or fragments from a variety of cultural sources ... His argument shows that people need cultural materials ... not ... that what they need is "a rich and secure cultural structure". It shows the importance of access to a variety of stories and roles; but it does not, as he claims, show the importance of something called *membership* in a culture.'[53]

Even if Waldron is wrong, and community membership is important in a stronger sense than he allows, Sonu Bedi points out a tension between the increasing tendency to view religion and religious belief as mutable and demands for the provision of 'religious exemptions'. Unless, she argues, religion is unchosen, an 'immutable and fixed belief system',[54] there is no basis to differentiate 'the Jew from the Rotarian ... the Sikh from the mere hat-wearer'. Bedi concedes that the cost of wearing a turban may be higher than not wearing a hat because it is part of an overall system which is threatened with collapse if an aspect of it is not complied with, and/or threatens estrangement from community, but she points out that the cost of not wearing a hat would be very high also if the wearer had bet all her money on being allowed to wear it. And although the turban

[49] *Ibid.*, p. 85.
[50] W. Kymlicka, *Liberalism, Community, and Culture* (Oxford University Press, 1989), p. 178.
[51] *Ibid.*, p. 165.
[52] See for example S. Okin, 'Equal Citizenship: Gender/Justice and Gender: An Unfinished Debate', *Fordham Law Review* 72 (2004), 1537; A. Phillips 'Defending Equality of Outcome', *The Journal of Political Philosophy* 1 (2004).
[53] J. Waldron, 'Minority Cultures and the Cosmopolitan Alternative', *University of Michigan Journal of Law Reform* 25 (1991–1992), 783–4.
[54] S. Bedi, 'Debate: What is so Special about Religion? The Dilemma of the Religious Exemption', *Journal of Political Philosophy* 15(2) (2007), 237.

is tied up with an ethical system, 'voluntary associations such as the Boy Scouts or Rotary also proffer ethical and moral guidelines that their members draw from.'[55]

If Bedi is right, as I think she is,[56] then there is no overriding reason to provide religious exemptions as a general rule. Religion is clearly not immutable, given the shifts in doctrine that occur over time. Indeed there are very good reasons *not* to provide such exemptions even over and above concerns about the equality and other rights of *outsiders.* Frances Raday points out that conflicts between equality rights and religion 'arise in the context of almost all religions and traditional cultures, since they rely on norms and social practices formulated or interpreted in a patriarchal context at a time when individual human rights, in general, and women's right to equality, in particular, had not yet become a global imperative'. [57]

The patriarchal norms that underpin much sex discrimination are also hostile to the subversion of gender roles associated with homosexuality. And as Yael Tamir argues, 'group rights strengthen dominant subgroups within each culture and privilege conservative interpretations of culture over reformative and innovative ones.'[58]

> Women rarely belong to the more powerful groups in society, and protectors of women's rights do not affiliate themselves with conservative segments. It follows, then, that women, and those who strive to protect their rights and equal status, are among the first to be harmed by group rights. Their plight, however, is not unique. It is shared by all those who wish to diverge from accepted social norms and question the traditional role of social institutions.[59]

---

[55] *Ibid.*, p. 244.

[56] See L. Vickers who argues (*Religious Freedom, Religious Discrimination and the Workplace* (Oxford: Hart, 2008), p. 40) that religious beliefs can be distinguished from others and their protection demanded on grounds of dignity because 'it is only those ... which feed into an individual's ability to make sense of the world, and through which they develop a sense of the good, that require protection.' Vickers concludes, on the basis of this assertion, that 'religious freedom is an important aspect of the individual autonomy and self-respect due to all people as a result of their humanity. If we accept that all humans are equal, we need to give equal concern and respect to the world views they develop.'

[57] F. Raday, 'Culture, religion, and gender' *International Journal of Constitutional Law* 4 (2002), 664–5.

[58] Y. Tamir, 'Siding with the Underdogs' in S. Moller Okin, J. Cohen, M. Howard and M. Nussbaum (eds.), *Is Multiculturalism Bad for Women?* (Princeton University Press, 1999), p. 47.

[59] *Ibid.*, p. 47.

Exempting religious organisations from the application of equality norms is likely to strengthen the hand of the more conservative elements within those organisations, rather than facilitating or encouraging greater respect within organisations for *internal* minorities (including women who, while often greater in numbers, are generally subordinate in terms of power).[60] And yet a further difficulty with the grant of exemptions on religious grounds is that it creates a pressure to characterise as 'religious' (and, impliedly, immutable, or at any rate, less mutable) cultural practices that may serve to disadvantage the less powerful within groups. A benign example is the turban, which, Bedi suggests, is not mandatory as a matter of Sikh doctrine.[61] Bedi cites Parekh's acknowledgement that:

> [m]inorities are naturally tempted to take advantage of this [modern Western society's sensitivity to religion], and demand recognition of their differences on the grounds that these are an integral part of their religion. The Sikh's turban no longer remains a cultural symbol, which is what it largely is, and becomes a badge of religious identity. The Hindu refusal to eat beef, the Muslim use of loudspeakers to call the faithful to prayer, and the Rastafarian dreadlock are all turned into mandatory religious requirements.[62]

The inability of the secular courts to determine what religion requires exacerbates the difficulties caused by protecting 'religious' over 'cultural' demands. It may be possible for a court to determine, on the balance of probabilities, whether an individual adheres, at least outwardly, to a certain set of religious or other beliefs (where, for example, he or she regularly

---

[60] See L. Green, 'Internal Minorities and their Rights' in J. Baker (ed.), *Group Rights* (University of Toronto Press, 1994). See also M. Sunder, 'Piercing the Veil', *Yale Law Journal* 112 (2003), 1402–3. Sunder characterises religious communities as 'internally contested, heterogeneous, and constantly evolving over time through internal debate and interaction with outsiders', and complains that law's failure to recognise this results in 'a legal veil, and not religion itself, [which] will increasingly insulate religious community from modernity and change'. See also Sunder's 'Cultural Dissent', *Stanford Law Review* 54 (2001), 495 and J. Tomasi, 'Kymlicka, Liberalism, and Respect for Cultural Minorities', *Ethics* 105(3) (1995), 581.

[61] B. Barry makes a similar point in relation to the Jewish *yarmulke*; see *Culture and Equality* (Cambridge: Polity Press, 2001), p. 33.

[62] Bedi, 'Debate', p. 239 citing B. Parekh, *Rethinking Multiculturalism: Cultural Diversity and Political Theory* (Basingstoke: Macmillan, 2000), p. 198. In 'French Sikhs threaten to leave country', *Guardian* (23 January 2004) reported a letter written by a leader of a French Sikh temple to Jacques Chirac, then President of France, in connection with the (then-proposed) French ban on the wearing of religious symbols in public schools in which Chain Singh, a leader of the Bobigny temple, argued that the turban was a cultural, rather than a religious, symbol, to which any ban should not therefore apply.

attends a particular religious service, or outwardly manifests over time a commitment to pacifism, veganism or Communism). But even the model of attendance as an indicator of religious affiliation is, as was pointed out by the English Administrative Court in *R (E)* v. *Governing Body of the Jews' Free School*,[63] of no application to a religion such as Orthodox Judaism in which 'attendance at the services of a synagogue has no bearing on a person's Jewish status as a matter of Jewish religious law. Being Jewish is a matter of Jewish status, under Jewish religious law.' More generally, while enquiry could be made as to whether the exemption sought by an individual or collective rationally relates to his or her commitment to an identifiable set of non-religious beliefs such as pacifism, veganism or Communism, the same is not true of an exemption sought on the basis of an asserted religious belief given the inability of secular courts to adjudicate doctrinal disputes within a religious collective, much less to determine the contents of an individual's religious belief.

In *R (Williamson)* v. *Secretary of State for Education and Employment and Others*,[64] the British House of Lords accepted that a belief in the mandatory nature of corporal punishment in the educational setting was a religious belief for the purposes of Article 9 ECHR. Lord Nicholls, with whom Lord Bingham agreed, stated that the Court could consider, if it was at issue, whether a belief was genuinely held. But:

> This is a limited inquiry. The court is concerned to ensure an assertion of religious belief is made in good faith, 'neither fictitious, nor capricious, and that it is not an artifice'[65]. But, emphatically, it is not for the court to embark on an inquiry into the asserted belief and judge its 'validity' by some objective standard such as the source material upon which the claimant founds his belief or the orthodox teaching of the religion in question or the extent to which the claimant's belief conforms to or differs from the views of others professing the same religion. Freedom of religion protects the subjective belief of an individual.[66]

---

[63] *R (E)* v. *Governing Body of the Jews' Free School* [2008] EWHC 1535 & 1536 (Admin), [2008] All ER (D) 54 (Jul). The Supreme Court took a different approach: [2010] 2, AC 728.

[64] *R (Williamson)* v. *Secretary of State for Education and Employment and Others* [2005] UKHL 15. Domestic law has always been inclined to deal with accommodation cases in this way – *See Ahmed* v. *ILEA* [1978] QB 31 in which the Court of Appeal, by contrast with the Commission, accepted that there had been an interference, though the Court ruled that it was justified.

[65] Citing Iacobucci J in the decision of the Supreme Court of Canada in *Syndicat Northcrest* v. *Amselem* (2004) 241 DLR (4th) 1 at 27 (para. 52).

[66] *R (Williamson*, para. 22, also citing Eur. Ct. H. R. (1st section), *Metropolitan Church of Bessarabia* v. *Moldova*, 13 December 2001, para. 117: 'in principle, the right to freedom

Lord Walker went on to express his disapproval of the suggestion made by Arden LJ in the Court of Appeal that 'to be protected by art 9, a religious belief, like a philosophical belief, must be consistent with the ideals of a democratic society, and that it must be compatible with human dignity, serious, important, and (to the extent that a religious belief can reasonably be required so to be) cogent and coherent',[67] doubting that 'it is right for the court (except in extreme cases such as the "Wicca" case ...) to impose an evaluative filter [in determining the existence of a belief], especially when religious beliefs are involved. For the court to adjudicate on the seriousness, cogency and coherence of theological beliefs is to take the court beyond its legitimate role.'[68]

While wearing a turban is not a practice which carries any overtones of gender inequality or subordination, or which imposes on its adherents any physical harm, practices such as coerced and polygamous marriage and compulsory restrictive dress codes are more or less damaging for those (generally or exclusively women) subject to them, while hostility to gay men and lesbians, sanctioned by a number of faiths, creates significant threats to those who practise (or are regarded as inclined to practise) the 'abomination' of same-sex sexual contact. The identification of many of these practices as 'religious' as distinct from 'cultural' is strongly contested, and providing protection against challenge to those which are accepted as 'religious', where such protection is not provided to the merely 'cultural', will create pressure to categorise them as matters of religious

---

of religion as understood in the convention rules out any appreciation by the state of the legitimacy of religious beliefs or of the manner in which these are expressed.'

[67] *R (Williamson)*, para. 258.

[68] *R (Williamson)* citing Richards J in *R (on the application of Amicus – MSF section)* v. *Secretary of State for Trade and Industry* [2004] IRLR 430, para. 36, and decisions of the High Court of Australia, the Supreme Court of Canada and the United States Supreme Court in the *Church of the New Faith* case (1983) 154 CLR 120, especially pp. 129–30, and 174; *Syndicat Northcrest* v. *Amselem* (2004) 241 DLR (4th) and *Employment Division, Department of Human Resources of Oregon* v. *Smith* (1990) 494 US 872 respectively. Note that the Wicca case (*X* v. *UK*, 1977) 11 DR 55) concerned an Article 9 complaint by a prisoner as to a governor's failure to register his asserted religious affiliation, which was dismissed as manifestly ill founded on the basis that the facilities for manifestation of his religion to which registration a prisoner was entitled were 'only conceivable if the religion to which the prisoner allegedly adheres is identifiable [whereas] ... in the present case the applicant has not mentioned any facts making it possible to establish the existence of the Wicca religion'. The applicant in *X* did not complain of any interference with his right to manifest his religion, or any failure on the part of the prison authorities to facilitate that manifestation in any specific way. The case does not stand as authority for any proposition that a court may exercise any veto over the recognition of a belief asserted to be 'religious' because of the content of that belief.

doctrine and, in so doing, helps to perpetuate them.[69] The difficulties associated with external challenge to this categorisation by religious collectives are considered above. Internal challenge is also rendered more difficult, and perhaps impossible for those at the bottom of the hierarchy, given the ossifying tendencies of 'religious' classification. Thus the provision of religious exemptions may result in the expansion of 'religious' obligation, and the reinforcement of religious hierarchies hostile to civil, political, social and economic rights for the 'unfavoured'.

Conclusion: religious demands and civic equality

There is every reason to curtail the influence of religious organisations in the public sphere, unless those organisations are prepared to 'play by the rules', if necessary undergoing internal change in order to render this possible. The interferences that this will entail with the internal organisation of religious collectives will be at most indirect, and many internal conflicts can be avoided by following the advice to snowmen to stay out of kitchens. It would of course be absurd to excuse an individual from a prohibition on race, sexual orientation or sex discrimination on the basis that he or she was racist, homophobic or sexist. But the question posed by the lack of engagement between religion and law, that is, by the law's powerlessness in the face of assertions about religion, is whether allowing religious exemptions to prohibitions on discrimination does not serve fatally to undermine those prohibitions. Where, as in the case of Article 9, accommodation of individual or collective religious practice is a qualified right at best, the belief whose accommodation is sought is open to scrutiny. (A court confronted with an Article 9 claim by a religious group with a racist ideology seeking exemption from a generally applicable prohibition on race discrimination in the provision of services would, it is to be presumed, have little hesitation in finding that any (indirect) interference was proportionate to a legitimate aim of the state.) But where a statutory exemption is provided to religious organisations or individuals there may be no such control. Thus, for example, if religious organisations are granted exemption from prohibitions on discrimination which are inconsistent with their ethos or beliefs, such exemptions cannot readily

---

[69] As Sunder points out in 'Piercing the Veil', p. 1441, discussing the experience of the network Women Living Under Muslim Laws, 'religious claims are particularly hard to challenge, and therefore [WLUML] expends effort to deconstruct religious claims as, in part, contingent and political'.

be denied on the basis that the discrimination at issue is not required by the organisation's ethos or belief as interpreted by a secular court, much less than the discrimination is inconsistent with the concept of 'religion' more generally.

This is not to say that it will never be appropriate to permit religious organisations some (limited) exemption from otherwise generally applicable rules. Where, for example, the discrimination can be characterised as purely internal (as in the case of male ministry or similar), Article 9 may trump questions of equality or other normative values. It may be the case that the non-neutral nature of the state as regards, for example, the arrangement of the working week and the school year requires a degree of accommodation of religious collectives whose pattern of worship differs from the 'background norm'. This question of accommodation, which may be better characterised as a matter of individual rather than collective right, is discussed further elsewhere. Finally, pragmatism may at times indicate a measure of accommodation. This point is made by Martha Minow who recognises the conflict between the free exercise of religion (in the USA) and equality rights, but warns of the risk of backlash which, in her words, can 'undermine initial reforms, erode public support for the government that was pursuing the reform, and further mobilize reactionary forces with even broader agendas for retrenchment', as well as 'eliminate[ing] informal accommodations that may have taken place and produc[ing] rigidity in the positions taken by competing groups that otherwise might reach practical accommodations'.[70]

Minow suggests that negotiation is the proper mechanism to the resolution of many of these disputes, blanket policies of exemption and non-exemption conceding too little and too much on the part of the state 'as arbiter of values or source of norms for public life',[71] while the creation of case-by-case exemptions based on the centrality of the discrimination at issue to the religious organisation's beliefs and practices involves undue interference with religious freedom, with the *government* reaching conclusions on religious doctrine. Her analysis points to the dangers of adopting an absolutist approach which may have the unintended effect of leaving everyone worse off. It may be, then, that any practical response to a particular conflict needs to be carefully considered in order to avoid such an outcome. But there is a difference in principle between accepting

---

[70] M. Minow, 'Should Religious Groups be Exempt from Civil Rights Laws?', *Boston College Law Review* 1(48) (2007), 43–4.

[71] *Ibid.*, p. 47.

that compromise may be necessary in order to make the 'best of a bad lot', and advocating such compromises as of right.[72] There must also, I would suggest, be strict limits on the extent to which such compromises might be allowed to intrude into the rights of others, whatever the apparent practical benefits. It may well be, as Minow suggests, that we ought to treat 'respect, flexibility, and humility as virtues themselves, even when the stakes seem high and the cause just'.[73] But whatever benefits religion may bring, it is hard to escape the conclusion that they come at a significant, and unevenly distributed, cost. Thus the concession of ground to the religious collective may result in what Ayelet Scachar calls 'the paradox of multicultural vulnerability', that is, the fact that 'individuals inside [groups protected by initiatives towards "multiculturalism"] can be injured by the very reforms that are designed to promote their status as group members in the accommodating, multicultural state'.[74]

---

[72] Similarly, as A. Favell suggests (in 'Applied Political Philosophy at the Rubicon: W. Kymlicka's *Multiculturalism Citizenship*', *Ethical Theory and Moral Practice* 1 (1998), 255, 258 and 261), W. Kymlicka's categorisation of a variety of cultural concessions, targeted arts funding, constitutional arrangements, etc. by which 'liberal institutions deal ... with their ethnic dilemmas' involves essentialising from 'descriptive facts' and aggrandising piecemeal accommodations. See also C. Joppke ('The retreat of multiculturalism in the liberal state: theory and policy', *British Journal of Sociology* 55 (2004), 237 and 238), on what Kymlicka refers to as 'multiculturalism' as pragmatic dealing with difference rather than recognition as of right, which would 'contradict the public-order-orientated way in which states have actually accommodated such claims'; J. Levy, *The Multiculturalism of Fear* (Oxford University Press, 2000).

[73] Minow, 'Should Religious Groups be Exempt from Civil Rights Laws?', p. 64.

[74] A. Scachar, *Multicultural Jurisdictions: Cultural Differences and Women's Rights* (Cambridge University Press, 2001), p. 3.

10

Is there a right not to be offended in one's religious beliefs?

GEORGE LETSAS

Introduction

This chapter explores the place of religion in Europe, which is the general theme of this volume, through the lens of European human rights law and the European Convention on Human Rights (ECHR) in particular. I will focus on the normative claim that freedom of religion requires respect for the religious convictions of believers when expressing oneself in public; or, put differently, the claim that there is a right not to be insulted in one's religious beliefs by the public expression of the views of others. This claim has been endorsed by the European Court of Human Rights in its judicial reasoning and is popular with many courts in Europe when reviewing criminal legislation that prohibits blasphemy, religious hate speech or the disparaging of (known) religious doctrines. The claim, if true, justifies the position that a liberal state may sanction or prevent the public expression of views for the reason that they offend, or are likely to cause offense to, religious convictions.

The claim has recently become the subject of much controversy and public debate, following the publication of the Danish cartoons and the subsequent riots around the world that resulted in the death of dozens of people. Various legal proceedings were initiated at national level complaining that the publication violated the right to freedom of religion of Muslims. Religious organizations called for stricter regulation of speech that offends religious doctrine. Meanwhile many liberal politicians, intellectuals and lawyers defended fiercely the freedom to publish cartoons and condemned

I am grateful to the participants of the EUI Conference on religion in the European Public sphere in May 2008 and to my respondent, Lorenzo Zucca, for very helpful comments and criticisms. I would also like to thank Stuart Lakin, Virginia Mantouvalou and Camil Ungureanu for their comments on earlier drafts of this chapter.

regulation as a violation of free speech. The debate is still raging and it is typically cast in terms of what the appropriate balance is between freedom of expression on one hand and freedom of religion on the other.

My aim in this chapter is to challenge the claim that there is a right not to be offended in one's religious beliefs in so far as such a right serves as a prima facie ground for restricting freedom of expression. If this challenge is successful, then the need to balance freedom of expression and freedom of religion in cases of religiously offensive expression evaporates. The argumentative strategy employed here is to show that there is a reason for the state not to protect religious convictions from offense, instead of showing that there are reasons (e.g. about the value of free speech) that, on balance, outweigh the reason to protect religious convictions. The choice of strategy is not accidental, as it is motivated (and is entailed) by some general theses about the nature of rights in law and political morality. Nor is the choice of strategy a matter of pure terminology: the claim that there is no right not to be offended in one's religious beliefs is not equivalent normatively to the claim that such a putative right loses in its competition with the right to freedom of expression.

The chapter is structured as follows. I begin in section 1 with some preliminaries that will help sharpen the normative claim under consideration. Section 2 provides a critical account of where the European Court's case law stands on the issue. My aim is to challenge the European Court's assumption that there is a right not to be insulted in one's religious beliefs which conflicts with, and must be balanced against, the right to free speech. I argue that balancing is warranted only if such a right exists and that the European Court begs an important question by resorting so quickly to the vague test of balancing free speech with religious freedom. In section 3 I discuss an argument which figures in the European Court's case law and which is based on the distinction between speech that contributes to public debate and speech that does not. I argue that this distinction fits nicely with a process-based understanding of democracy, which would afford political speech greater protection than religious or artistic expression. The Court's argument, however, does not justify the protection of religious beliefs *qua religious beliefs*, nor does it explain why there is a legal right not to be offended in one's beliefs in general, let alone in one's *religious* beliefs. In section 4 I advance an understanding of democracy and liberal equality that shows why there is no right to be insulted in one's religious beliefs in public space. In section 5 I conclude that in the absence of such right, the European Court's balancing methodology obscures an important matter of principle.

1   Religious offense and reasons for action

The claim that the state has a reason to sanction or prevent expression that offends religious convictions must be spelt out. This is because the claim is elliptical: it does not fully specify the fact(s) that grounds the reason. This is perfectly normal. Reasons for or against a particular action, including state action, are often stated in an elliptical fashion. Usually we do not cite all the facts that figure in the explanation or the justification of an action, but we focus on some of them depending on the context and the audience.[1] When we ask, for example, why the police shot a suspect dead, we may cite some but not necessarily all of the many facts that explain their action: the suspect was under surveillance; he ignored the police order to stop; he was about to board the train; he appeared to be armed with explosives; it was the only way to stop him boarding the train; and so on and so forth. The same applies to justificatory reasons. When we ask whether the police were justified in shooting a suspect dead, we may cite some but not necessarily all of the many facts that justify their action: the suspect posed an imminent threat to the public; there was at the time no other, non-lethal, means of protecting the public; there was no prior point in time at which the police could have intervened; and so on and so forth.

Of each of these many facts, seen in isolation, we may say that they are reasons that justify (or normatively support) the action. For example, the fact that the suspect was armed with explosives and was about to board a crowded train was a reason for the police to shoot him. But it is a further question whether the action in question is *all things considered* justified; this is the case if, and only if, other relevant facts obtain: for example, that the police were properly trained to respond to such situations or that the surveillance operation had been properly planned and executed. Moreover, there are facts that, seen in isolation, necessarily fail to justify a particular action: that the suspect was a member of an unpopular ethnic minority was no reason for the police to shoot him. When such inappropriate considerations motivate the acting agent, they might even taint the justifiability of the action, even though they do not directly constitute a reason against the action. So we might say that, for any possible action, there are some facts that ground reasons in favor of it, facts that ground reasons against it and facts that provide no ground either way.

---

[1] See J. Raz, *Practical Reasons and Norms* (Oxford University Press, 1999), pp. 22ff. See also more recently his "Reasons: Explanatory and Normative," available at: www.papers.ssrn.com/sol3/papers.cfm?abstract_id=999869# (last accessed August 15, 2011).

It is of course difficult, if not impossible, to provide *ex ante* a full list
of the facts that must figure in a complete account of the justifiability of
actions. This is why we study reasons in isolation: we say that *other things
being equal* this fact is a reason to perform that action and, other things
being equal, this other fact is a reason against performing the same action.
When, in real life, many of these facts obtain together, we seek to balance their weight either in order to act, or in order to assess *ex post facto*
whether the act was justified. Only facts that can count as reasons for a
particular action may be weighed in assessing that action's justifiability.
It would be wrong, for example, to say that, in planning a shoot-to-kill
operation, the fact that a suspect belongs to the same ethnic or religious
group as known terrorists must be balanced against the fact that he does
not appear to be carrying any explosives. Belonging to the same ethnic or
religious group as known terrorists is not a fact that grounds a prima facie
reason to shoot someone.

The preceding remarks help to sharpen the claim that is under scrutiny in this chapter. The claim is that the fact that some expression will
cause offense to religious believers is, other things being equal, a reason
for the state to sanction or prevent this expression. The claim is not just
that offense serves as a source of reasons for action; the claim is more specific. It contains two crucial elements. First, the claim is that the fact that
someone will be offended serves a source of reasons for *state* action, not
(or not only) *individual* action. This is an important moral distinction, as
not all reasons are agent-neutral.[2] Some reasons for action may apply to
collective action or to states but not to individuals. And second, that *religious* offense grounds special kinds of reasons for state action, that are not
co-extensive with reasons grounded by non-religious instances of offense
(such as offending someone's football team).[3] It is the claim thus understood that, I will argue, fails to lend normative support to the sanctioning
of expression that offends religious convictions.

I should note that part of the claim under scrutiny is that there is a
public dimension to the notion offense, in the sense that religious offense

---

[2] On the distinction between agent-neutral and agent-relative reasons, see T. Nagel, *The
View From Nowhere* (Oxford University Press, 1989).

[3] The claim that religious offense constitutes a special kind of offense can be easily attributed
to courts that, like the European Court of Human Rights, read into the right to freedom
of religion, the right not to be offended in one's religious beliefs by the public expression
of the views of others. The special nature of religious offense is manifested in the fact that
the Court takes prevention of religious offense to be an individual right, not simply a legitimate aim. It is also manifested in the fact that not all beliefs are taken by the Court to be
worthy of protection against offense.

occurs mainly as a result of acts that take place in public or as a result of being exposed to information that the public has a legal right to receive. It cannot be said that someone is offended in his religious beliefs because he knows that his lesbian neighbors have sex in their bedroom. It follows that the right not to be offended in one's religious beliefs, if it exists, necessarily affects the way public space is organized and shaped as well as the way public goods, such as culture, are produced and distributed.

By showing that the claim under consideration fails, one has not thereby established that the sanctioning of expressions that offend religious convictions is never justified. One has merely neutralized one source of reasons in favor of restriction. There may be other facts that, other things being equal, ground reasons for the state to sanction expression that offends religious beliefs. For example, the fact that offending religious beliefs is very likely to lead to violence and death grounds a reason in favor of state sanctioning. The same applies to the fact that offending someone's religious beliefs is very likely to cause severe psychological distress or damage to that person.[4] In both these examples, the operative reason for the state sanctioning is the imminence of violence and of psychological harm, not the likelihood of religious offense. In other words, in these two examples the fact that someone was offended and the fact that he was offended in his religious beliefs are *incidental* to, and not *constitutive* of, the normative explanation of the justifiability of state action.

2 The right not to be offended in the case law of the European Court of Human Rights

The Court's position on speech that offends religious feelings originated in a series of cases decided in the late 1980s and the early 1990s. In the leading judgment of *Otto-Preminger-Institut v. Austria*,[5] the European Court upheld the seizure and forfeiture by the Austrian authorities of Werner Schroeter's film *Das Liebeskonzil* (1981) prior to screening. The film was based on a play by Oskar Panizza, written in 1894, which portrayed God, Christ and the Virgin Mary in an unfavorable light,[6] agreeing with the Devil to punish mankind for its immorality by infecting it with

---

[4] The risk of emotional harm is of course a necessary but not sufficient condition. Other conditions may include knowledge of the risk, whether the offense was direct and personalized, etc.

[5] Eur. Ct. H. R., *Otto-Preminger-Institut v. Austria*, 20 September 1994.

[6] According to the description of the Austrian courts, the film presented God as a "senile, impotent idiot," Christ as a "cretin" and Mary ("slutty Mary") as "a wanton lady."

syphilis. The treatment received by the original play was no better than that received by the film: Oskar Panizza was charged with ninety-three counts of blasphemy and was found guilty by the Munich Assize Court in 1895, serving a twelve-month sentence in prison. Jes Petersen, who edited a new edition of *Das Liebeskonzil* in 1962, also got in trouble with the German authorities, being charged with publishing pornographic writings. In 1985 Otto-Preminger-Institut, a small private cinema association in Innsbruck, announced a series of six showings. The cinema was known for its preference for experimental and progressive cinema and the screening was going to be open to the public upon the payment of a fee. Soon after the announcement, the Public Prosecutor, at the request of the local diocese of the Roman Catholic Church, made an application for the seizure of the film and charged the cinema's manager with the criminal offense of "disparaging religious doctrines" under section 188 of the Austrian Penal Code.[7] The criminal prosecution was subsequently discontinued, but the Regional Court upheld the seizure order and ordered the forfeiture of the film. Appeals lodged with higher courts in Austria were deemed inadmissible and the case reached the European Court of Human Rights in 1993.

In its reasoning, the European Court made a series of important remarks in relation to expression that offends religious convictions. It noted that the state bears a responsibility to ensure the peaceful enjoyment of freedom of religion and that extreme ways of denying or opposing religious beliefs, like provocative portrayals of objects of religious veneration, may hinder the exercise of freedom of religion.[8] It noted further that freedom of expression carries with it duties and responsibilities, which may legitimately include "an obligation to avoid as far as possible expressions that are gratuitously offensive to others and thus an infringement of their rights."[9] Applying these principles to the case, the Court set up the legal question as one of conflict of rights: on one hand the right of the film institute to impart to the public controversial views and on the other hand the right

---

[7] Section 188 of the Penal Code reads as follows: "Whoever, in circumstances where his behaviour is likely to arouse justified indignation, disparages or insults a person who, or an object which, is an object of veneration of a church or religious community established within the country, or a dogma, a lawful custom or a lawful institution of such a church or religious community, shall be liable to a prison sentence of up to six months or a fine of up to 360 daily rates."

[8] *Otto-Preminger-Institut*, para. 47. Similar reasoning figures in the Court's earlier judgment in Eur. Ct. H. R., *Kokkinakis* v. *Greece*, 25 May 1993, para. 48.

[9] *Ibid.*, para. 49.

of other persons to proper respect for their freedom of religion. The Court found that the aim of protecting the religious feelings of believers from offensive speech is not only a legitimate one for restricting speech (under the limitation clause in Article 10, para. 2 ECHR) but that it is also part of the right to religious freedom (under Article 9, para. 1 ECHR). It said:

> The issue before the Court involves weighing up the conflicting interests of the exercise of two fundamental freedoms guaranteed under the Convention, namely the right of the applicant association to impart to the public controversial views and, by implication, the right of interested persons to take cognisance of such views, on the one hand, and the right of other persons to proper respect for their freedom of thought, conscience and religion, on the other hand.[10]

When it came to balance the two rights, the Court deferred to the judgment of the Austrian authorities, which were "better placed" to decide what is offensive to the Roman Catholics who form the majority of the Tyroleans and what is required in order to protect their rights against attacks on their religious convictions. It found no violation of the association's right to freedom of expression.

In the later case of *Wingrove v. United Kingdom*, the applicant complained that the refusal by the British Board of Film Classification (BBFC) to grant a certificate for the short film *Visions of Ecstasy* (1989) amounted to a violation of freedom of expression. The film, directed by Nigel Wingrove, portrays St. Teresa of Avila having ecstatic visions of Jesus Christ and being engaged in acts of sexual nature astride the body of Jesus on the cross. The Court reasoned that the English law of blasphemy, which was the legal basis for the restriction, pursued a legitimate aim, which was to protect the right of citizens not to be offended in their religious beliefs. The Court cited, with approval, the decision of the British Board of Film Classification according to which the aim of the interference was to protect against the treatment of a religious subject in such a manner "as to be calculated (that is bound, not intended) to outrage those who have an understanding of, sympathy towards and support for the Christian story and ethic, because of the contemptuous, reviling, insulting, scurrilous or ludicrous tone, style and spirit in which the subject is presented".[11] The Court noted that this aim is also "fully consonant with the aim of the protections afforded by article 9 (art. 9) to religious freedom."

---

[10]   *Ibid.*, para. 55.
[11]   Eur. Ct. H. R., *Wingrove* v. *United Kingdom*, 25 November 1996, para. 48.

When the Court moved to examine whether the interference with the director's right to freedom of expression was necessary, it repeated the *Otto-Preminger-Institut* dictum that there is a duty to avoid so far as possible an expression that is, in regard to objects of veneration, gratuitously offensive to others and profanatory. The Court granted again a wide margin of appreciation to the respondent state, as being in a better place to decide what counts as offensive to religious convictions. It added that the high degree of profanation that must be attained for an expression to constitute blasphemy under English law was an important safeguard against arbitrariness and ruled that there was no violation of the applicant's right to freedom of expression.

What are we to make of the European Court's reasoning in *Otto-Preminger-Institut* and *Wingrove*? The claim that there is a right not to be insulted in one's religious beliefs, which conflicts with freedom of speech, fits nicely with the European conception of rights. European courts employ what we may call the "balancing conception of rights": this is the idea, based on the wording of the European bills of rights, that fundamental rights, with a few exceptions, are not absolute; they are to be balanced against legitimate aims and/or other rights with which they may come into conflict. Courts view their task as one of performing a balancing test of assigning weight to the competing rights and legitimate aims.[12] In relation to free speech in particular, the approach of European courts is contrasted to the US doctrine of freedom of expression, which rejects content-based restrictions and balancing as detrimental to free speech.[13] The European Court of Human Rights is a balancer par excellence. Contrary to the US Supreme Court's approach of requiring the existence of very specific compelling governmental interests as a justified basis for limiting rights, the European Court is very generous in what it takes to be a legitimate aim and a protected interest, and proceeds fairly quickly to examine whether the limitation of the right is proportionate to the legitimate aim being pursued.[14] In examining whether the test of proportionality is met, it often grants a margin of appreciation to the respondent state, particularly when there is no consensus amongst contracting states.[15]

---

[12] See R. Alexy, *A Theory of Constitutional Rights* (Oxford University Press, 2002), Chapter 3.

[13] R. Post, "Religion and Freedom of Speech: Portraits of Muhammad," *Constellations* 14(1) (2007), 72–90.

[14] On the relationship between the test of proportionality and that of strict scrutiny see R. Fallon, "Strict Judicial Scrutiny," *UCLA Law Review* 54 (2007), 1267.

[15] I have criticized the Court's deferential stance in my book *A Theory of Interpretation of the European Convention on Human Rights* (Oxford University Press, 2009), Chapters 5 and 6.

Now one thing we might say about *Otto-Preminger-Institut* and *Wingrove*[16] is that the European Court got the balance wrong, say because the limitation was actually disproportionate to the legitimate aim. Perhaps freedom of artistic expression should have prevailed in *Otto-Preminger-Institut*, when balanced against freedom of religion: the film was going to be shown to a paying audience in an art cinema that catered for a relatively small public with a taste for experimental films. It was seized and forfeited prior to screening and there was little evidence that it was going to cause indignation to the general public. Besides, it was very unlikely that a Tyrolean Roman Catholic would go and see the film without knowing what it was about. It appears that there were many other alternatives, less restrictive of the right, that the Austrian authorities could have employed in order to protect the feelings of Roman Catholics, such as requiring the cinema to put up a sign saying that Roman Catholics may find the film offensive. It is a plausible criticism to make that the European Court deferred too quickly to the judgment of national authorities, whereas it should have itself applied the principle of proportionality to the facts of this case.

Be that as it may, I would like to take a step back and make a different point, which is to question whether there is a right (or a legitimate aim) not to be insulted in one's religious beliefs by the public expression of the views of others *in the first place*. For if there is no such right, then there is no conflict with other rights, like free speech, and no need for any balancing exercise whatsoever. I want to suggest, not that there is something wrong with balancing per se, but that there is something wrong with what was balanced. This is not a trivial point. The balancing methodology necessarily presupposes the view that the things we balance are of some independent value. As it has been mentioned already, the things we balance must be *actual* moral reasons for the action in question, not some impermissible considerations. We should not balance freedom of speech against something that has no independent moral value. We do not, for instance, say that there is a free speech right to incite imminent violence that is to be balanced against the right to physical integrity of others. Rather, we say that there is a prima facie reason not to incite imminent violence. The European Court's position therefore must assume that there is a reason *for the state* to protect religious people from offense that

---

[16] As well as other similar judgments of the 1980s and 1990s like *Müller and others* v. *Switzerland* (1991) 13 EHRR 212 and *Handyside* v. *United Kingdom* (1979–80) 1 EHRR 737.

is of the same status as the value inherent in free speech. Put differently: if the Court's reasoning is sound, we must regret the loss of some value each time we weigh up free speech against the right not to be offended (or any other right), no matter which right prevails at the end of the balancing process. For example, when free speech prevails over the right not to be offended (say because the offense was not gratuitous or profanatory), we should regret the fact that someone was offended, and perhaps try to find ways to prevent this from happening again. This is inherent in the balancing of reasons. When I fail to keep my promise to meet you for lunch because I heard that a close relative just had an accident and I rushed to the hospital, I should regret that I canceled our lunch, apologize and make amends.

What would be the argument for the assumption that there is some value in protecting religious people from offense? It appears that European courts make this assumption unreflectively without considering whether it is justified. They move from the premise that there is a right to freedom of religion, to the conclusion that it is a legitimate aim for the state to regulate speech in order to protect the exercise of people's religious freedom. And they read a duty that is correlative to the right not to be offended into freedom of expression: in publicly expressing oneself, one must avoid, so far as it is possible, offending religious convictions. Once respect for religious feelings is recognized as a legitimate aim or a right, courts bring in the scales and the balancing begins.

Of course the political history of Europe (which of course is very different to the American one) is part of the explanation why this assumption is made unreflectively. Historically, refraining from offending the religious doctrines of others helped move from religious wars to religious tolerance and to foster a national identity as a means of promoting peace and stability. But explaining why this assumption (i.e. that there is value in protecting religious sensibilities) is made in Europe is not the same as justifying it. Pointing to the existence and long history of blasphemy laws in Europe – which have most often been used to protect the majority religion – is certainly not an argument. History is full of moral mistakes – not to mention atrocities – and Europe probably has the largest share of those mistakes. Nor is it a good argument to say that there is a right not to be insulted in one's religious beliefs in Europe because most Europeans have widely shared expectations that religiously offensive speech be restricted. For we do not normally accept that the exercise of fundamental rights is conditioned by what others – let alone the majority – takes or expects these rights to be. To have a right is to insist on being treated in a certain way even if the majority would be better off if you were not treated in that way.[17] Nor, finally, can it be argued of course that we may limit speech on the grounds that there is only one true religion or that the majority has a right to impose its religion on everybody. Theocratic conceptions of free speech have no place in discussions, which assume, as this one does, the moral primacy of rights.

But you may think: is it not obvious that it is morally wrong deliberately to offend people's beliefs? Is it not obvious that there is a reason not to express views that one knows will upset others, by offending or insulting the beliefs they hold dear? Isn't this why it is called "offense," because it is an assault on people's personhood? What more needs to be said?

Recall that the claim we are considering is not whether it is wrong for individuals to offend someone's beliefs. The claim is whether it is wrong for us collectively, through state institutions and state action, to allow speech that offends religious convictions. And note that the intuitive appeal of the wrongness of individual action does not necessarily extend to state action. Just to give an example: it is clearly wrong for me to care the same about my children as I do about all children but it is not clearly wrong for the state to care the same about my children as it does about all children.

An argument is therefore needed to justify why peaceful, liberal democratic states, committed to constitutional protection of fundamental rights, should value the protection of religious feelings in regulating expression. This argument must be of the same kind as the argument in support of free speech, in the following sense: the value of protecting religious sensibilities must flow from, or at least be compatible with, the same cluster of values that justify the constitutional foundations of a liberal democracy. The argument must show that free and equal citizens, who hold very different ethical ideas about what life is good for them but who govern themselves collectively through democratic decision-making (as all ECHR members do), all have reason to accept special protection of religious feelings. Without such an argument, the balancing methodology, which assumes that there is such a value, must be seen as suspect and arbitrary.

3 Public debate and gratuitous offenses

Can such an argument be made? In *Otto-Preminger-Institut*, the European Court came close to offering one. It argued that one ought to "avoid, as

---

[17] R. Dworkin, "Rights as Trumps" in Jeremy Waldron (ed.), *Theories of Rights* (Oxford University Press, 1984).

far as possible, expressions that are gratuitously offensive to others and thus an infringement of their rights," as such expressions "*do not contribute to any form of public debate capable of furthering progress in human affairs.*"[18] The distinction between gratuitous insults on one hand and provocative speech that contributes to public debates on the other, figures prominently in subsequent case law. Contrast the following two more recent cases on speech that offends religious beliefs: *I.A.* v. *Turkey*[19] and *Giniewski* v. *France.*[20]

I.A. v. *Turkey* concerned the fine imposed on a publishing company in Turkey for publishing a novel that contained blasphemous remarks about the Prophet Muhammad.[21] The Public Prosecutor charged the director of the publishing company with the offense of blasphemy against "God, the Religion, the Prophet and the Holy Book", under Article 175 of the Criminal Code. He relied on an expert opinion that had been prepared, at his request, by the Dean of the Theology Faculty of Marmara University. The Court of First Instance, having received a second expert opinion by a committee of professors, convicted the applicant to two years' imprisonment and a fine. It commuted the prison sentence to a fine, so that the applicant was ultimately ordered to pay a total fine of 3,291,000 Turkish liras (equivalent at the time to 16 United States dollars).

When the case reached the European Court Human Rights, the Court – following the same principles as in *Otto-Preminger-Institut* – upheld the conviction as a proportionate limitation to freedom of expression. It found that the case concerned not only comments that offend or shock, or a "provocative" opinion (which are generally protected) but also "an abusive attack on the Prophet of Islam." Given that "believers may legitimately feel themselves to be the object of unwarranted and offensive attacks", the Court held that there was a "pressing social need" to restrict the publication of the book. It found that the 16-dollar fine was a proportionate restriction of the applicant's freedom of expression.

The Court did find a violation of freedom of expression by contrast in the case of *Giniewski* v. *France*. The case concerned the publication of a newspaper article in which the author criticized the 1993 papal encyclical

---

[18] *Otto-Preminger-Institut*, para. 49 (emphasis added).
[19] *I.A.* v. *Turkey*, Judgment of 13 September 2005, Application no. 42571/98.
[20] *Giniewski* v. *France*, Judgment of 31 January 2006, Application no. 64016/00.
[21] The book contained the following passage: "Some of these words were, moreover, inspired in a surge of exultation, in Aisha's arms ... God's messenger broke his fast through sexual intercourse, after dinner and before prayer. Muhammad did not forbid sexual intercourse with a dead person or a live animal."

"The Splendour of Truth" for containing principles of the Catholic religion that, on his view, are tainted with anti-Semitism and contributed to the Holocaust. The author, a respectable figure who had sought in all of his work to promote a rapprochement between Jews and Christians, was found guilty of the offence of publicly defaming a group of persons on the ground of membership of a religion. He was ordered to pay damages to the religious association that brought the action of public defamation and to publish, at his expense, the court ruling in a national newspaper. The European Court found a violation of freedom of expression on the grounds that the author's conviction did not meet a pressing social need.

The Court distinguished *Giniewski* from *Otto-Preminger* and *I.A.* on the grounds that in the former case the publication was neither gratuitously offensive (as in *Otto-Preminger*) nor insulting (as in *I.A.*). It emphasized that:

> the applicant sought primarily to develop an argument about the scope of a specific doctrine and its possible links with the origins of the Holocaust. In so doing he had made a contribution, which by definition was open to discussion, to a wide-ranging and ongoing debate without sparking off any controversy that was gratuitous or detached from the reality of contemporary thought.[22]

The European Court's claim that what makes an expression worthy of state protection is the contribution it makes to a public debate that is capable of furthering progress fits nicely with what we may call a process-based conception of democracy. It is the idea that democracy – which is a doctrine about how political power should be exercised – cannot allow the censoring of any competing view, no matter how implausible, about politics. For the legitimacy of the democratic process depends on allowing all people, upon whom the outcome of this process will be coercively enforced, to express their views about what that outcome should be. This conception of democracy would condemn the censoring of *political* views but it would not furnish a reason to protect provocative expressions about non-political aspects of our lives that are not subject to a collective and rational discussion. The conception is reflected in the European Court's case law, which has shown far greater willingness to protect political speech while upholding severe restrictions on religious and artistic expression. In *Wingrove* the European Court said that:

---

[22] *Giniewski* v. *France*, para. 50.

> Whereas there is little scope under Article 10 para. 2 of the Convention for restrictions on political speech or on debate of questions of public interest, a wider margin of appreciation is generally available to the Contracting States when regulating freedom of expression in relation to matters liable to offend intimate personal convictions within the sphere of morals or, especially, religion.[23]

And indeed much offensive expression does not inform, nor intends to inform, nor is perceived as informing any ongoing public debate. By wearing a T-shirt with the stamp "Jesus loves you but only as a friend," one hardly contributes to a rational debate about religion or homosexuality. Provocative and satirical portrayals of religious objects or doctrines need not contain any view about politics and culture and the role of religion in them. In fact, it is not accidental that offenses and insults in general typically do not convey a view that contributes to a rational debate. For often an expression is insulting precisely because it shows deliberate contempt for rational argumentation. When you burn a cross or the national flag, part of what you communicate is the view that the ideas of religion and national pride are not even worthy of rational discussion. You do not just think they are bad ideas, you think that they do not even qualify as ideas, as thoughts that are capable of being entertained, discussed, refuted and so on. They are more like material objects which, unlike ideas and concepts, cannot make demands on humanity's rational faculties. *That* is how low you think them. And it is this kind of contempt for rational argumentation that suffices to offend people: to be told that one's beliefs are not really beliefs is worse than to be told that one's beliefs are false, misguided, confused. It is to be told that one does not have the rational capacity worthy of a human being. Provocative expressions that offend someone's beliefs and that make no contribution to a rational debate can therefore be as much directed against the persons who hold those beliefs as they are against the beliefs themselves.

But still, to come back to our question: is there a right not to have one's beliefs and personality attacked in this manner? The distinction between speech that contributes to public debate and speech that does not (as well as the conception of democracy upon which it rests) may or may not be plausible. The principle upon which the distinction is premised, however, assumes, rather than grounds, a right not to be insulted in public space. Here is how the argument underlying the Court's reasoning goes: the

---

[23] *Wingrove* v. *United Kingdom*, para. 58. See also Eur Ct. H. R., *Lingens* v. *Austria*, 8 July 1986.

contribution to a public debate that is capable of furthering progress is what makes an expression worthy of state protection. We have reason to tolerate expressions that cause offense only in so far as they make a contribution to a public debate. But since offensive expressions typically do not, then the value of free speech gives no reason against restricting such expressions, while the value of preventing offense gives a reason in favor of restricting them. Note that the latter claim, which supports the restriction, is independent and separate from the first and it is still in need of argumentative support. All we have so far is an argument from speech that does not extend protection to offensive expression. But we have yet to see a positive argument to the effect that one has a right not to be offended in one's religious beliefs.

It is important to note, moreover, that the claim that there is a right not to be insulted in one's beliefs by provocative expressions that do not contribute to a public debate accords no special importance to religion as such. It just so happens that one way in which you can offend people is by insulting their religion. For it is possible to insult non-religious people and it is possible to insult religious people without insulting their religion. The category of gratuitously offensive speech that does not contribute to any public debate includes many expressions that have nothing to do with religion. Consider the expressions "Macs are camp" or "iPhones suck"; or consider the burning of the flag of Manchester United or the spitting on the British National Party logo. Such expressions and speech acts do not contribute to any public debate capable of furthering progress in human affairs. It is also possible that these expressions will cause offense to people who love Macs, iPhones, Manchester United or the BNP.

True, we know from experience that religious believers tend to get more agitated, disturbed and upset when their religion is insulted. But the question of the *degree* of one's reaction to an insult becomes relevant only if there is already a right not to be insulted in one's beliefs in the public space. Put differently: the claim that there something special about religious offense gets traction only if there is something special about offense, namely a right that collective force (the law) be used to sanction or prevent offense of beliefs in the public space. The conception of free speech put forward by the European Court of Human Rights only goes *half way* to justifying the position that a liberal state may sanction or prevent the public expression of views that offend religious convictions. The other half is provided by an assumed right not to be insulted in one's beliefs by the public expression of the views of others, which is still in need of justification.

4 Liberal equality and the value of the freedom to offend

So is there a right not to be insulted gratuitously in one's beliefs in the public space? I will argue, in this section, that we cannot make sense of such a right, at least not if we assume a half-decent theory of what rights are and what role they play in political morality.

Following the liberal tradition we may distinguish between the claim that something *is the right thing to do*, from the claim that others have *a right* that you do it, in the sense that they have a right that collective force be used against you if you don't.[24] Being faithful to your partner, not lying to your mother about skipping meals, not jumping the queue in the bank, stopping and chatting with your boring neighbor, remembering your friend's birthday and so on, are all "the right thing to do." Yet it does not follow that these people have a right that collective force be used to get you to do those things. Although my life will go better if I do those things – I will be a more sensitive human being, a nice guy to have as friend, a good neighbor – this is all my business and responsibility, not anyone else's and certainly not the state's. One should not move too quickly from the claim that it is right to treat people in a certain way to the claim that we collectively have a right to force you to treat them in that way. Cheating on one's partner is wrong; gratuitously cheating is even more wrong. But that does not entail that the state has a right to punish cheating. The state should not sanction behavior on the grounds that doing so will make me a better person or on the grounds that a particular way of life or conception of the good is superior to the one I currently have. Since it is my responsibility to decide that, and since we are all equals, the state should not take sides on whether the plan of life of some of us is ethically inferior to that of others.

Now, is gratuitously insulting people's beliefs by publicly available expressions found in books or films one of those activities that are my business and not the state's? We might think that it is not, since public insults are neither a personal (intimate) activity nor take place in private. Like littering and driving dangerously, expressions that offend beliefs may adversely affect the lives of others in the public space. And they might do so to a far greater degree than in the case of the boring neighbor who realized that you have been trying to avoid him. Deliberately and gratuitously

---

[24] See T. Nagel, "Personal Rights and Public Sphere," *Philosophy and Public Affairs* 24(2) (1995), 83–107. The discussion in this section draws heavily on Nagel's views in that article.

insulting religious doctrines may make the lives of the people who believe in them less enjoyable; they might become upset, disturbed or alienated from their fellow citizens. Words and images can upset and frustrate. Would it not be appropriate if we, collectively, decided to prevent so much frustration, caused simply because some people take pleasure in gratuitously provoking such frustration?

Consider for a moment, however, what constitutes religious offense. It is the disparaging of the doctrines, symbols or figures of a religion. Such doctrines, symbols and figures have value primarily within a particular conception of the good life and primarily for the people who believe in it. Offense, in other words, is subjective: not in the sense that there is no truth of the matter as to *what* offends (or is likely to offend) someone – this is objective; nor in the sense that there is no truth of the matter as to whether the belief that is under attack is worth holding, because it may well be; rather, in the sense that the subject matter of the beliefs belongs to the sphere of *partiality*: others are not expected to have found, or contemplated, or discovered whatever value exists in the object of those beliefs. This is because the good life is rich and multifaceted: there are not only many ethical values whose pursuit makes one's life better; there are also many ways in which the same value can be pursued. It is each person's responsibility to explore and choose both which ethical ideas to pursue and how to pursue them. Just like the atheist is not expected to have found the value in a religious way of life, the believer is not expected to have found the humorous value in religious jokes. It follows, therefore, that the state cannot force people into discovering particular ethical ideas, let alone particular interpretations of those ethical ideas.

Moreover, what counts as an insult depends on the interpretation of the conception of the good life that each one chooses to follow. As we know from the history of religion, even people of the same religion may find each other's interpretation offensive. A homosexual Christian need not find the statement "Jesus was gay" insulting. He is actually likely to be offended by Christians who find that statement blasphemous. This point further suggests that expressions we take to be offensive to our beliefs may well be part of a valuable way of life, like the pursuit of art or humor. In fact humor, like that found in the Danish cartoons, is – for those who are able to see it – precisely a function of them being provocative and insulting; they would not be humorous if they were not provocative. This is also why satirical blasphemy is often committed by people who believe in the very religion they satirize. Indeed, if you are a believer, you should hope that God has a sense of humor. And we can generalize from the examples of art and humor to say that something ethically valuable is likely to be involved in expressions that insult, provoke or offend beliefs others hold. There are many valuable things to learn about human nature for example, from watching Schroeter's *Council of Love* or Wingrove's *Visions of Ecstasy*: why is depicting holy figures in sexual activities a taboo for monotheistic religions? What is the relationship between religious faith and sexual morality? Undoubtedly, the aesthetic quality of blasphemous books or paintings varies immensely, but if provocation is constitutive of a valuable form of art, then we cannot punish people for trying to produce it.

Moreover, it makes no difference that offenses may be gratuitous and deliberate, making no contribution not only to a public debate but also to art. Insulting religious doctrines – through burning crosses, writing heretic books, publishing cartoons – is a way of expressing one's *own* conception of the good life that may well have value. To paraphrase Thomas Nagel's remark which he makes in relation to sadistic and masochistic fantasies: it is not that blasphemers are delighted by the same thing that revolts believers; it is something else, that we do not understand because it does not fit into the particular configuration of our imagination.[25]

So if there is ethical value in expressing oneself in a way that offends others' beliefs, then banning those expressions amounts to prioritizing one valuable ethical ideal over another. It amounts to using collective force in order to force some individuals to abandon one ethically valuable practice (provocative art) for the reason that others find it objectionable. And such use of collective force cannot be squared with the requirement that the liberal state treat people as free and equal agents, who are responsible for choosing their own ethical ideals.

It might be objected that the cost of the restriction on provocative expression is nowhere near that borne by religious believers who are offended. Some might argue that, for a great number of religious believers, changing or revising their ethical life so as to cope with public offense to their religion is simply not possible and that those who offend by contrast can still pursue what they deem valuable in other ways. It seems to me, however, that it is a mistake to view religious beliefs as an accident that has befallen upon people. Religious beliefs are not inseparable from a person's agency. An atheist is a religious zealot who has read Darwin and a religious zealot is an atheist who

---

[25] *Ibid.*, p. 105.

has read the Bible. It would be disrespectful of the rational agency of believers to assume that their religious convictions are unshakable, not subject to change.

In a liberal democracy, moreover, all citizens should have the opportunity to participate as equals, not just in voting and expressing their views about how we should be governed, but also in the forming of *public culture*. Public culture includes much more than public opinion about politics and the regulation of expression. It includes what clothes and lifestyles one sees in the streets, what products are fashionable to own, what books one finds in the bookshops, what music we are exposed to, what jokes one feels comfortable to tell and so on. It is fair that, in a liberal democratic state, public culture is shaped organically, as the result of the millions of (cultural, aesthetic, ethical) choices that all of us make every day. But it is not fair that the government deliberately regulates or assumes control of public culture on the grounds that some ethical or aesthetic ideas are wrong – as it does when it prohibits religiously offensive speech. If most of us like wearing T-shirts with the Danish cartoons or with the phrase "Jesus loves you but only as a friend" or "Fuck the BNP," then that is the public culture we are entitled to have. Nobody has a right for the government to intervene in public culture so as to make it more to her liking. Why should religious believers be an exception? As Ronald Dworkin puts it: "in a genuinely free society the world of ideas and values belongs to no one and to everyone."[26]

Conclusion

I have argued in this chapter that the European Court's argument, that gratuitous offenses do not contribute to any debate, does not justify a right not to be offended in one's religious beliefs. Nor is there an independent ground for justifying such a right – quite the opposite: the morality of human rights, as egalitarian constraints on the use of collective force provides strong reasons against recognizing such a right. It follows that in cases of expressions that offend religious beliefs, there is no need to balance free speech against freedom of religion: other things being equal, free speech prevails without any competition with other values.

[26] R. Dworkin, *Is Democracy Possible Here? Principles for a New Political Debate* (Princeton University Press, 2006), p. 89.

We must take care to distinguish the claim that there is a right not to be insulted in one's religious beliefs from two very different arguments. The first argument we have touched on already. It is that it is justified to restrict speech, not just religiously offensive speech but any kind of speech, which is likely to lead to imminent violence. This argument expresses a true moral principle, but it does not ground a right not to be insulted in one's religious beliefs; for the restriction is allowed only in order to avoid *violence*, not in order to protect the religious feelings of believers. The principle applies to speech that offends religion as much as it applies to shouting falsely "fire!" in a crowded theatre.

The second argument draws on the claim that allowing certain expressions (e.g. hate speech or pornography) reinforces patterns of discrimination which in turn cause harm against disadvantaged or minority groups, in the sense that there is a causal link between the use of such expressions and the resulting harm. Prohibiting such expressions may be a way of preventing the injustice and/or compensating the victims. This second argument claims that the just distribution of resources (employment, income, health care etc.) is obstructed or delayed by private conduct that is encouraged by public expressions of hate and offensive speech. This second argument is based on valid egalitarian reasons: we collectively have a duty to ensure that public goods are distributed in an egalitarian way. But the argument carries the burden of showing that there is a clear and direct causal link between allowing religiously offensive speech and inequalities in the distribution of important social goods. It also carries the burden of showing that there is no alternative means, less restrictive of speech, to combat these inequalities. In any case, however, this argument is not one that draws on the right not to be insulted in one's religious beliefs either: the reason for restricting speech is not to prevent offense but rather to promote distributive justice.

It is worth noting that both the above arguments would require the courts to scrutinize restrictions on rights in order to make sure that there is a direct causal link between the expression and the resulting distributive injustice or physical harm. Indeed, the European Court applied a similar test in the recent case of *Ollinger v. Austria*,[27] which concerned the prohibition of an assembly that the applicant had intended to hold on All Saints' Day in commemoration of the Salzburg Jews murdered by the SS

---

[27] Eur. Ct. H. R., *Ollinger v. Austria*, 29 June 2006. This case bears strong similarities to the famous *National Social Party of America v. Village of Skokie* 432 U.S. 43 (1977) case of the United States Supreme Court.

during the Second World War. The assembly would take place at the same time as an assembly of Comradeship IV in memory of the SS soldiers killed in the Second World War. The Court found the restriction disproportionate, and a violation of freedom of assembly, partly on the grounds that the planned assembly was likely to be peaceful and without incidents of violence. It is also useful to note in passing that the test of a clear and present danger and its variations need not be seen as a form of balancing between conflicting rights. The requirement that there be a close causal link between restricting a right and preventing harm may stem from the need to ensure that legitimate reasons (such as prevention of harm) are not used as a *pretext* for the pursuit of illegitimate purposes. This is a judicial task that is very different to the balancing methodology: it consists in finding diagnostic tests that *"smoke out" illegitimate reasons.*[28] It is not a form of judicial reasoning that presupposes the view that rights, properly understood, conflict and that balancing involves a compromise between two independently valuable goals.

In the landmark *Handyside* v. *United Kingdom* judgment, the European Court of Human Rights declared that free speech protects "not only 'information' or 'ideas' that are favorably received or regarded as inoffensive or as a matter of indifference, but also those that shock, offend or disturb the State or any sector of the population".[29] In *Otto-Preminger-Institut*, the Court qualified this principle by arguing that the right to express ideas that offend does not encompass a right to insult gratuitously the religious beliefs of others. It has maintained this position ever since. Three dissenting judges in *Otto-Preminger-Institut* disputed the existence of a right to protection of religious feelings. They argued that:

> it should not be open to the authorities of the State to decide whether a particular statement is capable of "contributing to any form of public debate capable of furthering progress in human affairs"; such a decision cannot but be tainted by the authorities' idea of "progress."[30]

Sixteen years later, perhaps most Europeans are still very reluctant to accept that the law should grant no protection to (their) religious beliefs as such and that it should permit blasphemy. I have argued in this chapter that the European Court of Human Rights has very good reasons to accept it and no reasons not to. In *I.A.* v. *Turkey*, the Court held that a

[28] On the idea of smoking out illegitimate reasons, see Fallon, "Strict Judicial Scrutiny," pp. 1308–12.

[29] *Handyside* v. *United Kingdom*, para. 49.

[30] Joint Dissenting Opinion of Judges Palm, Pekkanen and Makarczyk.

16-dollar fine was a proportionate limitation of the applicant's right to publish a book that contained blasphemous passages. But if nobody had a legal right not to be offended by that book, then there should not have been, as a matter of principle, any limitation of the applicant's right on *that* basis. What if the fine was only 16 dollars? For what the human right to free speech can afford, it was 16 dollars too many.

11

Religious pluralism and national constitutional traditions in Europe

DANIEL AUGENSTEIN

Introduction

This chapter explores the relationship between religious pluralism and national constitutional traditions in Europe through the lens of national and European human rights jurisprudence. The analysis suggests that persisting defensive attitudes towards religious diversity in Europe can be traced to the national corroboration of, and the European deference to, Europe's diverse national constitutional traditions. The first part of the chapter explores the treatment of religious pluralism in the German and the French constitutional tradition. Comparing the regulation of the display of religious symbols in educational institutions and the public sphere, it submits that, at the national level, negative and defensive attitudes towards religious diversity stem from majoritarian assertions of national cultures permeated by Christian values.

The second part of the chapter considers how the European Court of Human Rights (ECtHR) and the European Court of Justice (ECJ) protect religious pluralism against the backdrop of diverse national constitutional traditions. Both courts are transnational courts in that they operate outside the normative framework of the nation state that gives shape and contour to the decisions of their national counterparts. Accordingly, rather than endorsing any particular national model, the they are called on to develop a transnational reading of the relationship between religious pluralism and national constitutional traditions in the light of, respectively, the European Convention on Human Rights and the European Union legal order. The ECtHR tackles this problem by avoiding it, emphasising its limited role in implementing a common European minimum standard of human rights protection as correlative to a wide national margin of appreciation. The ECJ, by contrast, should pursue a strategy of integration that undercuts the linkage between the containment of religious pluralism and the perpetuation of majoritarian national cultures inherent in some of Europe's national constitutional traditions. The concluding section defends such a transnational strategy of human rights integration in the light of Europe's supranational telos and its self-image of open and pluralistic democracies.

1   Religious pluralism in the German and the French national constitutional tradition

A   *The German constitutional tradition*

The treatment of religious pluralism in the German constitutional tradition can be conceptualised on the basis of a twofold distinction: first, between Christianity as a distinctive religion, and Christianity as a general national culture; secondly, between freedom of religion as a positive right to express one's beliefs, and freedom of religion as a negative right to be free from undue religious influence. In conjunction, these distinctions are geared towards the perpetuation of a majoritarian national culture permeated by Christian values.

During what has become known as the 'crucifix debate' in Germany,[1] a Bavarian administrative court distinguished between the Christian faith (as *distinctive* religion) and the Christian culture (as merely religiously permeated *common* culture). On this basis it held that the display of crucifixes in classrooms was not the (in this context illegitimate) expression of a commitment to a particular religious faith but the (legitimate) affirmation of an essential component of the general Christian-occidental tradition and common property of its cultural realm.[2] The Federal Constitutional Court squashed this decision, amongst others, because it *did* consider the crucifix a specific symbol of the Christian faith which, when displayed in classrooms of public schools, violated the children's negative freedom of religion as protected by Article 4 of the German Constitution. The dissenting judges aligned with the reasoning of the Bavarian administrative court and held that such interference with non-Christian denominations was justified, having regard to the state's mandate to impart Christian values through education: 'The affirmation of Christianity does not bear

---

[1] That is, the question of whether German school laws can require the displaying of a cross or crucifix in classrooms of public schools.

[2] Beschluss des Bayrischen Verwaltungsgerichtshof of 3 June 1991 as cited by the German Federal Constitutional Court, BVerfG, 1 BvR 1087/91 of 16 May 1995 (Kruzifix), para. 10. All translations from German and French into English are mine.

on the content of its beliefs but on the appreciation of its formative cultural and educational components, and is therefore also justified towards non-Christians by virtue of the history of the occidental cultural realm.'[3]

In the subsequent 'headscarf controversy', a German school board rejected the application of a Muslim teacher unwilling to refrain from wearing her headscarf in school. It argued that the wearing of a headscarf in public schools would contravene the principle of state neutrality. Moreover, it considered the headscarf a symbol of cultural disintegration that would endanger social cohesion and school peace. The decision of the school board was upheld by two lower instance administrative courts and the Federal Administrative Court.[4] The latter confirmed that wearing a headscarf in public schools was not compatible with the principle of state neutrality that, given increasing religious diversity in Germany, had to be interpreted in a restrictive way. It further considered that because young children were not yet sufficiently educated in mutual respect and tolerance, a negative impact of Islam as 'symbolised' by the headscarf could not be excluded.[5]

The German Federal Constitutional Court, distinguishing the crucifix in classrooms as a symbol associated with the state from the headscarf as an individual statement of the person concerned, found that the latter was in principle covered by the teacher's fundamental right to freedom of religion. Accordingly, it ruled that the headscarf could not be prohibited through an administrative decree but only by means of a parliamentary statute.[6] The majority of judges suggested two possible interpretations of the relationship between religious pluralism and state neutrality under the German constitution: a negative one that bans the display of religious symbols in state schools to minimise the 'potential of possible conflicts' in an increasingly religiously diverse society; and a positive one that permits the display of such symbols in order to foster mutual tolerance and integration through the active encounter of religious difference.[7] The

---

[3] BVerfG, 1 BvR 1087/91, para. 72.
[4] VG Stuttgart, 15 K 532/99, *Neue Zeitschrift für Verwaltungsrecht* (2000) 959; VGH Baden-Wuerttemberg, 4 S 1439/00, *Neue Juristische Wochenschrift* (2001) 2899; BVerwG, 2 C 21.01, *Juristenzeitung* (2002) 254.
[5] BVerwG, 2 C 21.01, pp. 7–8.
[6] BVerfG, 2 BvR 1436/02 of 3 June 2003 (Kopftuch Ludin). According to German constitutional law, decisions with an essential impact on fundamental rights require a parliamentary statute (so-called *Wesentlichkeitstheorie*). Since in the German federal system the *Länder* have the competence for school legislation, it was their responsibility to draft the respective legislation.
[7] *Ibid.*, para. 65.

dissenting judges drew a different distinction. On the one hand, they considered the crucifix a (merely) cultural symbol that, while 'stemming from' and 'being bound by' Judeo-Christian values, also stood for 'openness' and 'tolerance'. On the other hand, they stressed that such openness and tolerance could not extend to symbols such as the headscarf that challenged dominant value standards and were therefore prone to provoking conflicts.[8]

By now, many of the German *Länder* have enacted legislation banning the headscarf while still sanctioning nuns teaching in their traditional costume. The laws of Hesse and Baden-Württemberg, for instance, provide that teachers shall not demonstrate any religious convictions that would contravene the principle of state neutrality. Manifestations of Christianity, however, are considered compatible with this requirement because they reflect the *Länder*'s Christian and humanistic traditions and fulfil the educational mandate conferred upon the state.[9] Similar laws have been passed in Lower Saxony, Saarland and Bavaria. The *Verwaltungsgerichtshof* Baden-Württemberg and the Bavarian Constitutional Court confirmed that the preferential treatment of Christian symbols was compatible with the principle of state neutrality because a Muslim teacher could not credibly convey to her pupils the Christian values and traditions anchored in the *Länder* constitutions and the respective school laws.[10]

Against this background, Chancellor Merkel's and the Bavarian Prime Minster Seehofer's recent 'Multiculturalism is dead' slogans appear representative of a majoritarian sentiment that associates the German constitutional tradition with a relatively homogenous national-as-Christian culture. This national Christian majoritarianism has a twofold impact on the protection of religious pluralism in the German constitutional tradition. On the one hand, the state is required to protect children's negative freedom of religion which, by implication, may justify the ban of headscarves from school. On the other hand, the state is encouraged to actively promote Christian values so that it may justifiably discriminate between the Muslim headscarf and the Christian habit.

While, as Gerstenberg says, 'a distinctive feature of the German approach is the emphasis of freedom of conscience as a principle, another feature of the German approach is the assumption that Christian culture

---

[8] *Ibid.*, paras. 113, 125.
[9] See s 86 (3) Hessisches Schulgesetz and s 38 (2) Schulgesetz Baden-Württemberg.
[10] Judgment of the Verwaltungsgerichtshof Baden-Württemberg of 14 March 2007, 4 S 516/07; Judgment of the Bayerischer Verfassungsgerichtshof of 15 January 2007, Vf. 11-VII-05.

occupies a privileged place in German public life and is, indeed, a postu-late of German political identity and social cohesion'.[11] Accordingly, while not hostile towards religion per se, the German constitutional tradition cognises religious diversity as something unwelcome and disruptive that needs to be contained, if not assimilated to the majoritarian Christian culture.

B The French constitutional tradition

The French constitutional tradition assimilates the *citoyen* to its *republican* identity, while leaving her free to pursue her religious beliefs as a *private* individual. This separation of citizens' public and private 'selves' is reflected in a broader societal distinction between a secular public sphere and a religious private sphere. It is legally entrenched through a rigid interpretation of *laïque* state neutrality that reacts with institutional blindness to the fact of religious and cultural diversity.[12]

The principle of *laïcité* that commits French public schools to a strictly secular education was challenged in 1989 when three schoolgirls insisted on wearing headscarves in class. The headmaster suspended the girls. In the same year, the Conseil d'État gave a legal opinion (*avis*) holding that the display of religious symbols in public schools was not per se incompatible with the principle of *laïcité* but could be restricted in case this (among other things) constituted an act of pressure or provocation, or perturbed the school order or the peaceful running of schools.[13] On this basis, the court reversed a number of school decisions suspending or excluding students who had refused to remove their headscarves. In *Kehrouaa*, for example, the court struck down a school regulation on the ground that it was too general and indiscriminate, thus violating the pupils' freedom of religion.[14] In *Mlle Saglamer*, the court stressed that penalties for wearing a headscarf could only be applied if it was established that the behaviour of the pupil amounted to an act of pressure or proselytism or interfered with the public order in school. In *Aoukili*, by contrast, it upheld the exclusion of students in the more specific context of physical education classes.[15]

---

[11] O. Gerstenberg, 'Freedom of Conscience in Public Schools', *International Journal of Constitutional Law* 3 (2005), 94–6.

[12] See, for example, S. Poulter, 'Muslim Headscarves in School: Contrasting Legal Approaches in England and France', *Oxford Journal of Legal Studies* 17 (1997), 43–50.

[13] Conseil d'État, Avis No. 346893, 27 November 1989.

[14] Conseil d'État, *Kherouaa, Kachour, Balo, Kizic*, No. 130.394, 2 November 1992.

[15] See, respectively, *Kherouaa, Kachour, Balo, Kizic*, No. 130.394, 2 November 1992; *Mlle Saglamer*, No. 169.522, 27 November 1996; *Aoukili*, No. 159.981, 10 March 1995.

On occasion of the publication of the Stasi Report in December 2003, Jacques Chirac called in a controversial speech for a 'national mobilization in defence of the republic's secular values'.[16] The Stasi Report, after asserting that the principle of *laïcité* required a complete neutrality of the state in religious matters, recommended that educational institutions should provide better instruction on the values of republicanism and *laïcité*, and that 'ostentatious' symbols manifesting a religious or political affiliation should be banned from public schools. These measures were deemed necessary to prevent 'identity conflicts' that could trigger violence, endanger individual liberties, and threaten the public order.[17] In 2004 the French parliament eventually passed a law prohibiting the wearing of any signs manifesting a religious affiliation in public schools.[18] Most recently, the French Senate overwhelmingly approved a bill that would make it illegal to wear garments such as the niqab or the burka (both forms of full-faced veil) anywhere in the public sphere.

In an insightful essay, Cecile Laborde distinguishes three different strands of the French constitutional tradition: *laïcité* as state neutrality *qua* abstention that endorses secular equality through the privatisation of religion; *laïcité* as promotion of individual autonomy that lies at the heart of a perfectionist morality; and *laïcité* as a communitarian ideal that fosters a civic sense of loyalty to a particular historical community. For all intents and purposes, Laborde concludes, '*laïcité* has never really formed part of an autonomous juridical, political or philosophical theory, isolated from concrete historical moments, and has always been intimately linked to the republican project of the entrenchment of the modern liberal society born out of the French revolution'.[19] What is more, this plausible interpretation of *laïcité* as a national tradition is rooted in a French national culture that continues to nourish secular *and* Christian values. As Hervieu-Léger notes, 'it is impossible to appreciate the discussion of many questions in French public life which have nothing strictly to do with religion ... without being aware of the extent to which French culture

---

[16] Cited in D. McGoldrick, *Human Rights and Religion – The Islamic Headscarf Debate in Europe* (Oxford University Press, 2006), p. 82.

[17] Commission de Réflexion sur l'application du principe de la laïcité dans la République, pp. 13, 51, 58.

[18] Loi no. 2004–225 du 15 mars 2004 encadrant, en application du principe de laïcité, le port de signes manifestant une appartenance religieuse dans les écoles, collèges et lycées public.

[19] C. Laborde, 'Toleration and *laïcité*' in C. McKinnon and D. Castiglione (eds.), *The Culture of Toleration in Diverse Societies* (Manchester University Press, 2003), p. 173.

is impregnated with Catholic values.'[20] The Christian roots of French constitutional tradition are traceable in all three dimensions of *laïcité* distinguished by Laborde.

Laïcité as state neutrality *qua* abstention is the result of a historical process coined by *the interrelation of* Christianity and secularisation in France, and therefore proves less neutral than it purports. Crudely put, European Christians will find it much easier to accept the distinction between a secular public sphere and a religious private sphere simply because they contributed to its creation in the first place. The French constitutional tradition does not require *them* to change their dress, behaviour and customs regarding the role of religion in the public sphere. Hence today the awkward alliance against the headscarf between French left-wing secular Republicanism and right-wing Christian Catholicism:

> The Right and the Left can define the prohibition on Islamic headscarves in the classroom as a defence of either French Christian or French secular culture, because the two are not at all mutually exclusive. Current Western Christian religious practice defines that women and men bare their heads in public, non-sacred buildings, and that convention – the absence of a religious marker – has been accepted as a secular practise [*sic*].[21]

For those who defend *laïcité* on grounds of individual autonomy, the ban of religious symbols from the public sphere is justified by virtue of liberating Muslim women from heteronymous social structures that persist in the private sphere – a position enthusiastically endorsed by President Sarkozy when advocating the French burka ban: 'The *burka* is not a religious sign. It is a sign of the subjugation, of the submission, of women ... We cannot accept in our country women imprisoned behind bars, cut off from social life, deprived of identity.'[22] The blemish of this heroic posture is that it is self-defeating: we foster the inclusion of Muslim women by excluding them from the 'autonomous' public sphere and forcing them back into the 'heteronymous' private sphere that deprives them of their 'identity'. Moreover, it categorically denies that Muslim women could embrace the headscarf as an autonomous choice, that is, as a self-conscious expression of their struggle to define their place as female Muslims in the secularised

---

[20] D. Hervieu-Léger, 'The Role of Religion in Establishing Social Cohesion' in K. Michalski (ed.), *Conditions of European Solidarity. Vol. II: Religion in the New Europe* (Budapest: Central European University Press: 2006), p. 51.

[21] N. Moruzzi, 'A Problem with Headscarves. Contemporary Complexities of Political and Social Identity', *Political Theory* 4 (1994), 664.

[22] Cited by D. Carvajal, 'Sarkozy Backs Drive to Eliminate the Burqa', *The New York Times* (23 June 2009), p. A4.

Christian nation-state. What gets lost in the relentless crusade of secular autonomy against sacred heteronomy is, as Balibar remarks, the tragic character of a situation in which Muslim women 'become the stake of a merciless struggle for prestige between two male powers which try to control them, one on behalf of patriarchal authority wrapped up in religion, the other on behalf of national authority wrapped up in secularism'.[23]

Ultimately, the 'neutrality' and 'autonomy' strands of *laïcité* are rooted in a communitarian notion of civic loyalty that strives to resurrect a 'traditional Catholic-inspired sociability'[24] in new national clothes. It is the French majoritarian national *and* secular *and* Christian conception of 'public' that directs the neutrality principle towards the exclusion of (certain) religions from the public sphere, as it is the French majoritarian national *and* secular *and* Christian conception of 'private' that reduces the political subject behind the veil to a false dichotomy between secular autonomy and sacred heteronomy.

Bereft of its neutralist pretentions, also the French constitutional tradition thrives on national majoritarianism that betrays the liberal promise not just to assimilate but to accommodate religious diversity. During the parliamentary debates of the 1994 French law, a member of the Assemblée Nationale used his '*bon sens paysan*' to provide a contemporary interpretation of the traditional French way of transforming (Catholic) 'peasants into Frenchmen': 'Islam has settled rather recently in our country. Its faith is absolutely respectable. But its adherents, as everybody else, must adapt to our values and traditions, not the other way around.'[25]

2   Religious pluralism and national constitutional traditions in European human rights jurisprudence

A   A strategy of avoidance

While both the German and the French constitutional tradition exhibit defensive attitudes towards religious diversity, they also appear irreconcilable *inter se* because they are embedded in different national cultures. Put cynically, what the controversy on including a reference to Christianity in the Draft Treaty establishing a Constitution for Europe has revealed is

---

[23] E. Balibar, 'Dissonances within Laïcité', *Constellations* 11 (2004), 359.
[24] C. Laborde, 'Toleration and *laïcité*', p. 170.
[25] Journal Officiel de la République Française, Année 2004. – No 17 [2] A.N. (C.R.), p. 1463.

that the greatest common denominator that the European nation states could consent to is to discriminate against their non-Christian populations. Beyond this 'negative integration', the differences between Europe's *national* constitutional traditions pose significant problems for an effective transnational vindication of *religious* pluralism.

The European Court of Human Rights, in spite of its lip-serving commitment to religious pluralism, de facto endorses the defensive attitudes towards religious pluralism inherent in Europe's different national constitutional traditions. The court uses the absence of a uniform European conception of the role of religion in the public sphere as a pretext for granting national authorities a wide margin of appreciation in dealing with religious diversity.

The most authoritative ECtHR case on freedom of religion and the Islamic headscarf is *Şahin* v. *Turkey*, decided in a split judgment of the Grand Chamber in 2005.[26] Ms Şahin, a medical student at Istanbul University, was refused permission to attend lectures and sit examinations because she insisted on wearing a headscarf. After having left Istanbul to continue her studies in Vienna, Ms Şahin brought a case against the Government of Turkey under the European Convention, arguing that her exclusion from university for reasons of wearing the headscarf violated her freedom of religion. All judges of the Chamber, and all but one judge of the Grand Chamber, while accepting that the applicant's exclusion from university interfered with her freedom of religion, found that this interference was justified and proportionate to the aims pursued. What is remarkable about both the Chamber and the Grand Chamber judgment is how the judges fail to engage critically with the concrete submissions of the parties. Both judgments suffer from want of evidence and balance in the courts' proportionality test.

The Grand Chamber, after reiterating its appraisal of pluralism, tolerance and broadmindedness as 'hallmarks of a democratic society', flatly states that 'pluralism and democracy must also be based on dialogue and a spirit of compromise necessarily entailing various concessions on the part of individuals or groups of individuals which are justified in order to maintain and promote the ideals and values of a democratic society'.[27] This circular reasoning – pluralism, while being a prerequisite of democratic societies, is also delimited in the name of maintaining and

---

[26] Eur. Ct. H. R. (Grand Chamber), *Leyla Şahin* v. *Turkey*, 10 November 2005, following on from Eur. Ct. H. R. (Fourth Section) *Leyla Şahin and Others* v. *Turkey*, 29 June 2004.

[27] *Şahin* (2005), para. 108.

promoting democratic values – serves to alleviate the court from scrutinising Turkey's submission that the headscarf ban was necessary and
proportionate in the light of Article 9(2) ECHR. The judges uncritically
accept the government's association of the headscarf with proselytism
and political Islam, despite the fact that there was no evidence of Ms Şahin
trying to pressure or even influence others, or of her being connected to
extremist political movements. The Chamber, instead of focusing on the
applicant's concrete behaviour, endorses the government's view that the
headscarf ban was justified as general 'preventive' measure.[28] Such rubber-
stamping of pre-emptive measures not warranted by tangible evidence
effectively reverses the burden of proof at the expense of the applicant and
comes dangerously close to granting the government a carte blanche for
unbuffered interference. While the court relies heavily on the unsubstantiated assumption that Muslim women wearing the headscarf are prone
to force their views on others, it appears oblivious to the coercive nature
of state intervention.[29] The Chamber's approach does not fare any better in this regard. After cursorily observing that 'the impugned interference primarily pursued the legitimate aim of protecting the rights and
freedoms of others and of protecting public order', the majority of judges
assert that 'having found that the regulations pursued a legitimate aim, it
is not open to the Court to apply the criterion of proportionality in a way
that would make the notion of an institution's "internal rules" devoid of
purpose'.[30] Such twofold deference to the views of the national government and the educational institution undermines the supervisory role of
the ECtHR. Both the Grand Chamber and the Chamber approach render
a meaningful proportionality test impossible, and an effective protection
of religious freedom illusionary.

The ECtHR's earlier *Dahlab* decision is even more problematic in this
regard.[31] In 1996 Ms Dahlab, a Swiss primary school teacher, was requested
to take off her headscarf in class as such conduct was deemed incompatible with section 6 of the Canton of Geneva Public Education Act, which
requires the public education system to respect pupils' and parents' political and religious beliefs. The ECtHR agreed with the Swiss government's
contention that Ms Dahlab's case was manifestly ill-founded. 'Weighing'
the right of the teacher to manifest her religion against the need to protect

[28] *Şahin* (2004), para. 96.
[29] C. Evans, 'The "Islamic Scarf" in the European Court of Human Rights', *Melbourne
Journal of International Law* 7 (2006), 65.
[30] *Şahin* (2005), paras. 99, 121.
[31] Eur. Ct. H. R., *Dahlab* v. *Switzerland*, 15 February 2001.

pupils by 'preserving religious harmony', the judges concluded that it 'appears difficult to reconcile the wearing of an Islamic headscarf with the message of tolerance, respect for others, and, above all, equality and non-discrimination that all teachers in a democratic society must convey to their pupils.'[32]

This is a surprisingly bold statement for a court that has repeatedly stressed that 'the State's duty of neutrality and impartiality is incompatible with any power on the State's part to assess the legitimacy of religious beliefs or the ways in which those beliefs are expressed'.[33] What is more, the court's analysis of the symbolic significance and impact of the headscarf is entirely detached from the concrete person and behaviour of the wearer. As a consequence, the court's association of the headscarf with intolerance and gender discrimination appears perfunctory and stereotypical. Furthermore, the assessment of the impact of the headscarf in the abstract leads the court to ignore the concrete evidence before it. It was uncontested between the parties that Ms Şahin had been wearing the headscarf in class for more than five years without causing any obvious disturbance or complaints from pupils or parents. The Swiss government's submission that the headscarf was a 'powerful religious symbol' likely to influence children's beliefs, by contrast, remained unsubstantiated and in want of evidence.

In two recent judgments, *Dogru* v. *France* and *Kervanci* v. *France*,[34] the ECtHR adopts a more case-sensitive approach, possibly encouraged by the jurisprudence of the French Conseil d'État.[35] Because both applications centred on the limited issue of whether the headscarf could be banned in physical education and sports classes, the court's consideration of Article 9(2) ECHR focuses on the school's internal rules on health and safety. In this context, the court notes that 'it transpires from these various sources that the wearing of religious signs was not inherently incompatible with the principle of secularism is schools, but became so according to the conditions in which they were worn and the consequences that the wearing of a sign might have'.[36] However, this promise of a more differentiated and contextualised approach is immediately mitigated by the

---

[32] *Ibid.*, at 8.

[33] *Leyla Şahin v. Turkey* (2005), para. 107; see also *Hasan and Chaush v. Bulgaria*, Application no 30985/96 (2000) para. 78, and *Manoussakis and Others* v. *Greece*, Application no 18748/91 (1996) para. 47.

[34] Eur. Ct. H. R., *Dogru* v. *France*, 4 December 2008; Eur. Ct. H. R., *Kervanci* v. *France*, 4 December 2008.

[35] See above, section 2B.   [36] *Dogru*, para. 70.

court's statement that because 'the ban was limited to the physical education class, [it] cannot be regarded as a ban in the strict sense of the term'.[37]
Accordingly, rather than scrutinising the proportionality of the ban in
the light of the alleged health and safety concerns, the ECtHR contents
itself with noting that it was 'not unreasonable'.[38] Having stressed that
the headscarf controversy had created a 'general atmosphere of tension'
within the school, the court fails to inquire as to the proper source of this
tension.[39] Instead, it jumps to the conclusion that the 'principle of *pluralism*' is an entirely legitimate ground for justifying the exclusion of pupils
wearing headscarves in school.[40]

The ECtHR's supervisory role is limited to ensuring a common minimum standard of human rights protection in Europe, leaving Convention
states free to provide higher levels of protection at the national level.
Where national constitutional traditions diverge on a contentious issue
such as the headscarf, this minimum approach results in the court granting Convention states a particularly wide margin of appreciation. The
ECtHR's dictum in *Dogru* is representative in this regard, and worth citing at length:

> Where questions concerning the relationship between State and religions
> are at stake, on which opinion in a democratic society may reasonably
> differ widely, the role of the national decision-making body must be
> given special importance. This will notably be the case when it comes to
> regulating the wearing of religious symbols in educational institutions,
> in respect of which the approaches in Europe are diverse. Rules in this
> sphere will consequently vary from one country to another according to
> national traditions and the requirements imposed by the need to protect
> the rights and freedoms of others and to maintain public order.[41]

The way the court applies these principles in its headscarf jurisprudence
undermines an effective transnational protection of religious pluralism
against the backdrop of diverse national constitutional traditions. The
margin of appreciation doctrine is used to water down the high burden of
'necessity' of interference to be discharged by the state. As Judge Tulkens

---

[37] *Ibid.*, para. 74.   [38] *Ibid.*, para. 73.

[39] *Ibid.*, para. 74. The applicant had submitted the unrest and disruption started with a
teachers' strike action against the headscarf on the pretext of defending secularism (para.
44), and that her proposal to wear a hat or balaclava instead of the headscarf was indicative of her conciliatory attitude and willingness to compromise (paras. 44, 75).

[40] *Ibid.*, para. 67, with reference to *Köse and 93 Others* v. *Turkey*, Application no 26625/02
(2006), my emphasis.

[41] *Dogru*, para. 63; see also *Kervanci*, para. 63 and *Şahin* (2005), paras. 108–9.

notes in her lone dissent to *Şahin*, 'only indisputable facts and reasons whose legitimacy is beyond doubt – not mere worries or fears – are capable of satisfying that requirement and justifying interference with a right guaranteed by the Convention'.[42] The Grand Chamber majority idly remarks that the 'State's role as the neutral and impartial organiser of the exercise of various religions' should not be discharged by way of removing 'the cause of tension by eliminating pluralism' but through ensuring that 'the competing groups tolerate each other'.[43] Yet the actual headscarf jurisprudence of the court speaks to different concerns.

B   A strategy of integration

My assessment of the ECJ's response to the tension between protecting religious pluralism and respecting Europe's diverse national constitutional traditions is more tentative as the court has not yet come to decide a case involving the display of religious symbols in educational institutions. Yet I shall argue that for systemic and normative reasons, the ECJ is unlikely to adopt an ECtHR-type minimum approach that accommodates national at the expense of religious diversity.

Freedom of religion has long been recognised as a general principle of Community law and receives the broad protection of Article 10 of the Charter of Fundamental Rights of the European Union that avouches each person's right to publicly manifest his religious beliefs. Post Lisbon, Article 10 legally binds the European institutions and the European member states when acting in the field of Community law. In the light of the increasingly dense web of European anti-discrimination legislation, it seems likely that European member state measures affecting the manifestation of religious beliefs in educational institutions and the broader public sphere will come under the scrutiny of the ECJ.[44]

---

[42] *Şahin* (2005), Dissenting Opinion of Judge Tulkens, para. 5.

[43] *Ibid.*, para. 107.

[44] Certain religious groups come under the scope of Council Directive 2000/43/EC of 29 June 2000 implementing the principle of equal treatment between persons irrespective of racial or ethnic origin. Council Directive 2000/78/EC of 27 November 2000 establishing a general framework for equal treatment in employment and occupation covers both conditions for access to employment and occupation, and access to all types and levels of vocational training. The European Commission's proposal COM (2008) 426 final for a Council Directive implementing the principle of equal treatment between persons irrespective of religion or belief, disability, age or sexual orientation states in Article 3 that the Directive shall be 'without prejudice to national legislation ensuring the secular nature of the State, State institutions or bodies, or education'. It remains to be seen

Having introduced fundamental rights as part of the general principles of Community law, the ECJ developed two guiding principles for
interpreting them. On the one hand, the court has consistently held
that EU fundamental rights must be interpreted in an autonomous way,
in the light of the Community legal order as an 'independent source
of law'.[45] On the other hand, it has stressed that such interpretation 'is
inspired by the constitutional traditions common to the Member States'
and their obligations under international law.[46] As the Court says in its
ERT ruling:

> Fundamental rights form an integral part of the general principles of
> law the observance of which the Court ensures. For that purpose, the
> Court draws inspiration from the constitutional traditions common to
> the Member States and from the guidelines supplied by international
> treaties for the protection of human rights on which the Member States
> have collaborated or to which they are signatories. The ECHR has special
> significance.[47]

At first sight, the 'special significance' accorded to the European
Convention may suggest that the ECJ should endorse the ECtHR's minimum approach. This interpretation was favoured by the French Conseil
Constitutionnel when scrutinising the consistency of Article 10 EU
Charter (then: Article II-70 of the Treaty establishing a Constitution
for Europe) with Article 1 of the French Constitution. According to
the Conseil Constitutionnel, Article 10 of the EU Charter should be
interpreted as having the same meaning and scope as Article 9 of the
European Convention. To ensure that the European Charter is interpreted 'in harmony' with Europe's diverse national constitutional
traditions, the ECJ should accord to member states a wide margin of

---

whether this will prevent the ECJ from scrutinising the alleged link between the ban of
religious symbols from the public sphere and the 'secular nature of the State', in particular with regard to countries that do not adhere to a strictly secular model of education.
The case law of the German Federal Constitutional Court, the French Conseil d'État and
the ECtHR considered in this chapter does not warrant the conclusion that the display
of religious symbols is per se incompatible with the secular nature of the state or state
education.

[45] See, e.g., Case 11/70 *Internationale Handelsgesellschaft* v. *Einfuhr- und Vorratstelle fuer
Getreide und Futtermittel* [1970] ECR 1125, para. 3.

[46] *Ibid.*, para. 4; since Maastricht, Article 6 (2) TEU obliges the EU to respect fundamental
rights as guaranteed by the ECHR and as they result from the constitutional traditions
common to the member states, as general principles of Community law.

[47] Case C-260/89 *Elliniki Radiophonia Tileorassi AE (ERT)* v. *Dimotiki Etaria Pliroforissis
and Sotirios Kouvelas* [1991] ECR I-2925, para. 41.

appreciation in 'reconciling' freedom of religion with the principle of secularism.[48]

However, such an approach proves unsatisfactory for at least three reasons. First, and regardless of the pending accession of the EU to the ECHR, the 'special significance' accorded to the latter can only provide a *negative* reference point for the ECJ, disqualifying measures in the Community 'which are incompatible with observance of the human rights thus recognised and guaranteed'.[49] To mistake this 'floor' of European human rights protection for its 'ceiling'[50] not only runs counter to the self-understanding of the Convention system, but also renders the proclaimed autonomous interpretation of general principles of EC law void of meaning. Secondly, adopting a common minimum standard disregards the systemic differences between human rights protection under the European Convention and in the European Union. The ECtHR uses the absence of a pan-European approach to freedom of religion in the public sphere as a pretext for granting Convention States a wide margin of appreciation, therewith effectively endorsing national *diversity* as a matter of ECHR law. The ECJ, by contrast, builds its fundamental rights jurisprudence on constitutional traditions *common* to the European member states, which is antagonistic to recognising national differences for the purpose of defining standards of human rights protection as a matter of EU law.[51] Since the early days of its human rights jurisprudence, the ECJ has stressed that a high level of convergence among member states' constitutional traditions is a functional imperative of European legal integration. Deference to national diversity would compromise the doctrinal supremacy and damage the coherence and efficacy of Community law,

---

[48] *Re EU Constitutional Treaty and the French Constitution* (French Constitutional Court) [2005] 1 CMLR 750.

[49] Case C-260/89 *ERT*, para. 41.

[50] For this terminology see P. Craig and G. de Búrca, *EU Law*, 4th edition (Oxford University Press, 2008), pp. 385–6; for earlier elaborations of the problem of minimum versus maximum standards in EU human rights protection, see L. Besselink, 'Entrapped by the Maximum Standard: On Fundamental Rights, Pluralism and Subsidiarity in the European Union', *Common Market Law Review* 35 (1998), 629–80; and J Weiler, 'Fundamental Rights and Fundamental Boundaries: On the Conflict of Standards and Values in the Protection of Human Rights in the European Legal Space' in *The Constitution of Europe* (Cambridge University Press, 1999), pp. 102–29.

[51] The problem of defining common *EU* human rights standards should be distinguished from the ECJ's practice of granting member states exceptions from Community law on the basis of conflicting *national* human rights standards; see e.g. Case C-36/02 *Omega Spielhallen- und Automatenaufstellungs-GmbH* v. *Oberbuergermeisterin der Bundesstadt Bonn* [2004] ECR I-9609.

effectively leading 'to the destruction of the unity of the Common Market and the jeopardizing of the cohesion of the Community'.[52]

Finally, the ECJ's endorsement of the ECHR minimum standard runs the risk of engendering a European 'race to the bottom' of human rights protection. There is already a tendency among some national courts to treat the ECtHR jurisprudence as an authoritative and exclusive, rather than merely a minimum, standard. If the ECJ were to adopt the same approach, the Strasbourg floor of human rights protection would become binding on the member states as a matter of European law. At the same time, the ECtHR has accorded the European Union a rebuttable presumption of compliance with the European Convention on Human Rights, accepting that the protection of fundamental rights under EU law was 'equivalent' to that of the Convention system.[53] Such mutual deference between the European courts risks undermining the effective protection of religious pluralism at all levels. Rather than developing an autonomous, transnational interpretation of the relationship between religious and national diversities, the ECJ would fall back on, and reinforce, the defensive attitudes towards religious pluralism inherent in Europe's national constitutional traditions.

The obvious alternative to adopting an ECtHR minimum approach is to derive a high standard of protection of religious pluralism from the constitutional traditions 'common to the Member States'. In this vein, Leonard Besselink advocates a 'universalised maximum standard approach' that functions as a 'decisional principle for the Court to apply the standard which offers the best protection in a concrete case'.[54] In a nutshell, the ECJ should adopt, on a case-by-case basis, the respectively highest national standard and apply it across the European Union. According to Besselink, this would ensure the uniform and full effect of Community law and a robust protection of human rights across the European Union.

Attractive as it may seem at first sight, the adoption of a maximum approach is also fraught with difficulties. First of all, it is difficult to explain how the scope of freedom of religion as a general principle of Community law could be derived from one particular national constitutional tradition. As regards the existence of particular rights not 'common' to the member states, the ECJ has either refused to recognise them

---

[52] Case 44/79 *Hauer* v. *Land Rheinland-Pfalz* [1979] ECR 3727.

[53] *M & Co* v. *Federal Republic*, Application no 13258/87 (1990); *Bosphorus* v. *Ireland*, Application no 45036/98 (2005), para. 165.

[54] Besselink, 'Entrapped by the Maximum Standard', p. 671.

as a matter of Community law,[55] or has construed them as general rights that could be said to be shared among all member states.[56] The latter approach – an induction from the particular to the general – appears not feasible once what is at stake is not merely the abstract recognition of a right but its concrete interpretation in European law.[57] Secondly, Besselink's maximum standard is also incompatible with the principle of autonomous interpretation. Rather than developing a genuine interpretation of EU human rights, it merely selectively incorporates particular national standards into European law to then impose them on the member states *qua* European law. Besselink rightly insists that an EU approach to human rights that effectively lowers national standards of protection risks stirring up anti-European feeling and jeopardising the integration process.[58] However, the imposition of one particular national constitutional tradition on other member states in European disguise is likely to have the same effect.

EU human rights protection cannot operate in a normative vacuum. Most significantly for the present purpose, the EU legal order lacks a relatively homogenous cultural pedigree comparable to those that underpin the protection of human rights in Europe's national constitutional traditions.[59] Yet it would be premature to conclude that this impedes an autonomous interpretation of EU human rights law on the basis of the EU legal order as an independent source of law.[60] Such argument fails to appreciate the particular nature of human rights protection in the European Union *qua* supranational polity. As Joseph Weiler has lucidly argued, European supranationalism dwells on the notion of a 'community as a transnational regime' that is 'not meant to eliminate the national state but to create a regime which seeks to tame the national interest with a new discipline'. Accordingly, it does not seek to redraw the actual political boundaries of the polity within the existing nation-state conceptual framework but to 'redefine the very notion of boundaries of the state, between the nation

---

[55] Cases 46/87 and 227/88, *Hoechst* v. *Commission* [1989] ECR 2859, para. 17.

[56] Case 155/79 *AM & S Europe Ltd* v. *Commission* (1982) ECR 1575, 1587 paras. 18–28; Case C-36/02 *Omega Spielhallen- und Automatenaufstellungs-GmbH*, paras. 34–8.

[57] For example, in the joint cases C-122/99 and C-125/99 *D and Sweden* v. *Council* (2001) ECR I-4319 the ECJ took the view that the meaning of the term 'married official' in the Staff Regulations could not be derived from the law of singular member states but was a matter for independent Community interpretation.

[58] See Besselink, 'Entrapped by the Maximum Standard', p. 670.

[59] See above, section 2 and, more generally, N. Walker, 'Legal Theory and the European Union: A 25th Anniversary Essay', *Oxford Journal of Legal Studies* 25 (2005), 590.

[60] See Besselink, 'Entrapped by the Maximum Standard'.

and the state, and within the nation itself'.[61] Placed in the context of EU human rights protection, such a redefinition of the boundaries between the state and the nation in the area of tension between national and religious diversities can neither content itself with adopting the ECtHR general minimum standard, nor can it simply replicate any particular national standard at the European level. Rather, and drawing 'inspiration' from the constitutional traditions of the member states, the ECJ must *reinterpret* the relationship between national and religious diversities 'within the framework and structure of the Community'.[62]

Having regard to the supranational telos of European integration, such a reinterpretation should start from the premise that the European member states accommodate religious diversity, rather than that religious minorities be assimilated to majoritarian national cultures. More precisely, it would consist of challenging the linkage between the perpetuation of majoritarian national cultures and the containment of religious diversity inherited from the formative period of the European nation states. This would take seriously the ECtHR's appraisal of religious pluralism as one of the foundations of democratic societies. Moreover, it could draw on Europe's diverse national constitutional traditions without collapsing into any particular national model. Neither the German Federal Constitutional Court nor the French Conseil d'État considers the ban of religious symbols from educational institutions and the broader public sphere as a national constitutional requirement per se. While the German court has proposed a positive interpretation of state neutrality that permits the display of religious symbols in educational institutions to foster mutual tolerance and integration through the active encounter of religious difference, the French court has attempted to restrict the headscarf ban to situations of concrete threats to the public order. A similar tendency can also be traced in the more recent case law of the ECtHR. The converging case law may prove indicative of a growing recognition on the part of national and European human rights courts that in increasingly pluralistic societies, the proper role of the state as a 'neutral arbitrator' may not be to contain or assimilate religious diversity, but to ensure that different religious groups tolerate each other.

---

[61] J. Weiler, 'To be a European citizen: Eros and civilization' in *The Constitution of Europe* (Cambridge University Press, 1999), pp. 350–1.

[62] See, respectively, Case C-260/89 *ERT*, para. 41 and Case 11/70 *Internationale Handelsgesellschaft*, para. 4.

Concluding Remarks

The present European scepticism vis-à-vis the prospects of a true '*révolution post-islamique*'[63] in the Middle East may in part be explainable by virtue of a deep-seated mistrust in Europe towards the liberal and tolerant credentials of Islam. It may also be considered the mirror image of an in itself not particularly liberal and tolerant tendency within various European member states to suppress religious diversity by assimilating religious minorities into majoritarian national cultures. As Evans notes with regard to *Dahlab*, it may not be the headscarf but its ban that sends a message of intolerance and discrimination:

> The Court's judgment makes clear that there were Muslim children in the school who wore traditional Muslim clothing and they might well wonder why dressing as they do or as their mothers do is so terrible that it requires an otherwise good teacher to be forced out of the school community. In addition, children who are already inclined towards mistrust, religious hatred or racial discrimination could be sent the message that their fears are justified and their stereotypes valid.[64]

Defensive attitudes towards religious diversity that feed on spurious notions of homogenous national cultures are difficult to square with Europe's self-image of open and pluralistic societies, and may (further) undermine the credibility of the European Union as an international human rights actor. Perhaps more fundamentally, they may hamper the very process of integrating the European Union, as they easily lend themselves to reciprocal segregation and misrecognition: on the part of national majorities because they ascertain majoritarian 'ways of life' as a legitimate criterion for distinction and discrimination; and on the part of religious minorities because they invite them to withdraw into angry and cynical indifference towards their societies.

Against this background, the present chapter suggested that EU human rights protection could yet have a fruitful role to play in averting that the bugbear of emerging 'parallel societies' in Europe becomes a self-fulfilling prophecy. A European Union that continues to renegotiate its multinational roots under the umbrella of European supranationalism constitutes a predestined vessel for overcoming defensive societal attitudes towards religious diversity that have formed in the shadow of

---

[63] I borrow this term from O. Le Roy, 'Révolution post-islamique', *Le Monde* (12 February 2011).

[64] Evans, 'The "Islamic Scarf" in the European Court of Human Rights', 65.

the nation state. The European experience of living together in national diversities may contribute to decentring socio-cultural parochialisms and may function as a catalyst for giving voice and recognition to religious pluralism. As Charles Taylor notes, European integration bears the hope of creating societies with an unprecedented degree of openness and inclusion: 'In its finest moments, Europe is blazing a trail for all of us.'[65]

---

[65] C. Taylor, 'Religion and European Integration' in K. Michalski (ed.), *Religion in the New Europe* (Budapest: Central European University Press, 2006), p. 21.

PART III

12

Rights, religion and the public sphere: the European Court of Human Rights in search of a theory?

JULIE RINGELHEIM

During deliberations over the drafting of a Constitution for Europe, the proposal to insert a reference to Christianity in its Preamble generated heated debates throughout the European Union (EU).[1] These discussions put into sharp relief disagreements among EU member states about the proper place of religion in public life. References to the European Court of Human Rights (ECtHR) and its case law were surprisingly absent from these discussions. This Court though, entrusted with ensuring respect for the 1950 European Convention on Human Rights (ECHR), has for several decades been confronted with the task of deciding religion-related disputes on the basis of one common European instrument. Whilst Article 9 of the European Convention guarantees the right to freedom of religion, Article 2 of its first Protocol creates an obligation for states to respect parents' religious convictions when assuming education and teaching functions. Cases brought under these provisions have long exposed this Court to the difficulty of developing a consistent stance on the scope and implications of religious freedom, while having regard to the varying conceptions and arrangements of states parties regarding the relations between religions and the state. Against this background, how has this institution conceptualised the place of religion in the public sphere? This is the subject of this chapter.

An important evolution can be discerned in the ECtHR's case law on religious rights. While in its first judgments the Court demonstrates great

---

This chapter was last updated in February 2011. It is based, therefore, on the examination of the European Court of Human Rights' case law until this date.

[1] The Intergovernmental Conference on the drafting of a Treaty establishing a Constitution for Europe lasted from October 2003 to October 2004. Its ratification was rejected by referendum in France and the Netherlands and this Treaty never entered into force. Large parts of it have, however, been included in the Lisbon Treaty signed on 13 December 2007 and in force since 1 December 2009.

caution in approaching religious issues, it has progressively become more assertive in its defence of religious freedom. Furthermore, especially remarkable in this jurisprudence, is an increasing attempt at going beyond casuistry and building a consistent vision of religious freedom and of its implications for state–religions relations that is valid across Europe. It is this attitude that I refer to as an effort at 'building a theory'. Alongside the core notion of pluralism, three major principles have progressively emerged in the ECtHR's jurisprudence: the right to autonomy of religious communities vis-à-vis the state; an obligation of neutrality for the state; and the necessity of the secularity of the legal order's foundations (section 1). These principles, it is submitted, are in line with the democratic ideal that underlies the European Convention. Yet the Court's approach to religion-related disputes is not without tensions and problems. These are especially manifest when the Court handles disputes that go beyond the issue of the respective autonomy of religion and public authority, and concern the multifaceted question of expression of religion in the public sphere, in particular, the status of religion in public discourse, the wearing of religious garments at public school or university and claims for accommodation of religious practice in the workplace. In some cases of this sort, the Court has adopted stances that are questionable from the viewpoint of the principles it has itself identified as central for religious freedom. In other instances, these principles themselves appear to be in need of further elaboration (section 3). But the significance of the tensions surrounding the treatment of religious disputes by the Court cannot be fully grasped without having regard to present-day discussions in social and political theory about the place of religion in the public sphere (section 2).

1   Building a European vision of religious freedom

A   *The early case law*

During the thirty-three first years of the Court's existence, from 1959 to 1992, cases bearing upon the right to religious freedom were dealt with exclusively by the European Commission of Human Rights.[2] Until 1989, in almost all cases brought under Article 9, it concluded that the facts at stake did not disclose any appearance of violation. These

---

[2] In the original system, applications were subject to a preliminary examination by the European Commission on Human Rights, which determined their admissibility. Pursuant to Protocol No. 11 to the Convention the system was reformed in 1998: the two existing organs, the Commission and the Court, were replaced by a single and permanent Court of Human Rights.

applications, therefore, were deemed inadmissible and never reached the Court.

In this early period the European Commission emphasised the distinction drawn in Article 9 between two aspects of religious freedom: whereas its internal dimension, namely the right to have or change religion or belief, cannot be subject to any limitation whatsoever, its external aspect, that is, 'the freedom, either alone or in community with others and in public or private, to manifest his religion or belief, in worship, teaching, practice and observance' may be restricted in some circumstances, under the conditions set forth in the second paragraph of Article 9. Based on this distinction, the Commission claimed that religious freedom firstly concerns internal beliefs; the individual's personal sphere, its inner self: 'Article 9 primarily protects the sphere of personal beliefs and religious creeds, that is the area which is sometimes called the *forum internum*.' The Commission acknowledged that it also 'protects acts which are intimately linked to these attitudes, such as acts of worship or devotion which are aspects of the practice of a religion or a belief in a generally recognised form'. However, in order to protect this personal sphere, Article 9 'does not always guarantee the right to behave *in the public sphere* in a way which is dictated by such a belief'.[3] Yet the Commission never specified what it exactly meant by 'public sphere'.

This view was to a large extent followed by the Court. The ECtHR also states that religious freedom 'is primarily a matter of individual concerns', while also implying the freedom to manifest one's religion.[4] Interestingly, while restating that 'Article 9 does not protect every act motivated or inspired by a religion or belief', the Court dropped the phrase 'in the public sphere', which may be the sign that it deemed the notion too hazy.[5] Nonetheless, the propensity to regard the protection provided by religious freedom as weaker when a religion is manifested outside the sphere of the family and the religious community can still be observed in recent case law of the Court (see section 3).

B   In search of a theory?

The Court issued its first judgment on religious freedom in 1993 in the case *Kokkinakis* v. *Greece*.[6] Since then the right guaranteed in Article 9

---

[3] Eur. Comm. H. R., *C.* v. *United Kingdom*, 15 December 1983, *D.R.* 37, p. 147, emphasis added.
[4] Eur. Ct. H. R., *Kokkinakis* v. *Greece*, 25 May 1993, para. 31.
[5] Eur. Ct. H. R. (Grand Chamber), *Leyla Şahin* v. *Turkey*, 10 November 2005, para. 121.
[6] 25 May 1993.

ECHR has been the subject of a burgeoning jurisprudential activity at the
ECtHR. From the start, two trends can be discerned in this case law. On
the one hand, the Court observes on various occasions that it is not possible 'to discern throughout Europe a uniform conception of the significance of religion in society; even within a single country such conceptions
may vary'.[7] Accordingly, the role of national decision-making bodies has
to be given special importance where questions concerning the relationship between state and religions are at stake, 'on which opinion in a democratic society may reasonably differ widely'.[8] Domestic authorities should
enjoy a wide margin of appreciation. Yet, this attitude of judicial restraint
is counterbalanced by an opposite tendency. Beginning with *Kokkinakis*
v. *Greece*, the Court demonstrates an increasing willingness to go beyond
the diversity of facts specific to each case and articulate general principles
stemming from religious freedom, valid throughout Europe for all states
party to the European Convention.

In this regard, one notion proves central: that of pluralism. Already in
Kokkinakis v. *Greece*, where Greece was found to be in violation of Article
9 for having prohibited a Jehovah's Witness from proselytising his religion, the Court observes:

> As enshrined in Article 9, freedom of thought, conscience and religion
> is one of the foundations of a 'democratic society' within the meaning
> of the Convention. It is, in its religious dimension, one of the most vital
> elements that go to make up the identity of believers and their conception
> of life, but it is also a precious asset for atheists, agnostics, sceptics and
> the unconcerned. The *pluralism, indissociable from a democratic society*,
> which has been dearly won over the centuries, depends on it.[9]

Noticeable in this passage is the assertion that freedom of thought, conscience and religion is important not only for believers but also for non-
believers – atheist, agnostics, sceptics and the unconcerned. Diversity of
beliefs, convictions and worldviews is conceived as a common good for the
whole society. Thus, pluralism, as referred to by the ECtHR, does not only
refer to a fact; it is also a value. It conveys the idea that in a democracy the
diversity of opinions and worldviews individuals may hold as a result of
the exercise of their freedoms should be respected and allowed to flourish.

---

[7] Eur. Ct. H. R., *Otto-Preminger-Institut* v. *Austria*, 20 September 1994, *Serie* A 295,
   para. 50.
[8] *Leyla Şahin* v. *Turkey*, para. 109.
[9] *Kokkinakis* v. *Greece*, para. 31, emphasis added.

Pluralism can be seen as both an outcome and a condition of the exercise of certain individual rights, such as freedom of speech, freedom of association and freedom of religion.[10] Expanding upon this notion, the Court, in subsequent jurisprudence, has highlighted three interrelated principles that, in its view, should govern relations between state and religions in a democracy. First, it proclaims the autonomy of religious communities vis-à-vis the state (i). Second, it derives from the right to religious freedom an obligation for states to remain neutral towards religions and beliefs (ii). Third, it asserts the necessity of the secularity of the foundations of the legal order (iii).

(i)   Autonomy of religious communities vis-à-vis the state

The rights protected under the ECHR are bestowed upon individuals, not groups. Article 9 only indirectly alludes to the communitarian component of religious practice: it guarantees individuals the freedom to manifest their religion 'individually *or collectively*'. Yet, the European Court has progressively recognised a collective dimension to religious liberty and a corresponding obligation for states to respect religious groups' autonomy. Most notably, in *Hasan and Chaush* v. *Bulgaria* (2000), it states that participation in the life of a religious community must in itself be deemed a manifestation of one's religion. Freedom of religion 'encompasses the expectation that the community will be allowed to function peacefully, free from arbitrary State intervention.'[11] Hence, Article 9 entails the right of the community of believers to manage autonomously their internal affairs, that is choose their leaders, create their own institutions, establish their religious doctrine, as well as define the manner in which new members are admitted and existing members excluded.[12]

This does not mean that there can never be legitimate reasons for a state to interfere with the internal life of a religious community. The Court has not had much occasion to delve into this issue. On one occasion, it observed that it is legitimate for a government to verify that a religious organisation aspiring to official recognition acts in accordance with the law, does not present any danger for a democratic society and does not carry out

---

[10] A. Nieuwenhuis, 'The Concept of Pluralism in the Case-Law of the European Court of Human Rights', *European Constitutional Law Review* 3 (2007), 367–84 and J. Ringelheim, *Diversité culturelle et droits de l'homme. La protection des minorités par la Convention européenne des droits de l'homme* (Brussels: Bruylant, 2006), 349–426.

[11] Eur. Ct. H. R. (Grand Chamber), *Hasan and Chaush* v. *Bulgaria*, 26 October 2000, para. 62.

[12] Eur. Ct. H. R., *Svyato-Mykhaylivska Parafiya* v. *Ukraine*, 14 May 2007, para. 150.

any activity threatening the public order or the rights and freedoms of others.[13] If a religious community carried out practices amounting to torture or inhuman or degrading treatment, the Court would certainly not consider it illegitimate for the state to intervene in order to protect individuals subject to such treatment. Given the case law on right violations committed by private persons, public authorities could even be deemed to have a positive obligation to act in defence of individuals whose fundamental rights are jeopardised by a religious group.[14] However, based on the autonomy of religious communities, the Court admits that where a church acts as an employer, it is entitled to impose on its employees specific duties of loyalty, which may entail a restriction to their freedom of speech (Article 10) or to their right to private life (Article 8).[15] Yet, the community's autonomy is not unlimited: the Court insists on its power to ensure in each case that a fair balance has been struck between the interests of the church and that of the individual.[16]

(ii)   State neutrality

A second fundamental principle emphasised by the Court is that of the state's duty of neutrality and impartiality vis-à-vis religions and creeds. It is again in *Hasan and Chaush* that for the first time the Court declared that freedom of religion entails such an obligation. When exercising its regulatory powers in the sphere of religious practice, and in its relations with the diverse denominations and beliefs, the state must remain neutral and impartial.[17] Its role consists in acting as 'the neutral and impartial organiser of the exercise of various religions, faiths and beliefs'.[18] The Court attaches various consequences to this duty of neutrality. First, the right to freedom of religion excludes in principle any discretion on the part of the state to determine whether religious beliefs or the means used to express them are legitimate. Furthermore, in case of divisions in

---

[13] Eur. Ct. H. R., *Carmuirea spirituala a musulmanilor din Republic Modlova* v. *Moldova*, 14 June 2005.

[14] See D. Spielmann, 'Obligations positives et effet horizontal des dispositions de la Convention' in F. Sudre (ed.), *L'interprétation de la Convention européenne des droits de l'homme* (Brussels: Bruylant, 1998), 133–74; A. Clapham, *Human Rights in the Private Sphere* (Oxford: Clarendon Press, 1993).

[15] See Eur. Ct. H. R., *Obst* v. *Germany*, 23 September 2010.

[16] See Eur. Ct. H. R., *Schüth* v. *Germany*, 23 September 2010 and Eur. Ct. H. R., *Lombardi Vallauri* v. *Italy*, 20 October 2009.

[17] *Hasan and Chaush* v. *Bulgaria*, para. 78.

[18] Eur. Ct. H. R. (Grand Chamber), *Refah Partisi (The Welfare Party) and others* v. *Turkey*, 13 February 2003, para. 9.

a religious community, the state should abstain from taking sides: state action seeking to compel a community to come together under a single leadership against its own wishes would constitute an interference with religious freedom.[19] The state is the 'ultimate guarantor of pluralism'.[20] The Court admits that where a religious community becomes divided, tensions might arise. But this 'is one of the unavoidable consequences of pluralism. The role of the authorities in such circumstances is not to remove the cause of tension by eliminating pluralism, but to ensure that the competing groups tolerate each other.'[21] They may, however, act as mediators between religious groups and endeavour to ensure pacific relations between them, provided that they remain strictly neutral.[22] Yet the Court's insistence on the state's duty to refrain from interfering with disputes within or between religious groups, is counterbalanced by its observation that 'in democratic societies, in which several religions coexist within one and the same population, it may be necessary to place restrictions on [the freedom to manifest one's religion] in order to reconcile the interests of the various groups and ensure that everyone's beliefs are respected'.[23] Depending on the context of the case, judges put the emphasis either on the first or on the second of these concerns.

The Court has yet to unravel the implications of this neutrality obligation as to the conformity with the ECHR of the various legal regimes of state–religions relations in Europe. Previous jurisprudence indicates that different systems can be compatible with the European Convention.[24] The establishment of a state church was declared by the Commission not to be per se incompatible with Article 9, provided that it includes appropriate safeguards for the freedom of religion of all individuals; first and foremost, people should be free to leave the state church.[25] More generally, public authorities are under no obligation to provide an identical legal status to each religious community.[26] They can establish an institutionalised form of collaboration with specific faith groups and grant them

---

[19] *Hasan and Chaush* v. *Bulgaria*, para. 78.

[20] Eur. Ct. H. R., *Sinan Isik* v. *Turkey*, 2 February 2010, para. 45.

[21] Eur. Ct. H. R., *Serif* v. *Greece*, 14 December 1999, para. 53.

[22] Eur. Ct. H. R., *Supreme Holy Council of the Muslim Community* v. *Bulgaria*, 16 December 2004, para. 80.

[23] *Kokkinakis* v. *Greece*, para. 31.

[24] J. Martinez-Torron, 'The European Court of Human Rights and Religion' in R. O'Dair and A. Lewis, *Law and Religion, Current Legal Issues*, vol. 4 (Oxford University Press, 2001), 189–90.

[25] Eur. Comm. H. R., *Darby* v. *Sweden*, Report of 9 May 1989, para. 45.

[26] Eur. Ct. H. R., *Canea Catholic Church* v. *Greece*, 16 December 1997, para. 47.

certain privileges such as tax exemptions.[27] Yet, pursuant to the rule of non-discrimination, any advantage conferred on a religious community to the exclusion of the others must rest on a legitimate justification and remain proportionate.[28] Read in this light, the neutrality concept, as elaborated by the ECtHR, does not amount to a requirement of strong separation between state and religion nor of strict uniformity of treatment. Instead, it points towards a duty of even-handedness and proportionality in the state's relations with the various faiths and beliefs.

Nonetheless, the rise of the neutrality obligation has led the Court to control with heightened severity the conformity with the Convention of arrangements in which a privileged position is granted to one religion.[29] The Court is increasingly concerned with ensuring that the state refrains from exerting pressure, even indirectly, on the religious choices of individuals. This emerges especially in the context of public education. In *Folgerø and others* v. *Norway* (2007), regarding instruction about religion in public schools, it insists that where the curriculum and teaching methods do not guarantee that information is conveyed in a strictly objective, critical and pluralistic manner, pupils should have the right to be fully exempted from it.[30] In *Lautsi* v. *Italy* (2009), it is the compulsory display of a crucifix in state school classrooms that is found to be in breach of the state obligation to respect parents' religious and philosophical convictions. The Court here emphasises that state's confessional neutrality is a condition of pluralism in education; it guarantees an open scholarly environment that favours inclusion of all pupils, regardless of their religious beliefs, ethnic origin or social background.[31] Schooling of children is said to be particularly sensitive because it involves the imposition of the compelling power of the state 'on minds which still lack ... the critical capacity

---

[27] Eur. Comm. H. R., *Iglesia Bautista 'El Salvador' and Jose Aquilino Ortega Moratilla* v. *Spain*, 11 January 1992, *D.R.* 72, at 256.

[28] See Eur. Ct. H. R., *Religionsgemeinschaft der Zeugen Jehovas and Others* v. *Austria*, 31 July 2008.

[29] F. Tulkens, 'The European Convention on Human Rights and Church–State Relations: Pluralism vs. Pluralism', *Cardozo Law Review* 30(6) (2009), 2575–91, 2585–6.

[30] Eur. Ct. H. R. (Grand Chamber), *Folgerø and others* v. *Norway*, 29 June 2007 (eight judges dissenting). See also Eur. Ct. H. R., *Hasan and Eylem Zengin* v. *Turkey*, 9 October 2007 and Eur. Ct. H. R., *Grzelak* v. *Poland*, 15 June 2010.

[31] Eur. Ct. H. R., *Lautsi* v. *Italy*, 3 November 2009 (not final), para. 47. This decision was reversed by the Grand Chamber in its 18 March 2011 judgment, which concludes that in deciding to maintain crucifixes in state school classrooms, Italian authorities have acted within the limits of their margin of appreciation. Accordingly, no violation of the European Convention or of its Protocols has occurred. This ruling was issued after this chapter was finished and could not thus be included in the analysis.

which would enable them to keep their distance from the message derived from a preference manifested by the State in religious matters.'[32] In such context, the exhibition of the crucifix in the classroom, a symbol which is clearly associated with one religion, is seen as amounting to the promotion of a belief by the state: 'children will feel that they have been brought up in a school environment marked by a particular religion. What may be encouraging for some pupils may be emotionally disturbing for pupils of other religions or those who profess no religion.'[33] This case, however, has been referred to the Grand Chamber for re-examination.[34]

(iii) Secularity of the foundations of the law

Closely related to the notion of state's neutrality, secularity of the legal system's foundations is another principle that has taken a prominent place in the Court's case law. It is mainly in *Refah Partisi (Welfare Party) and others* v. *Turkey* (2003) that European judges developed their views on the question.[35] The case concerns the dissolution of an Islamist political party which, according to the Turkish government, was planning to establish a theocratic regime in Turkey, based on Islamic law (sharia). The judgment, which does not find any breach of the European Convention, generated strenuous controversies. But what interests us here are the general observations made by the Court about the relation between democracy and religion. It declares that a political–legal system based on religious rules cannot be considered compatible with the Convention system, since such a societal model 'would do away with the State's role as the guarantor of individual rights and freedoms and the impartial organiser of the practice of the various beliefs and religions in a democratic society, since it would oblige individuals to obey, not rules laid down by the State ... but static rules of law imposed by the religion concerned.'[36] The Court thereby asserts the necessity, in a democracy, of the autonomy of the basis of the legal system with regard to religious beliefs: a democratic state within the meaning of the Convention cannot be founded on the norms of a religion.[37]

Also relevant here is *Buscarini and others* v. *San Marino* (1999). In it, the Court declares it incompatible with Article 9 to compel elected members

---

[32] *Ibid.*, para. 48.   [33] *Ibid.*, para. 55.   [34] See note 31.

[35] Eur. Ct. H. R. (Grand Chamber), *Refah Partisi (The Welfare Party) and others* v. *Turkey*, 13 February 2003.

[36] *Ibid.*, para. 119.

[37] See F. Margiotta-Broglio, 'Principio costituzionale di laicità e partiti politici islamici nell' ordinamento della Turchia', in A. Weiss und S. Ihli (eds.), *Flexibilitas iuris canonici, Festschrift für Richard Puza zum 60 Geburtsag* (Frankfurt: Peter Lang, 2003), 817–27.

of the parliament to take oath on the Gospel. This obligation, in its opinion, amounts to requiring elected representatives of the people to swear allegiance to a particular religion. And 'it would be contradictory to make the exercise of a mandate intended to represent different views of society within Parliament subject to a prior declaration of commitment to a particular set of beliefs.'[38] What seems to underlie the Court's ruling is the idea that by introducing a religious reference in the oath taken by the members of parliament, the state symbolically designates this religion as the foundation of the political system and obliges the population, through its representatives, to recognise its authority. The Court thus opposes the maintenance of religion in its function of legitimation of the political and social order; a stance reminiscent of Lefort's famous thesis that in modern democracies, the sovereign's place becomes 'empty'.[39]

2   The case law in context: the question of religion and the public sphere in political and social theory

The principles derived by the European Court from religious freedom – autonomy, neutrality and secularity – resonate with the classic tenets of liberal thought regarding state–religion relationships. Liberalism is often said to posit that the state should be neutral with respect to the various conceptions of the good life, in particular religious conceptions, that the citizens may hold.[40] Such neutrality is viewed as necessary to guarantee the freedom of citizens to pursue their own notion of the good. Neutrality is also seen as a corollary of the state obligation to treat individuals as equals.[41] Rawls, in particular, maintains in *Political Liberalism* that in a time where people are profoundly divided by reasonable though incompatible religious, philosophical and moral doctrines, a just and stable society of free and equal citizens can only exist if its constitutional regime is based on a conception of justice that is, as far as possible, independent from these conflicting comprehensive doctrines.[42]

---

[38] Eur. Ct. H. R. (Grand Chamber), *Buscarini and others* v. *San Marino*, 18 February 1999, para. 39.

[39] C. Lefort, 'Permanence du théologico-politique?' in *Essais sur le politique (XIXè-XXè siècles)* (Paris: Esprit/Seuil, 1986), p. 265.

[40] C. Larmore, 'Political Liberalism' in *Political Theory* 18 (1990), 339–60.

[41] R. Dworkin, 'Liberalism' in *A Matter of Principle* (Cambridge, MA: Harvard University Press, 1985), pp. 181–204.

[42] J. Rawls, *Political Liberalism* (New York: Columbia University Press, 2005 (expanded edition)), p. 9.

By identifying the aforementioned notions as guiding principles for understanding Article 9, the Court does contribute to the illumination of the implications of religious freedom in a democratic society and the anchoring of the interpretation of the European Convention within the liberal tradition.

This conceptual framework, however, presents a major limitation: it works best when the issue at stake is that of preserving the respective autonomy of the state and religious communities. Thus, it tends to pre-suppose that religion and the state belong to two distinct spheres of social life that can be easily disentangled. The trouble with this conception is twofold: first, it is doubtful that it actually captures contemporary social reality. The privatisation of faith in modern societies, which it seems to assume, is indeed widely contested in present-day sociology of religion. Second, from a normative viewpoint, political theory discussions have highlighted the ambiguities and uncertainty that surround the classic liberal concept of state's neutrality towards religion. In particular, the idea that as a general rule religion should be excluded from the public domain in order to preserve such neutrality has generated intense debates in recent times.

Underlying the Court's case law is the idea that religion is primarily an inward feeling; a 'matter of individual conscience'.[43] It can be exteriorised through rites and acts of cults, but these are in principle accomplished within the family and 'the circle of those whose faith one shares'.[44] The case law strongly suggests that manifestations of religion outside this domain are considered as of secondary importance. Faith is normally expressed in a specific, discrete, domain, which is distinct from the rest of social life.

This vision strikingly evokes the classic sociological paradigm of secu-larisation.[45] Classic proponents of this theory have long claimed that modernisation would necessarily bring in its wake both the decline of religiosity and the privatisation of religion. Importantly, the notion of privatisation differs from the 'differentiation thesis': whilst the latter refers to the process by which secular spheres, primarily the state, the

---

[43] See, e.g., Eur. Ct. H. R., *97 members of the Gldani Congregation of Jehovah's Witnesses and 4 others* v. *Georgia*, 3 May 2007, para. 130.

[44] See, e.g., *Leyla Şahin* v. *Turkey*, para. 105.

[45] See J. Casanova, *Public Religions in the Modern World* (University of Chicago Press, 1994); D. Martin, *On Secularization – Towards a Revised General Theory* (Aldershot: Ashgate, 2005); and B. R. Wilson, *Religion in Secular Society – A Sociological Comment* (Harmondsworth: Penguin Books, 1966).

economy and science, emancipate from the religious sphere with religion ceasing to be the central organising institution of society,[46] the privatisation thesis goes further and claims that religion is banished from the public domain; it retreats into the private sphere, if not the individual conscience, and becomes increasingly irrelevant and marginal to modern societies.[47]

Since the 1960s, however, both the 'decline of religion' and the 'privatisation' theses have been strongly contested.[48] Empirical research has highlighted that, outside Europe, modernity did not necessarily entail the fall of religiosity and marginalisation of religion.[49] In Europe itself, the secularisation process attained different levels of intensity, depending on the dominant religious tradition and on the history of state–church relations.[50] Besides, it has also been argued that privatisation of religion is not necessary to modernity: provided certain conditions are met, religious groups may enter the public sphere and assume the role of civil society actors without endangering individuals' freedom and modern differentiated structures.[51]

These discussions shed a particular light on the ECtHR's case law. The assumption, present in this jurisprudence, that there is a neat distinction between the public and the private spheres, and that religious expression is normally confined to the latter square with the privatisation thesis. To be sure, the Court's stance is not uniform and some of its rulings reflect other influences (see section 3A). But as a general matter the Court seems most comfortable when it has to scrutinise cases that can be seen either as an attempt by the state to control a religious community (e.g. *Hasan and Chaush*), or as endeavours by a religion to take control over the state (e.g. *Refah Partisi*); in other words, where the problem is that of preserving the boundary between religion and public authority. By contrast, when faced with contestations touching upon the issue of expression of religion in the public sphere, some uneasiness can be observed: as will be shown in the next section, the judges often appear hesitant and all too prone to leave the decision to the state by virtue of the margin of appreciation. This sort of case does indeed reveal a discrepancy

---

[46] Casanova, *Public Religions*, p. 19.   [47] *Ibid.*, pp. 35–9.
[48] See in particular J. A. Beckford and Th. Luckmann (eds.), *The Changing Face of Religion* (London: Sage, 1989) and S. Bruce (ed.), *Religion and Modernization: Sociologists and Historians Debate the Secularization Thesis* (Oxford: Clarendon Press, 1992).
[49] P. Berger (ed.), *The Desecularization of the World: Resurgent Religion and World Politics* (Washington DC: Eerdmans, 1999).
[50] Martin, *On Secularization*.   [51] Casanova, *Public Religions*.

between the privatisation theory and the facts with which the Court is confronted: they suggest that, even in modern European societies, religious expressions are not always easily contained within the boundaries of the home and places of worship. Some religious practices – like dietary requirements or the wearing of specific clothes – affect the entire life of individual believers, wherever they find themselves.[52] Further, believers or church authorities sometimes intervene in the democratic public debate to promote their creeds or take a stance on socio-political issues. Conversely, religious doctrines may themselves be subject to discussion, contestation or mockery through media and arts. From different angles, all these situations raise the question of religious expressions in the public square.

Social developments relating to the place of religion in the public sphere have also stirred vivid discussions in political theory in the last two decades. Classic liberal notions such as the state's neutrality have been subject to critical reappraisal. Importantly, different understandings of the 'public sphere' are at stake here. A first set of debates relates to the public sphere envisioned in a Habermasian sense, as encompassing the network of institutional and non-institutional sites where citizens express politically oriented opinions and deliberate common affairs.[53] Considerable attention has focused on the idea, defended by Rawls in the first edition of *Political Liberalism*,[54] that religious-based arguments cannot be accepted as valid in the democratic public sphere of deliberation. Advancing the notion of 'post-secular society', Habermas claims that in the 'informal public sphere' citizens should be allowed to express their convictions in a religious language if they cannot find secular 'translations' for them. By contrast, in the institutional public sphere, that is parliaments, courts, and so on, officials should have the obligation to justify their decisions only on the basis of secular reasons that are equally accessible to all citizens.[55] In fact, Rawls himself revised his position and admitted that in certain socio-historical situations, reasons

[52] T. Asad, 'Secularism, Nation-State, Religion', in T. Asad, *Formations of the Secular – Christianity, Islam, Modernity* (Stanford University Press, 2003), pp. 200–1.

[53] J. Habermas, *The Structural Transformation of the Public Sphere: An Inquiry into a Category of Bourgeois Society* (Cambridge, MA: MIT Press, 1991).

[54] J. Rawls, *Political Liberalism* (New York: Columbia University Press, 1993 (first edition)).

[55] J. Habermas, 'Religion in the Public Sphere', *European Journal of Philosophy* 14(1) (2006), 1–25.

rooted in religious doctrines could be presented in public discussions in non-official settings.[56]

A second set of discussions refer to the growing religious diversity in many Western countries. The core issue from this perspective is the question of what it means for the state to be neutral in a religiously plural society. The focus here is on the practice of religion in the public sphere understood either as state institutions (e.g. the case of civil servants or pupils in public schools) or as encompassing all domains external to the family and the religious community, mainly public institutions and the market.[57] Advocates of multiculturalism and minority rights have challenged the view, defended by some, that religious neutrality implies for the state an obligation to ignore religions and abstain from taking religious specificities into account in all circumstances. They point out that, in a context of diversity, general legislation may have the indirect effect of precluding some individuals from observing important precepts of their religion, while not affecting other communities. The dramatic rise in the domains regulated by the state in the modern era has increased the risk that such a situation arises. And this problem is much more likely to affect minority religious groups.[58] Indeed, public rules and institutions remain to a certain extent imbued with the traditions of the historically dominant faith, as reflected in public holidays or uniforms required in certain settings. Hence, promoters of minority rights argue that if neutrality means that the state may not unduly disadvantage a religious community compared to others, the specificities of a religion must sometimes be taken into account in order to avoid impairing its practice.[59]

These various debates point to a common concern, namely the issue how a democratic society should handle the plurality of faith and the variety of opinions about religions in the polity. It is to the analysis of the

[56] J. Rawls, 'The Idea of Public Reason Revisited', *University of Chicago Law Review* 64(3) (1997), included in *Political Liberalism* (New York: Columbia University Press, 2005), pp. 247–54.

[57] See J. Weintraub, 'The Theory and Politics of the Public/Private Distinction' in J. Weintraub and K. Kumar (eds.), *Public and Private Thought and Practice – Perspectives on a Grand Dichotomy* (The University of Chicago Press, 1997), pp. 1–42.

[58] N. L. Rosenblum, 'Pluralism, Integralism, and Political Theories of Religious Accommodation' in N. L. Rosenblum (ed.), *Obligations of Citizenship and Demands of Faith – Religious Accommodation in Pluralist Democracies* (Princeton University Press, 2000), pp. 3–31.

[59] W. Kymlicka, *Multicultural Citizenship* (Oxford University Press, 1995); B. Parekh, *Rethinking Multiculturalism: Cultural Diversity and Political Theory* (Basingstoke: Macmillan, 2000); T. Modood, *Multiculturalism* (Cambridge: Polity Press, 2007).

manner in which the Court approaches situations raising these questions that we now turn.

3   The European Court as a site of debate about the place of religion in the public sphere

In this section we will focus on three groups of cases, which are representative of some major preoccupations in contemporary Europe relating to the place of religion in the public realm: claims for religious accommodation in the workplace (A); the expression of opinions *based on* religion or *about* religion in the democratic public sphere (B); and the wearing of religious symbols, more particularly the Islamic headscarf, in public institutions (C). One common trend in this case law is the large discretion left to national authorities. Arguably, this is symptomatic of the difficulty the Court encounters in dealing with these questions and building a consistent vision of what pluralism entails with regard to the place of religion in the public sphere.

A   Claims for religious accommodation in the workplace

Where a legislation or policy has the unintended effect of precluding members of a minority religion from observing an important precept of their faith, is there an interference with religious freedom? Are individuals affected entitled to an accommodation of their religious needs? Such questions have been raised on a few occasions before the Convention's institutions, especially in relation to work schedules and religious holidays.[60]

The response of the Convention's institutions has been generally negative. It is in this sort of case that the influence of the idea that religious practice is normally restricted to a specific domain of social life is the most palpable. In the case of a Muslim teacher who complained that the London state school in which he worked had refused to arrange his timetable so as to enable him to take forty-five minutes off on Friday to attend prayers at the mosque, the European Commission finds no interference with his right under Article 9.[61] Determining this view is the fact that

---

[60] S. Stavros, 'Freedom of Religion and Claims for Exemption from Generally Applicable, Neutral Laws: Lessons from Across the Pond?', *European Human Rights Law Review* 6 (1997), 607–27; D. McGoldrick, 'Accommodating Muslims in Europe: From Adopting Sharia Law to Religiously Based Opt Outs from Generally Applicable Laws', *Human Rights Law Review* 9(4) (2009), 603–45.

[61] Eur. Comm. H. R., *X. v. United-Kingdom*, 12 March 1981, *D.R.* 22, p. 27.

he voluntarily accepted teaching obligations under his contract with the school and remained free to resign if he found that these duties conflicted with his religious duties.[62] The Commission thus presents the issue as one of free choice, obscuring the legal background against which the facts take place: the legislation guarantees workers the right not to work on Sunday, but does not provide any protection to those wishing to take time off for religious reasons on a different day. The applicant was not in a position to negotiate his work schedule: he could only accept it or resign.[63] At a deeper level, this reasoning suggests that religion has no standing in the work sphere. Religious claims must yield to the rules governing this domain, whether defined by the state or by the employer.

The Commission similarly dismisses the discrimination claim. It simply observes that 'in most countries, only the religious holidays of the majority of the population are celebrated as public holidays'.[64] There is thus no question of envisaging an obligation for the state to endeavour to promote wherever possible 'reasonable accommodation' that would allow the reconciliation of the employee's religious needs with work requirements, as was recognised in Canadian and US law.[65] For the Commission, it is natural that the norm is the norm of the majority and minority workers must adapt to it or resign.

The Court's case law, however, is not static. The evolution undergone by the notions of pluralism and non-discrimination in the first decade of the twenty-first century could entail a very different approach to this sort of issue. In *Thlimmenos v. Greece* (2000), the Court acknowledges that the right not to be discriminated against under Article 14 ECHR is not only violated when states treat persons in analogous situations differently, but also when they fail to treat differently persons whose situations are significantly different, without objective and reasonable justification.[66] Moreover, under certain circumstances, failing to introduce 'appropriate exceptions' to a general norm which unfairly disadvantages persons practising a certain religion may amount to discrimination.[67] In the same

---

[62] *Ibid.*, paras. 9 and 15. See also Eur. Comm. H. R., *Konttinen v. Finland*, 3 December 1996, *D.R.* 87-B, p. 68.

[63] See P. Cumper, 'The Accommodation of "Uncontroversial" Religious Practices' in M. L. P. Loenen and J. E. Goldschmidt (eds.), *Religious Pluralism and Human Rights in Europe: Where to Draw the Line?* (Antwerp: Intersentia, 2007), pp. 208–9.

[64] *X. v. United-Kingdom*, para. 28.

[65] See E. Bribosia, J. Ringelheim and I. Rorive, 'Reasonable Accommodation for Religious Minorities: A Promising Concept for European Antidiscrimination Law?', *Maastricht Journal of European and Comparative Law* 17(2) (2010), 137–61.

[66] Eur. Ct. H. R. (Grand Chamber), *Thlimmenos v. Greece*, 6 April 2000, para. 44.

[67] *Ibid.*, para. 48.

period, elaborating further its conception of pluralism, the Court emphasises that a 'pluralist and genuinely democratic society should not only respect the ethnic, cultural, linguistic and religious identity of each person belonging to a national minority, but also create appropriate conditions enabling them to express, preserve and develop this identity.'[68] These parallel evolutions could pave the way to the recognition of an obligation for the state to take the specificities of minority religions into account where necessary to avoid preventing without due reasons their followers from observing an important aspect of their religion.[69]

Yet later cases suggest that the Court at present is not prepared to recognise a right to 'reasonable accommodation' in the workplace. In *Kosteski v. the Former Yugoslav Republic of Macedonia* (2006), although the main issue at stake was different, the Court takes the opportunity to endorse the Commission's jurisprudence on the question of work schedule and religious holidays.[70] It even expresses doubts that taking a day off to celebrate a religious feast is a manifestation of religious beliefs protected by Article 9 ECHR.[71] Such position excludes any discussion of a possible duty to accommodate religious diversity at work.

B.   The place of religion in the democratic public sphere

European judges do not express a priori objections to religious figures participating in the public debate and defending views based on their religious convictions, even provocative ones, at least when the 'informal public sphere' is at stake. In *Gündüz v. Turkey* (2000), it castigates Turkey for having sanctioned the leader of an Islamic group who, during a television programme, had issued virulent criticisms of secularism and democracy in Turkey and declared his preference for a sharia-based regime. Such comments, expressed in the course of a pluralistic debate with other participants, could not be construed as a call to violence or as hate speech based on religious intolerance.[72] In a later judgment, the Court declares

---

[68] Eur. Ct. H. R. (Grand Chamber), *Gorzelik and others* v. *Poland*, 17 February 2004, para. 93.

[69] L. Vickers, *Religious Freedom, Religious Discrimination and the Workplace* (Oxford: Hart, 2008); Bribosia, Ringelheim and Rorive, 'Reasonable Accommodation'.

[70] Eur. Ct. H. R., *Kosteski* v. *The Former Yugoslav Republic of Macedonia*, 13 April 2006, para. 37.

[71] *Ibid.*, para. 38. See M. D. Evans, 'Freedom of Religion and the European Convention on Human Rights: Approaches, Trends and Tensions' in P. Cane, C. Evans and Z. Robinson (eds.), *Law and Religion in Theoretical and Historical Context* (Cambridge University Press, 2008).

[72] Eur. Ct. H. R., *Gündüz* v. *Turkey*, 4 December 2003, paras. 48 and 51.

that associations 'proclaiming or teaching religion' can play a role in civil society and contribute to the proper functioning of democracy.[73]

But what has proved especially contentious is the Court's treatment of the question as to what extent religions themselves can be criticised or ridiculed in the democratic public sphere. In *Otto-Preminger-Institut* v. *Austria* (1994), a small cultural association from Innsbruck in Tyrol complained about the decision of Austrian Courts to seize and forfeit the film it had planned to show on the ground that it mocked in provocative terms the Catholic religion. The Court finds no violation of the right to freedom of expression: taking into account the national margin of appreciation, the state's interference with the applicant's freedom pursued the legitimate aim of protecting the citizens' right 'not to be insulted in their religious feelings by the public expression of views of other persons'.[74] The Court indeed contends that religious freedom entails a right for believers to be protected against 'provocative portrayals of objects of religious veneration'.[75] This, however, goes beyond a protection against incitement to hatred or hostility: it is a right to have one's religious symbols or beliefs shielded from representations one considers provocative. The judges give no regard to the precautions taken by the association to dissuade people likely to be shocked by the film to go to see it: it had indeed warned the public in its programme about its sensitive character. By contrast, what the Court deems determining is the fact that the religion at stake is largely dominant in the population. It claims that it cannot 'disregard the fact that the Roman Catholic religion is the religion of the overwhelming majority of Tyroleans'. The Austrian Courts' ruling that the film constituted 'an abusive attack on the Roman Catholic religion' is said to reflect 'the conception of the Tyrolean public'.[76]

The problem here is not that the Court limits the protection of religious freedom to a too-restrictively-defined sphere of social life, but, on the contrary, that it permits the state to impose the viewpoint of the dominant faith on the whole population.[77] It disregards the efforts deployed

---

[73] Eur. Ct. H. R., *The Moscow Branch of the Salvation Army* v. *Russia*, 5 October 2006, para. 58.

[74] *Otto-Preminger-Institut* v. *Austria*, para. 48.

[75] *Ibid.*, para. 47.   [76] *Ibid.*, para. 56.

[77] See G. Letsas in this volume; D. Pannick, 'Religious Feelings and the European Court', *Public Law* (1995), 7–10; P. Wachsmann, 'La religion contre la liberté d'expression: sur un arrêt regrettable de la Cour européenne des droits de l'homme', *Revue universelle des droits de l'homme* 6(12) (1994), 441–9.

by the cine-club to render possible the coexistence of opposed views on a religion, by enabling those interested in the film to seeing it while sparing observant Catholics the risk of being exposed to portrayals of their religion that they would find offensive. It is sufficient that the movie exists and that some people can watch it for the offence to the believers to occur. In effect, the Court allows state authorities to silence public expressions that are virulently critical about the majority religion.

The reasoning held in *Otto-Preminger-Institut* was confirmed in *Wingrove v. United Kingdom* (1996)[78] and in *I.A. v. Turkey* (2005), in the case of a publishing house's director sentenced to a fine for having published a novel containing offensive statements against Islam.[79] In later rulings, however, while reasserting the *Otto-Preminger-Institut* doctrine, the Court seems concerned with restricting its scope: in *Aydin Tatlav v. Turkey*, where the applicant had been condemned for having published a book in which he virulently criticised Islam, it rules that the contentious statements were not of such nature as to justify a restriction to his freedom of speech. They represented the critical viewpoint of a non-believer on religion, but did not amount to an insult against believers or an abusive attack on sacred symbols.[80]

C.   Wearing religious symbols in educational institutions

The wearing of religious clothing or symbols within public institutions generates vehement debates in several European countries. Clearly, it is the headscarf worn by Muslim girls or women in public education institutions that creates the most ardent controversies. Yet, at present, most European states do not prohibit pupils from wearing it at school, except where it poses a safety or health hazard.[81] Some states, however, most notably France and Turkey, claim that the notion of *laïcité* or strict secularism, to which they officially adhere, requires precluding individuals from wearing religious signs in public schools as well as, in the case of Turkey, at universities. But the meaning and implications of *laïcité* are contested. In France, despite an apparent unanimity over this notion,

---

[78] Eur. Ct. H. R., *Wingrove* v. *United Kingdom*, 25 November 1996.
[79] Eur. Ct. H. R., *I.A.* v. *Turkey*, 13 September 2005 (three judges dissenting).
[80] Eur. Ct. H. R., *Aydin Tatlav* v. *Turkey*, 2 May 2006, esp. para. 28. See also Eur. Ct. H. R., *Giniewski* v. *France*, 31 January 2006 and Eur. Ct. H. R., *Klein* v. *Slovakia*, 31 October 2006.
[81] See D. McGoldrick, *Human Rights and Religion: the Islamic Headscarf Debate in Europe* (Hart, 2006); E. Bribosia and I. Rorive, 'Le voile à l'école: une Europe divisée', *Revue trimestrielle des droits de l'homme* 60 (2004), 941–73.

at least two different conceptions coexist:[82] the first understands *laïcité* as the confessional neutrality of the state;[83] while a second, based on a rather negative perception of religion, envisions it as the requirement of an exclusion of faith from public institutions, deemed necessary to preserve the separation of state and religion.[84] Interestingly, when in 1989 the French Council of State (Conseil d'État) was asked to provide an opinion on the issue, it stated that in educational institutions the wearing by pupils of signs through which they manifest their religion *is not by itself incompatible with the laïcité principle*, insofar as this act is protected by freedoms of religion and expression. Only specific reasons, pertaining to the preservation of the rights of others, safety, health or public order could justify a limitation of these freedoms.[85] It is only after heated discussions and the setting-up of a special official commission to examine the problem, that in 2004 French legislators passed a law prohibiting, in virtue of the *laïcité* principle, the wearing in state schools of signs through which pupils ostensibly manifest their religious belonging.[86]

In *Leyla Şahin* v. *Turkey* (2005),[87] the Court was asked to review the conformity with the European Convention of a similar prohibition in Turkish universities. Sitting as a Grand Chamber, it rules that no violation of Article 9 has occurred: the measure is deemed necessary to the protection of the rights of others and preservation of public order. In justifying its ruling, the Court uncritically praises the principle of secularism (meaning *laïcité*), as interpreted by the Turkish Constitutional Court. It declares that this latter principle is not only consistent with the values underpinning the Convention, but may be considered necessary to protect the democratic

---

[82] P.-H. Prélot, 'Définir juridiquement la laïcité' in G. Gonzalez (ed.), *Laïcité, liberté de religion et Convention européenne des droits de l'homme* (Brussels: Bruylant, 2006), pp. 115–49. On the historical background to the *laïcité* concept in France, see J. Baubérot, *Histoire de la laïcité en France* (Paris: Presses universitaires de France, 2003). For a critical discussion of the theoretical underpinnings of the French *laïcité*, see C. Laborde, *Critical Republicanism – The Hijab Controversy and Political Philosophy* (Oxford University Press, 2008).

[83] See Prélot, 'Définir juridiquement la laïcité', pp. 116–28.

[84] See, e.g., H. Pena-Ruiz, *Qu'est-ce que la laïcité?* (Paris: Gallimard, 2003).

[85] Opinion of the Council of State, 27 November 1989, *Revue française de droit administratif* (1990), 1.

[86] Law of 15 March 2004 regulating, by virtue of the principle of *laïcité*, the wearing of signs or attire manifesting a religious belonging in public schools, *Journal Officiel*, n. 65, 17 March 2004, 5190.

[87] Eur. Ct. H. R. (Grand Chamber), *Leyla Şahin* v. *Turkey*, 10 November 2005 (one judge dissenting).

system in Turkey.[88] Yet, the interpretation of the *laïcité* concept adopted by the Turkish Court is especially far-reaching: by virtue of this principle, the state may prohibit any religious manifestation for the sole reason of it being public.[89] The state's neutrality is seen as being jeopardised as soon as a person exteriorises his or her religious convictions in the public square, regardless of whether he or she is a state agent. This conception, however, contradicts Article 9 ECHR, which guarantees the freedom to manifest one's religious convictions *in public*, and authorises restrictions to this freedom only insofar as they are necessary to achieve one of the legitimate aims listed in its second paragraph. The potential conflict between the Turkish conception of *laïcité* and freedom of religion was indeed acknowledged a few years later in *Ahmet Arslan and others* v. *Turkey* (see below).

The Court also strongly insists on the specificity of the Turkish context, where Islam is the religion of the vast majority of the population and where fundamentalist movements seek to impose their worldviews on the whole society. Against this background, it considers that the wearing of a headscarf could by itself create a pressure on those who do not want to wear it, as the government argued.[90] The Court, however, eludes the difficult questions raised by this case. As a university student, Ms Şahin did not represent the state and was not in a position of authority with respect to other students.[91] It was not claimed that the way she had personally worn the headscarf had caused any disruption or been accompanied by provocative or proselyte behaviour. Yet the Court abstains from verifying whether less restrictive measures, such as sanctions limited to individuals who would have actually exerted pressure, would not have permitted the pursued aims to be reached. The measure taken by Turkish authorities is pretty radical, though: it excludes any possibility of coexistence, within the university, between students wearing a headscarf and those who do not share their beliefs.

In truth, the headscarf is treated by the Court as a symbol of fundamentalism and gender inequality.[92] Significantly, it declares that this

---

[88] *Ibid.*, para. 114.

[89] C. Grewe and Ch. Rumpf, 'La Cour constitutionnelle turque et sa décision relative au "foulard islamique"', *Revue universelle des droits de l'homme* (1991), 122–3.

[90] *Leyla Şahin*, para. 115.

[91] Compare with *Dahlab* v. *Switzerland*, 15 February 2001 (primary school teacher wishing to wear the headscarf at work).

[92] C. Evans, 'The "Islamic Scarf" in the European Court of Human Rights', *Melbourne Journal of International Law* 7 (2006), 52–73; T. Lewis, 'What not to Wear: Religious Rights, the European Court, and the Margin of Appreciation', *International and Comparative Law Quarterly* 56 (2007), 395–414.

practice is by itself difficult to reconcile with a 'message of tolerance, respect for others and, above all, equality and non-discrimination'.[93] This statement contrasts with the numerous sociological studies highlighting the ambiguous and plural meaning of the headscarf, as well as the ability of Muslim women to reappropriate this practice in various ways.[94] Judge Tulkens in her dissent observes:

> it is not the Court's role to make an appraisal of this type – in this instance a unilateral and negative one – of a religion or religious practice, just as it is not its role to determine in a general and abstract way the signification of wearing the headscarf or to impose its viewpoint on the applicant.[95]

By equating the headscarf with Islamic fundamentalism and gender inequality, the Court refuses to engage with the tensions, ambiguities and conflicting meanings associated with it.[96] Seen in this light, *Leyla Şahin* can be envisaged as an inverted mirror of *Otto-Preminger-Institut*: while in the latter ruling the Court allows the state to act as the protector of majority religious beliefs in the democratic public sphere, in *Leyla Şahin*, it permits public authorities to take action to exclude religion from the public realm. In both cases, either religious or anti-religious expressions are silenced to appease the fear or irritation of the secular or the religious dominant group.

Post-*Leyla Şahin* decisions confirm that the Court is prepared to leave considerable discretion to domestic authorities to ban the wearing of the headscarf in educational establishments. In a later case it was asked to review a headscarf interdiction imposed in public religious high schools in Turkey. These schools can hardly be said to be religiously neutral: they are designed to train religious professionals, such as imams and Koran readers, and 40 per cent of their curriculum concerns Islamic theology. Yet the Court declares that the prohibition of the headscarf can be regarded as necessary to protect the rights of other children and the neutrality of education. The state is even said to have a duty to ensure that manifestation of their beliefs by pupils within the school premises

---

[93] *Leyla Şahin*, para. 111.

[94] See in particular N. Göle, *Musulmanes et modernes – Voile et civilisation en Turquie* (Paris: La Découverte, 2003, 2nd edn.); N. Weibel, *Par-delà le voile – Femmes d'Islam en Europe* (Brussels: Complexe, 2000).

[95] Dissenting opinion of Judge Tulkens, para. 12.

[96] C. D. Belelieu, 'The Headscarf as a Symbolic Enemy of the European Court of Human Rights' Democratic Jurisprudence: Viewing Islam Through a European Legal Prism in Light of the *Şahin* Judgment', *Columbia Journal of European Law* 12 (2006), 573–623, 619 and 622.

does not become 'ostentatious' so as to constitute a source of pressure.[97] Unsurprisingly, the Court also deems that the exclusion of Muslim[98] and Sikh[99] pupils from high schools in France pursuant to the 2004 Act does not conflict with the ECHR.

In *Ahmet Arslan and others* v. *Turkey* (2010),[100] however, the Court draws a limit on what a state is entitled to do in the name of *laïcité*: convicting a group of persons for merely touring in the streets while wearing the distinctive dress of their religious movement, namely a turban, a tunic and a stick, constitutes a breach of religious freedom. The government maintained that this was necessary to protect the secular (*laïc*) and democratic principles on which the Turkish Republic is based. The Court rejects this contention: the argument of protecting state neutrality or *laïcité* does not hold where simple citizens express their religion in the public space, such as public streets and squares.

Conclusion

The European Court of Human Rights' attempts at theorising its conception of religious freedom and at developing a coherent model of relations between religion and the public sphere remain tentative and fragmentary. Nonetheless, throughout its case law it has progressively drawn from the individual right to religious freedom several principles regarding the proper relations between state and religions in a democratic society. Besides the notion that religious and philosophical pluralism must be respected, the Court proclaims the autonomy of religious communities vis-à-vis the state: the religious life of faith groups constitutes an autonomous sphere in which the state, as a rule, should not interfere. Further, it infers from the right to religious freedom an obligation of neutrality: in its relations with the various denominations and beliefs, the state must remain neutral and impartial. Lastly, the secularity of the legal system's foundations is considered a necessary condition of democracy.

These principles are consistent with the basic ideals that underlie the European Convention. They cast an important light on the fundamental concerns that govern relations between political authority and religions in a democratic society. Their meaning and implications, however, are

---

[97] Eur. Ct. H. R., *Sefika Köse and 93 others* v. *Turkey*, 24 January 2006.

[98] Eur. Ct. H. R., *Aktas* v. *France*; *Ghazal* v. *France*; *Bayrak* v. *France* and *Gamaleddyn* v. *France*, 30 June 2009.

[99] Eur. Ct. H. R., *Jasvir Singh* v. *France* and *Ranjit Singh* v. *France*, 30 June 2009.

[100] Eur. Ct. H. R., *Ahmet Arslan and Others* v. *Turkey*, 23 February 2010.

still in need of further clarification. Thus, to what extent the modalities of an established church regime can be regarded as compatible with state neutrality, as construed by the Court, remains to be seen. To be sure, such elaboration should not attain the same level of precision as it does within one single polity: the Court must identify minimal common norms, valid for all European democracies. Importantly, the duty of neutrality, as construed in the case law, does not entail that the state must necessarily grant identical treatment to all religious communities: national authorities are allowed to accord different legal status to certain faith groups provided that any difference of treatment can be justified on legitimate grounds. State neutrality fundamentally implies a requirement of even-handedness in its relations with the various religions. Moreover, it also means that the state should refrain from exerting pressure on citizens' religious choices.

But when one considers the Court's jurisprudence on contestations regarding expressions of religion, or about religion, in the public sphere, whether in the democratic public debate, in public institutions or in the workplace, the weaknesses of its present conceptualisation of religious freedom come into light. The large discretion it often grants to national authorities in such cases is symptomatic of its difficulty in dealing with them. Yet cases of this sort confront the Court with a question of critical importance for contemporary European societies: how to guarantee pluralism, while ensuring state neutrality and equal rights to all? This is a question that should not be evaded by an international Court tasked with protecting human rights in Europe. The ECtHR's jurisprudence already contains important resources on which the judges could build to specify further their conception of pluralism and of its relation with state neutrality. Meanwhile, despite its gaps, ambiguities and limitations, the European Court's case law has the merit of promoting a trans-European reflection on the relations between religion and the public square.

13

Europe and religion: an ambivalent nexus

CAMIL UNGUREANU

Introduction

Europe is the arena of a competition between different models of democracy, law and religion. This is unsurprising given the practical–normative questions and dilemmas that mark the current European predicament. Firstly, how to square the development of a consistent European approach to religion beyond the nation state, with the recognition of the often conflictive diversity of the continent's models. Secondly, how to combine the recognition of religious pluralism with the desideratum of the construction of a society free of gender inequality and coercion. As it becomes apparent from the various contributions of this book, there is neither a short-term nor an algorithmic solution for such questions and dilemmas. The outcome of the debate over the Preamble of the Constitutional Treaty as well as the European Court of Human Rights' and the Council of Europe's support of the liberal principles of neutrality and separation have been either deplored by Christian conservatives as the result of European Christophobia, or celebrated by certain atheists as a confirmation of the saga of secularism.[1] But are the European institutions agents of a secularism inimical to religion? And does integration into Europe mean "signing on

---

For useful discussions I am indebted to Julie Ringelheim, Lorenzo Zucca, Daniel Gamper and Marisa Iglesias. I also want to thank Clare Sheppard for proofreading this text.

[1] See J. Weiler, *Un'Europa cristiana. Un saggio esplorativo* (Milan: Rizzoli, 2003); J. Weiler, "State and Nation; Church, Mosque and Synagogue – the trailer", *I-CON* 8 (2010), 157–66; I. T. Plesner, *The European Court on Human Rights Between Fundamentalist and Liberal Secularism* (Strasbourg Consortium, 2006), available at www.strasbourgconsortium.org/document.php?DocumentID=3849 (last accessed 31 August 2011). In this chapter I use "secularization" to refer to an empirically verifiable socio-historical phenomenon, and "secularism" to refer to an ideology according to which modernization generates the ineluctable and desirable decline of religion.

the Eurosecularity?"[2] In this chapter I shall argue for a more nuanced view by analyzing four approaches that aim at providing orientation to European citizens and institutions faced with renewed claims of religion in the public sphere – a *Christian Europe* (section 1), *laïcité* (section 2), *liberal constitutionalism* (section 3), and *dialogical post-secularism* (section 4). I will maintain that institutions such as the European Court of Human Rights (ECtHR) and the Council of Europe (CoE) have often questioned biased aspects of the inherited regimes of privilege between state and majority religion so as to provide protection of individual liberty, neutrality and religious pluralism.[3] Yet these institutions have not erected a European "wall of separation" between state and religion; instead, they have at key moments enhanced a minimal liberal–constitutionalist framework that incorporates the principle of pluralism as positive recognition of the value of (non)religious diversity. From within this constitutional framework, the state is not "purely" neutral, but has a positive obligation to protect pluralism and enhance a culture of mutual tolerance, respect and dialogue amongst citizens. This framework has at times been linked to the claim that religious and non-religious pluralism represents a positive contribution to identity building and democratic life. In particular, the ECtHR has, despite its ambiguities, advanced such a justificatory discourse that is at odds with the ideology of secularism. This justificatory trend of the ECtHR takes as its basis Article 9 of the Convention, according to which religious manifestations in the public sphere are legitimate, and develops the claim that these manifestations can contribute to democratic life, and should be recognized as being able to do so.[4]

The point of this chapter is, however, not to argue that a unique European model is emerging, or that such a model should be uniformly imposed throughout Europe. A mono-colored Europe is something of a bad dream. In effect, the aforementioned liberal–constitutional trend does *not* advance one alternative model to replace the existing ones, but a

---

[2] P. Berger, "Religion in the West," *The National Interest* (Summer 2005), 113.

[3] It is beyond the purpose of the chapter to make an analysis of the complex development of and differences between the Council of Europe "system" and that of the European Union. It is noteworthy that Article 6 of the Lisbon Treaty (2007) establishes the legal basis for the EU's accession to the European Convention on Human Rights (ECHR).

[4] For instance, in *Gorzelik* v. *Poland*, the Court argued that "proclaiming or teaching religion … are also important to the proper functioning of democracy. For pluralism is also built on the genuine recognition of, and respect for, diversity and the dynamics of cultural traditions, ethnic and cultural identities, religious beliefs"; Eur. Ct. H. R. (Grand Chamber), *Gorzelik and others* v. *Poland*, 17 February 2004, para. 92 (see also section 3).

minimal framework of reference that sets *limitations* to them. There is a diversity of European models from those based on *laïcité* to those based on state religion, all of which are, as a matter of principle, recognized as legitimate by the European institutions. Still, Europe is profoundly divided between the defence of individual freedom and (non)religious pluralism as opposed to an ever-increasing wave of anti-Islamic and anti-immigration populism. This division is reflected by the ECtHR's inability to advance a nuanced position on issues involving Islam, in contrast to its propensity to be overprotective towards Christian majorities. The Court's development and implementation of a liberal–constitutional minimal framework could act as a buffer against the current rise of populism, yet so far its approach has been deeply ambivalent.

Finally, political and legal discourse in Europe has also moved towards incorporating the principle of dialogue between democracy and religion. This "postsecular" development focused on dialogue has been developed most systematically in the Council of Europe's *White Paper of Intercultural Dialogue* (2008), which displays a striking resemblance to Habermas' dialogical view. The practical consequences of this goodwill postsecular trend remain uncertain, but one should be wary of idealizing it according to Habermasian rationalist "script." The existence of a variety of forms of communicative interaction is vital for aspiring to mutual respect and learning in society. Yet reducing this variety to a form of rational argument working as the beating heart of a "postsecular Europe" is no more than a philosophical chimera.

1   A Christian Europe

The history of Europe and Christianity are inextricably entwined. Nonetheless, what is the role of Christianity in the process of European polity-building? J. Ratzinger and J. Weiler argue that Christianity should be placed at the heart of Europe. Ratzinger's view is built on a gloomy diagnostic of the current European situation.[5] That Europe is in a deep crisis is due to what Ratzinger calls the "dialectic of modernity," a process whereby rational progress turns against itself.[6] Modernity has brought about rational–scientific progress, but it has also engendered an aggressive secularism. This is based on instrumental rationality that threatens

---

[5] In the following, I will refer to Ratzinger's writings before and after he became Pope. Here I cannot discuss the issue of the development of and changes in Ratzinger's view.

[6] J. Ratzinger, *Europe: Today and Tomorrow* (San Francisco: Ignatius Press, 2007).

to reduce moral–political life to the utilitarian calculus of subjective preferences, and so to sever it from the belief in Absolute and the traditional
objective values. In particular, law and democracy have turned into the
mere outcome of the mechanical sum of ephemeral preferences, being
exposed "to the whim of the majority."[7] The blend of aggressive secularism, utilitarianism and subjectivism has, in short, corroded Europe's
umbilical bond with the Christian tradition and its objective values,
and has undermined the democratic practice. For Ratzinger, religion's
sleep has brought about the monsters of a derailed reason and atheistic
totalitarianism.[8]

What is the way out of this quandary? Ratzinger's answer is unam-
biguous: Christianity should regain its position at the center of the construction of Europe. This is not to return to a political regime for which
God and the Book of Revelation are the direct foundation of the state.
In Ratzinger's political-theological view, the state is autonomous, and
the church is to be separated from it. The autonomy of the political order
is premised on the fact that God endowed us with a self-standing *ratio*.
In Ratzinger's interpretation, the Catholic tradition maintains that the
objective norms governing just actions are accessible to reason, independently of one's faith in God and the Bible. However, while democracy
and religion are autonomous, they should not be separated. Reason without faith, democracy without church, are crippled. In a Europe in crisis,
reason and faith, political authority and the church should be brought
together in a new reconciling synthesis. At the basis of it lies the idea that
the church should influence in an *indirect* way the political process by
means of clarifying and supporting objective moral values: "the formation of just structures is not directly the duty of the Church, but belongs
to the world of politics, the sphere of the autonomous use of reason. The
Church has an indirect duty here, in that she is called to contribute to the
purification of reason and to the reawakening of those moral forces without which just structures"[9] cannot be established.

The church's "indirect influence" is to be achieved, in good part,
through the constitution of a Christian civil religion ("*religione civile cristiana*"). Ratzinger's model of civil religion is distinct from the

[7] J. Ratzinger, "Crises of Law," in J. F. Thornton and S. B. Varenne (eds.), *The Essential Pope Benedictus XVI. His Essential Writings and Speeches* (London: HarperCollins e-books, 2007), p. 378.
[8] "Pope's Speech: 'Faith remains a mighty force for good in the UK'," *Guardian* (16 September 2010).
[9] Benedictus XVI, *Deus Caritas Est* (2006), para. 28.

republican and liberal versions of it. With respect to Europe, he neither proposes a state civil religion (Rousseau) nor a social civil religion (Tocqueville). Ratzinger acknowledges that a European civil religion would not be able either to form a state religion or to reproduce the American religious ethos. In Europe secularization has had a strong impact – much stronger than in the United States. And, deplores Ratzinger, even American civil religion is not what it used to be. For him, American Protestantism and Catholicism have made too many concessions to secular modernity, resulting in their weakening. There is, however, one inspiring exception: the American evangelicals.[10] Interestingly, American evangelicalism, and not American Catholicism, provides Ratzinger with a paradigmatic example of what he calls a *creative religious minority*. The constitution of an analogous religious minority in Europe should fight secularism, defend tradition and provide the building bloc of a pan-European civil religion. In Ratzinger's view, "one needs to agree with Toynbee that the destiny of a society always depends on creative minorities. The faithful Christians should conceive themselves as a creative minority and contribute to Europe's re-conquering the best of its tradition."[11]

How convincing is Ratzinger's proposal? The idea of civil religion is surely compatible with democracy, but Ratzinger's interpretation of it is questionable on normative and practical grounds. In effect, Ratzinger urges Catholic politicians to abide by their religious conscience when they take commonly binding decisions.[12] However, it is a stand which attempts to *directly* influence the legal–political processes. This attempt brings into question the autonomy of politics that Ratzinger claims to defend. More importantly, it is likely to lead to commonly binding decisions that are at odds with democratic inclusiveness, and which are potentially discriminatory for non-Catholics. It is significant that evangelical movements such as Moral Majority aim at shaping directly the legal–political framework. In addition, Ratzinger's model of an exemplary religious minority is not an emblematic case of creativity, but rather of closure and over-politicization of religion, namely of the conversion of civil religion into a political one.

---

[10] J. Ratzinger, "Europa oggi" in M. Pera and J. Ratzinger, *Senza Radici. Europa, relativismo, cristianesimo, islam* (Milan: Mondadori, 2004), p. 102.

[11] *Ibid.*, p. 72 (my translation).

[12] For Ratzinger's position on this issue, see his "Nota Dottrinale circa alcune questioni riguardanti l'impegno e il comportamento dei cattolici nella vita politica" (2002); see also *Compendio de la Doctrina Social de la Iglesia*, para. 571.

Ratzinger's view is also in dissonance with current transformations of religion in Europe. As Grace Davie argues, Europe is witnessing a passage from a culture of obligation to a culture of choice – to a culture of "believing without belonging." What was "until recently simply imposed (with all the negative conceptions of the word), or inherited (a rather more positive spin), becomes instead a matter of personal choice."[13] There is a growing trend in Europe towards the diversification of the religious and spiritual search, taking often more hybrid, fluid and individualized forms. This trend, involving a transformation of Christianity, creates tension with strongly hierarchical religious organizations like the Catholic Church, and questions the feasibility of a European–Catholic civil religion. It is noteworthy, for instance, how divided the current Pope and Archbishop of Canterbury are over the issues of pluralism and multiculturalism: the former tends to see in them the danger of relativism undermining (Christian) objective values, while the latter regards them as a necessity and an opportunity for broadening and deepening democratic and religious practices in a society of "interconnected differences."[14] In short, given the growing pluralism and desideratum of democratic Europe, Ratzinger's proposal is questionable: the formation of a European civil-political religion led by a minority is as unattractive as it seems unworkable.

In turn, Joseph Weiler develops a distinctive line of argumentation by combining comparative constitutionalism, political philosophy and reflections on the Catholic theology after the Second Vatican Council (1962–1965).[15] Weiler departs from Habermas' view of constitutional patriotism by maintaining that a viable democracy cannot be based on a lackluster consensus on abstract constitutional principles, but only on a "thick" ethical identity and community. However, Weiler does not advance, as it was claimed, a communitarian argument based on a

---

[13] G. Davie, "Is Europe an exceptional case?", in *State and Religion in Europe* (Istanbul: Center for Islamic Studies, 2006), p. 26.

[14] For the Archbishop of Canterbury, "[p]roperly understood ... a political pluralism that is fully conscious of the potential of interactive variety (a refinement of 'interconnected difference') is a fruitful context for an interreligious encounter that does not compromise convictions but is also ready to envisage growth and change." Archbishop's Chevening Lecture at the British Council, New Delhi (October 15, 2010), at www.archbishopofcanterbury.org/articles.php/569/archbishops-chevening-lecture-at-the-british-council-new-delhi (last accessed August 16, 2011). Compare this stand with Ratzinger's criticism of ethical pluralism in his "Nota Dottrinale," II.2.

[15] Weiler, *Un'Europa cristiana*. See also J. Weiler, "Invocatio Dei and the European Constitution" (2003), available at www.project-syndicate.org/commentary/weiler1 (last accessed August 16, 2011).

presumed consensus on the Christian identity.[16] His view incorporates a pluralist–agonistic element that sets him apart from communitarianism.[17] Weiler's starting point is the plurality of European constitutional arrangements and identities. Some European countries include a reference to God or Christianity in their constitution (e.g. Ireland, Germany), while others do not (e.g. France, Romania). Thus, in order to achieve real pluralism and neutrality, the European constitutional framework should adopt something like the Polish solution. The merit of the Polish model is, for Weiler, that it does not advocate secularism under the mask of neutrality, but grants recognition to *both* "thick" identities or worldviews, laic and Christian, without privileging any of them. Therefore, only a solution similar to the Polish one would be truly pluralist and neutral: pluralist because it would include them both, and neutral because it would not favor either of the two. This double recognition is, for Weiler, not meant as a constitutional ornament. The symbolic function of the constitution expresses deep value commitments of the political community, and should entail concrete consequences: decisions will be taken sometimes on the basis of laic values, and other times of Christian ones.[18]

Weiler backs this constitutional argument with a reflection on European identity. In building their identity, Europeans need not shy away from publicly assuming Christian heritage as a fundamental element of who they are. A viable European polity cannot be reduced to a market system or an abstract set of universal rights, but it has to assert itself as an ethical community endowed with a "thick" identity anchored in European history. For Weiler, the public assertion of Christianity as an essential part of European history and identity does not have discriminatory effects for Muslims and other religious minorities. Paraphrasing a dictum of the Catholic Church, Weiler maintains that Europe should

---

[16] A. J. Menéndez, "A pious Europe? Why Europe should not define itself as Christian," *Arena Working Papers* 10 (2004).

[17] Religion did not play a role in Weiler's earlier writings. However, the combination between agonistic pluralism and communitarianism is already present. For Weiler's taste for the paradoxes and the *agon* inherent in our current predicament, see his "Epilogue: The European Courts of Justice: Beyond 'Beyond Doctrine' or the Legitimacy Crisis of European Constitutionalism" in A.-M. Slaughter, A. S. Sweet, and J. H. H. Weiler (eds.), *The European Court and National Courts – Doctrine and Jurisprudence. Legal Change in its Social Context* (Oxford: Hart Publishing, 1998), p. 387; see also J. Weiler, "Fundamental Rights and Fundamental Boundaries: On the Conflict of Standards and Values in the Protection of Human Rights in the European Legal Space," *The Constitution of Europe* (Cambridge University Press, 1999) pp. 102–29.

[18] Weiler, *Un'Europa cristiana*, see esp. pp. 81–3.

"propose, not impose" her Christian identity. In addition, for Weiler, even Muslims would favor this Christian–European perspective, since it is a precondition of mutual respect. Being respectful to the other (i.e. the Muslim) is not premised on the Europeans hiding their identity, but on assuming and asserting it openly.

Weiler's plea is masterful in showing the deep interconnection of the history of Europe and Christianity, but it implies the bizarre conclusion that true pluralism and neutrality are ensured when (Christian/laic) "thick" values can directly ground commonly binding decisions. This stand is objectionable on normative and practical grounds, as it introduces a patent bias in the European legal system and a strong element of legal incoherence. It is indeed difficult to see how taking legal decisions founded on Christian values could be neutral with regard to Muslim and other minorities. Such decisions would impose, and not propose, Christian values to those who do not share them. Neutrality as a principle of legitimacy does not result from the "mechanical" addition of "thick" worldviews, and of the "votes" of their followers. The consequence of Weiler's "mechanical" procedure of addition is not state neutrality, but *agonistic majoritarianism*: sometimes religious citizens form the majority and impose their values, at other times the laic citizens do. Weiler's "mechanical" view of European constitutionalism further misses the current transformation of the nexus between religion and politics in Europe. As Ferrari points out, a "convergence from extreme positions towards the center is taking place in Europe, where the extremes are church-of-state systems on the one hand and rigid separation on the other."[19] There is, at the European level, a normatively appealing trend of moving away from the opposite poles of the state religion model and the strictly laic one, which have traditionally had difficulties with the respect of freedom of religion, pluralism and minority rights. Despite their ambiguities, leading European institutions have, at key moments, supported this trend in tune with the growing pluralism of society and the legitimacy of public manifestation of a diversity of (non) religious voices (see sections 3 and 4).

2   Une Europe laïque

The argument that *laïcité* is the point of convergence of current European developments has been recently proposed by the influential Stasi

---

[19] S. Ferrari, "State regulation of religion in the European democracies: the decline of the old pattern," in G. Motzkin and Y. Fischer (eds.), *Religion and Democracy in Contemporary Europe* (London: Alliance Publishing Trust, 2008), p. 109.

Commission (2003) and French public intellectuals.[20] But has Europe become increasingly *laïque* or is *laïcité* a French idiosyncrasy?

Laïcité has emerged from a process that can be usefully distinguished from that of *secularization*.[21] Secularization involves neither a systematic conflict between state and religion, nor the attempt to exclude the latter from the formation of the body politic. To illustrate, in the secularized Scandinavian countries the adoption of Lutheran Protestantism has supported the emergence of a modern nation whose pillars have been the church and the state. The presence of political–theological elements such as the "theology of the two reigns" and the absence of fundamental differences between laymen and clergy worked as premises of the construction of a relatively autonomous nation state that did not have to assert itself against the church. In Protestantism there is no equivalent of the *Syllabus Errorum* of the Catholic Church: for a long time Protestantism did not oppose democratization and individualization but contributed, sometimes unintentionally, to these processes.

The dynamic of Scandinavian secularization is different from that of French laicization. Before the French Revolution the model of the relation between society and religion was, to use Charles Taylor's terms, "paleo-Durkheimian":[22] the Catholic Church imbued all aspects of French society, and political authority was personified by an absolutist monarch acting as God's representative on earth. The Revolution inaugurated a "tradition" of conflict between state and religion; the laic state attempted to exclude the church from the construction of the body politic so as to create a unitary and indivisible French republic. As Gauchet notes, in the clash with the church, the new laic state adopted the paraphernalia of its enemy so as to remove its spell over people's imagination and feelings. This resulted in a quasi-theology of the state based on the "sacralization" of republican virtues, and can be seen to be celebrated, in all their ambiguities, in Jacques-Louis David's paintings *Oath of the Horati* and *The Death of Marat*. *Laïcité* became a civil "religion," a "religion" of the *citoyens* united in the pursuit of public good (*res publica*) and virtue. According to this

---

[20] J.-P. Willaime, "European Integration, *Laïcité* and Religion," in L. N. Leustean and J. T. S. Madeley (eds.), *Religion, Politics and Law in the European Union* (London: Routledge, 2009), pp. 17–29.

[21] For more on the complex history and ambiguities of *laïcité*, see J. Baubérot, *Laïcité 1905–2005, entre passion et raison* (Paris: Seuil, 2004); O. Roy, *La laïcité face à l'islam* (Paris: Stock, 2005); C. Laborde, *Critical Republicanism: The Hijab Controversy and Political Philosophy* (Oxford University Press, 2008); C. Laborde, *Français, encore un effort pour être républicains!* (Paris: Seuil, 2010); M. Gauchet, *La réligion dans la démocratie: parcours de la laïcité*, Romanian trans., (Bucharest: Humanitas, 2001).

[22] C. Taylor, *A Secular Age* (Cambridge, MA: Harvard University Press, 2007) p. 487.

model of integration, individuals turn into "faithful" *citoyens* when they strip themselves of their religious particularities in the public sphere.

This model of "missionary" *laïcité* is currently undergoing a process of relative transformation. The 2003 Report of the Stasi Commission is representative of the attempt of the French state to revisit the laic model in a new historical–intellectual configuration where a modernized church abandons the role of competing against the laic state, and the Muslim minority occupies a central place in the debate.[23] The Stasi Report advocates an "active laicism" ("*laïcité active*") as a central characteristic of the French state, and opposes it to the "lazy neutrality" (*neutralité paresseuse*) of a liberal sort.[24] In the Commission's interpretation, "active laicism" abandons much of its "sacral aura," and in part loosens the idea of a religious-blind public sphere. Instead, it envisages a "reasonable approach to religions as facts of civilization,"[25] and backs the attempt to engage in a dialogue with religious organizations. In particular, the Stasi Report points out approvingly that the French state has granted certain facilities to the French Muslim minority, and has become actively involved in organizing the French Council of the Muslim Cult as a dialogue partner representative of Islam. The Report further argues that the laic conception is not a French idiosyncrasy. Europe has become increasingly *laïque*. To illustrate this, the Commission underlines that the ECtHR implements a laic view, a case in point being its support for the veil ban.

The advocates of *laïcité* are rightly concerned with the importance of public values and political integration: one must admit that the panorama of the disaffected European democracies is disheartening. Apart from the common concern with integration, there are other significant commonalities between *laïcité* and the European discourses on religion, for instance the agnostic refusal of an official religion and of imposing religion-based prescriptions by means of civil law, as well as the growing concern with integration. So far, so good. Nonetheless, the Stasi Report falls short on two accounts: first, it is misguided in arguing that Europe has become ever more *laïque* (see point 1 below). Second, the Report does

---

[23] The Report of the Stasi Commission is available at www.fil-info-france.com/actualites-monde/rapport-stasi-commission-laicite.htm (last accessed August 16, 2011).

[24] Stasi Report, para. 4.3.1.

[25] Cf. R. Debray, "L'enseignement du fait religieux dans l'école laïque" (2002), www.lesrapports.ladocumentationfrancaise.fr/BRP/024000544/0000.pdf (last accessed August 16, 2011).

not question the deep ambivalences of the French practice of *laïcité* (see point 2 below).

1. The French "neo-Durkheimian" model based on the bond between state, "civil religion" and nation, remains the product of a specific historical–political context, and is difficult to extrapolate it to a Europe characterized by growing pluralism and individualism. At the European level, there is nothing analogous to the attempt of constituting a homogenous republican identity based on public virtues and the misrecognition of minority rights.[26] Certainly, European institutions such as ECtHR or the CoE acknowledge that *laïcité* is not incompatible with the European Convention; but this does not entail that they adopt the model of *laïcité* in its specificities, or that they impose it on other states. It is true that the Court has supported the veil ban. Yet its stand is not rooted in anything specific to *laïcité*, but in a broader suspicion towards Islam.[27] At the level of principles, the ECtHR and the CoE have in fact advanced an approach that is in dissonance with the ideal typical *laïcité*, and is based on the principle of legitimacy of religious manifestations in the public sphere, the principle of minority rights, and that of the positive contribution of religious pluralism to democratic life. In contrast, according to *laïcité*, the individual becomes a citizen proper if she brackets her religious opinions and particularities. If, for instance, the French state grants a form of recognition to the Muslim minority, this is not a matter of principle, but an exception justified circumstantially. The Muslim minority is thus regarded as a partner in dialogue by virtue of the situational concern for potential social disintegration and rise of fundamentalism, and not on the basis of principles such as positive recognition of minorities, and intercultural dialogue as mutual exchange and learning (see sections 3 and 4 below).

2. Second, the French practice of *laïcité* and its justification by the Stasi Commission remain profoundly ambivalent. The "untouchable" core of the laic model is the 1905 "Law concerning the separation of the Churches and the State." The Law stipulates that "(t)he Republic does not recognize, pay for or subsidize any cult" (Article 2). However, above all Catholicism has been granted a range of substantial state privileges, so much so that C. Laborde speaks of a "*catho-laïque*" tradition in France.[28]

---

[26] See Willaime, "European Integration," p. 20.

[27] J. Cesari and S. McLoughlin (eds.), *European Muslims and the Secular* State (Aldershot: Ashgate, 2005).

[28] C. Laborde, "Virginity and Burqa: Unreasonable Accommodations? Considerations on the Stasi and Bouchard-Taylor Reports" (2008), www.booksandideas.net/Virginity-and-Burqa-Unreasonable.html (last accessed August 16, 2011).

The compatibility of these privileges with the laic principles of neutrality and separation is plainly dubious. It is ironic that, when it comes to these privileges, the Stasi Report does not resort to the treasured principles of *laïcité*; however, when it comes to Muslims and issues such as the head-scarf ban, invoking the deep commitment to these rigorous principles of *laïcité* proves convenient.

For the influential intellectual and policy-maker R. Debray, "*laïcité* is an opportunity for Islam in France."[29] But legal and socio-economic practices do not confirm this optimism. The Stasi Report and French jurisprudence do not make a serious attempt to critically challenge the biased relationship towards Catholicism,[30] and to envision a situation of equality between various religious groups in France. This failure of *laïcité* is reflected by socio-economic inequalities, in part caused by the "wrong" religious affiliation. According to a recent study, anti-Muslim discrimination exists in the French labor market: a Muslim candidate is 2.5 times less likely to receive a job interview call-back than his or her Christian counterpart, and Muslim workers earn only 15 percent of the average wage.[31] Religious diversity is a thorn in the flesh of *laïcité*: diversity remains either a problem to be overcome, or a threat to be kept under control. The French state's dialogue with the Muslim community is the hypocritical homage that a "pure" *laïcité* pays to the necessity of providing fair conditions of integration.

The laic model is at loggerheads with at least two European developments to which I am going to turn now. First, at the level of the ECtHR, the principle of pluralism has become part of what I call a minimal liberal–constitutional framework (see section 3). Second, especially at the political level of the Council of Europe, the principles of liberal constitutionalism have been connected to that of dialogue. According to a European post-secular trend, the principle of dialogue does not merely have a situational and instrumental function of controlling certain religious groups perceived by the securitizing state as "problematic." Dialogue is regarded, from this standpoint, as having two other functions: an instrumental one of fostering pluralist integration, and a substantial one of involving reciprocal learning and mutually enriching exchanges (see section 4).

---

[29] Debray, "L'enseignement du fait religieux dans l'école laïque," p. 21.
[30] Laborde, "Virginity and Burqa."
[31] C. L. Adida, D. D. Laitin, and M.-A. Valfort, "Identifying barriers to Muslim integration in France," *Proceedings of the National Academy of Sciences of the United States of America* (PNAS, November 2010).

3   Minimal liberal constitutionalism

While the ECtHR's case law is inconsistent at key moments (see below), my hypothesis is that minimal liberal constitutionalism captures an important trend in it. "Liberal constitutionalism" refers here to the combination of two aspects. It includes, first, the secular principles of the European liberal tradition as they emerged in the aftermath of the wars of religion, that is, freedom of religion and state neutrality. But this classic liberal constitutionalism, with its focus on individual freedom and rights, did not require the state to have the obligation of recognizing (non)religious pluralism as a contribution to "good" democratic politics. In contrast, a revisited liberal constitutionalism presupposes that the state should grant equal recognition to the diversity of (non)religious relevant particularities. As a consequence, state neutrality, when interconnected with the principle of pluralism, acquires a double dimension: negative, that is the absence of a biased relation between the state and (non)religious communities, and positive, that is one founded upon the principle of equal recognition of diversity.

By *minimal* liberal constitutionalism, I refer to the fact that the role of the Convention "machinery" is subsidiary. As established by case law, national authorities are, by virtue of the margin of appreciation, in principle better placed than an international court to assess national and local needs and circumstances. However, the Court, as the main European instance of judicial review concerning religious issues, aims to define minimal limitations with respect to the existing models. In so doing, the Court has developed a liberal–constitutionalist framework that brings together the principles of freedom of religion, neutrality and pluralism that help it justify these limitations of the margin of appreciation granted to national authorities.[32] While it is beyond the scope of this chapter to give an overview of the principles of the Court's jurisprudence (see Ringelheim, Chapter 12), I briefly analyze this liberal–constitutionalist trend with respect to some representative cases dealing with religious symbols, education and freedom of speech. I shall discuss my hypothesis by examining two key decisions: *Folgerø and others* v. *Norway* (2007) and

---

[32] See also F. Tulkens, "The European Convention on Human Rights and Church–State Relations. Pluralism v Pluralism," *Cardozo Law Review* 30(6) (2009), 2575–91, and A. Nieuwenhuis, "The Concept of Pluralism in the Case-Law of the European Court of Human Rights," *European Constitutional Law Review* 3 (2007), 367–84.

Lautsi v. *Italy* (2009).[33] Then I shall briefly deal with the ECtHR's ambivalence as it emerges from decisions such as *Dahlab* v. *Switzerland* (2001) and *Otto-Preminger-Institut* v. *Austria* (1994).

Folgerø deals with complaints lodged by non-Christian parents and their children in reaction to the 1998 Education Act and its introduction of the compulsory subject of "Christianity, Religion, and Philosophy" (the KRL subject).[34] The legal conflict resulted from the fact that the Norwegian authorities rejected the full exemption from KRL demanded by non-Christian parents. The ECtHR examined this conflict under Article 2 of Protocol No. 1, as the *lex specialis* in the area of education, according to which the state must respect the parents' rights to educate their children according to their religious and philosophical convictions. In the Court's interpretation of Article 2, the state "is forbidden to pursue an aim of indoctrination that might be considered as not respecting parents' religious and philosophical conviction."[35]

The Court's interpretation of the Article 2 is not reduced to this "negative" aspect of freedom of religion and state neutrality whereby the state should avoid religious indoctrination. *Folgerø* has the merit of strengthening the link between freedom of religion, neutrality and the protection of pluralism. For the Court, Article 2 aims at safeguarding the possibility of pluralism in education as "essential for the preservation of the democratic society as conceived by the Convention."[36] Following the previous decision in *Kjeldsen, Busk Madsen and Pedersen* v. *Denmark* (1976),[37] the Court argues that the state must take care that "information or knowledge included in the curriculum is conveyed in an objective, critical and pluralistic manner."[38] Furthermore, the Court claims that the state has a *positive obligation* to recognize pluralism, and foster a culture of mutual respect: "article 2 ... enjoins the State to respect parents' convictions, be they religious or philosophical, throughout the entire State education programme ... The verb 'respect' means more than 'acknowledge' or 'take into account.' In addition to a primarily negative undertaking, it implies some positive obligation on the part of the State."[39]

---

[33] This chapter was written before the reversal of the *Lautsi* decision in March 2011. This reversal raises strong doubts as to the ECtHR's capacity to protect, in a more consistent way, diversity in Europe as well as to its bias in favor of Christian majorities.

[34] Eur. Ct. H. R. (Grand Chamber), *Folgerø and others* v. *Norway*, 29 June 2007.

[35] *Ibid.*, para. 84 (h).   [36] *Ibid.*, para. 84 (b).

[37] Eur. Ct. H. R., *Kjeldsen, Busk Madsen and Pedersen* v. *Denmark* (7 December 1976).

[38] *Ibid.*, para. 71.   [39] *Ibid.* para. 84 (c).

The Court's support of freedom of religion, neutrality and pluralism does not exclude its recognition of the special role of the majority religion in education in Norway. To the contrary, the fact that knowledge about Lutheranism represented, according to the Education Act, a more substantial part of the curriculum was regarded as legitimate, given the place occupied by Christianity in the national history of Norway. In addition, Article 2 "does not embody any right for parents that their child be kept ignorant about religion and philosophy in their education."[40]

However, the Court argued against the government that the implementation of the KRL subject entailed that not only *quantitative* but also *qualitative* differences applied to the teaching of Christianity as compared to that of other religions and philosophies. For a variety of activities such as prayers, the singing of hymns, church services and school plays, the national authorities proposed a partial exemption, by claiming that proposed observation by attendance could unproblematically replace involvement through participation. Yet, as the Court persuasively argued, the distinction between observation and involvement was hard to implement in practice, and "parents might have misapprehensions about asking teachers to take on the extra burdens of differentiated teaching."[41] Furthermore, under the "Christian object clause" of the Education Act, the "[p]rimary school shall, with the understanding and co-operation of the home, assist in giving pupils a Christian and moral education and in developing their abilities, spiritual as well as physical."[42] Yet it is apparent that the Christian and "spiritual" education goes beyond transmitting knowledge about Christianity and moral education, and represents a bias in favor of Christians. Pluralism, argued the Court, entailed the protection of minorities, and democracy should not be confused with majoritarianism.[43] Given the qualitative difference in teaching of the KRL subject, the Court persuasively argued that the explicit objectives of the Education Act itself such as fostering mutual respect and intercultural dialogue were not fully fulfilled, and that the information and knowledge included in

---

[40] *Ibid.*, para. 89   [41] *Ibid.*, para. 95.

[42] *Ibid.*, para. 12. The Court's reasoning is *not* devoid of problems. The Court argues that the "[t]he difference as to emphasis was also reflected in the Curriculum, where approximately half of the items listed referred to Christianity alone whereas the remainder of the items were shared between other religions and philosophies" (*ibid.*, para. 92). Yet it is difficult to see why a state where the overwhelming majority are Lutherans should not have the right to dedicate approximately 50 percent to a subject like KRL to the Christian tradition, and why doing so would automatically lead to indoctrination (see Leigh, Chapter 8, although I differ from his general conclusion).

[43] *Ibid.*, para. 84.

the curriculum were not conveyed in an objective, critical and pluralistic manner for the purposes of Article 2.

In short, the Court recognizes the importance of the special relation between the majority religion and the state. In particular, education is not to take place in a moral and historical–religious vacuum. Nonetheless, the requirement to recognize the plurality of systems of education in Europe should not work as a pretext for curtailing the principles of liberal constitutionalism. In granting a full exemption, the Court aimed at protecting freedom of religion, educational neutrality and a minority from majoritarianism – that is from "indoctrination" into the majority religion.

The Court pursued a more ambiguous stand in decisions such as *Lautsi* (2009), which banned the crucifix from the walls of Italian public schools. This decision has generated a huge controversy: is the *absence* of the crucifix as supported by the Court a *symbol in itself* – one that is in favor of the ideology of secularism? Does the Court's invoking of freedom of religion and the neutrality of the Italian state camouflage a bias against Christianity?

The criticism implicit in these questions is, to an important extent, misleading.[44] The Court points out that pupils could very well interpret the presence of the crucifix in the classrooms as a specific *religious* sign, and not as a cultural one. This could be supportive for Catholic pupils, but unsettling for non-Catholic pupils.[45] Further, respect for parents' religious convictions and children's convictions "implies the right to believe in a religion or not to believe in any religion. The freedom to believe and the freedom not to believe (negative freedom) are both protected by Article 9 of the Convention."[46] Given that the symbol may be reasonably associated with the majority religion in Italy, the Court also rejected the claim that the display of the crucifix respected state neutrality and was able to serve the educational pluralism that is essential for the preservation of a democratic society. The ECtHR argues in *Lautsi* that the state should protect pluralism especially when minorities are at stake.[47] This is all the more salient in the context of public education, where attending classes is obligatory irrespective of religion.

As a result, arguing that *absence* of the crucifix means nothing less than the *presence* of an anti-religious or atheist symbol is a non sequitur. In fact, the Court explicitly rejects the replacement of a religious symbol with an atheist symbol. The "absence" could be understood as a

---

[44] Weiler, "State and Nation," which also contains Weiler's intervention in front of the Great Chamber of June 30, 2010.

[45] Eur. Ct. H. R. (2nd section), *Lautsi v. Italy*, 3 November 2009 (not final), para. 55.

[46] *Ibid.*, para. 47.   [47] *Ibid.*, para. 47.

precondition for pupils being able to build freely their own religious or non-religious "presence", namely for the principles of freedom of religion, state neutrality and the protection of pluralism.

However, while *Lautsi* (2009) aims at implementing the principles of liberal constitutionalism, it is not devoid of problems. It is arguable that a "conditional removal" approach (i.e. removal of the crucifix only upon request and preceded by a local deliberative process) to the issue of the crucifix, analogous to the one adopted in Spain in 2009, would have been more convincing.[48] Such an approach has important merits: it neither imposes a uniform model pre-deciding the significance of the crucifix nor does it accept uncritically the status quo to the detriment of minorities and their freedom of religion. This approach avoids over-juridification, and it advances a democracy-oriented solution more suited to the dynamic and complexity of the contexts of interpretation of the meaning of the crucifix, and it avoids over-juridification. Instead of freezing the dynamic of signification of the crucifix by the fiat of a European Court far from the diversity of concrete circumstances, an alternative solution would have given citizens more opportunity to reflect on, negotiate and decide on it at the level of their communities and neighborhoods. This approach would have also avoided the failure of the *Lautsi* to consider the doctrine of the margin of appreciation. It could have better balanced both the limitation of the ECtHR as a sub-sidiary instance and the necessity to protect minorities and freedom of religion.

In other representative cases the Court has abandoned the liberal–constitutionalist stand in a more straightforward way. To illustrate this, consider the first headscarf case, *Dahlab* v. *Switzerland* (2001), which concerned a primary school teacher.[49] The Court maintained that, during Ms. Dahlab's three years of teaching, no complaints whatsoever were

---

[48] The Spanish "solution" was advanced in 2009 by the *Tribunal Superior de Justicia de Castilla y León* in Valladolid. According to the Spanish Court, the removal of the crucifix should be interpreted as conditional upon the existence of a "request of withdrawal of the religious symbols" ("*petición de retirada de símbolos religiosos*") from the part of the parents, and for a determined period. In this case, the so-called School Council (*Consejo Escolar*) should withdraw the crucifix from the classroom in question, and for the school year in which the petition was made. The final decision (2009) of the Valladolid Court can be found at: www.stecyl.es/juridica/091214_sentencia_TSJ_CyL.pdf (last accessed September 6, 2011). Note that the Spanish decision does not give any importance to the issue of deliberation.

[49] Eur. Ct. H. R., *Dahlab* v. *Switzerland*, 15 February 2001. See D. McGoldrick, *Human Rights and Religion: The Islamic Headscarf Debate in Europe* (Oxford: Hart Publications, 2006).

made with respect to the "content or quality" of the teaching.[50] The Court further acknowledged that it could *not* be established that Ms. Dahlab's wearing of the headscarf had had a negative impact on the pupils. However, the Court submitted that this possibility could not be ruled out, all the more since wearing the headscarf was based on an imposition pre-scribed by the Koran. According to the Court, since the Koran is at log-gerheads with gender equality, "[i]t … appears difficult to reconcile the wearing of an Islamic headscarf with the message of tolerance, respect for others and, above all, equality and non-discrimination that all teachers in a democratic society must convey to their pupils."[51] The Swiss authorities were, therefore, seen as justified in pursuing the aim of protecting the rights and freedoms of others, public order and public safety.

The ECtHR's inferential "logic," however, raises important difficulties. First, it remains unexplained how Ms. Dahlab's wearing of the headscarf, an issue which had not raised any complaint whatsoever, could be rea-sonably considered a menace to public order and public safety. The Court is completely silent as to the grounds of invoking Article 9.2 to justify an inference with the freedom of religion (Article 9.1). Second, the ECtHR mistakenly maintains that wearing the headscarf was a clear-cut obliga-tion imposed on women by the Koran.[52] In addition, the Court's sweeping negative judgment concerning the Koran as being at odds with gender equality, democracy and tolerance was, at best, unfortunate. The role of a Court is not to "put on trial" books like Koran – the milestone of a hugely complex and changing religious tradition of practice and interpretation. Regrettably, such generalizing verdicts with respect to Islam do not con-stitute an exception, for instance, in influential decisions such as *Refah Partisi* v. *Turkey* (2003), where the Court intimated that there is a prin-cipled incompatibility between democracy and sharia.[53] It is also note-worthy that the ECtHR has double standards: the Court has never passed such sweeping negative verdicts over the Bible, even if one can easily find statements that are at loggerheads with the contemporary understanding of democracy and gender equality.[54]

---

[50] *Dahlab* v. *Switzerland.*   [51] *Ibid.*

[52] See, for instance, F. Zouari, *Le Voile Islamique: Histoire et Actualité, du Coran à L'Affaire du Foulard* (Paris: Favre, 2002).

[53] Eur. Ct. H. R. (Grand Chamber), *Refah Partisi (The Welfare Party) and others* v. *Turkey*, 13 February 2003, para. 44.

[54] I do *not* want to suggest that the stand of the Court in cases involving Islam is completely problematic. For instance, in Eur. Ct. H. R. (2nd section), *Ahmet Arslan and Others* v. *Turkey*, 23 February 2010 (not final), the Court upheld the right of women to wear the headscarf in the street.

Third, the conjecture that wearing the veil may negatively influence pupils cannot be taken for granted, especially when it is not backed by expert studies. If building a society based on mutual respect and tolerance is a desideratum, it is reasonable to envisage that pupils be exposed in schools to a plurality of opinions and lifestyles. A neutral and pluralist educational system need not exclude contact with a plurality of options; real freedom of choice grows not in a "purely" neutral social vacuum, but by exposure to a rich and pluralistic context of choice. To respect differences and to be willing to learn from them are "aptitudes" that can be formed by acquaintance with differences, not by hiding them.

Another significant ambivalence of the Court plagues the area of freedom of speech. The Court has made important steps in protecting freedom of speech from abusive state interferences.[55] Yet in *Otto-Preminger-Institut*, and in a series of subsequent decisions,[56] the Court has supported a majoritarian position by choosing to restrict freedom of speech on the shaky ground of protecting the religious feelings of Christian majorities (see also Letsas, Chapter 10).

The bone of contention in *Otto-Preminger* was the Austrian authorities' ban of the film *Council in Heaven* promoted by the Otto-Preminger-Institut, and which portrayed key figures of the Christian religion in a polemic way.[57] The Court's argument that the ban does not violate Article 10 of the European Convention raises significant difficulties (see also Letsas, Chapter 10).[58] The film was also intended for a paying audience in an "art cinema", namely a cinema theatre with a small audience interested in experimental movies.[59] Showing a movie in such a theatre hardly qualified as a real menace to peace.[60] Furthermore, if religious people did not wish to feel offended, they could simply not go to see it. Nobody in any sense forced the film's images on the religious spectator: seeing the film was not an imposition, but a matter of individual choice, which included the cost of buying the ticket. As a result, by granting such a broad margin of appreciation to the state, the Court supported a "majoritarian" position in conflict

[55] See C. Evans, "Religious Freedom in European Human Rights Law: The Search for a Guiding Conception" in M. W. Janis and C. Evans (eds.), *Religion and International Law* (Leiden: Hotei Publishing, 2004), pp. 385–6.

[56] E.g. Eur. Ct. H. R., *Wingrove* v. *United Kingdom*, 25 November 1996; Eur. Ct. H. R., *Murphy* v. *Ireland*, 10 July 2003.

[57] Eur. Ct. H. R., *Otto-Preminger-Institut* v. *Austria*, 20 September 1994, *Serie* A 295, para. 21.

[58] *Ibid.* Joint Dissenting Opinion of Judges Palm, Pekkanen and Mazaryk, para. 6.

[59] *Ibid.*, para. 9.   [60] *Ibid.*, para. 56.

with the necessity to protect freedom of artistic expression, including when the exercise of freedom is "eccentric" (J. S. Mill) with respect to the existing moral and social rules. However, almost by definition artists challenge, in radical ways, existing social, moral and artistic codes. The "scandal" in the tradition of European art is a trait as important as the originality or the aesthetic rules. Accusations of blasphemy have characterized almost all the important moments of post-Renaissance art. Therefore, history, art historians and philosophers are generally better judges than a Court as to the meaning of an artistic performance, including as to whether an artistic performance can further human progress in aesthetic or ethical terms.

Decisions such as *Otto-Preminger-Institut* enhance "majoritarianism" by providing overprotection to local Christian majorities. This is all the more questionable given the tendency to politicize religious offence that goes beyond Europe. Especially since 1999, various non-binding resolutions condemning defamation of religion, and supported by the Organization of the Islamic Conference, have been voted on and accepted by the United Nations. The current politicization and juridication of religious offense gives grist to the mill of majoritarianism and, even worse, to Islamist governments that do not stand out for their human rights record. It is useful to remember George Orwell's words: "[i]f liberty means anything, it means the right to tell people what they don't want to hear."[61]

4   Dialogical postsecularism

The notion of "postsecularism," launched by J. Habermas, has received different interpretations and has generated a good deal of confusion.[62] Let me first clarify this notion by referring to its main proponent and theorist,

---

[61] G. Orwell, Preface to *Animal Farm*, available at www.home.iprimus.com.au/korob/ Orwell.html (last accessed September 6, 2011).

[62] J. Habermas, *Between Naturalism and Religion* (Cambridge: Polity, 2008). For different interpretations of Habermas' work on religion, see C. Lafont, "Religion in the Public Sphere: Remarks on Habermas's Conception of Public Deliberation in Postsecular Societies," *Constellations* 14(2) (2007), 239–59; K. Wenzel and T. M. Schmidt (eds.), *Moderne Religion? Theologische und religionsphilosophische Reaktionen auf Jürgen Habermas* (Freiburg: Herder Verlag, 2009); M. Cooke, "A Secular State for a Postsecular Society? Postmetaphysical Political Theory and the Place of Religion," *Constellations* 14(2) (2007), 224–38; C. Ungureanu, "The Contested Relation between Religion and Democracy", *European Journal of Political Theory* 7(4) (2008), 405–29. For a comprehensive bibliography on Habermas and religion, see www.habermasforum.dk. See also H. de Vries (ed.), *Political Theologies: Public Religions in a Post-Secular World*, (Fordham University Press, 2006), for a usage of postsecularism in a quite different way than Habermas', and J. Caputo, *On Religion* (Routledge, 2001). Both de Vries and Caputo

Habermas, and then move to its relevance for some of the latest developments in the European discourses on religion.

In recent writings Habermas has developed his dialogical model of democracy in a novel "postsecular" direction by granting an important role to religious values, imagination and motivations. In so doing, Habermas has not abandoned the secular principles of religious freedom, separation and state neutrality. These remain key elements of the "grammar" of a postsecular democracy. Nonetheless, Habermas severs them from the narrative of secularism that shaped his earlier post-Marxist theory, as advanced in *A Theory of Communicative Action*.[63] Especially after the collapse of communism, Habermas departs from the post-Marxist tradition and the idea that religion is at loggerheads with democracy and public reason. In contrast, Habermas' postsecular "turn" appeals to the continuing relevance of religious values, imagination and motivations for shaping and supporting public reason through dialogical exchanges in the informal or social public spaces. From this perspective, public reason obtains part of its moral content by the dialogical processes of translating religious language into secular reasons acceptable to all citizens. Rational dialogue is, in its translating capacity, able to reconcile democracy and a modernized religion. The process of "reconciliation through public reason"[64] has two facets. It refers to the instrumental role of religion in motivating people to participate in the democratic practice and in building relations of solidarity. Second, it refers to the substantial role of dialogue in nourishing an impoverished democratic practice through collective translations from religious into secular discourse.

Habermas' image of dialogical postsecularism finds a middle ground between the two opposite models of multiculturalism and *laïcité*. For

---

reject the Habermasian understanding of postsecularism in terms of public reason and deliberation. Instead, they define postsecularism by reappropriating Schmitt's political-theological reflections or, respectively, Derrida's deconstruction of the relation between reason and faith. For reasons of space, here I deal only with Habermas' influential interpretation of postsecularism.

[63] See J. Habermas, *Theory of Communicative Action: Vol. 1: Reason and Rationalization of Society* (Boston: Beacon Press, 1985). Therein Habermas advanced a post-Marxist theory of religion and modernity, by arguing that religion represented a distortion of reality and rational dialogue. Even universalistic religions such as Judaism or Christianity represented the ideological product of large and stratified class-societies, and a political tool of preserving a non-egalitarian status quo. From this perspective, he regarded religion as incompatible with the formation of an emancipated and modern post-class democracy.

[64] I borrow this phrase from Habermas' "Reconciliation through the public use of reason: remarks on John Rawls' Political Liberalism," *Journal of Philosophy* 92 (1995), 109–31.

Habermas, cultural–religious communities should benefit from public recognition, but not in the form of collective rights. Collective rights tend to "freeze" the cultural–religious traditions under a legal "straightjacket", and to undermine political integration. From Habermas' perspective, individuals and communities can and should be seen as open and willing to engage in translations and arguments in the public sphere. In so doing, they could build a common political culture able to reconcile the diversity of religious, non-religious and atheist voices.

Starting from this image of dialogical postsecularism, let me move now to the recent European discourse on religion. Much of the postsecular emphasis on the dialogue between democracy and religion has initially characterized the European *political* discourse (see 1 below), but it has of late gained certain *legal* salience as well (see 2 below). Certainly, it is an *intellectual fallacy* to interpret this postsecular trend at the level of European discourse by projecting Habermas' philosophical view onto it is an *intellectualistic fallacy*. Still, the parallelism is illuminating given the remarkable overlapping between Habermas' image of postsecular democracy and the model proposed by the Council of Europe's *White Paper* (2008).[65]

1. The European Commission was the first to start developing an informal dialogue with churches and communities of conviction, in particular as part of its broader governance "turn" in the 1990s. However, the Commission's tack on the principle of dialogue remains on the whole underarticulated. In turn, the Council of Europe proposed the most systematic treatment of the European dialogue-based model of integration in the *White Paper on Intercultural Dialogue* (2008).[66] Here I limit myself to analyzing this "moment" in the Council of Europe's development of a discourse on religion. The 2008 *White Paper* has the double merit of defining, for the first time, the Council as "a regular forum for intercultural dialogue,"[67] and of methodically analyzing "intercultural dialogue" as the cornerstone of a theory of integration. Not unlike Habermas, the *White Paper* proposes an intercultural model of integration as a middle ground between the multicultural and the assimilationist models. The dialogic approach aims to merge the positive elements of the multicultural and assimilationist models. According to the *White Paper*, "[the

---

[65] The *White Paper* is available at www.coe.int/t/dg4/intercultural/Source/Pub_White_Paper/White%20Paper_final_revised_EN.pdf (last accessed August 16, 2011).

[66] I do not argue that the *White Paper* fully represents the 'Council of Europe's stand. The reconstruction of its development is beyond the limit of this chapter.

[67] *White Paper*, p. 40.

dialogical approach] … takes from assimilation the focus on the individual; it takes from multiculturalism the recognition of cultural diversity."[68] The resulting model is premised on the view that identities are not closed, but in a relation of mutual interpenetration, and that dialogue is "critical of integration and social cohesion," and leads to mutual learning and improvement.[69] In a way similar to Habermas, the *White Paper* grants intercultural dialogue a double role in forming a democratic culture: first, instrumental, in that it is seen as helping to avoid conflict and bring about integration; second, *substantive*, in that it is perceived as contributing to social–political learning. As the *White Paper* argues, democratic culture is based on "open-mindedness, willingness to engage in dialogue and allowing others to express their point, a capacity to resolve conflicts by peaceful means and recognition of the well-founded arguments of others."[70] By dialogue, religious and non-religious people have a say in shaping the moral structure of society: "(t)hose holding non-religious world views have an equal right to contribute, alongside religious representatives, to debates on the moral foundations of society and to be engaged in forums for intercultural dialogue."[71] Whereas the *White Paper* does not (and need not) aim to advance a philosophical conception of dialogue, the Habermasian ring of some of its phrasings is unmistakable: dialogue, it is claimed, is "governed by the force of argument rather than the argument of force."[72]

2. "Dialogue" has been sporadically mentioned in ECtHR's decisions, but so far it has not been defined, and it has not had any significant practical effect. The principle of dialogue has, however, gained legal weight in Europe, although not under the "system" of the CoE, but under that of the European Union: in tune with the rhetoric of the European Commission, the Lisbon Treaty has advanced the principle of an "open, transparent and regular dialogue" with religious groups, giving legal status to what developed initially as an informal political practice. Whereas it is too early to evaluate its consequences, the Treaty brings the rhetoric of dialogue to a new phase. The Treaty stipulates that "(r)ecognising their identity and their specific contribution, the Union shall maintain an open, transparent and regular dialogue with these churches and organisations" (Article 17 C).[73] Certainly, some European traditions include a consultative dimension between state and church: state–church concordats or agreements are not an exception in Europe. Nonetheless, there are at least

---

[68] *Ibid.*   [69] *Ibid.*, p. 19.   [70] *Ibid.*, p. 17.   [71] *Ibid.*, p. 23.   [72] *Ibid.*, p. 19.
[73] www.eur-lex.europa.eu/JOHtml.do?uri=OJ:C:2007:306:SOM:EN:HTML

three distinguishing traits of the dialogical approach as enhanced by the Lisbon Treaty: it is not merely at the discretion of the state to establish dialogical exchanges with religious actors; it is instead a matter of supranational duty. This approach goes beyond the previous European treaties, the European Convention, as well as the current state–constitutional frameworks. Second, dialogical relations are not to be established on a preferential basis, but on an egalitarian one. This is also a new element, even if the Treaty mitigates it by incorporating a tension characteristic to the European "approach": on the one hand, the Treaty adopts the principle of dialogue with religious organizations on an equalitarian basis, while on the other stipulates the recognition of the state systems. Third, dialogical links are to be established with a *plurality* of religious organizations, as well as with philosophical and non-confessional ones. In tune with other European institutions, the *Treaty* aims at protecting pluralism, either religious or non-religious.

How convincing is the postsecular approach? A central commonality of the view of integration proposed by Habermas and the *White Paper* is that, while the state and religion are separated, religious and non-religious individuals and groups can generate a culture of dialogue, exchange and mutual learning in the public sphere. This image is, to a certain extent, appealing. It rejects the myth of closed identities by arguing that these are open, dynamic and intermingling. It also sustains that religious traditions and organizations can have a positive role in building peace-making dialogical links, in addition to providing inspiring motives and exemplary stories for believers, non-believers and even atheists. Furthermore, by emphasizing the desideratum of mutual engagement of citizens in the currently disaffected public sphere, the dialogical view usefully complements the liberal–constitutionalist trend (see section 3).

There are, however, two main difficulties with the postsecularism, one related to the Habermasian-rationalistic reading of it (see 1 below), and the other to the current juridification of the principle of dialogue at the European level (see 2 below).

1. Habermas' rationalistic gesture of placing dialogue at the center of the relationship between democracy and religion is, on balance, overburdening. Empirical research suggests that rational dialogue is not the rule in our current democratic practices.[74] Argumentative exchange is too infrequent an occurrence and thus the ice is too thin for the construction

---

[74] L. Sanders, "Against Deliberation," *Political Theory* 25(3) (1997), 347–76; J. Steiner, A. Bachtiger, M. Sprondli (eds.), *Deliberative Politics in Action: Analyzing Parliamentary Discourse* (Cambridge University Press, 2004).

of a democratic community. The image of the citizen–translator granting positive recognition and willing to learn from those he disagrees with is too demanding for building a relationship between democracy and religion. The Habermasian projection of a "postsecular society" or a "postsecular Europe" made of citizens–deliberators remains no less utopian than a state of nature made of noble savages. This line of objection does *not*, however, invalidate the contribution of the postsecular approach, but aims at severing it from Habermas' overtaxing rationalism. A postsecularism devoid of rationalistic illusions becomes more open and modest. First, Habermas' specific interpretation of dialogue is restrictive, as it tends to reduce communicative exchanges to a certain form of rational argument or deliberation. His stand is insensitive to the variety of communicative styles, and to the plurality of the contexts of their formation. Rational dialogue is, as Young pointed out, one of the forms of communicative interaction whose importance depends on context.[75] Rational argument, rhetoric, symbolic communication and exemplary storytelling can, in different ways, foster a democratic culture of mutual exchange and tolerance. Alternatively, postsecularism could designate not a new type of society, but – less ambitiously – one dimension of a democratic culture. It thus refers to mutual argumentative and non-argumentative engagement of religious, non-religious and atheist citizens in the public sphere.

2. The conversion of dialogue into a legal principle at the European level may have problematic consequences. Lawmaking is not a "soul craft" (Rousseau) able to produce deliberative citizens, but a limited tool. If the European Courts were to enhance a "duty of dialogue," this could deepen the current overpoliticization and overjuridification of religion. It is noteworthy that the 2008 *White Paper on Intercultural Dialogue* assumes that the institutionalization of dialogue secures integration and efficiency, and does not generate conflicts. Such documents do not contain any serious attempt to deal with the relation between dialogue and power, just as they do not tackle the variety of tensions and conflicts involving religion. Likewise, Habermas' postsecular approach focused on "reconciliation though public reason" underestimates empirical research, according to which more dialogue in public spaces does not necessarily lead to reconciliation and the protection of pluralism.[76] Dialogue can privilege established actors, deepen divergences and even foster radicalization, all the more when deep religious and atheist commitments are concerned. It is

---

[75] See esp. I. M. Young, *Justice and the Politics of Difference* (Princeton University Press, 1990).
[76] Sanders, "Against Deliberation."

thus doubtful whether, in a climate already marked by overpoliticization and overjuridification, and where majority religions and their churches are often reluctant to accept pluralism, it is really useful to turn a policy recommendation regarding the salience of dialogue between political and religious organizations into a legal principle.[77]

Conclusion

The recent history of Europe has not confirmed the triumphant secularist saga of the linear withering away of religion. In Europe, religious and non-religious experiences exist in a conflictive space made of religious, spiritual and exclusive–materialist options. This conflictive pluralism is unlikely to be conducive to a postsecular reconciliation (Habermas) whereby citizens would recognize as positive the values and opinions of others, and would be willing to learn from them by means of dialogue. A Habermasian goodwill interpretation of a "post-secular Europe" centered unilaterally on dialogue is not only overoptimistic with respect to the place of argument in public life, but it also underestimates the deep moral–political conflicts between religious, agnostic and atheist allegiances. In turn, the "conservative" image of rebuilding a Christian Europe does not appear either realistic or desirable.

In practice, European institutions such as the ECtHR have aimed at providing protection of individual liberty and (non)religious pluralism by questioning certain biased aspects of the inherited regimes of privilege between state and majority religion. Such institutions have thus made important steps in developing a framework based on the minimal principles of freedom of religion and state neutrality, in addition to that of pluralism. This trend is consonant with the increasing pluralism and individualism of the socio-religious landscape in Europe, and is part of a broader process of revisiting the traditional compromises between state and religion in a more diverse world where different religious voices can find a legitimate place in public sphere.

However, the ECtHR has, at key moments, undermined the principles of liberal constitutionalism. In particular, I have pointed out two of its major failings: the Court has generally had a black-and-white approach to Islam

---

[77] I do not suggest that the juridification of the principle of dialogue can be derived from Habermas' view. In effect, Habermas is very keen on preserving a clear border between the informal public sphere (which is the privileged site of dialogical exchanges) and the formal public sphere.

and, in turn, it has been overprotective with respect to Christian major-ities. Underlying these failings has been the Court's incapacity to develop a flexible but coherent understanding of the margin of appreciation, and a more consistent understanding of its main principles. The ECtHR will hopefully be more nuanced with respect to Islam in the near future, for instance in the case of the ban of building minarets in Switzerland. The predicament of the Muslim minority in Switzerland is not an exception in Europe. Carl Schmitt is back in the limelight: the other (Muslim, immi-grant, etc.) has become the enemy. The ghost of the Muslim enemy – the "non-European" *par excellence* – is being summoned up by the alliance of past arch-adversaries: old extremist right-wingers, (neo)conservatives and radical laicist left-wingers.

"The role of the authorities," maintains the ECtHR in *Serif* v. *Greece*, "is not to remove the cause of tension by eliminating pluralism, but to ensure that the competing groups tolerate each other."[78] A more consist-ent reliance on this stand on part of the European institutions could be an asset in a political environment where states aim anew at assimilation, and even sober figures like Angela Merkel fall into the populist rhetoric of the death of multiculturalism. Indeed, it is not the specter of religion in general, but that of reactive populism and extremism that haunts an undecided Europe. How exactly Europe will combine the defense of neu-trality and pluralism, separation and dialogue, the need for more legal coherence and the recognition of the diversity of existing models, is a question yet to be answered.

[78] Eur. Ct. H. R., *Serif* v. *Greece*, 14 December 1999, para. 53.

INDEX

adequate reason, for an action, 77–8
Agbetu, Tony, 93–4, 95
Ahmad v. *UK*, 224
Ahmet Arslan and others v. *Turkey*, 303,
    305
Alberti, Leon Battista, 44
Al-Qa'eda, 129
Ambrogio Lorenzetti's *Sala dei Nove*,
    10, 24–30, 34
American Catholicism, 311
American civil religion, 311
American evangelicalism, 311
American Protestantism, 311
Angeleni v. *Sweden*, 208
anti-Semitism, 96
Arbitration Act 1996, 106
Archbishop of Canterbury, 115, 116
Aristotelianism, 39
Aryan Nations, 217
Audi, Robert, 11–12, 65
    accessible reasons and religious
      ideas, 87–90
    church–state separation, 71–5
    coercion, 66–71
    defining religion, 79
    freedom of expression v.
      governmental laws and policies,
      75–6
    governmental neutrality towards
      religion, 73–5
    pluralism of society, 66
    principle of natural reasons, 80–5
    principle of religious rationale, 85–7
    principle of secular rationale, 76–80
    relation between rationality and
      consensus, 79
Augenstein, Daniel, 16

Bartolo, Taddeo di, 35
Bavarian Crucifix Order, 177
Bayle, Pierre, 57–60
Bayle's theory, 11
Bedi, Sonu, 231–2, 233
behavioral liberty, 71
Berger, P., 2
biblical heros, statues of, 36
Bottici, Chiara, 13
British Board of Film Classification
    (BBFC), 245
British Muslim family norms,
    see Muslim 'Sharia' law
Bruni, Leonardo, 44
Buscarini and others v. *San-Marino*,
    291

Calvinist minority, suppression of,
    51–3
Canadian law, 104
caritas, 32, 42, 44
caritas patriae, 33
Catholic faith, 23, 310
Challand, Benoit, 13
charity, 34
Christian civil religion, 310
Christian Knights of the Ku Klux Klan,
    217
Christianity, as the religion of virtue,
    42–8, *see also* God concept
    civil virtues, 46
    and earthly life, 43
    love of country, 42–3
    political virtue, 46
    principle of charity, 45–7
    tasks in life, 45
    Valla's views, 45–6

Christianity, in Europe, 309–14
Christs du Seigneur, 39
Cicero's ideal of civil virtue, 43
citizenship, ethics of, 12
civic liberalism, 195
civil Christianity, 21–2
civil religion
  Ambrogio Lorenzetti's painting,
    30, 34
  for Aristotle, 35
  artistic representation in Florence,
    36–8
  Christian, 310
  'Cycle of Famous Men', 35
  European, 309–14
  Maurizio Viroli's reflections, 10–11
  principle of the common good,
    30–3
  within republican cities' culture and
    custom, 22–8
  in Roman times, 35
  in Simone Martini's *Maestà*, 29
  Viroli's views, 21–2
civil virtues, 46
classical evolutionism, history
  of ideas of, 97–9
coercion and liberty, 66–71, 89
common good, principle of, 30–3
  Aristotelian context, 30, 32–3
  Lorenzetti's views, 31–2
  love of country, 34
  Rubinstein's views, 31–2
  Skinner's views, 31–2
  Tolomeo's views, 33
communes, of Italy
  and Bible, 23–4
  birth, 22
  duties of ruler, 24
  functions and duties of the Podestà,
    22, 24
  invective of justice against bad
    rulers, 24–5
  religious dimension, 22–3
  religious identity, 23
  republican ideology, 23–8
  statutes, 22–3
  in Vicenza, 22
compulsory education, 75

constituenda religione, 51
constituenda republica, 51
constitutional treatment of religion,
    160–5
  religious tolerance and cultural
    Christianity, 165–6
constitutionalism and religious
    pluralism, 160–5
Corpus Vaticanum, 150
Council Directive 2000/43/EC (the
    Race Directive), 217–18
Council Directive 2000/78/EC, 217
Council of Europe (CoE), 308
Council of Trent, 40
crucifix, display of, 166–71
  debate, in Germany, 262–3
cultural racism, issue of, 95–7
Curtius, Marcus, 33

da Lucca, Tolomeo, 33
da Viterbo, Giovanni, 25–6
Dahlab v. *Switzerland*, 3–4, 178, 225,
    270, 323, 325
Danish cartoons, case of, 116
Danish sex education case, 199
Dante's *Divine Comedy*, 1
Dante's *Convivio*, 34
Das Liebeskonzil (film), 243–4
David, statue of, 36
De bono communi, 32
De bono pacis, 32
De dignitate hominis, 47
de facto monopoly, 153
de jure monopolies, 153
De Officiis, 25
*De regimine et sapientia
    potestatis*, 25
de' Girolami, Remigio, 32
Dei gratia dux formula, 41
democracy *tout court*, 182
democratic societies
  accessible reasons and religious
    ideas, 87–90
  characteristics, 65
  freedom of expression v.
    governmental laws and policies,
    75–6
  liberty and equality in, 65–71

democratic societies (*cont.*)
  and principle of secular rationale,
    76–80
  separation of church and state as an
    element in, 71–5
  issue of non-Western cultures
dialogical model of democracy, 327
dialogical post secularism, 16, 326–8
Dictionaire historique and critique, 60
Discourses on Livy, 47
Divorce (Religious Marriages) Act
    2002, 106
Dogru v. *France*, 178, 271
dominant conception of toleration, 64
Do-unto-others principle, 80, 88
Duplessis-Mornay, Monarch, 55
duty-imposing norms, 14, 139–40

Edict of Nantes, 51–3, 54
Elgin County case, 200–1
EM (Lebanon) (Fc) (Appellant) (Fc) v.
    *Secretary of State For The Home
    Department Appellate Committee*,
    110–12
English colonialism, 95–7
English law, 105
Enlightenment project, 187–91
Enlightenment tradition, 13
equality-centered religious conflict, 5
Establishment Clause, 165
ethnological thinking, about races, 97
European approach, to religion, 7
  autonomy of religious communities,
    288
  Christianity, 309–14
  in contemporary Europe, 297–305
  context of Islamic headscarf, 100–1
  in the context of political and social
    theory, 292–7
  to cultural and religious differences,
    99–101
  in democratic public sphere,
    299–301
  images and stereotypes about Islam,
    116–21
  issue of non-Western cultures, 97–9
  non-Christian minorities, 94–7
  pluralist perspective, 8–9

  in public sphere, 94–7
  relationship between Orientalism
    and feminism, 99
  religious accommodation in
    workplace, 297–9
  religious organizations and
    movements, 9–10
  and secularity of legal system,
    291–2
  state neutrality, 288–91
  Tony Agbetu's protest, 93–4
  wearing of religious clothing and
    symbols, 301–5
European civil religion, 309–14
European Court law and freedom of
    religion, 243–9, 297–305
European Court of Human Rights
    (ECtHR), 16, 283, 308
  article 2, 138–43, 283, 320
  article 8, 141–3
  article 9, 145–4, 219–21, 223–6,
    227–30, 234, 245, 270, 271, 283,
    288, 297, 324
  article 10, 144–5, 245, 274
  Dahlab decision, 270–1
  early case law, 284–5
  Elgin County case, 200–1
  issue of free speech, 15
  jurisprudence, 16
  normative principles of, 16
  Refah Partisi decision, 112, 145–7
  religious education, 14, 202–13
  suicide and euthanasia, 142–3
  supervisory role, 272–3
  veil case at, 3–4, 97, 177–81
European institutions and claims of
    religion, 16–17
European legal systems and polygamy,
    148–9
euthanasia, 142–3

Ficino, Marsilio, 46
Florence, 1
Florentine art, 36–8
Foe Nesi religious faith, 47
Folgerø and others v. *Norway*, 14, 192,
    202, 209, 290, 320
Forst, Rainer, 11

case of *Lautsi* v. *Italy*, 49
components of tolerance, 50–1
critical theory of toleration, 54–5
justification of tolerance, 60–3
permission conception of toleration,
    53–4
respect conception of tolerance,
    56–7
toleration–democracy, relationship,
    63–4
France and veil law, 174–7
France's laic state model, 4
Free Exercise Clause, 165
free speech and religion, 144–5
freedom of conscience, 57
freedom of expression v. governmental
    laws and policies, 75–6, 157
freedom of religion, 273
    and democracy and liberal equality,
        254–7
    European Court's balancing
        methodology, 257–60
    European Court's case law, 243–9
    normative claims, 241–3
    political speech v. religious/artistic
        expression, 249–53
freedom-centered religious
    conflict, 5
French *burka* ban, 267
French *Conseil Constitutionnel*, 274
French constitutional tradition, on
    religious pluralism, 261–8
French Council of State (*Conseil
    d'Etat*), 302
functioning coercively, notion of, 70
fundamental rights and conflict
    between law and religion
    article 2 v. artice 8, 141–3
    article 9 v. rights of others, 143–4
    article 10, 144–5
    article 11, 145–7
    concept of dignity, 140
fundamentalist religions, 160–5

gay marriage, 55
generality, 61
German constitutional tradition and
    religious pluralism, 262–5

Germany and prohibition of Islamic
    symbols, 171–3
Ghibellins, 1
Giniewski v. *France*, 250–1
God concept, *see also* Christianity, as
    the religion of virtue
    the Bible, 23–4
    functions and duties of the Podestà,
        22, 24
    invective of Justice against bad
        rulers, 24–5
    Italian dimension, 22
    in *Liber de regimine civitatum*,
        25–6
    in *Livres dou Tresor*, 26–8
    and public of equals, 131
    religious people v. non-religious
        people, 141–3
    republican ideology, 23–8
Goliath, statue of, 36
good citizenship, ethics of, 76
Gospel of John, 25
Guelfs, 1
Gündüz v. *Turkey*, 299

Habermas, 326–32
Hale, Lady, 101
Hanbali legal school of jurisprudence,
    124
Handyside v. *United Kingdom*, 259
Hasan and Chaush v. *Bulgaria*, 288,
    294
headscarf controversy
    at ECtHR, 3–4, 97, 177–81
    in Germany, 263–5
Hollywood films, Muslims in,
    119–20
Holmes, Justice Oliver Wendell, 9
holy king, 40
homosexual Christian, 255

I.A. v. *Turkey*, 250, 259, 301
informal public sphere, 295
International Covenant on Civil and
    Political Rights, 200
Islam and presupposition of equality,
    130
Islam in Europe, 13

books and intellectual discourses,
119–20
case of Islamic headscarf, 100–1
France, 174–7
Germany, 171–3
John Rawls' imagined Kazanistan,
118–19
as political myth, 118–19
public reason and imagination,
116–21
relationship between Islam and the
ideal of public sphere, 121–7
United Kingdom, 173–4
Islamic finance, 126
Islamic jurisprudence, 123–6
Islamic public sphere, 121–7
Islamophobia in France, 121
islamo-phobias, 14
istislah, concept of, 123–4, 129
Italian laws, 149
Italian republicanism, 21

Jacobin fundamentalist tendency of
anti-pluralism, 130
Jewish *kippah*, 172–3
Jewish law, 222
judicial preference for state abstention,
222
judicialization of politics, 9
Judith and Holofernes, statue of,
36

Kantian morality, 184
Karaduman v. *Turkey*, 225
Kazakhstan, 118–19
KC and NNC v. *City of Westminster
Social and Community Services
Department*, 110
Kervanci v. *France*, 178, 271
Kjeldsen, Busk Madsen and Pedersen v.
Denmark, 320
Kokkinakis v. *Greece*, 143
Kosteski v. *the Former Yugoslav
Republic of Macedonia*, 299
Kymlicka, Will, 231

laïcité, principle of, 152, 265–8, 301,
314–18

Lateran pacts of 1929, 137
Latini, Brunetto, 26–8
Lautsi v. *Italy*, 49, 55, 290, 322, 325
law v. religion
church–state relationship, 149–50
conflict of laws and, 148–9
core of conflicts, 139–40
dealing with, 151–8
and fundamental rights, 140–7
management of conflicts, 138–9
power-conferring norms, 147–8
Leigh, Ian, 14–15
Letsas, George, 15
Letter Concerning Toleration, 56
Levinson, 195
Leyla Şahin's case, 100, 144, 302, 304
Liber de regimine civitatum, 25–6
liberal constitutionalism, 16–17,
319–26
liberal democracy, 67, 72–3, 80,
91, 104
and display of religious symbols, 168
and religious freedom, 73–5
liberalism, 12
Malik's perspective, 12
liberty
and coercion, 66–71
limitation on protection of, 72–3
and pluralism, 66
religious, 66
Libri della famiglia, 44
Lisbon Treaty, 9
Livres dou Tresor, 26–8
love of country, concept of, 28–34
Lutheran Protestantism, 315
Lynch v. *Donnelly*, 168

McColgan, Aileen, 15
McConnell, Michael, 87–90
Macedo, Stephen, 196
Machiavelli, Niccolò, 10, 47
Malik, Maleiha, 12
Mancini, Susanna, 13
Manetti, Giannozzo, 45
Marketplace of Religions, 151–5
maslahah, concept of, 124–6, 129–31
mediatic Islamophobia, 121
membership in a culture, 231

Metropolitan Church of Bessarabia v. *Moldova*, 220–1
minimal liberal constitutionalism, 319–26
Mirandola, Giovanni Pico della, 47
modernization, as secularization, 1
monotheistic law, 132
moral respect, 11
multicultural state model, 5
multiculturalism, 107
Muslim Arbitration Tribunal (MAT), 105, 140, 147–8
Muslim duty of solidarity, 131
Muslim 'Sharia' law, 101–12, 147–8
  and Boyd's report, 109
  dispute resolution, 104
  EM (Lebanon) (Fc) (Appellant) (Fc) v. *Secretary of State For The Home Department Appellate Committee*, 110–12
  issue of accommodating, 104, 108
  KC and NNC v. *City of Westminster Social and Community Services Department*, 110
  marriages and divorce, 105–6
  on mortgages, 103
  'right to exit' argument, 107
  Talaq divorce, 149
  and women, 108
mutual toleration, 57

natural reasons, principle of, 80–5
  Aquinas' views, 81
  Habermas' views, 84
  public health rationales for inoculations, 84
  and religious identity, 83–5
  theoretical aspects, 81
Nesi, Giovanni, 46
Nicomachean Ethics, 32–3
non-Christian minorities, in Europe, 94–7
non-European cultures, 97–9
Norwegian state schools, religious education in, 202–13

Oculus pastoralis, 22, 23
Ollinger v. *Austria*, 258

Oratio de Caritate, 47
Oratio de humilitate, 47
oriental despotism, 117
Orientalism, 99, 117
Otto-Preminger-Institut doctrine, 301
Otto-Preminger Institute v. *Austria*, 15, 177, 243, 246, 259, 300

Palmieri, Matteo, 44
paternalistic state model, 4
Pensées diverses sur la Comète, 57
permission conception, of toleration, 53–4, 57
persistent disagreement, 86
Philosophy of Political Myth, A, 13
phobia-free polity, 155–8
political constructivism, 8
Political Liberalism, 7–8, 292, 295
political myths, 118–19
postsecular democracy, 326–32
power-conferring norms, 14, 139–48
Presbyterian Church v. *Hull Church*, 222
Privat-Exercitium of religious duties, 53
proselytism, 143
Protestantism, 315
Psalms, the, 25
public of equals, 131
public sphere, concept of, 127–32
  democratic, 299–301
  Habermas' account, 128
  and Islam, 129–32
  Kant's definition, 129
  religious engagement, 216
  and state relations, 4
  as third sphere, 128
  transnational Islamic public, 130

R (E) v. *Governing Body of the Jews' Free School*, 234
R (Williamson) v. *Secretary of State for Education and Employment and Others*, 234
R v. *Chief Rabbi, ex parte Wachmann*, 222
rabbinical court, 106
race, as a 'biological' construct, 96

Racial and Religious Hatred Act 2006,
    157
rational disagreement
    between epistemic peers, 86
    principle of, 12
Ratzinger, J., 309–14
reciprocity, principle of, 11, 61
Refah Partisi decision, 112, 141, 146,
    291, 294, 324
Regulus, Attilius, 33
religion of liberty, idea of, 11
religion of the Counter-reformation,
    47–8
religion, conflicts involving, 5
    case of headscarf, 6
    European approach, 7
    and globalization, 160–5
    Rawls' views, 7
    Skinner's views, 8
    Zucca's typology, 14
religion–secular state relations
    Audi's views, 11–12
    in the context of modern political
        and legal theory, 1
    at political-legal level, 3–4
    in public sphere, 2
religiosity, 2
religious citizens, 84
religious collectives, 229–30
religious education, 14
    confessional approach, 193
    ECtHR approach, 202–13
    neutrality in, 194
    phenomenological approach, 195
    practical and human rights
        implications, 198–202
    in public schools, rationale for,
        193–8
    secularist approach, 197
    separatist approach, 196–7
religious engagement in the public
    sphere, 216
religious exemptions, 231–2
religious fundamentalism, 181–3
religious liberty, 66
religious pluralism
    and ECJ's response, 273–8
    in French constitutional tradition,
        265–8

German constitutional tradition,
    262–5
    in trans-national human rights
        jurisprudence, 268–78
religious pluralism v. social cohesion,
    16
religious rationale, principle of, 78–87
religious symbols, 14
    analysis of conflicts, 182–3
    cultural Christianity, 165–6
    display of Christian symbols, 166–71
    display of Islamic symbols, 171–81
    ideal conditions for displaying,
        183–7
    in public spaces, 164
    and secularism, 181–3
religious tolerance and cultural
    Christianity, 165–6
religious unity, 51
religious-based discrimination
    conflicts of conscience, 227–9
    direct internal interferences, 220–3
    and European law, 217–18
    and freedom of religion, 219–29
    indirect interference, 223–6
    on patriarchal norms, 232
    and religious collectives, 229–30
    value and cost of religion, 230–6
republican good government, principle
    of, 28
republican ideology, about God, 23–8
republican religion, 23–8, 38–42
    fundamental expressions, 41
    v. royal religion, 40–1
respect conception, of tolerance, 56–7,
    64
right to free speech, 15
right to freedom of speech, 14
right to justification, 61
Ringelheim, Julie, 16
Rosenfeld, Michel, 13
royal ointment, 40
royal religion, concept of, 40
    v. republican religion, 40–1
Rubinstein, Nicolai, 30–3

Sacchi, Bartolomeo, 46
Şahin v. *Turkey*, 269
Salazar v. *Buono*, 170

Sandel, Michael, 230
Sansovino, Francesco, 42
Scandinavian secularization, 315
science education, 74
secular rationale, principle of, 76–80
secular reason, for an action, 77
secularism, 13
    v. article 11, 139–47
    and display of religious symbols,
        181–3
    dynamic between intra-communal
        and inter-communal dealings,
        188–91
    modernization as, 1
    necessity of, 157–8
    robust, 14
    in Turkey, 144
secularization of Europe, 3, 315
self-evident principles, 82
Shabina Begum case, 101, 174
Sharia Councils, 102–3
Sharia Courts, 97
Sikh doctrine, 233
Skinner, Quentin, 31
social cohesion limitation, of freedom
    of religion, 16
South Asian Muslims, 97
Stasi Report, 266, 314, 316–18
state, models of
    laic model, 4
    multicultural model, 5
    paternalistic model, 4
    security state, 3–4
Stedman v. *UK*, 225
Stocking, George W. Jr., 97
suicide, 142–3
Sunni legal schools, 124

Talaq divorce, 149
Taylor, Charles, 230
Thlimmenos v. *Greece*, 228, 298
Tocqueville, 21
*Toledo Guiding Principles on Teaching
    about Religion and Beliefs in
    Public Schools*, 198–9, 201, 204
tolerance, principle of, 11, 87
    Augustine's arguments, 58
    Calvinist suppression and Edict of
        Nantes, 51–3

Catholicism enforcement in
    Netherlands, 55–7
components, 50–1, 63
critical theory, 54–5
criticism, 52, 54
cultural Christianity, 165–6
and democracy, 63–4
dominant conception, 64
and equal rights, 55
forms, 54
historical discourses, 57–60
interpretation of, 50
of Jews, 54
Jonas Proast's critique, 58
justification, 60–3
mutual, 57
permission conception, 53–4, 57
on pragmatic and normative
    grounds, 53, 62
respect conception, 56–7, 64
Toleranzpatente of the Habsburg
    Emperor Joseph II, 53
Toleration Act of 1689, 52
transformative civic liberalism, 196
transnational Islamic public, 130
truths of religion, 11
Tully, James, 96

Ubaldis, Baldus de, 38
ulama, 124
Ülke v. *Turkey*, 228
umma, moral order of, 124
Un'Europa Cristiana, 312
Ungureanu, Camil, 16–17
United Kingdom and display of
    religious symbols, 173–4

Vatican laws, 149–50
Vecchio, Palazzo, 36
Venetian doge, 40–1
Viroli, Maurizio
    on civil religion, 10, 21–2
    God concept, 22, 28
Visions of Ecstasy (film), 245, 256
Vita civile, 44

Waldron, Jeremy, 231
Weiler, Joseph, 312–14
Western feminism, 99

Western societies, 91
Williams, Archbishop Rowan,
    101–12
Wingrove v United Kingdom, 245, 301
Wingrove, Nigel, 245
Wolterstorff, Nicholas, 69–70, 78
women and Islam, 108–5, 131

Zagrebelsky, Gustavo, 170
zakaat, 131
Zengin v. *Turkey*, 14, 192, 211
Zénon Bernard v. *Luxembourg*, 208
Zucca, Lorenzo, 14